LOEB CLASSICAL LIBRARY
FOUNDED BY JAMES LOEB 1911

EDITED BY
JEFFREY HENDERSON

EARLY GREEK PHILOSOPHY
IV

LCL 527

EARLY GREEK PHILOSOPHY

VOLUME IV

WESTERN GREEK THINKERS
PART 1

EDITED AND TRANSLATED BY
ANDRÉ LAKS AND GLENN W. MOST

IN COLLABORATION WITH
GÉRARD JOURNÉE

AND ASSISTED BY
LEOPOLDO IRIBARREN

HARVARD UNIVERSITY PRESS
CAMBRIDGE, MASSACHUSETTS
LONDON, ENGLAND
2016

Copyright © 2016 by the President and Fellows
of Harvard College
All rights reserved

First published 2016

LOEB CLASSICAL LIBRARY® is a registered trademark
of the President and Fellows of Harvard College

Library of Congress Control Number 2015957358
CIP data available from the Library of Congress

ISBN 978-0-674-99692-2

*Composed in ZephGreek and ZephText by
Technologies 'N Typography, Merrimac, Massachusetts.
Printed on acid-free paper and bound by
The Maple-Vail Book Manufacturing Group*

CONTENTS

PYTHAGORAS AND THE PYTHAGOREAN SCHOOL

General Introduction to Chapters 10–18	3
10. Pythagoras	8
a. The Person	14
b. The Institution	58
c. Doctrines Attributed by Name; Sayings and Precepts	98
11. Hippasus	128
12. Philolaus	145
13. Eurytus	187
14. Archytas	196
15. Hicetas	265
16. Ecphantus	269
17. Pythagorean Doctrines Not Attributed by Name	277
18. Pythagoras, Pythagoreans, Pythagoreanism: Reception	337

PYTHAGORAS AND THE
PYTHAGOREAN SCHOOL

GENERAL INTRODUCTION TO CHAPTERS 10–18

The presentation of the transmitted information relating to Pythagoras and the Pythagorean school is rendered particularly difficult by three partially interdependent factors: the evanescent and quasi-mythical character of the personality and teaching of Pythagoras; the anonymity of a large part of the information transmitted; and the existence of a vast pseudepigraphic literature, which, though in most cases it can be recognized as such, also includes texts about which one might well wonder whether they ought not to be attributed to the older Pythagoreans, especially Philolaus and Archytas. To these three difficulties must be added the sheer abundance of the material to be considered, given that more texts survive regarding the Pythagorean school than all the rest of the early Greek philosophers put together: besides the Pseudo-Pythagorean texts, two biographies of Pythagoras, composed by the Neoplatonic philosophers Porphyry and Iamblichus, have been preserved in their entirety; to these must be added the existence of works influenced by a more or less diffuse and more or less identifiable form of Pythagoreanism, like Nicomachus of Gerasa's *Introduction to Arithmetic* and *Manual of Harmonics* or Theon of Smyrna's *On Mathematics Useful for the Understanding of*

Plato. The singular character of the transmission of the Pythagorean corpus derives from the character, itself singular, of the history of ancient Pythagoreanism, which is itself principally marked by two factors: first, the very nature of its identity, which varies from epoch to epoch but displays at its origin a set of features corresponding simultaneously to a political formation (*hetairia,* literally an association of "friends" or "companions"), a religious congregation, and an educational institution, implying structures, attitudes, and processes familiar from the sociology of groups, such as hierarchization, solidarity, apostasy, diversification, and mythicization of the founder; and second, the fact that the Pythagorean doctrine and perhaps, even more, its spirit were claimed by Plato for himself, in a manner so decisive that Pythagoreanism became an integral part of the—itself very complex—history of Platonism and of Neoplatonism.

In order to try to take account of this exceptional configuration, we have felt obliged to modify the tripartition **P/D/R** that is used in most other chapters. Indeed, Diels himself, in his presentation of this material, was obliged to abandon his own division into A (testimonia) and B (fragments), and used a classification from A to E, which is indicated in our lemmata.

The chapter dedicated to Pythagoras (chap. 10) is divided into three subchapters: the first ("Pythagoras a"), designated **P,** collects, besides the biographical data, the earliest references to the person of Pythagoras (these are particularly important, given that his was a figure that rapidly became mythicized) and a series of texts in which he appears with the canonical features of a 'divine man'; the second ("Pythagoras b"), designated **T,** focuses on the or-

ganization and early history of the institution of Pythagoreanism, but, given that certain features of this organization cannot be separated from the person of Pythagoras himself, it also completes the preceding subchapter; in the third ("Pythagoras c"), designated **D,** we have put together, besides some teachings that may be attributed to Pythagoras himself—it being understood that any such attribution is uncertain and contestable—a selection of anonymous formulas and precepts that (in particular on the basis of Aristotle's testimony) can reasonably be assigned to the oldest form of Pythagoreanism—if not to Pythagoras himself, then at least to his 'congregation.'

The six chapters that follow are dedicated to the person (**P**), when this is appropriate, and to the doctrines attributed by name (**D**) to the principal Pythagoreans who can be situated between Pythagoras and Plato—in chronological order (uncertain in the case of the last two) Hippasus (chap. 11), Philolaus (chap. 12), Eurytus (chap. 13), Archytas (chap. 14), Hicetas (chap. 15), and Ecphantus (chap. 16). This list excludes, not without some degree of arbitrariness, certain authors who were reputed to be Pythagoreans or to have belonged to the Pythagorean movement, such as Menestor and Damon, whom considerations of space and significance have induced us to omit within the framework of this edition. But there are also a large number of doctrines that are attributed in a general manner to 'Pythagoreans' who are not further identified by name. In most of these cases, it is at the best imprudent, and at the worst impossible, to assign these doctrines to this or that individual Pythagorean; this is the reason why we have chosen—following Diels' example—to collect these texts in a specific chapter dedicated to Pythagorean

doctrines not attributed by name (chap. 17). Nonetheless, a certain number of these unattributed doctrines clearly coincide with, or are very close to, those that are known to belong to Philolaus, so that this chapter includes a number of texts that complete the **D** section of the chapter specifically dedicated to him. Finally, we have collected in a single chapter (chap. 18) the elements relating to the reception of Pythagoras and of the Pythagorean 'school' in antiquity—including the reception of the authors who are the objects of chapters 11 to 16. This is a particularly complex reception, and one whose presentation, given the abovementioned abundance of the available documentation, cannot help but be incomparably more selective than most of the other chapters of the present edition. We only hope that our choice will be sufficiently representative to suggest, to those who wish them, paths for possible further research, starting out from the bibliographical references we provide. The particular problems connected with the transmission of the works of Philolaus and Archytas, which are due to the production of pseudepigraphic texts, are discussed in the specific introductions to these two chapters.

BIBLIOGRAPHY

General Works

W. Burkert. *Lore and Science in Ancient Pythagoreanism*, trans. E. L. Minar Jr. (Cambridge, MA, 1972).

C. A. Huffman, ed. *A History of Pythagoreanism* (Cambridge, 2014).

PYTHAGORAS

- C. H. Kahn. *Pythagoras and the Pythagoreans: A Brief History* (Indianapolis, 2001).
- L. Zhmud. *Pythagoras and the Early Pythagoreans* (Oxford, 2012).

On the Musical Theory

- A. D. Barker. *Greek Musical Writings*. Vol. 2, *Harmonic and Acoustic Theory* (Cambridge, 1989).

10. PYTHAGORAS
[PYTH. a, PYTH. b, PYTH. c]

The ancient sources situate Pythagoras' maturity in 540 or 530 BC, and his name is explicitly mentioned twice by Heraclitus, at the end of the sixth century. Hence he can be considered a contemporary of Anaximenes. Born on Samos, not far from Miletus, he seems to have emigrated to southern Italy at the time of Polycrates' tyranny over the island. Whether or not the reason for this departure was political, the institution that he goes on to found at Croton is marked by features that are resolutely political. Doubtless this is, in a certain sense, a school of thought, but that aspect is combined with a group of 'companions' (the technical term is *hetairia*) of a conservative tendency, who attained considerable success, if it is true that for a certain time many south Italian cities were governed by Pythagoreans, until these oligarchic governments were themselves overthrown. Pythagoras himself was obliged to leave Croton for Metapontum as the result of a revolt (this is dated ca. 500), and other violent uprisings occurred around 450 and led to a dispersal of the community and to the exile of individuals as far away as continental Greece. An idea of the size of these communities, even if only an indirect one, is provided by the impressive catalog of the principal Pythagorean men (and women) that is

transmitted by Iamblichus in his *Life of Pythagoras* (**PYTH. b T30**). It seems to be clear that the Pythagorean *hetairia* is intimately linked to the charisma and exceptional authority of its founder. A certain number of its characteristic features—silence, degrees of initiation, the practice of secrecy—place this institution in the proximity of religious sects. Its relation with the nature of the teachings imparted is difficult to establish. The doctrines that can be attributed to Pythagoras are few in number and heterogeneous in character; it seems certain that they included a role for number, under whose aegis a significant part of the later destiny of Pythagoreanism is played out; the idea of a survival after death seems equally certain, although the notion of metempsychosis, which constitutes the other pillar of the later destiny of Pythagoreanism, is not so well attested. The very numerous attested prescriptions of a ritual and moral character are difficult to date, but their core is certainly ancient, and they fit the idea of a community that, according to the available evidence, was quickly perceived as being connected with a distinctive way of life. The category of 'divine man' that one finds applied to Pythagoras derives from a later typology, but Herodotus' reports, Heraclitus' invectives, and a possible allusion in Empedocles show that Pythagoras was soon thought of as a person endowed with supernatural faculties. Master of the truth, director of conscience, magus, charlatan—these are notions that can help situate the largely ungraspable figure of that man who, of all the early Greek philosophers, without a doubt exerted the longest-lasting influence until the beginning of modern times, and who continues to exercise a fascination that none of his peers can vaunt.

EARLY GREEK PHILOSOPHY IV

BIBLIOGRAPHY

C. Riedweg. *Pythagoras. His Life, Teaching, and Influence* (2nd ed. Ithaca-London, 2005).

See also the titles listed in the General Introduction to Chapters 10–18.

OUTLINE OF THE CHAPTER

Pythagoras a
Biographical Elements and Legend

P

Biographical Elements (P1–P24)
  Birthplace (P1–P2)
  Chronology (P3–P5)
  Longevity (P6–P7)
  Alleged Parentage and Family (P8–P11)
  Alleged Greek Teachers (P12–P17)
  Alleged Travels in the Orient and Initiation into Barbarian Wisdom (P18–P22)
  Departure for Southern Italy (P23–P26)
    The Reason for His Departure (P23)
    Impact at Croton and in the Rest of Italy (P24–P26)
Earliest References to Pythagoras' Person and to Various Aspects of His Activity (P27–P33)
  References by Name (P27–P31)
    In Heraclitus (P27–P28)
    In Ion of Chios (P29)
    In Herodotus (P30)

PYTHAGORAS

In Democritus (P31)
Other References (P32–P33)
  In Xenophanes (P32)
  In Empedocles? (P33)
Later Reports about the Sage and Holy Man (P34–P42)
  Between God and Man (P34–P36)
  Earlier Lives (P37–P39)
  His Descent to the Underworld, or Katabasis *(P40–P41)*
    His Encounter with Hesiod and Homer (P40)
    A Rationalizing Interpretation of the Katabasis *(P41)*
  The Harmony of the Spheres (cf. P33)
  Other Prodigies and Marvels (P42)
A Caricature by the Skeptic Timon of Phlius (P43)
Four Versions of Pythagoras' Death (P44)
Civic Honors and Religious Aura (P45–P46)
Iconography (P47)

Pythagoras b
The Institution

T

The Community of Life and of Teaching (T1–T6)
  The Pythagorean Way of Life (T1)
  Friendship (T2–T3)
  Diet (T4–T6)
The School: Characteristics and History (T7–T28)
  Admission into the School (T7)
  Pythagoras' Authority (T8–T10)
  The Practice of Silence (T11–T13)
  Pythagoras' Audiences and Rhetoric (T14)

EARLY GREEK PHILOSOPHY IV

'Knowers' (mathêmatikoi) and 'Listeners' (akousmatikoi) (T15–T20)
    The Nature of the Difference (T15–T18)
    A Rationalizing Explanation of This Difference (T19)
    Secrets and Betrayals (T20)
Political Vicissitudes (T21–T28)
    At Croton (T21–T23)
    In the Rest of Italy (T24)
    Anti-Pythagorean Revolts (T25–T27)
    The Dispersal of the Pythagoreans (T28)
The Pythagoreans in the Course of Time (T29–T36)
    Longevity of the School (T29)
    The Catalog of Male and Female Pythagoreans Transmitted by Iamblichus (T30)
    Some Other Names and Reports (T31–T36)
        Cercops (T31)
        Democedes of Croton (T32–T33)
        Brontinus (or Brotinus)
        Iccus of Tarentum (T34)
        Ameinas (T35)
        Telauges
        Lysis (T36)

Pythagoras c
Doctrines Attributed by Name; Sayings and Precepts

D

Did Pythagoras Write Anything? (D1–D3)
Traces of Doctrines Attributable to Pythagoras (D4–D8)
    Immortality, Transmigration, Eschatology (D4–D5)
    Numbers: Justice Is a Square (D6)

PYTHAGORAS

Geometry: The Pythagorean Theorem (D7)
Music (D8)
The First Inventor (prôtos heuretês) *(D9–D14)*
The Term 'Philosophy' (D9)
Mathematics (D10–D12)
The Decad and the tetraktys *(D10)*
Geometry (D11)
Weights and Measures (D12)
The Term 'Cosmos' (D13)
The Identity of the Morning Star and the Evening Star (D14)
'Symbols' (symbola) *or 'Sayings'* (akousmata) *(D15–D25)*
The Three Kinds of 'Sayings' (D15)
Exegetical Traditions (D16–D19)
Examples (D20–D25)
A List Transmitted by Iamblichus (D20)
Some Shorter Reports That Go Back to Aristotle (D21–D23)
Two Other Reports (D24–D25)

PYTHAGORAS a

BIOGRAPHICAL ELEMENTS AND LEGEND

P

Biographical Elements (P1–P24)
Birthplace (P1–P2)

P1 (> 14.8) Diog. Laert. 8.1

[. . .] Πυθαγόρας Μνησάρχου δακτυλιογλύφου, ὥς φησιν Ἕρμιππος [Frag. 19 Wehrli], Σάμιος ἤ, ὡς Ἀριστόξενος, Τυρρηνός [Frag. 11a Wehrli], ἀπὸ μιᾶς τῶν νήσων ἃς ἔσχον Ἀθηναῖοι Τυρρηνοὺς ἐκβαλόντες.

P2 (≠ DK) Porph. *VP* 5

Λύκος[1] δ' ἐν τῇ τετάρτῃ τῶν ἱστοριῶν καὶ περὶ τῆς πατρίδος ὡς διαφωνούντων τινῶν μνημονεύει λέγων· "[. . .] λέγουσι γὰρ αὐτὸν οἱ μὲν εἶναι Σάμιον, οἱ δὲ Φλιάσιον, οἱ δὲ Μεταποντῖνον."

[1] λεῦκος mss., corr. Holstenius

PYTHAGORAS a

BIOGRAPHICAL ELEMENTS AND LEGEND

P

Biographical Elements (P1–P24)
Birthplace (P1–P2)

P1 (> 14.8) Diogenes Laertius[1]

[. . .] Pythagoras, son of the gem-cutter Mnesarchus; he was from Samos, as Hermippus says, or, as Aristoxenus says, a Tyrrhenian, from one of the islands [i.e. Lemnos and neighboring islands] occupied by the Athenians after they had expelled the Tyrrhenians from them [scil. in 510 BC].

[1] For more details, see Porphyry, *VP* 1–2; his source is Neanthes, who is probably Diogenes Laertius' as well.

P2 (≠ DK) Porphyry, *Life of Pythagoras*

Lycus in Book 4 of his *Histories* reports that certain people disagree also about his fatherland. He writes, "[. . .] for some say that he came from Samos, others from Phlius, others from Metapontum."

EARLY GREEK PHILOSOPHY IV

Chronology (P3–P5)

P3 (< 14.10) Diog. Laert. 8.45

ἤκμαζε δὲ καὶ[1] κατὰ τὴν ἑξηκοστὴν[2] Ὀλυμπιάδα.

[1] καὶ del. Cobet   [2] τὴν ‹δευτέραν καὶ› ἑξακοστὴν Jacoby

P4 (≠ DK) Eus. *Chron.* (Hier.), p. 104b12 Helm

[ad Ol. 62.3] Pythagoras physicus philosophus clarus habetur.

P5 (<14.8) Ps.-Iambl. *Theol.*, p. 52.18–53.5 (< Aristox. Frag. 12 Wehrli)

[. . . = **P39**] φ′ γὰρ καὶ ιδ′ ἔτη ἔγγιστα ἀπὸ τῶν Τρωικῶν ἱστορεῖται μέχρι Ξενοφάνους τοῦ φυσικοῦ καὶ τῶν Ἀνακρέοντός τε καὶ Πολυκράτους χρόνων καὶ τῆς ὑπὸ Ἁρπάγου τοῦ Μήδου Ἰώνων πολιορκίας καὶ ἀναστάσεως, ἣν Φωκεῖς φυγόντες Μασσαλίαν ᾤκησαν· πᾶσι γὰρ τούτοις ὁμόχρονος ὁ Πυθαγόρας· [. . . = **P19**] ὅ τε Καμβύσης τῇ Πολυκράτους μάλιστα τυραννίδι συνεχρόνει, ἣν φεύγων εἰς Αἴγυπτον μετῆλθε Πυθαγόρας [. . . = **P6**].

PYTHAGORAS a

Chronology (P3–P5)

P3 (< 14.10) Diogenes Laertius

He reached his full maturity in the 60th Olympiad [540–536].

P4 (≠ DK) Eusebius, *Chronicle* (Jerome)

[Third year of the 62nd Olympiad = 530]: Pythagoras the natural philosopher is considered famous.

P5 (< 14.8) Ps.-Iamblichus, *Theology of Arithmetic*

[. . .] For nearly 514 years are recorded from the Trojan War until Xenophanes the natural philosopher, the times of Anacreon and Polycrates, the siege and removal of the Ionians by Harpagus the Mede; the Phocians who fled this founded Marseille. For Pythagoras was contemporary with all these; [. . .] and Cambyses was exactly contemporary with the tyranny of Polycrates, which Pythagoras was fleeing when he went to Egypt [. . .] [cf. **P19**].

EARLY GREEK PHILOSOPHY IV

Longevity (P6–P7)

P6 (< 14.8) Ps.-Iambl. *Theol.*, p. 53.5–7 (< Aristox. Frag. 12 Wehrli)

[. . . = **P5**] δὶς οὖν ἀφαιρεθείσης τῆς περιόδου, τουτέστι δὶς τῶν σιϛ´ ἐτῶν, λοιπὰ γίνεται τὸ τοῦ βίου αὐτοῦ πβ´.

P7 (≠ DK) Diog. Laert. 8.44

ὁ δ᾽ οὖν Πυθαγόρας, ὡς μὲν Ἡρακλείδης φησὶν ὁ τοῦ Σαραπίωνος [Heraclides Lembos Frag. 6 Müller, Sotion Frag. 23 Wehrli], ὀγδοηκοντούτης ἐτελεύτα, κατὰ τὴν ἰδίαν ὑπογραφὴν τῶν ἡλικιῶν· ὡς δὲ οἱ πλείους, ἔτη βιοὺς ἐνενήκοντα.[1]

[1] ἐνενήκοντα ‹ἐννέα› Casaubon

Alleged Parentage and Family (P8–P11)

P8 (≠ DK) Porph. *VP* 2

Ἀπολλώνιος δ᾽ ἐν τοῖς περὶ Πυθαγόρου καὶ μητέρα ἀναγράφει Πυθαΐδα, ἀπόγονον Ἀγκαίου[1] τοῦ οἰκιστοῦ τῆς Σάμου. τινὰς δὲ Ἀπόλλωνος αὐτὸν ἱστορεῖν καὶ Πυθαΐδος τῷ γόνῳ, λόγῳ δὲ Μνησάρχου φησὶν Ἀπολλώνιος.

[1] ἀγγαίου mss., corr. edd.

PYTHAGORAS a

Longevity (P6–P7)

P6 (< 14.8) Aristoxenus in Ps.-Iamblichus, *Theology of Arithmetic*

[. . .] So when this period (that is, twice 216 years) is subtracted twice, the remainder is the length of his life, eighty-two years.

P7 (≠ DK) Diogenes Laertius

Pythagoras, as Heraclides the son of Serapion [i.e. Heraclides Lembus] says, died at the age of eighty, in conformity with his own schema of the periods of a lifetime; but most people say that it was at the age of ninety.

Alleged Parentage and Family (P8–P11)

P8 (≠ DK) Porphyry, *Life of Pythagoras*

Apollonius, in his book on Pythagoras, also records as his mother Pythaïs, a descendant of Ancaeus, the founder of Samos. Apollonius says that some people stated that he was the son of Apollo and Pythaïs according to birth, and of Mnesarchus according to report.

EARLY GREEK PHILOSOPHY IV

P9 (≠ DK) Diog. Laert. 8.2

ἔσχε δὲ καὶ[1] ἀδελφούς, πρεσβύτερον μὲν Εὔνομον, μέσον δὲ Τυρρηνόν· καὶ δοῦλον Ζάμολξιν, ᾧ Γέται θύουσι, Κρόνον νομίζοντες, ὥς φησιν Ἡρόδοτος.[2]

[1] καὶ BP[1]: om. FP[4]   [2] ὥς φησιν ἡρόδοτος ante Κρόνον transp. Stephanus, om. F

P10 (> 17.1, < 31 B155) Diog. Laert. 8.42–43

[42] ἦν δὲ τῷ Πυθαγόρᾳ καὶ γυνή, Θεανὼ ὄνομα, Βροντίνου τοῦ Κροτωνιάτου θυγάτηρ· οἱ δέ, γυναῖκα μὲν εἶναι Βροντίνου, μαθήτριαν δὲ Πυθαγόρου. ἦν αὐτῷ καὶ θυγάτηρ Δαμώ, ὥς φησι Λῦσις ἐν ἐπιστολῇ τῇ πρὸς Ἵππασον[1] [. . .]. [43] ἦν καὶ Τηλαύγης υἱὸς αὐτοῖς, ὃς καὶ διεδέξατο τὸν πατέρα καὶ κατά τινας Ἐμπεδοκλέους καθηγήσατο.

[1] ἵππασον BP: ἵππαρχον F[2] (cf. Iambl. VP 75)

P11 (<14.6, < 14.13) Porph. VP 3, 4

[3] Δοῦρις δ' ὁ Σάμιος ἐν δευτέρῳ τῶν Ὡρῶν παῖδά τ' αὐτοῦ ἀναγράφει Ἀρίμνηστον [. . .]. [4] ἄλλοι δ' ἐκ Θεανοῦς τῆς Πυθώνακτος τὸ γένος Κρήσσης υἱὸν Τηλαύγη Πυθαγόρου ἀναγράφουσι καὶ θυγατέρα Μυῖαν, οἱ δὲ καὶ Ἀριγνώτην [. . .].

PYTHAGORAS a

P9 (≠ DK) Diogenes Laertius

He also had brothers, an older one, Eunomus, and one in the middle, Tyrrhenus; and a slave, Zamolxis, to whom the Getans sacrifice, thinking he is Cronus, as Herodotus says (*Histories* 4.95).

P10 (> 17.1, < 31 B155) Diogenes Laertius

[42] Pythagoras also had a wife named Theano, daughter of Brontinus of Croton; other people say that she was the wife of Brontinus and a disciple of Pythagoras. He also had a daughter, Damo, as Lysis says in his letter to Hippasus [cf. **PYTHS. R54**].[1] [43] They also had a son, Telauges, who was his father's successor and according to some was the teacher of Empedocles [cf. **EMP. P11**].

[1] By confusion, for Hipparchus.

P11 (< 14.6, < 14.13) Porphyry, *Life of Pythagoras*

[3] Duris of Samos, in the second book of his [scil. *Samian*] *Annals*, records as his son Arimnestus [. . .]. [4] Others record Telauges as a son of Pythagoras and of Theano, who was a daughter of Pythonax and of Cretan origin, and Myia as a daughter, and others also Arignotê [. . .].

EARLY GREEK PHILOSOPHY IV

Alleged Greek Teachers (P12–P17)

P12 (≠ DK) Diog. Laert. 8.2

οὗτος ἤκουσε μέν [. . .] Φερεκύδου τοῦ Συρίου· μετὰ δὲ τὴν ἐκείνου τελευτὴν ἧκεν εἰς Σάμον καὶ ἤκουσεν Ἑρμοδάμαντος τοῦ ἀπογόνου Κρεωφύλου, ἤδη πρεσβυτέρου.

P13 (53b Schibli) Tzetz. *Chil.* 11.74–75

[. . .] οὗτος ὁ Πυθαγόρας
σὺν τῷ Θαλῇ κατήκουσε τοῦ Σύρου Φερεκύδους
[. . .].

P14 (≠ DK) Porph. VP 2

διακοῦσαι δ' οὐ μόνον Φερεκύδου[1] καὶ Ἑρμοδάμαντος ἀλλὰ καὶ Ἀναξιμάνδρου φησὶν οὗτος.

[1] φερεκύδους ἀλλὰ mss., corr. edd.

P15 (≠ DK) Iambl. VP 11–12

[. . .] μετὰ τοῦ Ἑρμοδάμαντος [. . .] πρὸς τὸν Φερεκύδην διεπόρθμευσε καὶ πρὸς Ἀναξίμανδρον τὸν φυσικὸν καὶ πρὸς Θαλῆν εἰς Μίλητον [. . .]. καὶ δὴ καὶ ὁ Θαλῆς ἄσμενος αὐτὸν προσήκατο, [. . .], μεταδούς τε ὅσων[1] ἠδύνατο μαθημάτων [. . .].

[1] ὅσον ms., corr. Küster

PYTHAGORAS a

Alleged Greek Teachers (P12–P17)

P12 (≠ DK) Diogenes Laertius

He studied [. . .] with Pherecydes of Syros [cf. **PHER. P9**]; after the latter's death he went to Samos and studied with Hermodamas, a descendant of Creophylus, who was already quite old.

P13 (≠ DK) Tzetzes, *Chiliads*

[. . .] This Pythagoras, together with Thales, studied with Pherecydes of Syria.[1]

[1] Tzetzes seems to have confused the Greek island of Syros, the home of Pherecydes, with the Near Eastern country Syria.

P14 (≠ DK) Porphyry, *Life of Pythagoras*

He [i.e. Apollonius] says that he studied not only with Pherecydes and Hermodamas, but also with Anaximander.

P15 (≠ DK) Iamblichus, *Life of Pythagoras*

[. . .] accompanied by Hermodamas [. . .], he crossed over [scil. from Samos] to Miletus in order to visit Pherecydes, Anaximander the natural philosopher, and Thales. [. . .] And Thales was pleased to welcome him and [. . .] imparted to him all the knowledge he could [. . .].

P16 (14.3) Diog. Laert. 8.8.

φησὶ δὲ καὶ Ἀριστόξενος [Frag. 15 Wehrli] τὰ πλεῖστα τῶν ἠθικῶν δογμάτων λαβεῖν τὸν Πυθαγόραν παρὰ Θεμιστοκλείας τῆς ἐν Δελφοῖς.[1]

[1] ἐν Δελφοῖς Aldobrandini: ἀδελφῆς mss.

P17

a (≠ DK) Iambl. *VP* 146

οὐκέτι δὴ οὖν ἀμφίβολον γέγονε τὸ τὰς ἀφορμὰς παρὰ Ὀρφέως λαβόντα Πυθαγόραν συντάξαι τὸν περὶ θεῶν λόγον [. . .].

b (≠ DK) Procl. *Theol.* 1.5, p. 25

[. . .] πρώτου μὲν Πυθαγόρου παρὰ Ἀγλαοφήμου τὰ περὶ θεῶν ὄργια διδαχθέντος [. . .].

Alleged Travels in the Orient and Initiation into Barbarian Wisdom (P18–P22)

P18 (< 14.4) Isocr. *Bus.* 28

[. . .] ὃς ἀφικόμενος εἰς Αἴγυπτον καὶ μαθητὴς ἐκείνων γενόμενος τήν τ' ἄλλην φιλοσοφίαν πρῶτος εἰς τοὺς Ἕλληνας ἐκόμισεν, καὶ τὰ περὶ τὰς θυσίας καὶ τὰς ἁγιστείας τὰς ἐν τοῖς ἱεροῖς ἐπιφανέστερον τῶν ἄλλων ἐσπούδασεν [. . .].

PYTHAGORAS a

P16 (14.3) Diogenes Laertius

Aristoxenus also says that Pythagoras derived most of his ethical doctrines from Themistocleia of Delphi.

P17

a (≠ DK) Iamblichus, *Life of Pythagoras*

So it can no longer be doubted that it was by taking his starting point from Orpheus that Pythagoras composed his discourse about the gods [. . .].

b (≠ DK) Proclus, *Platonic Theology*

[. . .] Pythagoras being the first to have been taught by Aglaophamus[1] about the divine rites [. . .].

[1] The man who supposedly initiated Pythagoras into the Orphic mysteries.

Alleged Travels in the Orient and Initiation into Barbarian Wisdom (P18–P22)

P18 (< 14.4) Isocrates, *Busiris*

[. . .] after he went to Egypt and became their [i.e. the Egyptians'] student, he was the first to bring to the Greeks philosophy in general and in particular he practiced more conspicuously than the others the sacrifices and rites in the temples [. . .].

P19 (< 14.8) Ps.-Iambl. *Theol.*, p. 53.1–3 (< Aristox. Frag. 12 Wehrli)

[. . . = **P5**] ὑπὸ Καμβύσου γοῦν ἱστορεῖται Αἴγυπτον ἑλόντος συνηχμαλωτίσθαι ἐκεῖ συνδιατρίβων τοῖς ἱερεῦσι καὶ εἰς Βαβυλῶνα μετελθὼν τὰς βαρβαρικὰς τελετὰς μυηθῆναι [. . .].

P20 Porph. *VP* 6 et 11

a (14.9)

[6] ἔτι καὶ περὶ τῆς διδασκαλίας αὐτοῦ οἱ πλείους τὰ μὲν τῶν μαθηματικῶν καλουμένων ἐπιστημῶν παρ' Αἰγυπτίων τε καὶ Χαλδαίων καὶ Φοινίκων φασὶν ἐκμαθεῖν· γεωμετρίας μὲν γὰρ ἐκ παλαιῶν χρόνων ἐπιμεληθῆναι Αἰγυπτίους, τὰ δὲ περὶ ἀριθμούς τε καὶ λογισμοὺς Φοίνικας, Χαλδαίους δὲ τὰ περὶ τὸν οὐρανὸν θεωρήματα· περὶ ‹δὲ›[1] τὰς τῶν θεῶν ἁγιστείας καὶ τὰ λοιπὰ τῶν περὶ τὸν βίον ἐπιτηδευμάτων παρὰ τῶν Μάγων φασὶ[2] διακοῦσαί τε καὶ λαβεῖν.

[1] ‹δὲ› edd. plerique   [2] φασὶ V: φησὶ B

b (≠ DK)

[11] [. . .] ἀφίκετο δὲ καὶ πρὸς Αἰγυπτίους, φησίν, ὁ Πυθαγόρας καὶ πρὸς Ἄραβας καὶ Χαλδαίους καὶ Ἑβραίους, παρ' ὧν καὶ τὴν περὶ ὀνείρων γνῶσιν ἠκριβώσατο.

PYTHAGORAS a

P19 (<14.8) Aristoxenus in Ps.-Iamblichus, *Theology of Arithmetic*

[. . .] it is reported that when Cambyses took Egypt [= 525 BC], he [i.e. Pythagoras] was taken prisoner by him too while he was spending time with the priests [cf. **P5**], and that he then went on to Babylon and was initiated into the barbarian mysteries [. . .].

P20 Porphyry, *Life of Pythagoras*

a (14.9)

[6] Regarding his education, most people say that he learned what belongs to what are called the mathematical sciences from the Egyptians, the Chaldaeans, and the Phoenicians. For the Egyptians have cultivated geometry since ancient times, the Phoenicians arithmetic and calculation, and the Chaldaeans the observation of the heavens. As for the rituals of the gods and the other practices regarding life, they say that he studied and took them over from the Magi.

b (≠ DK)

[11] Pythagoras traveled to the Egyptians, he [i.e. Antonius Diogenes] says, the Arabs, the Chaldaeans, and the Hebrews, among whom he perfected his knowledge of dreams.

EARLY GREEK PHILOSOPHY IV

P21 (14.11) (Ps.-?) Hippol. *Ref.* 1.2.12

Διόδωρος δὲ ὁ Ἐρετριεὺς [*FGrHist* 1103 F1] καὶ Ἀριστόξενος ὁ μουσικός [Frag. 13 Wehrli] φασι πρὸς Ζαράταν τὸν Χαλδαῖον ἐληλυθέναι Πυθαγόραν.

P22 (≠ DK) Iambl. *VP* 151

[. . .] ἃ μὲν μαθόντα παρὰ τῶν Ὀρφικῶν, ἃ δὲ παρὰ τῶν Αἰγυπτίων ἱερέων, ἃ δὲ παρὰ Χαλδαίων καὶ μάγων, ἃ δὴ παρὰ τῆς τελετῆς τῆς ἐν Ἐλευσῖνι γινομένης, ἐν Ἴμβρῳ τε καὶ Σαμοθρᾴκῃ καὶ Λήμνῳ,[1] καὶ εἴ[2] τι παρὰ Τουσκανοῖς,[3] καὶ περὶ τοὺς Κελτοὺς δὲ καὶ τὴν Ἰβηρίαν.

[1] Λήμνῳ Chapoutier: δήλῳ ms.   [2] εἴ Scaliger: ἀεί ms.
[3] Τουσκανοῖς Rohde: Τυρρηνοῖς Nauck: τοῖς κοινοῖς mss.

Departure for Southern Italy (P23–P26)
The Reason for His Departure (P23)

P23 (14.8) Porph. *VP* 9

γεγονότα δ᾽ ἐτῶν τεσσαράκοντα,[1] φησὶν ὁ Ἀριστόξενος [Frag. 16 Wehrli], καὶ ὁρῶντα τὴν τοῦ Πολυκράτους τυραννίδα συντονωτέραν οὖσαν ὥστε καλῶς ἔχειν ἐλευθέρῳ ἀνδρὶ τὴν ἐπιστατείαν[2] τε καὶ δεσποτείαν ὑπομένειν,[3] οὕτως δὴ τὴν εἰς Ἰταλίαν ἄπαρσιν ποιήσασθαι.

PYTHAGORAS a

P21 (14.11) (Ps.-?) Hippolytus, *Refutation of All Heresies*

Diodorus of Eretria and Aristoxenus the writer on music say that Pythagoras went to see Zaratas [i.e. Zoroaster] the Chaldaean.

P22 (≠ DK) Iamblichus, *Life of Pythagoras*

[...] he had learned some things from the Orphics, others from the Egyptian priests, others from Chaldaeans and Magi, still others from the initiations performed at Eleusis, Imbros, Samothrace, and Lemnos, and everything else there might be from the Etruscans, and again among the Celts and in Iberia.

Departure for Southern Italy (P23–P26)
The Reason for His Departure (P23)

P23 (14.8) Porphyry, *Life of Pythagoras*

Aristoxenus says that the reason he departed for Italy was that when he was forty years old he saw that Polycrates' tyranny was too harsh for it to be proper for a free man to endure that dominion and despotism.

---

¹ τεσσαράκοντα] μ′ BV   ² ἐπιστατίαν mss., corr. Nauck
³ μὴ ante ὑπομένειν hab. mss., secl. Cobet

EARLY GREEK PHILOSOPHY IV

*Impact at Croton and in the
Rest of Italy (P24–P26)*

P24 (< 14.4) Isocr. *Bus.* 29

[. . .] τοσοῦτον γὰρ εὐδοξίᾳ τοὺς ἄλλους ὑπερέβαλεν ὥστε καὶ τοὺς νεωτέρους ἅπαντας ἐπιθυμεῖν αὐτοῦ μαθητὰς εἶναι, καὶ τοὺς πρεσβυτέρους ἥδιον ὁρᾶν τοὺς παῖδας τοὺς αὑτῶν ἐκείνῳ συγγιγνομένους ἢ τῶν οἰκείων ἐπιμελουμένους.

P25 (< 14.8a) Porph. *VP* 18–19

[18] ἐπεὶ δὲ τῆς Ἰταλίας ἐπέβη καὶ ἐν Κρότωνι ἐγένετο, φησὶν ὁ Δικαίαρχος [Frag. 33 Wehrli], ὡς ἀνδρὸς ἀφικομένου πολυπλάνου τε καὶ περιττοῦ καὶ κατὰ τὴν ἰδίαν φύσιν ὑπὸ τῆς τυχης εὖ κεχορηγημένου [. . .] οὕτως διαθεῖναι τὴν Κροτωνιατῶν πόλιν ὥστ' ἐπεὶ τὸ τῶν γερόντων ἀρχεῖον ἐψυχαγώγησεν πολλὰ καὶ καλὰ διαλεχθείς, τοῖς νέοις πάλιν ἡβητικὰς ἐποιήσατο παραινέσεις ὑπὸ τῶν ἀρχόντων κελευσθείς· μετὰ δὲ ταῦτα τοῖς παισὶν ἐκ τῶν διδασκαλείων ἀθρόοις συνελθοῦσιν· εἶτα ταῖς γυναιξί,[1] καὶ γυναικῶν σύλλογος αὐτῷ κατεσκευάσθη. [19] γενομένων δὲ τούτων μεγάλη περὶ αὐτοῦ[2] ηὐξήθη δόξα, καὶ πολλοὺς μὲν ἔλαβεν ἐξ αὐτῆς τῆς πόλεως ὁμιλητάς, οὐ μόνον ἄνδρας ἀλλὰ καὶ γυναῖκας, ὧν μιᾶς γε Θεανοῦς καὶ διεβοήθη τοὔνομα, πολλοὺς δ' ἀπὸ τῆς σύνεγγυς βαρβάρου χώρας βασιλεῖς τε καὶ δυνάστας.

PYTHAGORAS a

Impact at Croton and in the Rest of Italy
(P24–P26)

P24 (< 14.4) Isocrates, *Busiris*

[. . .] He surpassed the others in fame so much that all the younger men wanted to be his disciples and the older ones were more pleased to see their children associating with him than caring for their household affairs.

P25 (< 14.8a) Dicaearchus in Porphyry, *Life of Pythagoras*

[18] Dicaearchus says that when he landed in Italy and arrived at Croton, on his arrival, being a man who had traveled much, was extraordinary, and whose nature had been richly endowed by fortune [. . .], he had such an effect upon the city of the Crotonians that after he had won over the souls of the council of the elders by delivering long and fine speeches, he in turn bestowed upon the young men, at the request of the magistrates, advice adapted to their age, and after this upon the children who had gathered as a crowd on leaving their schools; and then upon the women, and he organized an assembly of women. [19] After these events, his reputation grew very great, and in this same city he acquired many companions, not only men, but also women (the name of one of these, Theano, became famous), and also kings and rulers of the neighboring barbarian country.

---

¹ γυναιξίν, ⟨ἐπεὶ⟩ Westermann
² αὐτὸν mss., corr. Wakefield

P26 (≠ DK) Diog. Laert. 8.14–15

οὕτω δὲ ἐθαυμάσθη, ὥστε ἔλεγον[1] τοὺς γνωρίμους[2] αὐτοῦ ⟨παραγγέλλειν⟩[3] παντοίας[4] θεοῦ φωνάς [. . .]. τοιγὰρ καὶ προσεκαρτέρουν αὐτῷ καὶ τῶν λόγων ἕνεκα προσῄεσαν καὶ Λευκανοὶ καὶ Πευκέτιοι καὶ Μεσσάπιοί τε καὶ Ῥωμαῖοι. [. . .] τῶν τε ἑξακοσίων οὐκ ἐλάττους ἐπὶ τὴν νυκτερινὴν ἀκρόασιν ἀπήντων αὐτοῦ· καὶ εἴ[5] τινες ἀξιωθεῖεν αὐτὸν θεάσασθαι, ἔγραφον πρὸς τοὺς οἰκείους ὡς μεγάλου τινὸς τετυχηκότες [. . .].

[1] ἔλεγον BPF: λέγειν Kühn   [2] post γνωρίμους ⟨τὰ⟩ Kühn, ⟨τὰ λεγόμενα⟩ Marcovich   [3] ⟨παραγγέλλειν⟩ nos   [4] παντοίας BP: παντοίους F: τὰς παραγγελίας coni. Delatte: μάντιας Cobet: παντελῶς Marcovich   [5] εἴ PFΦ: οἱ B

Earliest References to Pythagoras' Person and to Various Aspects of His Activity (P27–P33)
References by Name (P27–P31)
In Heraclitus (P27–P28)

P27 [= HER. D20]

πολυμαθίη νόον οὐ διδάσκει· Ἡσίοδον γὰρ ἂν ἐδίδαξε καὶ Πυθαγόρην αὖτίς τε Ξενοφάνεά τε καὶ Ἑκαταῖον.

P26 (≠ DK) Diogenes Laertius

He was so greatly admired that they said of his disciples ⟨that they transmitted⟩ all kinds of words of a god [. . .]. And that is why the Lucanians and the Peucetians, the Messapians and the Romans remained attached to him and came to him to listen to his discourses [. . .]. Not fewer than six hundred people went to his evening lecture; and any who were considered worthy of seeing him wrote to their relatives as though something extraordinary had happened to them.

Earliest References to Pythagoras' Person and to Various Aspects of His Activity (P27–P33)
References by Name (P27–P31)
In Heraclitus (P27–P28)

P27 [= HER. D20]

Much learning does not teach intelligence: for otherwise it would have taught it to Hesiod and Pythagoras, and again to Xenophanes and Hecataeus.

P28 [= HER. D26]

Πυθαγόρης Μνησάρχου ἱστορίην ἤσκησεν ἀνθρώπων μάλιστα πάντων, καὶ ἐκλεξάμενος ταύτας τὰς
συγγραφὰς ἐποιήσατο ἑαυτοῦ σοφίην, πολυμαθίην,
κακοτεχνίην.

In Ion of Chios (P29)

P29 (< 36 B4) Ion Chius in Diog. Laert. 1.120

Ἴων δ' ὁ Χῖός φησιν περὶ αὐτοῦ·

[. . . cf. **PHER. R1**]
εἴπερ Πυθαγόρης ἐτύμως ὁ σοφὸς περὶ πάντων
ἀνθρώπων γνώμας εἶδε καὶ ἐξέμαθεν.

In Herodotus (P30)

P30 (14.2) Hdt. 4.95–96

[95] ὡς δὲ ἐγὼ πυνθάνομαι τῶν τὸν Ἑλλήσποντον καὶ
Πόντον οἰκεόντων Ἑλλήνων, τὸν Σάλμοξιν τοῦτον
ἐόντα ἄνθρωπον δουλεῦσαι ἐν Σάμῳ, δουλεῦσαι δὲ
Πυθαγόρῃ τῷ Μνησάρχου· ἐνθεῦτεν δὲ αὐτὸν γενόμενον ἐλεύθερον χρήματα κτήσασθαι συχνά, κτησάμε-
νον δὲ ἀπελθεῖν ἐς τὴν ἑωυτοῦ· ἅτε δὲ κακοβίων τε
ἐόντων τῶν Θρηίκων καὶ ὑπαφρονεστέρων, τὸν Σάλμοξιν τοῦτον ἐπιστάμενον δίαιτάν τε Ἰάδα καὶ ἤθεα

PYTHAGORAS a

P28 [= **HER. D26**]

Pythagoras, son of Mnesarchus, devoted himself to investigation more than all other men, and after he had made a selection of these writings [scil. probably: the writings of other people] he devised his own wisdom: much learning, evil artifice.

In Ion of Chios (P29)

P29 (< 36 B4) Ion of Chios in Diogenes Laertius

Ion of Chios says about him [i.e. Pherecydes, cf. **PHER. R1**]:

[...]
If indeed Pythagoras, truly wise beyond all [or: about all things],
    Made acquaintance with men's thoughts and knew them thoroughly.

In Herodotus (P30)

P30 (14.2) Herodotus, *Histories*

[95] As I have learned from the Greeks who live on the Hellespont and the Black Sea, this Salmoxis, who was a human being [scil. although the Thracians venerated him as a god], had been a slave in Samos, a slave of Pythagoras the son of Mnesarchus. When he was set free there, he acquired great wealth, and once he had done so he returned home. As the Thracians were poor and rather stupid, while Salmoxis knew the Ionian way of life, and manners more refined than the Thracians', since he had

βαθύτερα ἢ κατὰ Θρήικας, οἷα Ἕλλησί τε ὁμιλήσαντα καὶ Ἑλλήνων οὐ τῷ ἀσθενεστάτῳ σοφιστῇ Πυθαγόρῃ, κατασκευάσασθαι ἀνδρεῶνα, ἐς τὸν πανδοκεύοντα τῶν ἀστῶν τοὺς πρώτους καὶ εὐωχέοντα ἀναδιδάσκειν ὡς οὔτε αὐτὸς οὔτε οἱ συμπόται αὐτοῦ οὔτε οἱ ἐκ τούτων αἰεὶ γινόμενοι ἀποθανέονται, ἀλλ' ἥξουσι ἐς χῶρον τοῦτον ἵνα αἰεὶ περιεόντες ἕξουσι τὰ[1] πάντα ἀγαθά. ἐν ᾧ δὲ ἐποίεε τὰ καταλεχθέντα καὶ ἔλεγε ταῦτα, ἐν τούτῳ κατάγαιον οἴκημα ἐποιέετο. ὡς δέ οἱ παντελέως εἶχε τὸ οἴκημα, ἐκ μὲν τῶν Θρηίκων ἠφανίσθη, καταβὰς δὲ κάτω ἐς τὸ κατάγαιον οἴκημα διαιτᾶτο ἐπ' ἔτεα τρία· οἱ δέ μιν ἐπόθεόν τε καὶ ἐπένθεον ὡς τεθνεῶτα. τετάρτῳ δὲ ἔτει ἐφάνη τοῖσι Θρήιξι, καὶ οὕτω πιθανά σφι ἐγένετο τὰ ἔλεγε ὁ Σάλμοξις. ταῦτά φασί μιν ποιῆσαι. [96] ἐγὼ δὲ περὶ μὲν τούτου καὶ τοῦ καταγαίου οἰκήματος οὔτε ἀπιστέω οὔτε ὦν πιστεύω τι λίην, δοκέω δὲ πολλοῖσι ἔτεσι πρότερον τὸν Σάλμοξιν τοῦτον γενέσθαι Πυθαγόρεω.

[1] τὰ del. Krüger

In Democritus (P31)

P31 (< 14.6) Diog. Laert. 9.38

[. . .] ἀλλὰ καὶ αὐτοῦ Πυθαγόρου μέμνηται, θαυμάζων αὐτὸν ἐν τῷ ὁμωνύμῳ συγγράμματι [. . .] [= **ATOM. P24**].

associated with Greeks and, among the Greeks, with one who was not at all the weakest, the sage Pythagoras, he had a residence built for himself, where he received and entertained the first of the citizens, teaching them that neither he nor his guests nor their descendants would ever die, but that they would come to a place where they would live forever and would possess all good things. But while he was doing this and saying what I have said, at the same time he had a subterranean dwelling built for himself. When the dwelling was finished, he vanished from the sight of the Thracians, and having descended into the subterranean dwelling he spent three years there. They missed him and mourned him, thinking that he had died. But in the fourth year he appeared to the Thracians, and thus what Salmoxis had said seemed credible to them. This is what they say he did. [96] As for me, I neither disbelieve the story about him and his subterranean dwelling, nor do I believe it very much, but I think that this Salmoxis lived many years earlier than Pythagoras.

In Democritus (P31)

P31 (< 14.6) Thrasyllus in Diogenes Laertius

[. . .] in fact, he mentions Pythagoras himself admiringly in the work of his that bears his name [. . .] [cf. **ATOM. D2 [1.1], P21;** cf. **P5**].

EARLY GREEK PHILOSOPHY IV

Other References (P32–P33)
In Xenophanes (P32)

P32 (21 B7) Diog. Laert. 8.36

περὶ δὲ τοῦ ἄλλοτε ἄλλον αὐτὸν γεγενῆσθαι Ξενοφάνης ἐν ἐλεγείᾳ προσμαρτυρεῖ [. . . = **XEN. D64**].

In Empedocles? (P33)

P33 (31 B129) Porph. VP 30

αὐτὸς δὲ τῆς τοῦ παντὸς ἁρμονίας ἠκροᾶτο συνιεὶς τῆς καθολικῆς τῶν σφαιρῶν καὶ τῶν κατ' αὐτὰς κινουμένων ἀστέρων ἁρμονίας, ἧς ἡμᾶς μὴ ἀκούειν διὰ σμικρότητα τῆς φύσεως. τούτοις καὶ Ἐμπεδοκλῆς μαρτυρεῖ λέγων περὶ αὐτοῦ [. . . = **EMP. D38**].

Later Reports about the Sage and
Holy Man (P34–P42)
Between God and Man (P34–P36)

P34 (14.7) Ael. *Var. hist.* 2.26

Ἀριστοτέλης λέγει [Frag. 191 Rose] ὑπὸ τῶν Κροτωνιατῶν τὸν Πυθαγόραν[1] Ἀπόλλωνα Ὑπερβόρειον προσαγορεύεσθαι.

[1] πύθιον mss., corr. Gessner

PYTHAGORAS a

Other References (P32–P33)
In Xenophanes (P32)

P32 (21 B7) Diogenes Laertius

About the fact that he [i.e. Pythagoras] became a different person at different times, Xenophanes provides testimony in his elegiac poem [. . . = **XEN. D64**].

In Empedocles? (P33)

P33 (31 B129) Porphyry, *Life of Pythagoras*

He himself heard the harmony of the whole, because he had understood the universal harmony of the spheres of the heavenly bodies that move because of them—something that we other people do not hear because of the smallness of our nature. This is what Empedocles testifies to when he says about him, [. . . = **EMP. D38**].

Later Reports about the Sage and
Holy Man (P34–P42)
Between God and Man (P34–P36)

P34 (14.7) Aristotle in Aelian, *Historical Miscellany*

Aristotle says that Pythagoras was called 'Hyperborean Apollo' by the Crotonians.

P35 (≠ DK) Iambl. *VP* 30

[. . .] οἱ μὲν τὸν Πύθιον, οἱ δὲ τὸν ἐξ Ὑπερβορέων Ἀπόλλωνα, οἱ δὲ τὸν Παιᾶνα, οἱ δὲ τῶν τὴν σελήνην κατοικούντων δαιμόνων ἕνα, ἄλλοι δὲ ἄλλον τῶν Ὀλυμπίων θεῶν φημίζοντες[1] [. . .].

[1] ἐφήμιζον F, corr. Deubner

P36 (14.7) Iambl. *VP* 31

ἱστορεῖ δὲ Ἀριστοτέλης ἐν τοῖς περὶ τῆς Πυθαγορικῆς φιλοσοφίας [Frag. 192 Rose] διαίρεσίν τινα τοιάνδε ὑπὸ τῶν ἀνδρῶν ἐν τοῖς πάνυ ἀπορρήτοις διαφυλάττεσθαι· τοῦ λογικοῦ ζῴου τὸ μέν ἐστι θεός, τὸ δὲ ἄνθρωπος, τὸ δὲ οἷον Πυθαγόρας.

Earlier Lives (P37–P39)

P37 (< 14.8) Diog. Laert. 8.4–5

[4] τοῦτόν φησιν Ἡρακλείδης ὁ Ποντικὸς [Frag. 89 Wehrli] περὶ αὑτοῦ τάδε λέγειν, ὡς εἴη ποτὲ γεγονὼς Αἰθαλίδης καὶ Ἑρμοῦ υἱὸς νομισθείη· τὸν δὲ Ἑρμῆν εἰπεῖν αὐτῷ ἑλέσθαι ὅ τι ἂν βούληται πλὴν ἀθανασίας. αἰτήσασθαι οὖν ζῶντα καὶ τελευτῶντα[1] μνήμην ἔχειν τῶν συμβαινόντων. ἐν μὲν οὖν τῇ ζωῇ πάντων διαμνημονεῦσαι, ἐπεὶ δὲ ἀποθάνοι τηρῆσαι τὴν αὐτὴν μνήμην. χρόνῳ δ' ὕστερον εἰς Εὔφορβον ἐλθεῖν καὶ ὑπὸ Μενέλεω τρωθῆναι. ὁ δ' Εὔφορβος ἔλεγεν ὡς

PYTHAGORAS a

P35 (≠ DK) Iamblichus, *Life of Pythagoras*

[. . .] some said that he was the Pythian [i.e. Delphic Apollo], others the Apollo from the Hyperboreans, others the god Paean, others one of the divinities (*daimones*) that live on the moon, others some other Olympian god [. . .].

P36 (14.7) Aristotle in Iamblichus, *Life of Pythagoras*

Aristotle reports in his writings on Pythagoras' philosophy that these men preserved among their most secret doctrines the following classification: among rational living beings, one kind is divine, another is human, and another is such as Pythagoras.

Earlier Lives (P37–P39)

P37 (< 14.8) Heraclides of Pontus in Diogenes Laertius

[4] Heraclides of Pontus says that he [i.e. Pythagoras] used to say about himself that he had once been Aethalides and was considered to be Hermes' son; and that Hermes had said to him that he could choose whatever he wanted except immortality. So he had asked to preserve, both living and dead, a memory of what happened. So he remembered all things during his lifetime; and when he died, he preserved the same memory. Later in time he entered into Euphorbus and was wounded by Menelaus. And Euphor-

---

¹ τελευτήσαντα Cobet

Αἰθαλίδης ποτὲ γεγόνοι καὶ ὅτι παρ' Ἑρμοῦ τὸ δῶρον λάβοι καὶ τὴν τῆς ψυχῆς περιπόλησιν, ὡς περιεπολήθη καὶ εἰς ὅσα φυτὰ καὶ ζῷα παρεγένετο καὶ ὅσα ἡ ψυχὴ ἐν τῷ Ἅιδῃ² ἔπαθε καὶ αἱ λοιπαὶ τίνα ὑπομένουσιν. [5] ἐπειδὴ δὲ Εὔφορβος ἀποθάνοι, μεταβῆναι τὴν ψυχὴν αὐτοῦ εἰς Ἑρμότιμον [. . .] ἐπειδὴ δὲ Ἑρμότιμος ἀπέθανε, γενέσθαι Πύρρον τὸν Δήλιον ἁλιέα· καὶ πάντα πάλιν μνημονεύειν, πῶς πρόσθεν Αἰθαλίδης, εἶτ' Εὔφορβος, εἶτα Ἑρμότιμος, εἶτα Πύρρος γένοιτο. ἐπειδὴ δὲ Πύρρος ἀπέθανε, γενέσθαι Πυθαγόραν καὶ πάντων τῶν εἰρημένων μεμνῆσθαι.

² ἐν Ἅιδου Cobet

P38 (≠ DK) Porph. *VP* 45

ἀνέφερεν δ' αὑτὸν εἰς τοὺς πρότερον γεγονότας, πρῶτον μὲν Εὔφορβος λέγων γενέσθαι, δεύτερον δ' Αἰθαλίδης,¹ τρίτον Ἑρμότιμος, τέταρτον δὲ Πύρρος, νῦν δὲ Πυθαγόρας. δι' ὧν ἐδείκνυεν ὡς ἀθάνατος ἡ ψυχὴ καὶ τοῖς κεκαθαρμένοις εἰς μνήμην τοῦ παλαιοῦ βίου ἀφικνεῖται.

¹ πρῶτον μὲν Αἰθαλίδης . . . δεύτερον δ' Εὔφορβος coni. Nauck

P39 (< 14.8) Ps.-Iambl. *Theol.*, p. 52.8–18

Ἀνδροκύδης τε ὁ Πυθαγορικὸς ὁ Περὶ τῶν συμβόλων γράψας καὶ Εὐβουλίδης ὁ Πυθαγορικὸς καὶ Ἀριστό-

bus said that he had once been Aethalides and that he had received from Hermes this gift and the wandering of the soul, how it had wandered and all the plants and animals it had been in and everything that his soul had experienced in Hades and that the other souls endure there. [5] And when Euphorbus died, his soul passed into Hermotimus [. . .]. And when Hermotimus died, he became Pyrrhus, the Delian fisherman; and once again he remembered everything, how he had formerly been Aethalides, then Euphorbus, then Hermotimus, then Pyrrhus. And when Pyrrhus died, he became Pythagoras and remembered everything I have mentioned.

P38 (≠ DK) Porphyry, *Life of Pythagoras*

He himself traced himself back to people who had lived earlier, saying that first he had been Euphorbus, second Athalides, third Hermotimus, fourth Pyrrhus, and now Pythagoras, and in this way he showed that the soul is immortal and that in those who are pure it succeeds in remembering its earlier life.

P39 (< 14.8) Ps.-Iamblichus, *Theology of Arithmetic*

Androcydes the Pythagorean, who wrote *On Symbols*, Aristoxenus, Hippobotus, and Neanthes, who have writ-

ξένος καὶ Ἱππόβοτος καὶ Νεάνθης οἱ τὰ[1] κατὰ τὸν
ἄνδρα ἀναγράψαντες σιϛ´ ἔτεσι τὰς μετεμψυχώσεις
τὰς αὐτῷ συμβεβηκυίας ἔφασαν γεγονέναι. μετὰ τοσ-
αῦτα γοῦν ἔτη εἰς παλιγγενεσίαν ἐλθεῖν Πυθαγόραν
καὶ ἀναζῆσαι ὡσανεὶ μετὰ τὴν πρώτην ἀνακύκλησιν[2]
καὶ ἐπάνοδον τοῦ ἀπὸ ἐξ ψυχογονικοῦ κύβου, τοῦ δ᾽
αὐτοῦ καὶ ἀποκαταστατικοῦ διὰ τὸ σφαιρικόν, ὡς δὲ
καὶ ἄλλοτε[3] διὰ τούτων ἀνάζησιν ἔσχεν· ᾧ καὶ συμ-
φωνεῖ τὸ Εὐφόρβου τὴν ψυχὴν ἐσχηκέναι κατά γε[4]
τοὺς χρόνους [. . . = **P5**].

[1] τὰ A, om. cett.   [2] ἀνακύκλησιν xA: ἀνακύκλωσιν p
[3] ἄλλοτε yA: ἄλλο Pp: ἄλλην Ast   [4] γε Ast: τε xAp

His Descent to the Underworld, or
Katabasis (*P40–P41*)
His Encounter with Hesiod and Homer (*P40*)

P40 (≠ DK) Diog. Laert. 8.21

φησὶ δ᾽ Ἱερώνυμος [Frag. 42 Wehrli] κατελθόντα αὐτὸν
εἰς Ἅιδου τὴν μὲν Ἡσιόδου ψυχὴν ἰδεῖν πρὸς κίονι
χαλκῷ δεδεμένην καὶ τρίζουσαν, τὴν δὲ Ὁμήρου κρε-
μαμένην ἀπὸ δένδρου καὶ ὄφεις περὶ αὐτήν, ἀνθ᾽ ὧν
εἶπον περὶ θεῶν, κολαζομένους δὲ καὶ τοὺς μὴ θέλον-
τας συνεῖναι ταῖς ἑαυτῶν γυναιξί· καὶ δὴ καὶ διὰ
τοῦτο τιμηθῆναι ὑπὸ τῶν ἐν Κρότωνι.

ten about this man, stated that the metempsychoses he experienced lasted 216 years. So it was after this number of years that Pythagoras came to be reborn and to live again—just like after the first cycle and return of the cube of six, generator of the soul, which is also recurrent by reason of its spherical character, as he also obtained a second life at other times for these reasons. This agrees with his having received the soul of Euphorbus at that time [. . .].

His Descent to the Underworld, or
Katabasis *(P40–P41)*
His Encounter with Hesiod and Homer (P40)

P40 (≠ DK) Hieronymus of Rhodes in Diogenes Laertius

Hieronymus says that when he [i.e. Pythagoras] descended to Hades he saw Hesiod's soul bound to a bronze column and shrieking, and Homer's hung from a tree and surrounded by snakes, because of what they had said about the gods, and that he also saw that those who did not want to have sexual intercourse with their own wives were punished; and this is precisely why the Crotonians honored him.

EARLY GREEK PHILOSOPHY IV

A Rationalizing Interpretation of the
Katabasis *(P41)*

P41 (≠ DK) Diog. Laert. 8.41

λέγει γὰρ [Hermippus Frag . 20 Wehrli] ὡς γενόμενος ἐν Ἰταλίᾳ κατὰ γῆς οἰκίσκον ποιήσαι καὶ τῇ μητρὶ ἐντείλαιτο τὰ γινόμενα εἰς δέλτον γράφειν σημειουμένην καὶ τὸν χρόνον, ἔπειτα καθιέναι αὐτῷ[1] ἔστ' ἂν ἀνέλθῃ. τοῦτο ποιῆσαι τὴν μητέρα. τὸν δὲ Πυθαγόραν μετὰ χρόνον ἀνελθεῖν ἰσχνὸν[2] καὶ κατεσκελετευμένον· εἰσελθόντα τε εἰς τὴν ἐκκλησίαν φάσκειν ὡς ἀφῖκται ἐξ Ἅιδου· καὶ δὴ καὶ ἀνεγίνωσκεν αὐτοῖς τὰ συμβεβηκότα. οἱ δὲ σαινόμενοι τοῖς λεγομένοις ἐδάκρυόν τε καὶ ᾤμωζον καὶ ἐπίστευον εἶναι τὸν Πυθαγόραν θεῖόν τινα, ὥστε καὶ τὰς γυναῖκας αὐτῷ παραδοῦναι, ὡς καὶ μαθησομένας τι τῶν αὐτοῦ· ἃς καὶ Πυθαγορικὰς κληθῆναι. καὶ ταῦτα μὲν ὁ Ἕρμιππος [. . .].

[1] αὐτῷ B²FΦ: αὐτὸν B¹: αὐτὸ P   [2] ἰσχνὸν BPF: στυγνὸς Φ

The Harmony of the Spheres

See **P33**

PYTHAGORAS a

A Rationalizing Interpretation of the Katabasis *(P41)*

P41 (≠ DK) Hermippus in Diogenes Laertius

Hermippus also says something else about Pythagoras: that after he arrived in Italy, he built a small subterranean dwelling and ordered his mother to note and write down on a tablet what happened and when, and then to send this down to him until he came back up. His mother did this. After some time Pythagoras came back up, withered and reduced to a skeleton. He went into the Assembly and said he was returning from Hades; and he read out to them what had happened. They were so moved by what he said that they wept, groaned, and were convinced that Pythagoras was someone divine, so that they even entrusted their wives to him so that they would learn some of his teachings; and these were also called the Pythagorean women. And this is what Hermippus says [. . .].[1]

[1] Hermippus' story is derived from the one Herodotus tells about Zalmoxis (see **P30**).

The Harmony of the Spheres

See **P33**

EARLY GREEK PHILOSOPHY IV

Other Prodigies and Marvels (P42)

P42 (14.7) Apoll. *Mir.* 6

τούτοις δὲ ἐπιγενόμενος Πυθαγόρας Μνησάρχου υἱὸς τὸ μὲν πρῶτον ἐπονεῖτο περὶ τὰ μαθήματα καὶ τοὺς ἀριθμούς, ὕστερον δέ ποτε καὶ τῆς Φερεκύδου τερατοποιίας οὐκ ἀπέστη. καὶ γὰρ ἐν Μεταποντίῳ πλοίου εἰσερχομένου[1] φορτίον ἔχοντος[2] καὶ τῶν παρατυχόντων εὐχομένων σωστὸν εἶναι κατελθεῖν[3] διὰ τὸν φόρτον, ἑστῶτα τοῦτον εἰπεῖν· "νεκρὸν[4] τοίνυν φανήσεται ὑμῖν σῶμα ἄγον τὸ πλοῖον τοῦτο." πάλιν δὲ ἐν Καυλωνίᾳ, ὥς φησιν Ἀριστοτέλης [Frag. 191 Rose], ‹προυσήμηνε τὴν λευκὴν ἄρκτον. καὶ ὁ αὐτὸς Ἀριστοτέλης›[5] γράφων περὶ αὐτοῦ πολλὰ μὲν καὶ ἄλλα λέγει καὶ τὸν ἐν Τυρρηνίᾳ, φησίν, δάκνοντα θανάσιμον ὄφιν, αὐτὸς δάκνων, ἀπέκτεινεν. καὶ τὴν γινομένην δὲ στάσιν τοῖς Πυθαγορείοις προειπεῖν· διὸ καὶ εἰς Μεταπόντιον ἀπῆρεν ὑπὸ μηδενὸς θεωρηθείς, καὶ ὑπὸ τοῦ Κόσα[6] ποταμοῦ διαβαίνων ἤκουσε φωνὴν μεγάλην ὑπὲρ ἄνθρωπον· "Πυθαγόρα, χαῖρε." τοὺς δὲ παρόντας περιδεεῖς γενέσθαι· ἐφάνη δέ ποτε καὶ ἐν Κρότωνι καὶ ἐν Μεταποντίῳ τῇ αὐτῇ ἡμέρᾳ καὶ ὥρᾳ· ἐν θεάτρῳ δὲ καθήμενός ποτε ἐξανίστατο,[7] ὥς φησιν

---

[1] ἐν Μεταποντίῳ πλοίου εἰσερχομένου Rose: τῷ ποντίῳ πλοίῳ εἰσερχομένῳ ms.

[2] ἔχοντι ms., corr. Keller

[3] κατελθεῖν ms.: καὶ ἐλθεῖν Teucher

PYTHAGORAS a

Other Prodigies and Marvels (P42)

P42 (14.7) Aristotle in Apollonius, *Wonders*

Pythagoras, son of Mnesarchus, who lived after these men [i.e. Epimenides, Aristeas, Hermotimus, Abaris, and Pherecydes], at first worked on the sciences and numbers, but later he did not refrain from the miracle-working of Pherecydes. For one day when a boat was sailing in at Metapontum bearing a cargo and the bystanders prayed that it arrive safely because of its cargo, he stood up and said, "Well, it will be revealed to you that what this ship is carrying is a dead body." And another time, in Caulonia, as Aristotle says ⟨he predicted the appearance of the white bear. The same Aristotle⟩, who has written many things about him, also says, "he killed, by biting it himself, the Tyrrhenian snake, whose bite is deadly." And he predicted to the Pythagoreans that there would be a revolt. And that is why he left for Metapontum without letting anyone observe him. And while he was crossing the Cosas river together with other people he heard from it a great, superhuman voice: "Hail, Pythagoras!"; the people present were terrified. And once he appeared on the same day and at the same hour both in Croton and in Metapontum. And once when he was sitting in the theater he stood up, as

---

4 νεκρὸν Meursius ex Iambl. *VP* 142: μικρὸν ms.

5 add. Diels post Rose ex. Iambl. *VP* 142

6 Κόσα Rose (cf. Ael. *Var. hist.* 2.26): κατὰ σάμον ms.

7 ἐξανίσταται ms., corr. Hercher

Ἀριστοτέλης, καὶ τὸν ἴδιον μηρὸν παρέφηνε[8] τοῖς καθημένοις[9] χρυσοῦν.

[8] παρέφηνε Rose ex Aeliano VH 2.26 et 4.17.: παρέφαινε ms   [9] εἰς post καθημένοις hab. ms., del. Westermann post Rittershausen

A Caricature by the Skeptic Timon of Phlius (P43)

P43 (≠ DK) Diog. Laert. 8.36 (et al.)

τὴν δὲ σεμνοπρέπειαν τοῦ Πυθαγόρου καὶ Τίμων ἐν τοῖς Σίλλοις [Frag. 57 Di Marco] δάκνων αὐτὸν ὅμως οὐ παρέλιπεν, εἰπὼν οὕτως·

Πυθαγόρην τε γόητας ἀποκλίνοντ᾽[1] ἐπὶ δόξας
θήρῃ ἐπ᾽ ἀνθρώπων, Σεμνηγορίης[2] ὀαριστήν.

[1] ἀποκλίνοντ᾽ Plut. Num. 8.8: ἀπόκλινον BP[1]: ἀπο κλεινὸν FP[4]: ἀποκλίναν τὲ D   [2] Σεμνηγορίης Di Marco: σεμν- mss.

Four Versions of Pythagoras' Death (P44)

P44 (≠ DK) Diog. Laert. 8.39–40

a

[39] ἐτελεύτα δ᾽ ὁ Πυθαγόρας τοῦτον τὸν τρόπον. συνεδρεύοντος μετὰ τῶν συνήθων ἐν τῇ Μίλωνος οἰκίᾳ τοῦ ‹ἀθλη›τοῦ,[1] ὑπό τινος τῶν μὴ παραδοχῆς ἀξιω-

PYTHAGORAS a

Aristotle says, and showed to the spectators his own thigh, which was of gold.

See also **PHER. P10, R13**

A Caricature by the Skeptic Timon of Phlius (P43)

P43 (≠ DK) Diogenes Laertius

Pythagoras' solemn dignity was not ignored by Timon in his *Satires (Silloi)* either, biting him though he was; he speaks as follows:

> [. . .] and Pythagoras, inclining toward magical opinions
> In his hunt for humans, the lover of Lofty Utterance.

Four Versions of Pythagoras' Death (P44)

P44 (≠ DK) Diogenes Laertius

a

[39] Pythagoras died in the following way. While he was sitting with his companions in the athlete Milo's house, it happened that the house was set on fire out of envy by one

---

¹ τοῦ ‹ἀθλη›τοῦ Cobet: τούτου mss.

θέντων διὰ φθόνον ὑποπρησθῆναι τὴν οἰκίαν συνέβη (τινὲς δ᾽ αὐτοὺς τοὺς Κροτωνιάτας τοῦτο πρᾶξαι, τυραννίδος ἐπίθεσιν εὐλαβουμένους). τὸν δὴ Πυθαγόραν καταλειφθῆναι διεξιόντα· καὶ πρός τινι χωρίῳ γενόμενος² πλήρει κυάμων, ἵνα <μὴ>³ διέρχοιτο,⁴ αὐτόθι ἔστη, εἰπὼν ἁλῶναι <ἂν>⁵ μᾶλλον ἢ πατῆσαι, ἀναιρεθῆναι δὲ κρεῖττον ἢ λαλῆσαι·⁶ καὶ ὧδε πρὸς τῶν διωκόντων ἀποσφαγῆναι [. . .].

² γενόμενος Frobenius: γενόμενον mss.
³ <μὴ> Delatte   ⁴ διέρχοιτο Delatte: διήρχετο Suda Π. 3020: om. mss.   ⁵ <ἂν> Cobet
⁶ ἀναιρεθῆναι . . . λαλῆσαι del. Cobet

b

[40] φησὶ δὲ Δικαίαρχος [Frag. 35b Wehrli] τὸν Πυθαγόραν ἀποθανεῖν καταφυγόντα εἰς τὸ ἐν Μεταποντίῳ ἱερὸν τῶν Μουσῶν, τετταράκοντα ἡμέρας ἀσιτήσαντα.

c

Ἡρακλείδης δέ φησιν ἐν τῇ τῶν Σατύρου βίων ἐπιτομῇ [Satyr. Frag. 11 Schorn] μετὰ τὸ θάψαι Φερεκύδην ἐν Δήλῳ ἐπανελθεῖν εἰς Ἰταλίαν καὶ πανδαισίαν εὑρόντα Κύλωνος τοῦ Κροτωνιάτου εἰς Μεταπόντιον ὑπεξελθεῖν κἀκεῖ τὸν βίον καταστρέψαι ἀσιτίᾳ, μὴ βουλόμενον περαιτέρω ζῆν.

PYTHAGORAS a

of the people who were not considered worthy of being admitted to him; but some say it was the Crotonians themselves who did this, to prevent the establishment of a tyranny. Pythagoras was caught as he was going out: he got as far as a field full of beans, where he stopped so that he would ‹not› cross it, saying that he would rather be captured than trample them, and would rather be killed than talk nonsense; and this is how his pursuers cut his throat [. . .].

b

[40] But Dicaearchus says that Pythagoras died after he had fled into the temple of the Muses at Metapontum, when he spent forty days without eating.

c

Heraclides in his *Epitome of Satyrus' Biographies* says that after he had buried Pherecydes at Delos he returned to Italy and having attended a sumptuous banquet given by Cylon of Croton he withdrew to Metapontum and there ended his life by starvation, since he did not wish to live any longer.

d

Ἕρμιππος δέ φησι [Frag. 20 Wehrli], πολεμούντων Ἀκραγαντίνων καὶ Συρακουσίων, ἐξελθεῖν μετὰ τῶν συνήθων τὸν Πυθαγόραν καὶ προστῆναι τῶν Ἀκραγαντίνων· τροπῆς δὲ γενομένης περικάμπτοντα αὐτὸν τὴν τῶν κυάμων χώραν ὑπὸ τῶν Συρακουσίων ἀναιρεθῆναι [. . .].

Civic Honors and Religious Aura (P45–P46)

P45 (< 14.5) Arist. *Rhet.* 2.23 1398b9–16

[. . .] καὶ ὡς Ἀλκιδάμας [= Frag. 10 Avezzù], ὅτι πάντες τοὺς σοφοὺς τιμῶσιν. [. . .] καὶ Ἰταλιῶται Πυθαγόραν [. . .] ἔθαψαν καὶ τιμῶσιν ἔτι καὶ νῦν [. . .].

P46

a (≠ DK) Diog. Laert. 8.15

Μεταποντῖνοί γε μὴν τὴν μὲν οἰκίαν αὐτοῦ Δήμητρος ἱερὸν ἐκάλουν, τὸν στενωπὸν δὲ[1] Μουσεῖον, ὥς φησι Φαβωρῖνος ἐν Παντοδαπαῖς ἱστορίαις [Frag. 78 Amato].

[1] δὲ P^x.: om. BP^{1}F

PYTHAGORAS a

d

But Hermippus says that when the Agrigentines and Syracusans were at war, Pythagoras went out with his companions and fought in the frontline of the Agrigentines; and when they were routed, he was killed by the Syracusans as he was going around the bean field [. . .].

Civic Honors and Religious Aura (P45–P46)

P45 (< 14.5) Aristotle, *Rhetoric*

[. . .] and as Alcidamas says, that everyone honors the sages; [. . .] and the Italians buried [. . .] Pythagoras and honor him to this very day [. . .].

P46

a (≠ DK) Diogenes Laertius

Indeed, the Metapontians called his house 'the temple of Demeter' and his little street 'the Museum,' as Favorinus says in his *Miscellaneous Histories*.

b (> 14.13) Just. *Epitoma* 20.4

Pythagoras autem cum annos XX Crotone egisset, Metapontum emigravit ibique decessit; cuius tanta admiratio fuit, ut ex domo eius templum facerent eumque pro deo colerent.

c (< 14.13) Porph. *VP* 4

τὴν δ' οἰκίαν Δήμητρος ἱερὸν ποιῆσαι τοὺς Κροτωνιάτας, τὸν δὲ στενωπὸν καλεῖν Μουσεῖον.

b (> 14.13) Justin, *Epitome of Pompeius Trogus*

After Pythagoras had spent twenty years at Croton, he emigrated to Metapontum and died there; the admiration for him was so great that they made his house a temple and worshipped him as a god.

c (< 14.13) Porphyry, *Life of Pythagoras*

The Crotonians made his house a temple of Demeter, and call his little street 'the Museum.'

Iconography (P47)

P47 (cf. vol. 1, p. xii) Richter I, pp. 79–80 and Figures 302–5; Richter-Smith, p. 193 and Figures 152–53; Koch, "Ikonographie," in Flashar, Bremer, Rechenauer (2013), I.1, pp. 220–22; see also Zhmud 2012, p. 44, n. 71.

PYTHAGORAS b
THE INSTITUTION

The Community of Life and of Teaching (T1–T6)
The Pythagorean Way of Life (T1)

T1 (14.10) Plat. *Rep.* 10 600a–b

ἀλλὰ δὴ εἰ μὴ δημοσίᾳ, ἰδίᾳ τισὶν ἡγεμὼν παιδείας αὐτὸς ζῶν λέγεται Ὅμηρος γενέσθαι, οἳ ἐκεῖνον ἠγάπων ἐπὶ συνουσίᾳ καὶ τοῖς ὑστέροις ὁδόν τινα παρέδοσαν βίου Ὁμηρικήν, ὥσπερ Πυθαγόρας αὐτός τε διαφερόντως ἐπὶ τούτῳ ἠγαπήθη, καὶ οἱ ὕστεροι ἔτι καὶ νῦν Πυθαγόρειον τρόπον ἐπονομάζοντες τοῦ βίου διαφανεῖς πῃ δοκοῦσιν εἶναι ἐν τοῖς ἄλλοις.

Friendship (T2–T3)

T2 (16 Mansfeld) Diog. Laert. 8.10

εἶπέ τε πρῶτος, ὥς φησι Τίμαιος [*FGrHist* 566 F13b], κοινὰ τὰ φίλων εἶναι καὶ φιλίαν ἰσότητα. καὶ αὐτοῦ οἱ μαθηταὶ κατετίθεντο τὰς οὐσίας εἰς ἓν ποιούμενοι.

PYTHAGORAS b

THE INSTITUTION

The Community of Life and of Teaching (T1–T6)
The Pythagorean Way of Life (T1)

T1 (14.10) Plato, *Republic*

Homer is said to have been, if not publicly, then privately, by his mode of life, a leader in education for some people who loved to associate with him and who transmitted to posterity a certain 'Homeric' way of life, just as Pythagoras himself was extraordinarily loved for this reason, and later, men who even now call their way of life 'Pythagorean' seem to be distinguished in some way from the others.

Friendship (T2–T3)

T2 (≠ DK) Diogenes Laertius

As Timaeus says, he was the first to say that friends' possessions are in common and that friendship is equality. And his disciples deposited their possessions, combining them into one.

T3 (< 58D.7) Iambl. *VP* 233, 237 (et al.)

[233] ἀλλὰ μὴν τεκμήραιτο ἄν τις καὶ περὶ τοῦ μὴ παρέργως αὐτοὺς[1] τὰς ἀλλοτρίας ἐκκλίνειν φιλίας, ἀλλὰ καὶ πάνυ σπουδαίως περικάμπτειν αὐτὰς καὶ φυλάττεσθαι, καὶ περὶ τοῦ δὲ μέχρι πολλῶν γενεῶν τὸ φιλικὸν πρὸς ἀλλήλους ἀνένδοτον διατετηρηκέναι, καὶ ἐξ[2] ὧν Ἀριστόξενος ἐν τῷ περὶ Πυθαγορικοῦ βίου αὐτὸς διακηκοέναι φησὶ Διονυσίου τοῦ Σικελίας τυράννου [cf. Aristox. Frag. 31 Wehrli] [. . .]. [237] λέγεται δὲ ὡς καὶ ἀγνοοῦντες ἀλλήλους οἱ Πυθαγορικοὶ ἐπειρῶντο φιλικὰ ἔργα διαπράττεσθαι ὑπὲρ[3] τῶν εἰς ὄψιν μηδέποτε ἀφιγμένων, ἡνίκα τεκμήριόν τι λάβοιεν τοῦ μετέχειν τῶν αὐτῶν λόγων [. . .].

[1] αὐτοὺς Porph. *VP* 59: αὐτὸν ms.   [2] ita Porph., ἔκ τε ms.   [3] ὑπὲρ Scaliger: ὑπὸ ms.

Diet (T4–T6)

T4

a (14.9) Arist. in Aul. Gell. *Noct.* 4.11 (= Arist. Frag. 194 Rose)

Ἀριστοτέλης δὲ μήτρας καὶ καρδίας καὶ ἀκαλήφης καὶ τοιούτων τινῶν ἄλλων ἀπέχεσθαί φησιν τοὺς Πυθαγορικούς, χρῆσθαι δὲ τοῖς ἄλλοις.

b (cf. 58C.6) Diog. Laert. 8.19 (= Arist. Frag. 194 Rose)

παντὸς δὲ μᾶλλον ἀπηγόρευε μήτ' ἐρυθῖνον ἐσθίειν

PYTHAGORAS b

T3 (< 58D.7) Iamblichus, *Life of Pythagoras*

[233] But one might also conclude from what Aristoxenus, in his *Life of Pythagoras,* says that he himself heard from Dionysius the tyrant of Sicily, both that it was not merely a secondary issue that they [i.e. the Pythagoreans] refused friendships with strangers, but that they took the greatest care to avoid these and to guard against them, and also that for many generations they firmly maintained the friendship that bound them with one another [. . .]. [237] It is also reported that, even when they did not know one another, the Pythagoreans tried to render friendly services to people they had never seen before, so long as they had proof that they shared the same doctrines [. . .].

Diet (T4–T6)

T4

a (14.9) Aristotle in Aulus Gellius, *Attic Nights*

Aristotle says that the Pythagoreans abstain from the womb, the heart, the sea anemone, and some other things of this sort, but that they eat the others.

b (cf. 58C.6) Aristotle in Diogenes Laertius

Above all he prohibited them from eating sea bream (?)

μήτε μελάνουρον, καρδίας τ' ἀπέχεσθαι καὶ κυάμων·
Ἀριστοτέλης δέ φησι καὶ μήτρας καὶ τρίγλης ἐνίοτε.

c (< 58C.6) Porph. *VP* 43, 45

[43] ἔλεγε δ' ἀπέχεσθαι τῶν καταθυομένων ὀσφύος καὶ διδύμων καὶ αἰδοίων καὶ μυελοῦ καὶ ποδῶν καὶ κεφαλῆς. [. . .] ἴσα δὲ κυάμων παρῄνει ἀπέχεσθαι καθάπερ ἀνθρωπίνων σαρκῶν [. . .]. [45] ἀπέχεσθαι δὲ καὶ ἄλλων παρῄνει, οἷον μήτρας τε καὶ τριγλίδος καὶ ἀκαλήφης, σχεδὸν δὲ καὶ τῶν ἄλλων θαλασσίων ξυμπάντων.

T5 (≠ DK) Porph. *Abst.* 1.26

ὅτι δὲ οὐκ ἀσεβὲς τὸ κτείνειν καὶ ἐσθίειν, δηλοῖ τὸ καὶ αὐτὸν τὸν Πυθαγόραν, τῶν μὲν πάλαι διδόντων γάλα πίνειν τοῖς ἀθλοῦσι καὶ τυροὺς δὲ ἐσθίειν ὕδατι βεβρεγμένους, τῶν δὲ μετ' ἐκείνους ταύτην μὲν ἀποδοκιμασάντων τὴν δίαιταν, διὰ <δὲ>[1] τῶν ξηρῶν σύκων τὴν τροφὴν ποιουμένων τοῖς ἀθληταῖς, πρῶτον περιελόντα τὴν ἀρχαίαν κρέα διδόναι τοῖς γυμναζομένοις καὶ πολὺ διαφέρουσαν πρὸς ἰσχὺν εὑρεῖν δύναμιν. ἱστοροῦσι δέ τινες καὶ αὐτοὺς ἅπτεσθαι τῶν ἐμψύχων τοὺς Πυθαγορείους, ὅτε θύοιεν θεοῖς.

[1] add. nos

and the blacktail fish (?), and he ordered them to abstain from the heart and beans; Aristotle says also from the womb and red mullet sometimes.

c (< 58C.6) Porphyry, *Life of Pythagoras*

[43] He told them to abstain, among the sacrificial parts, from the loins, the testicles, the genitals, the marrow, the feet, and the head. [. . .] So too, he advised them to abstain from beans as though from human flesh [. . .]. [45] And he advised them to abstain from other things too, like the womb, the small red mullet, and the sea anemone, and from almost all creatures of the sea.

T5 (≠ DK) Porphyry, *On Abstinence*

The fact that it is not impious to kill and eat them [scil. animals] is proven by the fact that Pythagoras himself—while formerly they gave athletes milk to drink and cheese dipped in water to eat, and those who lived later rejected this diet and provided athletes with nutrition based on dry figs—was the first to reject the ancient [scil. diet] and to give meat to athletes, discovering a power that was much better for developing strength. And some people report that the Pythagoreans themselves laid hand upon living beings when they sacrificed to the gods.

EARLY GREEK PHILOSOPHY IV

T6 (< 58C.4) Iamb. *VP* 85

εἰς μόνα τῶν ζῴων οὐκ εἰσέρχεται ἀνθρώπου ψυχή, οἷς θέμις ἐστὶ τυθῆναι· διὰ τοῦτο τῶν θυσίμων χρὴ ἐσθίειν μόνον (οἷς ἂν τὸ ἐσθίειν καθήκῃ), ἄλλου δὲ μηδενὸς ζῴου.

The School: Characteristics and History (T7–T28)
Admission into the School (T7)

T7 (≠ DK) Iambl. *VP* 71

παρεσκευασμένῳ δὲ αὐτῷ οὕτως εἰς τὴν παιδείαν τῶν ὁμιλητῶν, προσιόντων τῶν νεωτέρων[1] καὶ βουλομένων συνδιατρίβειν οὐκ εὐθὺς συνεχώρει, μέχρις ἂν αὐτῶν τὴν δοκιμασίαν καὶ τὴν κρίσιν ποιήσηται, πρῶτον μὲν πυνθανόμενος πῶς τοῖς γονεῦσι καὶ τοῖς οἰκείοις τοῖς λοιποῖς πάρεισιν ὡμιληκότες, ἔπειτα θεωρῶν αὐτῶν τούς τε γέλωτας τοὺς ἀκαίρους καὶ τὴν σιωπὴν καὶ τὴν λαλιὰν παρὰ[2] τὸ δέον, ἔτι δὲ τὰς ἐπιθυμίας τίνες εἰσὶ καὶ τοὺς γνωρίμους οἷς ἐχρῶντο καὶ τὴν πρὸς τούτους ὁμιλίαν καὶ πρὸς τίνι μάλιστα τὴν ἡμέραν σχολάζουσι καὶ τὴν χαρὰν καὶ τὴν λύπην ἐπὶ τίσι τυγχάνουσι ποιούμενοι. προσεθεώρει δὲ καὶ τὸ εἶδος καὶ τὴν πορείαν καὶ τὴν ὅλην τοῦ σώματος κίνησιν, τοῖς τε τῆς φύσεως γνωρίσμασι φυσιογνωμονῶν αὐτοὺς σημεῖα τὰ φανερὰ ἐποιεῖτο τῶν ἀφανῶν ἠθῶν ἐν τῇ ψυχῇ.

PYTHAGORAS b

T6 (< 58C.4) Iamblichus, *Life of Pythagoras*

The only animals into which a human soul does not enter are those that it is licit to sacrifice: and this is why those for whom it is appropriate to eat must eat only those animals that one may sacrifice, but not any other animal.

The School: Characteristics and History (T7–T28)
Admission into the School (T7)

T7 (≠ DK) Iamblichus, *Life of Pythagoras*

When young men who wished to spend time with him came to him, prepared as he was in this way for the education of disciples, he did not admit them immediately, but waited until he had examined and judged them. First he found out how their relations were with their parents and their other relatives; then he observed them for inopportune fits of laughter and inappropriate silence and chattering, and [scil. observed] what their desires were, the friends they spent time with, their relation with these, how they mostly spent the day, and what caused them joy and grief. He also observed their appearance, their gait, the whole motion of their body, and, by examining them physiognomically using the traits of their nature, he made what was visible into signs for the invisible character in their soul.

---

¹ νεωτέρων Timaeus Taur. in schol. in Plat. *Phdr.* 279c: ἑταίρων ms.

² ⟨τὴν⟩ παρὰ Nauck

EARLY GREEK PHILOSOPHY IV

Pythagoras' Authority (T8–T10)

T8 (< 18.4) Iambl. *VP* 88

[. . .] εἶναι δὲ πάντα ἐκείνου τοῦ ἀνδρός· προσαγορεύουσι γὰρ οὕτω τὸν Πυθαγόραν, καὶ οὐ καλοῦσιν ὀνόματι.

T9 (12 Mansfeld) Diog. Laert. 8.46

[. . .] ἐφ' οὗ καὶ τὸ "αὐτὸς ἔφα" παροιμιακὸν εἰς τὸν βίον ἦλθεν.

T10 (< 58D.1) Iambl. *VP* 164

ᾤοντο δὲ δεῖν κατέχειν καὶ διασῴζειν ἐν τῇ μνήμῃ πάντα τὰ διδασκόμενά τε καὶ φραζόμενα, καὶ μέχρι τούτου συσκευάζεσθαι τάς τε μαθήσεις καὶ τὰς ἀκροάσεις, μέχρι ὅτου δύναται παραδέχεσθαι τὸ μανθάνον καὶ διαμνημονεῦον, ὅτι ἐκεῖνό ἐστιν ᾧ[1] δεῖ γιγνώσκειν καὶ ἐν ᾧ[2] γνώμην φυλάσσειν.

[1] ᾧ Küster post Obrechtum: ὅ ms.   [2] ᾧ Kiessling: τῷ ms.

The Practice of Silence (T11–T13)

T11 (≠ DK) Porph. *VP* 19

ἃ μὲν οὖν ἔλεγε τοῖς συνοῦσιν οὐδὲ εἷς ἔχει φράσαι βεβαίως· καὶ γὰρ οὐχ[1] ἡ τυχοῦσα ἦν παρ' αὐτοῖς σιωπή.

PYTHAGORAS b

Pythagoras' Authority (T8–T10)

T8 (< 18.4) Iamblichus, *Life of Pythagoras*

[...] everything belongs to the 'great man.' For this is how they designate Pythagoras, and they do not call him by his name.

T9 (≠ DK) Diogenes Laertius

It is about him [i.e. Pythagoras] that the proverbial phrase, "He himself said it," originated.

T10 (< 58D.1) Iamblichus, *Life of Pythagoras*

They thought that it was necessary to preserve and retain in memory everything that had been taught and said [scil. by Pythagoras], and to work on what they had learned and heard as far as the faculty of learning and memorizing was capable of assimilating it, because it is by means of this that one must learn, and in this that one must preserve one's thought.

The Practice of Silence (T11–T13)

T11 (≠ DK) Porphyry, *Life of Pythagoras*

What he said to his disciples, no one is able to report with certainty. For an extraordinary silence reigned among them.

---

¹ οὐχ Nauck: οὐδ' mss.

EARLY GREEK PHILOSOPHY IV

T12 (< 14.4) Isocr. *Bus.* 29

ἔτι γὰρ καὶ νῦν τοὺς προσποιουμένους ἐκείνου μαθητὰς εἶναι μᾶλλον σιγῶντας θαυμάζουσιν[1] ἢ τοὺς ἐπὶ τῷ λέγειν μεγίστην δόξαν ἔχοντας.

[1] θαυμάζουσιν ΓΕ: -ζομεν ΘΛ

T13 (16 Mansfeld) Diog. Laert. 8.10

πενταετίαν θ' ἡσύχαζον, μόνον[1] τῶν λόγων κατακούοντες καὶ οὐδέπω Πυθαγόραν ὁρῶντες εἰς ὃ δοκιμασθεῖεν· τοὐντεῦθεν δὲ ἐγίνοντο τῆς οἰκίας αὐτοῦ καὶ τῆς ὄψεως μετεῖχον.

[1] μόνων mss.: corr. Frobenius

Pythagoras' Audiences and Rhetoric (T14)

T14 (≠ DK) Schol. in Hom. *Od.* 1.1 (= Antisth. Frag. 51, V A 187 G²)

οὕτω καὶ Πυθαγόρας λέγεται πρὸς παῖδας ἀξιωθεὶς ποιήσασθαι λόγους διαθεῖναι πρὸς αὐτοὺς λόγους παιδικούς, καὶ πρὸς γυναῖκας γυναιξὶν ἁρμοδίους, καὶ πρὸς ἄρχοντας ἀρχοντικούς, καὶ πρὸς ἐφήβους ἐφηβικούς· τὸν γὰρ ἑκάστοις πρόσφορον τρόπον τῆς σοφίας ἐξευρίσκειν σοφίας ἐστίν.

PYTHAGORAS b

T12 (< 14.4) Isocrates, *Busiris*

Even now people admire more for their silence those who claim to be his disciples than those who enjoy the greatest reputation for their speeches.

T13 (≠ DK) Diogenes Laertius

They remained silent for five years, only listening to what Pythagoras said but not yet seeing him until they were tested; but from that moment on they belonged to his household and had a share in the opportunity of seeing him.

Pythagoras' Audiences and Rhetoric (T14)

T14 (≠ DK) Antisthenes the Socratic in Scholia on Homer's *Odyssey*

They say that when Pythagoras was asked to make a speech to children he composed discourses suitable for children, when it was to women, ones suitable for women, when it was to rulers, ones suitable for rulers, when it was to ephebes, ones suitable for ephebes. For it belongs to wisdom to discover the kind of wisdom appropriate for each person.

EARLY GREEK PHILOSOPHY IV

'Knowers' (mathêmatikoi) *and 'Listeners'*
(akousmatikoi) *(T15–T20)*
The Nature of the Difference (T15–T18)

T15 (21 Mansfeld) Diog. Laert. 8.15

ἔλεγόν τε καὶ οἱ ἄλλοι Πυθαγόρειοι μὴ εἶναι πρὸς πάντας πάντα ῥητά, ὥς φησιν Ἀριστόξενος ἐν δεκάτῳ Παιδευτικῶν νόμων [Frag. 43 Wehrli].

T16 (18.2) Porph. *VP* 37

διττὸν γὰρ ἦν αὐτοῦ τῆς διδασκαλίας τὸ σχῆμα. καὶ τῶν προσιόντων οἱ μὲν ἐκαλοῦντο μαθηματικοί, οἱ δ' ἀκουσματικοί· καὶ μαθηματικοὶ μὲν οἱ τὸν περιττότερον καὶ πρὸς ἀκρίβειαν διαπεπονημένον τῆς ἐπιστήμης λόγον ἐκμεμαθηκότες, ἀκουσματικοὶ δ' οἱ μόνας τὰς κεφαλαιώδεις ὑποθήκας τῶν γραμμάτων ἄνευ ἀκριβεστέρας διηγήσεως ἀκηκοότες.

T17 (< 58C.4) Iambl. *VP* 82

ἔστι δὲ ἡ μὲν τῶν ἀκουσματικῶν φιλοσοφία ἀκούσματα ἀναπόδεικτα καὶ ἄνευ λόγου, ὅτι οὕτω πρακτέον, καὶ τἆλλα, ὅσα παρ' ἐκείνου ἐρρέθη, ταῦτα πειρῶνται διαφυλάττειν ὡς θεῖα δόγματα, αὐτοὶ δὲ παρ' αὑτῶν οὔτε λέγειν προσποιοῦνται οὔτε λεκτέον εἶναι, ἀλλὰ καὶ αὑτῶν ὑπολαμβάνουσι τούτους ἔχειν βέλτιστα πρὸς φρόνησιν, οἵτινες πλεῖστα ἀκούσματα ἔσχον [. . .].

PYTHAGORAS b

'Knowers' (mathêmatikoi) and 'Listeners'
(akousmatikoi) (T15–T20)
The Nature of the Difference (T15–T18)

T15 (≠ DK) Diogenes Laertius

The other Pythagoreans too used to say that not everything could be said to everyone, as Aristoxenus says in the tenth book of his *Rules of Education*.

T16 (18.2) Porphyry, *Life of Pythagoras*

His mode of instruction was double. And among those who came to him, the ones were called 'knowers' (*mathêmatikoi*), the others 'listeners' (*akousmatikoi*). The 'knowers' were the ones who learned completely the scientific discourse that was superior and had been elaborated precisely, and the 'listeners' those who heard only the summary instructions of the writings without the more precise explanations.

T17 (< 58C.4) Iamblichus, *Life of Pythagoras*

The philosophy of the 'listeners' (*akousmatikoi*) consists in acousmatic statements [cf. **PYTH. c D15–D25**] that are not demonstrated and lack a justification, ones asserting that one must act in such and such a way; and in general they try to respect everything that that man said as though they were divine teachings, while they themselves claim that on their own they neither say nor should say anything, but they suppose that among themselves those men are best fitted for wisdom who possess the largest number of acousmatic statements.

T18 (< 18.2) Iambl. *VP* 81 (et al.)

δύο γὰρ ἦν γένη καὶ τῶν μεταχειριζομένων αὐτήν, οἱ μὲν ἀκουσματικοί, οἱ δὲ μαθηματικοί. τουτωνὶ δὲ οἱ μὲν μαθηματικοὶ[1] ὡμολογοῦντο Πυθαγόρειοι εἶναι ὑπὸ τῶν ἑτέρων, τοὺς δὲ ἀκουσματικοὺς[2] οὗτοι οὐχ ὡμολόγουν, οὔτε τὴν πραγματείαν αὐτῶν εἶναι Πυθαγόρου, ἀλλὰ Ἱππάσου [. . .].

[1] μαθηματικοὶ P: μαθητικοὶ F: ἀκουσματικοὶ Iambl. *Comm.* 25, p. 76.19   [2] ἀκουσματικοὺς] μαθηματικοὺς *Comm.* 25, p. 76.21

*A Rationalizing Explanation of
This Difference (T19)*

T19 (20 Mansfeld) Iambl. *VP* 87–88

[87] οἱ δὲ περὶ τὰ μαθήματα τῶν Πυθαγορείων τούτους τε ὁμολογοῦσιν εἶναι Πυθαγορείους, καὶ αὐτοί φασιν ἔτι μᾶλλον, καὶ ἃ λέγουσιν αὐτοί, ἀληθῆ εἶναι. τὴν δὲ αἰτίαν τῆς ἀνομοιότητος τοιαύτην γενέσθαι φασίν. [88] ἀφικέσθαι τὸν Πυθαγόραν ἐξ Ἰωνίας καὶ Σάμου κατὰ τὴν Πολυκράτους τυραννίδα, ἀκμαζούσης Ἰταλίας, καὶ γενέσθαι συνήθεις αὐτῷ τοὺς πρώτους ἐν ταῖς πόλεσι. τούτων δὲ τοῖς μὲν πρεσβυτέροις καὶ ἀσχόλοις διὰ τὸ ἐν πολιτικοῖς πράγμασι κατέχεσθαι, ὡς χαλεπὸν ὂν διὰ τῶν μαθημάτων καὶ ἀποδείξεων ἐντυγχάνειν, ψιλῶς διαλεχθῆναι, ἡγούμενον οὐδὲν ἧττον ὠφελεῖσθαι καὶ ἄνευ τῆς αἰτίας εἰδότας τί δεῖ

PYTHAGORAS b

T18 (< 18.2) Iamblichus, *Life of Pythagoras*

There were also two categories of those who practiced it [i.e. the philosophy of Pythagoras], the 'listeners' (*akousmatikoi*) and the 'knowers' (*mathematikoi*). Among these, the 'knowers' were recognized as Pythagoreans by the others, but they did not recognize the 'listeners' as being such, and they said that their doctrine was not that of Pythagoras, but that of Hippasus [... cf. **HIPPAS. P2**].[1]

[1] In a parallel passage in Iamblichus, *On General Mathematical Science* 25, the words 'knowers' and 'listeners' in the second sentence are inverted, presumably erroneously.

A Rationalizing Explanation of This Difference (T19)

T19 (≠ DK) Iamblichus, *Life of Pythagoras*

[87] But those among the Pythagoreans who practice the sciences agree that these [i.e. the 'listeners'] are Pythagoreans, and they themselves say that they are even more so, and that what they say is true. They say that the reason for this difference is the following: [88] Pythagoras came from Ionia and Samos during the tyranny of Polycrates, while Italy was flourishing, and the most distinguished men in the cities became his comrades. But since it was difficult to conduct discussions in terms of sciences and demonstrations with the older men, for they had little time, being occupied as they were by political activities, he spoke with them in a plain manner, as he thought that they would still benefit if they knew what they had to do, even if they did

πράττειν, ὥσπερ καὶ οἱ ἰατρευόμενοι, οὐ προσακούοντες διὰ τί αὐτοῖς ἕκαστα πρακτέον, οὐδὲν ἧττον τυγχάνουσι τῆς ὑγείας· ὅσοις δὲ νεωτέροις ἐνετύγχανε καὶ δυναμένοις πονεῖν[1] καὶ μανθάνειν, τοῖς τοιούτοις δι' ἀποδείξεως καὶ μαθημάτων ἐνετύγχανεν.[2] αὐτοὶ μὲν οὖν εἶναι ἀπὸ τούτων, ἐκείνους δὲ ἀπὸ τῶν ἑτέρων.

[1] πονεῖν Rittershusius: ποιεῖν F (et Iambl. Comm. 25, p. 76.24)   [2] ἐντυγχάνειν Herwerden

Secrets and Betrayals (T20)

T20 (18.4) Iambl. VP 246–47

[246] τὸν γοῦν πρῶτον ἐκφάναντα τὴν τῆς συμμετρίας καὶ ἀσυμμετρίας φύσιν τοῖς ἀναξίοις μετέχειν τῶν λόγων οὕτω φασὶν ἀποστυγηθῆναι, ὡς μὴ μόνον ἐκ τῆς κοινῆς συνουσίας καὶ διαίτης ἐξορισθῆναι, ἀλλὰ καὶ τάφον αὐτοῦ κατασκευασθῆναι, ὡς δῆτα ἀποιχομένου ἐκ τοῦ μετ' ἀνθρώπων βίου τοῦ ποτε ἑταίρου γενομένου. [247] οἱ δέ φασι καὶ τὸ δαιμόνιον νεμεσῆσαι τοῖς ἐξώφορα τὰ τοῦ Πυθαγόρου ποιησαμένοις· φθαρῆναι γὰρ ὡς ἀσεβήσαντα ἐν θαλάσσῃ τὸν δηλώσαντα τὴν τοῦ εἰκοσαγώνου σύστασιν (τοῦτο δ' ἦν δωδεκάεδρον, ἓν τῶν πέντε λεγομένων στερεῶν σχημάτων) εἰς σφαῖραν ἐκτείνεσθαι. ἔνιοι δὲ τὸν περὶ τῆς ἀλόγου καὶ τῆς ἀσυμμετρίας ἐξειπόντα τοῦτο παθεῖν ἔλεξαν.

not know the reason, just as patients still become healthy, even if they are not told why they should do each thing. But with all the younger ones he encountered who were capable of working hard and learning, he conducted discussions in terms of demonstration and the sciences. So they [i.e. the 'knowers'] come from the latter, these [i.e. the 'listeners'] from the former.

Secrets and Betrayals (T20)

T20 (18 A4) Iamblichus, *Life of Pythagoras*

[246] They say that the first man who revealed the nature of commensurability and incommensurability to those who were not worthy to share in these doctrines was so abhorred that not only was he banished from the community and their way of life, but also a tomb was erected for him, since he who had once been their companion had now departed far from the life of men. [247] But others say that the divinity too took vengeance on those who made Pythagoras' doctrines public. For the man who revealed that the figure with twenty angles (that is, the dodecahedron, one of the five figures called solid) could be inscribed within a sphere, died at sea for his sacrilege. And some said that it was the man who had divulged irrationality and incommensurability who suffered this fate.[1]

[1] This story is sometimes connected with Hippasus (cf. **HIPPAS. P2**).

EARLY GREEK PHILOSOPHY IV

Political Vicissitudes (T21–T28)
At Croton (T21–T23)

T21 (15 Mansfeld) Diog. Laert. 8.3

κἀκεῖ νόμους θεὶς τοῖς Ἰταλιώταις ἐδοξάσθη σὺν τοῖς μαθηταῖς, οἳ πρὸς τοὺς τριακοσίους ὄντες ᾠκονόμουν ἄριστα τὰ πολιτικά, ὥστε σχεδὸν ἀριστοκρατίαν εἶναι τὴν πολιτείαν.

T22 (< 14.13) Porph. VP 4

Τίμαιος δ' ἱστορεῖ [FGrHist 566 F131] τὴν Πυθαγόρου θυγατέρα καὶ παρθένον οὖσαν ἡγεῖσθαι τῶν παρθένων ἐν Κρότωνι καὶ γυναῖκα τῶν γυναικῶν.

T23 (< 14.14) Diod. Sic. 12.9.4

[. . .] Πυθαγόρου τοῦ φιλοσόφου συμβουλεύσαντος σώζειν τοὺς ἱκέτας, μετέπεσον ταῖς γνώμαις καὶ τὸν πόλεμον ὑπὲρ τῆς τῶν ἱκετῶν σωτηρίας ἀνείλοντο [. . .].

PYTHAGORAS b

Political Vicissitudes (T21–T28)
At Croton (T21–T23)

T21 (≠ DK) Diogenes Laertius

And there [scil. in Croton], after he had established laws for the Italians, he became celebrated together with his disciples, who were about three hundred in number and governed the city's affairs excellently, so that the political system was practically a government by the best men (*aristokratia*).

T22 (< 14.13) Porphyry, *Life of Pythagoras*

Timaeus reports that Pythagoras' daughter, when she was a girl, was the head of the girls in Croton, and also, when she was a woman, of the women.

T23 (< 14.14) Diodorus Siculus

[. . .] after Pythagoras the philosopher had advised them [i.e. the Crotonians] to save the suppliants [scil. a group of wealthy refugees whom Sybaris demanded be surrendered to them], they changed their mind and went to war in order to save the suppliants.

Cf. **PYTH. a P25, P46b, c**

EARLY GREEK PHILOSOPHY IV

In the Rest of Italy (T24)

T24 (> 14.12) Porph. *VP* 21–22

[21] ἃς δ' ἐπιδημήσας Ἰταλίᾳ τε καὶ Σικελίᾳ κατέλαβε πόλεις δεδουλωμένας ὑπ' ἀλλήλων, τὰς μὲν πολλῶν ἐτῶν τὰς δὲ νεωστί, φρονήματος ἐλευθερίου πλήσας διὰ τῶν ἐφ' ἑκάστης ἀκουστῶν αὐτοῦ ἠλευθέρωσε, Κρότωνα καὶ Σύβαριν καὶ Κατάνην καὶ Ῥήγιον καὶ Ἱμέραν καὶ Ἀκράγαντα καὶ Ταυρομένιον καὶ ἄλλας τινάς, αἷς καὶ νόμους ἔθετο διὰ Χαρώνδα τε τοῦ Καταναίου καὶ Ζαλεύκου τοῦ Λοκροῦ, δι' ὧν ἀξιοζήλωτοι τοῖς περιοίκοις ἄχρι πολλοῦ γεγόνασιν. Σίμιχος δ' ὁ Κεντοριπίνων[1] τύραννος ἀκούσας αὐτοῦ τήν τ' ἀρχὴν ἀπέθετο καὶ τῶν χρημάτων τὰ μὲν τῇ ἀδελφῇ τὰ δὲ τοῖς πολίταις ἔδωκεν. [22] προσῆλθον δ' αὐτῷ, ὥς φησιν Ἀριστόξενος [Frag. 17 Wehrli], καὶ Λευκανοὶ καὶ Μεσσάπιοι καὶ Πευκέτιοι καὶ Ῥωμαῖοι. ἀνεῖλεν δ' ἄρδην στάσιν οὐ μόνον ἀπὸ τῶν γνωρίμων, ἀλλὰ καὶ τῶν ἀπογόνων αὐτῶν ἄχρι πολλῶν γενεῶν καὶ καθόλου ἀπὸ τῶν ἐν Ἰταλίᾳ τε καὶ Σικελίᾳ πόλεων πασῶν πρός τε ἑαυτὰς καὶ πρὸς ἀλλήλας.

[1] Κεντοριπίνων Holstenius: κεντοροπίων mss.

Anti-Pythagorean Revolts (T25–T27)

T25 (cf. 14.16) Iambl. *VP* 248–49 (< Aristox. Frag. 18 Wehrli)

[248] ἦσαν δέ τινες, οἳ προσεπολέμουν τοῖς ἀνδράσι

PYTHAGORAS b

In the Rest of Italy (T24)

T24 (> 14.12) Porphyry, *Life of Pythagoras*

[21] When he found that the cities he traveled to in Italy and Sicily had been enslaved by one another, the ones for many years, the others recently, he filled them with a spirit of liberty and liberated them thanks to the disciples he had in each of them: Croton, Sybaris, Catania, Rhegium, Himera, Agrigentum, Tauromenium, and certain other ones, to which he also gave laws, by means of Charondas of Catania and Zaleucus of Locri, on account of which they were envied by their neighbors for a long time. When the tyrant Simichus of Centuripe heard him, he renounced his power and gave part of his wealth to his sister and the rest to the citizens. [22] As Aristoxenus says, there came to him Lucanians, Messapians, Peucetians, and Romans. He completely suppressed discord not only among his disciples but also among their descendants for many generations, and in general in all the cities of Italy and Sicily, both internally and among each other.

Anti-Pythagorean Revolts (T25–T27)

T25 (< 14.16) Iamblichus, *Life of Pythagoras*

[248] There were some who waged war against these men

τούτοις καὶ ἐπανέστησαν αὐτοῖς. ὅτι μὲν οὖν ἀπόντος Πυθαγόρου ἐγένετο ἡ ἐπιβουλή, πάντες συνομολογοῦσι, διαφέρονται δὲ περὶ τῆς τότε ἀποδημίας, οἱ μὲν πρὸς Φερεκύδην τὸν Σύριον, οἱ δὲ εἰς Μεταπόντιον λέγοντες ἀποδεδημηκέναι τὸν Πυθαγόραν. αἱ δὲ αἰτίαι τῆς ἐπιβουλῆς πλείονες λέγονται, μία μὲν ὑπὸ τῶν Κυλωνείων λεγομένων ἀνδρῶν τοιάδε γενομένη. Κύλων, ἀνὴρ Κροτωνιάτης, γένει μὲν καὶ δόξῃ καὶ πλούτῳ πρωτεύων τῶν πολιτῶν, ἄλλως δὲ χαλεπός τις καὶ βίαιος καὶ θορυβώδης καὶ τυραννικὸς τὸ ἦθος, πᾶσαν προθυμίαν παρασχόμενος πρὸς τὸ κοινωνῆσαι τοῦ Πυθαγορείου βίου καὶ προσελθὼν πρὸς αὐτὸν τὸν Πυθαγόραν ἤδη πρεσβύτην ὄντα, ἀπεδοκιμάσθη διὰ τὰς προειρημένας αἰτίας. [249] γενομένου δὲ τούτου πόλεμον ἰσχυρὸν ἤρατο καὶ αὐτὸς καὶ οἱ φίλοι αὐτοῦ πρὸς αὐτόν τε τὸν Πυθαγόραν καὶ τοὺς ἑταίρους, καὶ οὕτω σφοδρά τις ἐγένετο καὶ ἄκρατος ἡ φιλοτιμία αὐτοῦ τε τοῦ Κύλωνος καὶ τῶν μετ' ἐκείνου τεταγμένων, ὥστε διατεῖναι μέχρι τῶν τελευταίων Πυθαγορείων. ὁ μὲν οὖν Πυθαγόρας διὰ ταύτην τὴν αἰτίαν ἀπῆλθεν εἰς τὸ Μεταπόντιον, κἀκεῖ λέγεται καταστρέψαι τὸν βίον, οἱ δὲ Κυλώνειοι λεγόμενοι διετέλουν πρὸς τοὺς Πυθαγορείους στασιάζοντες καὶ πᾶσαν ἐνδεικνύμενοι δυσμένειαν. ἀλλ' ὅμως ἐπεκράτει μέχρι τινὸς ἡ τῶν Πυθαγορείων καλοκαγαθία καὶ ἡ τῶν πόλεων αὐτῶν βούλησις, ὥστε ὑπ' ἐκείνων οἰκονομεῖσθαι βούλεσθαι τὰ περὶ τὰς πολιτείας. τέλος δὲ εἰς τοσοῦτον ἐπεβούλευσαν[1] τοῖς ἀνδράσιν, ὥστε ἐν τῇ

PYTHAGORAS b

[i.e. the Pythagoreans] and rebelled against them. Everyone agrees that the conspiracy took place while Pythagoras was absent, but they disagree about the details of his voyage at that time. Some say that Pythagoras had gone to Pherecydes of Syros, others to Metapontum. As for the causes of the conspiracy, there are a number of different reports. According to one of them, it was brought about by the men called Cylonians: Cylon, a man of Croton, one of the first citizens by birth, reputation, and wealth, but otherwise of a difficult character, violent, turbulent, and tyrannical, had conceived a great desire to participate in the Pythagorean way of life; he had come to see Pythagoras himself, who was already old, but he had been rejected for the reasons I have just mentioned. [249] When this happened, he and his friends began a violent war against Pythagoras and his companions, and the rivalry of Cylon and his allies was so fierce and absolute that it extended to the very last Pythagoreans. This is the reason why Pythagoras left for Metapontum, and he is said to have died there. But the so-called Cylonians continued to rebel against the Pythagoreans and to manifest a total hostility against them. But all the same, for a certain time the Pythagoreans' virtue and valor and the will of the cities themselves had the upper hand, so that they wished to be governed by them. But in the end they went so far in their conspiracy against these men that they set on fire the

---

[1] ἐπεβούλευσαν Kiessling: ἐπεβούλευσε ms.

EARLY GREEK PHILOSOPHY IV

Μίλωνος οἰκίᾳ ἐν Κρότωνι συνεδρευόντων τῶν Πυθαγορείων καὶ βουλευομένων περὶ πολιτικῶν[2] πραγμάτων ὑφάψαντες τὴν οἰκίαν κατέκαυσαν τοὺς ἄνδρας, πλὴν δυεῖν, Ἀρχίππου τε καὶ Λύσιδος.

[2] πολιτικῶν Mahne: πολεμικῶν ms.

T26 (< 14.16) Polyb. 2.39

καθ᾽ οὓς γὰρ καιροὺς ἐν τοῖς κατὰ τὴν Ἰταλίαν τόποις κατὰ τὴν Μεγάλην Ἑλλάδα τότε προσαγορευομένην ἐνεπρήσθη τὰ συνέδρια τῶν Πυθαγορείων, μετὰ ταῦτα γενομένου κινήματος ὁλοσχεροῦς περὶ τὰς πολιτείας, ὅπερ εἰκός, ὡς ἂν τῶν πρώτων ἀνδρῶν ἐξ ἑκάστης πόλεως οὕτω παραλόγως διαφθαρέντων, συνέβη τὰς κατ᾽ ἐκείνους τοὺς τόπους Ἑλληνικὰς πόλεις ἀναπλησθῆναι φόνου καὶ στάσεως καὶ παντοδαπῆς ταραχῆς.

T27 (> 14.16) Porph. *VP* 56

Δικαίαρχος δὲ [Frag. 34 Wehrli] καὶ οἱ ἀκριβέστεροι καὶ τὸν Πυθαγόραν φασὶν παρεῖναι τῇ ἐπιβουλῇ· Φερεκύδην γὰρ πρὸ τῆς ἐκ Σάμου ἀπάρσεως τελευτῆσαι.

The Dispersal of the Pythagoreans (T28)

T28 (< 14.16) Iambl. *VP* 250–51

[. . .] [250] γενομένου δὲ τούτου καὶ λόγον οὐδένα ποι-

house of Milon in Croton, where the Pythagoreans had gathered to deliberate about political matters, and burned alive all the men except for two, Archippus and Lysis.

T26 (< 14.16) Polybius, *Histories*

At that time [ca. 455], in the part of Italy then called Magna Graecia the meeting places of the Pythagoreans were burned down, after which there was a general upheaval in the political regimes, as was to be expected, given that the first men of each city had been killed so unexpectedly; and it came about that the Greek cities in those parts were filled with murder, civil strife, and all kinds of turmoil.

T27 (> 14.16) Porphyry, *Life of Pythagoras*

Dicaearchus and the more precise authors say that Pythagoras too was present during the conspiracy. For Pherecydes had already died before his departure from Samos [cf. **PHER. P15**].

The Dispersal of the Pythagoreans (T28)

T28 (< 14.16), Iamblichus, *Life of Pythagoras*

[...] [250] After this happened [scil. the burning of Milon's

ησαμένων τῶν πόλεων περὶ τοῦ συμβάντος πάθους ἐπαύσαντο τῆς ἐπιμελείας οἱ Πυθαγόρειοι. συνέβη δὲ τοῦτο δι' ἀμφοτέρας τὰς αἰτίας, διά τε τὴν ὀλιγωρίαν τῶν πόλεων (τοῦ τοιούτου γὰρ καὶ τηλικούτου γενομένου πάθους οὐδεμίαν ἐπιστροφὴν ἐποιήσαντο), διά τε τὴν ἀπώλειαν τῶν ἡγεμονικωτάτων ἀνδρῶν. τῶν δὲ δύο τῶν περισωθέντων, ἀμφοτέρων Ταραντίνων ὄντων, ὁ μὲν Ἄρχιππος ἀνεχώρησεν εἰς Τάραντα, ὁ δὲ Λῦσις μισήσας τὴν ὀλιγωρίαν ἀπῆρεν εἰς τὴν Ἑλλάδα καὶ ἐν Ἀχαΐᾳ διέτριβε τῇ Πελοποννησιακῇ, ἔπειτα εἰς Θήβας μετῳκίσατο σπουδῆς τινος γενομένης, οὗπερ ἐγένετο Ἐπαμινώνδας ἀκροατὴς καὶ πατέρα τὸν Λῦσιν ἐκάλεσεν. ὧδε καὶ τὸν βίον κατέστρεψεν. [251] οἱ δὲ λοιποὶ τῶν Πυθαγορείων ἀπέστησαν τῆς Ἰταλίας, πλὴν Ἀρχύτου[1] τοῦ Ταραντίνου.[2] ἀθροισθέντες δὲ εἰς τὸ Ῥήγιον ἐκεῖ διέτριβον μετ' ἀλλήλων. προϊόντος δὲ τοῦ χρόνου καὶ τῶν πολιτευμάτων ἐπὶ τὸ χεῖρον προβαινόντων ‹...›[3] ἦσαν δὲ οἱ σπουδαιότατοι Φάντων τε καὶ Ἐχεκράτης καὶ Πολύμναστος καὶ Διοκλῆς, Φλιάσιοι, Ξενόφιλος δὲ Χαλκιδεὺς τῶν ἀπὸ Θράκης Χαλκιδέων. ἐφύλαξαν μὲν οὖν τὰ ἐξ ἀρχῆς ἤθη καὶ τὰ μαθήματα καίτοι ἐκλειπούσης τῆς αἱρέσεως, ἕως[4] εὐγενῶς ἠφανίσθησαν. ταῦτα μὲν οὖν Ἀριστόξενος διηγεῖται [Frag. 18 Wehrli] [...].

PYTHAGORAS b

house], the Pythagoreans stopped taking care of the cities, which took no account of the calamity that had occurred. This happened for two reasons: the neglect on the part of the cities (for they paid no attention to a calamity of this kind and of such magnitude) and the annihilation of the most important leaders. Of the two survivors, both of them from Tarentum, Archippus returned to Tarentum, while Lysis, filled with hatred for this neglect, left for Greece and spent some time in Achaea in the Peloponnese and then moved to Thebes, where a certain enthusiasm for him had developed. Here Epaminondas became his student and called Lysis his father; and here he died. [251] The remaining Pythagoreans left Italy, except for Archytas[1] of Tarentum. They gathered at Rhegium and lived together there. As time passed and the political regimes became worse ‹. . .›. The most zealous ones were Phanton, Echecrates, Polymnastus, and Diocles, all from Phlius; Xenophilus of Chalcidia, among the Chalcidians from Thrace. They preserved the original mores and knowledge even though the school had come to an end, until they passed away nobly. This is what Aristoxenus reports.

[1] Iamblichus mentions at §104 an 'older Archytas' who, he says, was a disciple of Pythagoras at the same time as Empedocles [cf. **ARCHY. P3**]. 'Archytas' here is sometimes corrected to 'Archippus.'

---

[1] Ἀρχύτου] Ἀρχίππου Fr. Beckmann   [2] ἀπέστησαν . . . Ταραντίνου transp. post προβαινόντων et δὲ post ἀθροισθέντες del. Rose   [3] lac. indic. Wyttenbach   [4] ἕως Küster: ὡς F

EARLY GREEK PHILOSOPHY IV

*The Pythagoreans in the Course of
Time (T29–T36)
Longevity of the School (T29)*

T29 (< 14.10) Diog. Laert. 8.45–46

[. . .] καὶ αὐτοῦ τὸ σύστημα διέμεινε μέχρι γενεῶν ἐννέα ἢ καὶ δέκα· τελευταῖοι γὰρ ἐγένοντο τῶν Πυθαγορείων, οὓς καὶ Ἀριστόξενος εἶδε, Ξενόφιλός τε ὁ Χαλκιδεὺς ἀπὸ Θρᾴκης καὶ Φάντων ὁ Φλιάσιος καὶ Ἐχεκράτης καὶ Διοκλῆς καὶ Πολύμναστος, Φλιάσιοι καὶ αὐτοί. ἦσαν δὲ ἀκροαταὶ Φιλολάου καὶ Εὐρύτου τῶν Ταραντίνων.

*The Catalog of Male and Female Pythagoreans
Transmitted by Iamblichus (T30)*

T30 (58A.) Iambl. VP 267

τῶν δὲ συμπάντων Πυθαγορείων τοὺς μὲν ἀγνῶτάς τε καὶ ἀνωνύμους τινὰς πολλοὺς εἰκὸς γεγονέναι, τῶν δὲ γνωριζομένων ἐστὶ τάδε τὰ ὀνόματα.

[1] Κροτωνιᾶται Ἱππόστρατος, Δύμας, Αἴγων, Αἴμων, Σύλλος, Κλεοσθένης, Ἀγέλας, Ἐπίσυλος, Φυκιάδας,

---

[1] This catalog of male (218 names) and female (17 names) Pythagoreans, classified by city of origin (29), probably goes back to Aristoxenus of Tarentum. The Pythagorean identity of at least some of them is doubtful or is the result of invented filiations (this is the case of Parmenides, for example); inversely, we know of

PYTHAGORAS b

*The Pythagoreans in the Course of
Time (T29–T36)
Longevity of the School (T29)*

T29 (< 14.10) Diogenes Laertius

[. . .] Its [i.e. the school's] organization lasted nine or ten generations. For the last Pythagoreans, whom Aristoxenus saw, were Xenophilus of Chalcis in Thrace, Phanton of Phlius, Echecrates, Diocles, and Polymnastus, these too of Phlius. They were students of Philolaus and of Eurytus of Tarentum.

*The Catalog of Male and Female Pythagoreans
Transmitted by Iamblichus (T30)*[1]

T30 (58A.) Iamblichus, *Life of Pythagoras*

Of all the Pythagoreans, it is only to be expected that many are unknown and anonymous, but here are the names of those that are known:

[1] From Croton: Hippostratus, Dymas, Aegon, Haemon, Syllus, Cleosthenes, Agelas, Episylus, Phyciadas, **Ecphan-**

certain older Pythagoreans who are not included in the catalog (for example, Ameinias or Telauges, Pythagoras' son and Empedocles' alleged teacher). Many of these names are otherwise unknown. We have printed in boldface in the translation the names that appear elsewhere (in one way or another) in our edition and some that appear in Diels-Kranz's but not in ours (cf. the General Introduction to Chapters 10–18).

Ἔκφαντος, Τίμαιος, Βοῦθος, Ἔρατος, Ἰταναῖος, Ῥόδιππος, Βρύας, Εὔανδρος, Μυλλίας, Ἀντιμέδων, Ἀγέας, Λεόφρων, Ἄγυλος, Ὄνατας, Ἱπποσθένης, Κλεόφρων, Ἀλκμαίων, Δαμοκλῆς, Μίλων, Μένων.

[2] Μεταποντῖνοι Βροντῖνος, Παρμίσκος, Ὀρεστάδας, Λέων, Δαμάρμενος, Αἰνέας, Χειλᾶς, Μελησίας, Ἀριστέας, Λαφάων, Εὔανδρος, Ἀγησίδαμος, Ξενοκάδης, Εὐρύφημος, Ἀριστομένης, Ἀγήσαρχος, Ἀλκίας, Ξενοφάντης, Θρασέας, Εὔρυτος, Ἐπίφρων, Εἰρίσκος, Μεγιστίας, Λεωκύδης, Θρασυμήδης, Εὔφημος, Προκλῆς, Ἀντιμένης, Λάκριτος, Δαμοτάγης, Πύρρων, Ῥηξίβιος, Ἀλώπεκος, Ἀστύλος, Λακύδας, Ἀνίοχος, Λακράτης, Γλυκῖνος.

[3] Ἀκραγαντῖνος Ἐμπεδοκλῆς.

[4] Ἐλεάτης Παρμενίδης.

[5] Ταραντῖνοι Φιλόλαος, Εὔρυτος, Ἀρχύτας, Θεόδωρος, Ἀρίστιππος, Λύκων, Ἑστιαῖος, Πολέμαρχος, Ἀστέας, Καινίας, Κλέων, Εὐρυμέδων, Ἀρκέας, Κλειναγόρας, Ἄρχιππος, Ζώπυρος, Εὔθυνος, Δικαίαρχος, Φιλωνίδης, Φροντίδας, Λῦσις, Λυσίβιος, Δεινοκράτης, Ἐχεκράτης, Πακτίων, Ἀκουσιλάδας, Ἴκκος, Πεισικράτης, Κλεάρατος, Λεοντεύς, Φρύνιχος, Σιμιχίας, Ἀριστοκλείδας, Κλεινίας, Ἁβροτέλης, Πεισίρροδος, Βρύας, Ἔλανδρος, Ἀρχέμαχος, Μιμνόμαχος, Ἀκμονίδας, Δικᾶς, Καροφαντίδας.

[6] Συβαρῖται Μέτωπος, Ἵππασος, Πρόξενος, Εὐάνωρ, Λεάναξ, Μενέστωρ, Διοκλῆς, Ἔμπεδος, Τιμάσιος, Πολεμαῖος, Ἔνδιος, Τυρσηνός.

PYTHAGORAS b

tus, Timaeus, Bouthus, Eratus, Itanaeus, Rhodippus, Bryas, Euandrus, Myllias, Antimedon, Ageas, Leophron, Agylus, Onatas, Hipposthenes, Cleophron, **Alcmaeon,** Damocles, **Milon,** Menon.

[2] From Metapontum: **Brontinus,** Parmiscus, Orestadas, Leon, Damarmenus, Aeneas, Cheilas, Melesias, Aristeas, Laphaon, Euandrus, Agesidamus, Xenocades, Euryphemus, Aristomenes, Agesarchus, Alcias, Xenophantes, Thraseas, **Eurytus,** Epiphron, Eiriscus, Megistias, Leocydes, Thrasymedes, Euphemus, Procles, Antimenes, Lacritus, Damotages, Pyrrhon, Rhexibius, Alopecus, Astylus, Lacydas, Haniochus, Lacrates, Glykinus.

[3] From Agrigentum: **Empedocles.**

[4] From Elea: **Parmenides.**

[5] From Tarentum: **Philolaus, Eurytus, Archytas,** Theodorus, Aristippus, Lycon, **Hestiaeus,** Polemarchus, Asteas, Caenias, Cleon, Eurymedon, Arceas, Cleinagoras, Archippus, **Zopyrus,** Euthynus, Dicaearchus, Philonides, Phrontidas, **Lysis,** Lysibios, Deinocrates, **Echecrates,** Paction, Acousiladas, **Iccus,** Peisicrates, Clearatus, Leonteus, Phrynichus, Simichias, Aristocleidas, Cleinias, Habroteles, Peisirrhodus, Bryas, Helandrus, Archemachus, Mimnomachus, Acmonidas, Dicas, Carophantidas.

[6] From Sybaris: Metopus, **Hippasus,** Proxenus, Euanor, Leanax, **Menestor,** Diocles, Empedus, Timasius, Polemaeus, Endius, Tyrsenus.

[7] Καρχηδόνιοι Μιλτιάδης, Ἄνθην, Ὁδίος, Λεώκριτος.

[8] Πάριοι Αἰήτιος, Φαινεκλῆς, Δεξίθεος, Ἀλκίμαχος, Δείναρχος, Μέτων, Τίμαιος, Τιμησιάναξ, Εὔμοιρος, Θυμαρίδας.

[9] Λοκροὶ Γύττιος, Ξένων, Φιλόδαμος, Εὐέτης, Εὔδικος, Σθενωνίδας, Σωσίστρατος, Εὐθύνους, Ζάλευκος, Τιμάρης.

[10] Ποσειδωνιᾶται Ἀθάμας, Σῖμος, Πρόξενος, Κραναός, Μύης, Βαθύλαος, Φαίδων.

[11] Λευκανοὶ Ὄκελλος καὶ Ὄκιλλος ἀδελφοί, Ἀρέσανδρος, Κέραμβος.

[12] Δαρδανεὺς Μαλίων.

[13] Ἀργεῖοι Ἱππομέδων, Τιμοσθένης, Εὐέλθων, Θρασύδαμος, Κρίτων, Πολύκτωρ.

[14] Λάκωνες Αὐτοχαρίδας, Κλεάνωρ, Εὐρυκράτης.

[15] Ὑπερβόρειος Ἄβαρις.

[16] Ῥηγῖνοι Ἀριστείδης, Δημοσθένης, Ἀριστοκράτης, Φύτιος, Ἑλικάων, Μνησίβουλος, Ἱππαρχίδης, Εὐθοσίων, Εὐθυκλῆς, Ὄψιμος, Κάλαις, Σελινούντιος.

[17] Συρακούσιοι Λεπτίνης, Φιντίας, Δάμων.

[18] Σάμιοι Μέλισσος, Λάκων, Ἄρχιππος, Ἑλώριππος, Ἕλωρις, Ἵππων.

[19] Καυλωνιᾶται Καλλίμβροτος, Δίκων, Νάστας, Δρύμων, Ξενέας.

[20] Φλιάσιοι Διοκλῆς, Ἐχεκράτης, Πολύμναστος, Φάντων.

PYTHAGORAS b

[7] From Carthage: Miltiades, Anthen, Hodius, Leocritus.

[8] From Paros: Aeetius, Phaenecles, Dexitheus, Alcimachus, Deinarchus, Meton, **Timaeus,** Timesianax, Eumoirus, Thumaridas.

[9] From Locri: Gyttius, Xenon, Philodamus, Euetes, Eudicus, Sthenonidas, Sosistratus, Euthynous, **Zaleucus,** Timares.

[10] From Poseidonia: Athamas, Simus, Proxenus, Cranaus, Mues, Bathylaus, **Phaedon.**

[11] From Lucania: **Occelus** and Occilus, brothers; Aresandrus, Cerambus.

[12] From Dardania: Malion.

[13] From Argos: Hippomedon, Timosthenes, Euelthon, Thrasydamus, Criton, Polyctor.

[14] From Laconia: Autocharidas, Cleanor, Eurycrates.

[15] From Hyperborea: **Abaris.**

[16] From Rhegium: Aristeides, Demosthenes, Aristocrates, Phytius, Helicaon, Mnesiboulus, Hipparchides, Euthosion, Euthycles, Opsimus, Calais, Selinountius.

[17] From Syracuse: Leptines, **Phintias, Damon.**

[18] From Samos: **Melissus,** Lacon, Archippus, Helorippus, Heloris, **Hippo.**

[19] From Caulonia: Callimbrotus, Dicon, Nastas, Drymon, Xeneas.

[20] From Phlius: **Diocles, Echecrates, Polymnastus, Phanton.**

[21] Σικυώνιοι Πολιάδης, Δήμων, Στράτιος, Σωσθένης.
[22] Κυρηναῖοι Πρῶρος, Μελάνιππος, Ἀριστάγγελος, Θεόδωρος.
[23] Κυζίκηνοὶ Πυθόδωρος, Ἱπποσθένης, Βούθηρος, Ξενόφιλος.
[24] Καταναῖοι Χαρώνδας, Λυσιάδης.
[25] Κορίνθιος Χρύσιππος.
[26] Τυρρηνὸς Ναυσίθοος.
[27] Ἀθηναῖος Νεόκριτος.
[28] Ποντικὸς Λύραμνος.
οἱ πάντες σιη'.
[29] Πυθαγορίδες δὲ γυναῖκες αἱ ἐπιφανέσταται· Τιμύχα γυνὴ Μυλλία τοῦ Κροτωνιάτου, Φιλτὺς θυγάτηρ Θεόφριος τοῦ Κροτωνιάτου, Βυνδάκου ἀδελφὴ, Ὀκελλὼ καὶ Ἐκκελὼ ‹ἀδελφαὶ Ὀκκέλω καὶ Ὀκκίλω›[1] τῶν Λευκανῶν, Χειλωνίς θυγάτηρ Χείλωνος τοῦ Λακεδαιμονίου, Κρατησίκλεια Λάκαινα γυνὴ Κλεάνορος τοῦ Λακεδαιμονίου, Θεανὼ γυνὴ τοῦ Μεταποντίνου Βροτίνου, Μυῖα γυνὴ Μίλωνος τοῦ Κροτωνιάτου, Λασθένεια Ἀρκάδισσα, Ἀβροτέλεια Ἀβροτέλους θυγάτηρ τοῦ Ταραντίνου, Ἐχεκράτεια Φλιασία, Τυρσηνὶς Συβαρῖτις, Πεισιρρόδη Ταραντινίς, Θεάδουσα Λάκαινα, Βοιὼ Ἀργεία, Βαβέλυκα Ἀργεία, Κλεαίχμα ἀδελφὴ Αὐτοχαρίδα τοῦ Λάκωνος.
αἱ πᾶσαι ιζ'.

PYTHAGORAS b

[21] From Sycion: Poliades, Demon, Stratius, Sosthenes.
[22] From Cyrene: Prorus, Melanippus, Aristangelus, Theodorus.
[23] From Cyzicus: Pythodorus, Hipposthenes, Boutherus, **Xenophilus.**
[24] From Catania: **Charondas,** Lysiades.
[25] From Corinth: Chrysippus.
[26] From Etruria: Nausithous.
[27] From Athens: Neocritus.
[28] From Pontus: Lyramnus.
All in all 218.
[29] The most notable female Pythagoreans: Timycha, wife of Myllias of Croton; Philtys, daughter of Theophris of Croton, sister of Byndacus, Occelo and Eccelo, ‹sisters of Occelus and Occilus› of Lucania; Cheilonis, daughter of Cheilon of Sparta; Cratesicleia of Sparta, wife of Cleanor of Sparta; **Theano,** wife of **Brotinus** of Metapontum; Myia, wife of **Milon** of Croton, Lastheneia of Arcadia; Habroteleia, daughter of Habroteles of Tarentum; Echecrateia of Phlius, Tyrsênis of Sybaris, Peisirrhodê of Tarentum, Theadousa of Sparta, Boeo of Argos, Babelyca of Argos; Cleaechma, sister of Autocharidas of Laconia.
All in all 17.

---

¹ nomina persaepe corrupta in ms., corr. edd.   1 suppl. Deubner

EARLY GREEK PHILOSOPHY IV

Some Other Names and Reports (T31–T36)
Cercops (T31)

T31 (15) Cic. *Nat. deor.* 1.38.107

Orpheum poetam docet Aristoteles [Frag. 7 Rose] numquam fuisse, et hoc Orphicum carmen Pythagorei ferunt cuiusdam fuisse Cercopis.[1]

[1] nomen varie corruptum in mss., corr. Victorius

Democedes of Croton (T32–T33)

T32 (< 19.1) Hdt. 3.125

[. . .] Δημοκήδεα τὸν Καλλιφῶντος Κροτωνιήτην ἄνδρα, ἰητρόν τε ἐόντα καὶ τὴν τέχνην ἀσκέοντα ἄριστα τῶν κατ' ἑωυτόν.

T33 (< 18 A5) Iambl. *VP* 257

[. . .] τῶν Πυθαγορείων Ἀλκιμάχου καὶ Δεινάρχου καὶ Μέτωνος καὶ Δημοκήδους [. . .].

Brontinus (or Brotinus)

See **PYTH. a P10; HIPPAS. P3; ALCM. D4**

PYTHAGORAS b

Some Other Names and Reports (T31–T36)
Cercops (T31)

T31 (15) Cicero, *On the Nature of the Gods*

Aristotle reports that a poet Orpheus never existed and they say that this Orphic poem is the work of a certain Pythagorean named Cercops.

Democedes of Croton (T32–T33)

T32 (< 19.1) Herodotus, *Histories*

[. . .] Democedes, son of Calliphon, a man of Croton, a doctor and the most expert practitioner of that art of his time.

T33 (< 18 A5) Iamblichus, *Life of Pythagoras*

[. . .] the Pythagoreans Alcimachus, Deinarchus, Meton, Democedes[1] [. . .].

[1] Herodotus 3.137 reports that Democedes was married to the daughter of the Pythagorean athlete Milon of Croton.

Brontinus (or Brotinus)

See **PYTH. a P10; HIPPAS. P3; ALCM. D4**

EARLY GREEK PHILOSOPHY IV

Iccus of Tarentum (T34)

T34 (< 25.1) Plat. *Prot.* 316d

[ΠΡ.] [. . .] ἐνίους δέ τινας ᾔσθημαι καὶ γυμναστικήν, οἷον Ἴκκος τε ὁ Ταραντῖνος [. . .].

Ameinas (T35)

T35 (27) Diog. Laert. 9.21

ἐκοινώνησε δὲ καὶ Ἀμεινίᾳ Διοχάρτα[1] τῷ Πυθαγορικῷ, ὡς ἔφη Σωτίων [Frag. 27 Wehrli], ἀνδρὶ πένητι μέν, καλῷ δὲ καὶ ἀγαθῷ.

[1] Διοχάρτα Bechtel: διοχαίτη BP: καὶ διοχέτη F: Διοχαίτα Diels: alii alia

Telauges

See **PYTH. a P10; HIPPAS. P3; EMP. P8, P11, P12**

Lysis (T36)

T36 (< 46.3) Diog, Laert. 8.7

[. . .] Λύσιδος [. . .] τοῦ Ταραντίνου Πυθαγορικοῦ, φυγόντος εἰς Θήβας καὶ Ἐπαμεινώνδα καθηγησαμένου [. . .].

PYTHAGORAS b

Iccus of Tarentum (T34)

T34 (< 25.1) Plato, *Protagoras*

[Protagoras:] [. . .] certain ones [scil. of the ancient 'sophists,' who conceal their art under a different art], I have heard, under gymnastics too, like Iccus of Tarentum [. . .].

Ameinas (T35)

T35 (27) Diogenes Laertius

As Sotion says, he [i.e. Parmenides] also spent time with Ameinias the Pythagorean, son of Diochartes, a poor man but of a noble character (*kalos kagathos*) [cf. **PARM. P8**].

Telauges

See **PYTH. a P10; HIPPAS. P3; EMP. P8, P11, P12**

Lysis (T36)

T36 (< 46.3) Diogenes Laertius

[. . .] Lysis of Tarentum, a Pythagorean, who escaped to Thebes and was the teacher of Epaminondas [. . .].[1]

[1] Given that the Theban general Epaminondas was born around 410, this presupposes either a late date for Lysis or a very long life.

See also **PYTHS. R45a;** cf. **R54**

PYTHAGORAS c

DOCTRINES ATTRIBUTED BY NAME; SAYINGS AND PRECEPTS

Did Pythagoras Write Anything? (D1–D3)

D1 Diog. Laert.

a (≠ DK) 1.16

καὶ οἱ μὲν αὐτῶν κατέλιπον ὑπομνήματα, οἱ δ' ὅλως οὐ συνέγραψαν, ὥσπερ [. . .] κατά τινας Πυθαγόρας [. . .].

b (< 14.19) 8.6–7

ἔνιοι μὲν οὖν[1] Πυθαγόραν μηδὲ ἓν καταλιπεῖν σύγγραμμά φασιν διαπεσόντες.[2] Ἡράκλειτος γοῦν ὁ φυσικὸς μονονουχὶ κέκραγε καί φησι· [. . . = **HER. D126**]. οὕτω δ' εἶπεν, ἐπειδήπερ ἐναρχόμενος ὁ Πυθαγόρας τοῦ Φυσικοῦ συγγράμματος λέγει ὧδε· [. . . = **PYTHS. R45b**].

[1] οὖν P: om. BF [2] διαπεσόντες Reiske: διαπέζοντες B: διαπαίζοντες PF: παίζοντες Diels

PYTHAGORAS c

DOCTRINES ATTRIBUTED BY NAME; SAYINGS AND PRECEPTS

Did Pythagoras Write Anything? (D1–D3)[1]

[1] The data make a negative answer likelier, but the opposite opinion has also had its defenders.

D1 Diogenes Laertius

a (≠ DK)

Some of them [i.e. philosophers] left behind treatises, while others did not write anything at all, like [. . .], according to some people Pythagoras, [. . .].

b (< 14.19)

Some people claim erroneously that Pythagoras did not leave behind even one written treatise. In any case Heraclitus, the natural philosopher, almost shouts when he says, [. . . = **HER. D26**]. He said this because Pythagoras at the beginning of his treatise *On Nature* said, [. . . = **PYTHS. R45b**].

c (< 36 B2) 8.8

Ἴων δὲ ὁ Χῖος ἐν τοῖς Τριαγμοῖς φησιν αὐτὸν ἔνια ποιήσαντα ἀνενεγκεῖν εἰς Ὀρφέα.

d (≠DK) 8.15

μέχρι τε Φιλολάου οὐκ ἦν τι γνῶναι Πυθαγόρειον δόγμα· οὗτος δὲ μόνος ἐξήνεγκε τὰ διαβόητα τρία βιβλία, ἃ Πλάτων ἐπέστειλεν ἑκατὸν μνῶν ὠνηθῆναι.[1]

[1] ἐωνηθῆναι mss., corr. Cobet

D2 (46.2) Porph. *VP* 57

οὔτε γὰρ τοῦ[1] Πυθαγόρου σύγγραμμα ἦν, οἵ τ' ἐκφυγόντες Λῦσίς τε καὶ Ἄρχιππος καὶ ὅσοι ἀποδημοῦντες ἐτύγχανον, ὀλίγα διέσῳσαν ζώπυρα τῆς φιλοσοφίας ἀμυδρά τε καὶ δυσθήρατα.

[1] τοῦ mss.: αὐτοῦ Rohde

D3 (< 44 B22) Claud. Mam. *Stat. an.* 2.3, p. 105.5–6

Pythagorae igitur, quia nihil ipse scriptitaverat,[1] a posteris quaerenda sententia est [. . . = **PYTHS. R49**].

[1] scriptitaverat *aut* -veret *mss.*: scriptaverit *Schott*

PYTHAGORAS c

c (< 36 B2)

Ion of Chios in his *Triagmoi* says that he [i.e. Pythagoras] composed some poems and attributed them to Orpheus.

d (≠ DK)

Until the time of Philolaus it was not possible to know anything about Pythagorean doctrine; it was he alone who published those celebrated three books which Plato ordered to be bought for a hundred minas.

D2 (46.2) Porphyry, *Life of Pythagoras*

For there was no writing by Pythagoras himself, and Lysis and Archippus, who had escaped [scil. after the Pythagorean residence at Croton was burned down], as well as all those who went into exile, preserved from his philosophy nothing more than a few embers that were faint and hard to understand.

D3 (< 44 B22) Claudianus Mamertus, *On the State of the Soul*

Pythagoras' opinion, since he himself wrote nothing, must be sought from his successors [. . .].

EARLY GREEK PHILOSOPHY IV

*Traces of Doctrines Attributable to
Pythagoras (D4–D8)
Immortality, Transmigration,
Eschatology (D4–D5)*

D4 (14.1) Hdt. 2.123

πρῶτοι δὲ καὶ τόνδε τὸν λόγον Αἰγύπτιοί εἰσι οἱ εἰπόντες, ὡς ἀνθρώπου ψυχὴ ἀθάνατός ἐστι, τοῦ σώματος δὲ καταφθίνοντος ἐς ἄλλο ζῷον αἰεὶ γινόμενον ἐσδύεται· ἐπεὰν δὲ πάντα περιέλθῃ τὰ χερσαῖα καὶ τὰ θαλάσσια καὶ τὰ πετεινά, αὖτις ἐς ἀνθρώπου σῶμα γινόμενον ἐσδύνειν· τὴν περιήλυσιν δὲ αὐτῇ γίνεσθαι ἐν τρισχιλίοισι ἔτεσι. τούτῳ τῷ λόγῳ εἰσὶ οἳ Ἑλλήνων ἐχρήσαντο, οἱ μὲν πρότερον, οἱ δὲ ὕστερον, ὡς ἰδίῳ ἑωυτῶν ἐόντι· τῶν ἐγὼ εἰδὼς τὰ οὐνόματα οὐ γράφω.

D5 (< 14.8a) Porph. *VP* 19

[. . .] μάλιστα μέντοι γνώριμα παρὰ πᾶσιν ἐγένετο πρῶτον μὲν ὡς ἀθάνατον εἶναί φησι τὴν ψυχήν, εἶτα μεταβάλλουσαν εἰς ἄλλα γένη ζῴων, πρὸς δὲ τούτοις ὅτι κατὰ περιόδους τινὰς τὰ γινόμενά[1] ποτε πάλιν γίνεται, νέον δ' οὐδὲν ἁπλῶς ἔστι, καὶ ὅτι πάντα τὰ

[1] γενόμενά Westermann

PYTHAGORAS c

Traces of Doctrines Attributable to Pythagoras (D4–D8)[1]
Immortality, Transmigration, Eschatology (D4–D5)

[1] Any attribution to Pythagoras himself is uncertain. We present here *exempli gratia* some of the doctrines that have most frequently been considered original, or possibly so.

D4 (14.1) Herodotus, *Histories*

The Egyptians are the first to have said the following too: that a human's soul is immortal, and when the body has been destroyed it enters each time into another living being that is being born; and after it has gone through all the animals, terrestrial, marine, and winged, it enters once again into a human body that is being born (it completes this cycle in three thousand years). There are some Greeks who have professed this doctrine, some of them earlier, others later, as though it were their own. I know their names but I do not write them down.[1]

[1] Herodotus is usually thought to be referring to Pythagoras. But since he refers to both earlier and later Greeks, it is not impossible that he is also alluding to Empedocles [cf. **EMP. D13–D20**].

D5 (< 14.8a) Porphyry, *Life of Pythagoras*

[. . .] What has become best known of all is first that he said that the soul is immortal; then that it passes into other species of animals; and also that what is born is born again sometime after determinate periods of time; and that there is absolutely nothing new; and that it must be

EARLY GREEK PHILOSOPHY IV

γινόμενα ἔμψυχα ὁμογενῆ δεῖ[2] νομίζειν. φαίνεται[3] γὰρ εἰς τὴν Ἑλλάδα τὰ δόγματα πρῶτος κομίσαι ταῦτα Πυθαγόρας.

[2] δὲ mss., corr. Holste   [3] φέρεται Nauck

Numbers: Justice Is a Square (D6)

D6 (58B.4) Ps.-Arist. *MM* 1.1 1182a11–14

πρῶτος μὲν οὖν ἐνεχείρησεν Πυθαγόρας περὶ ἀρετῆς εἰπεῖν, οὐκ ὀρθῶς δέ· τὰς γὰρ ἀρετὰς εἰς τοὺς ἀριθμοὺς ἀνάγων οὐκ οἰκείαν τῶν ἀρετῶν τὴν θεωρίαν ἐποιεῖτο· οὐ γάρ ἐστιν ἡ δικαιοσύνη ἀριθμὸς ἰσάκις ἴσος.

Geometry: The Pythagorean Theorem (D7)

D7

a (≠ DK) Diog. Laert. 8.12

φησὶ δ' Ἀπολλόδωρος ὁ λογιστικὸς ἑκατόμβην θῦσαι αὐτόν, εὑρόντα ὅτι τοῦ τριγώνου ὀρθογωνίου ἡ ὑποτείνουσα πλευρὰ ἴσον δύναται ταῖς περιεχούσαις.

thought that things that are born ensouled belong to the same race. For Pythagoras seems to have been the first to have introduced these doctrines into Greece.

See also **PHER. R1; XEN. D64**

Numbers: Justice Is a Square (D6)

D6 (58B.4) Ps.-Aristotle, *Magna Moralia*

Pythagoras was the first who tried to speak about virtue, but he did not do so correctly. For in referring the virtues to numbers he did not establish an appropriate way to study the virtues. For justice is not a number equal times equal [i.e. a square number].

See also e.g. **PYTHS. ANON. D20**

Geometry: The Pythagorean Theorem (D7)

D7

a (≠ DK) Diogenes Laertius

Apollodorus the mathematician says that he [i.e. Pythagoras] offered a hecatomb in sacrifice because he had discovered that the side subtending the right angle in a right triangle is equal in power to the sides containing the right angle [i.e. the square on the hypotenuse is equal to the sum of the squares on the sides].

b (58B.19) Procl. *In Eucl.* Prop. 47, theor. 33 (p. 426.1–9 Friedlein)

"ἐν τοῖς ὀρθογωνίοις $\overline{\Delta}$ τὸ ἀπὸ τῆς τὴν ὀρθὴν γωνίαν ὑποτεινούσης πλευρᾶς τετράγωνον ἴσον ἐστὶ τοῖς ἀπὸ τῶν περὶ τὴν ὀρθὴν γωνίαν πλευρῶν τετραγώνοις." τῶν μὲν ἱστορεῖν τὰ ἀρχαῖα βουλομένων ἀκούοντας τὸ θεώρημα τοῦτο εἰς Πυθαγόραν ἀναπεμπόντων ἐστὶν εὑρεῖν καὶ βουθύτην λεγόντων αὐτὸν ἐπὶ τῇ εὑρέσει [. . .].

Music (D8)

D8 (≠ DK) Porph. *In Ptol. Harm.* 30.1–3

γράφει δὲ καὶ Ἡρακλείδης περὶ τούτων ἐν τῇ Μουσικῇ εἰσαγωγῇ ταῦτα· "Πυθαγόρας, ὥς φησι Ξενοκράτης [Frag. 9 Heinze], εὕρισκε καὶ τὰ ἐν μουσικῇ διαστήματα οὐ χωρὶς ἀριθμοῦ τὴν γένεσιν ἔχοντα [. . .]."

The First Inventor (prôtos heuretês) *(D9–D14)*
The Term 'Philosophy' (D9)

D9 (≠ DK) Diog. Laert.

a 1.12

φιλοσοφίαν δὲ πρῶτος ὠνόμασε Πυθαγόρας καὶ ἑαυτὸν φιλόσοφον [. . . = **PYTHS. R29a**].

b (58B.19) Proclus, *Commentary on Euclid*

["In right-angled triangles, the square on the side subtending the right angle [i.e. the hypotenuse] is equal to the squares on the sides containing the right angle [scil. added together]" = Euclid, *Elements,* Book 1, Proposition 47]. One can find, if one reads the authors who investigate antiquity, some who attribute this theorem to Pythagoras and say he sacrificed an ox when he discovered it [. . .].

Music (D8)

D8 (≠ DK) Xenocrates in Porphyry, *Commentary on Ptolemy's* Harmonics

Heraclides writes the following about this in his *Introduction to Music:* "As Xenocrates says, Pythagoras also discovered that the musical intervals are not generated independently of number [. . .]."

The First Inventor (prôtos heuretês) *(D9–D14)*
The Term 'Philosophy' (D9)

D9 (≠ DK) Diogenes Laertius

a

Pythagoras was the first to use the term 'philosophy' and to call himself a 'philosopher' [. . .].

b 8.8

Σωσικράτης δ' ἐν Διαδοχαῖς φησιν αὐτὸν ἐρωτηθέντα ὑπὸ Λέοντος τοῦ Φλιασίων τυράννου τίς εἴη, φιλόσοφος εἰπεῖν [... = **PYTHS. R29b**].

Mathematics (D10–D12)
The Decad and the tetraktys *(D10)*

D10 (cf. 58B.15) Sext. Emp. *Adv. Math.* 7.94

καὶ τοῦτο ἐμφαίνοντες οἱ Πυθαγορικοὶ ποτὲ μὲν εἰώθασι λέγειν τὸ

– ∪ ∪ | – ∪ ∪ | – ἀριθμῷ δέ τε πάντ' ἐπέοικεν,

ὁτὲ δὲ τὸν φυσικώτατον ὀμνύναι ὅρκον οὑτωσί,

οὐ μὰ τὸν ἁμετέρᾳ κεφαλᾷ παραδόντα τετρακτύν,
παγὰν ἀενάου φύσεως ῥιζώματ' ἔχουσαν,

τὸν μὲν παραδόντα λέγοντες Πυθαγόραν [. . .], τετρακτὺν δὲ ἀριθμόν τινα, ὃς ἐκ τεσσάρων τῶν πρώτων ἀριθμῶν συγκείμενος τὸν τελειότατον ἀπήρτιζεν, ὥσπερ τὸν δέκα· ἓν γὰρ καὶ δύο καὶ τρία καὶ τέσσαρα δέκα γίνεται.

b

Sosicrates says in his *Successions* that he [i.e. Pythagoras] was asked by Leon, the tyrant of Phlius, who he was, and he said, "A philosopher" [. . .].

See also **PYTH. a P18, PYTHS. R29**

Mathematics (D10–D12)
The Decad and the tetraktys *(D10)*

D10 (cf. 58B.15) Sextus Empiricus, *Against the Logicians*

To indicate this [scil. that the criterion of all things is number], the Pythagoreans had the habit of saying sometimes,

> all things resemble number,

and at other times of swearing this oath, which was in the greatest conformity with nature:

> No, by the man who bequeathed to our very self the tetraktys,
> The source that holds the roots of ever-flowing nature,

meaning by 'the man who bequeathed' Pythagoras [. . .] and by 'tetraktys' a certain number that, composed out of the four first numbers, produces the most perfect number, i.e. ten: for one plus two plus three plus four makes ten.

EARLY GREEK PHILOSOPHY IV

Geometry (D11)

D11 (< 58B.1) Procl. *In Eucl.*, Prol. 2 (p. 65.15–21 Friedlein) (< Eudem. Frag. 133 Wehrli)

ἐπὶ δὲ τούτοις Πυθαγόρας τὴν περὶ αὐτὴν φιλοσοφίαν εἰς σχῆμα παιδείας ἐλευθέρου μετέστησεν, ἄνωθεν τὰς ἀρχὰς αὐτῆς ἐπισκοπούμενος καὶ ἀύλως καὶ νοερῶς τὰ θεωρήματα διερευνώμενος, ὃς δὴ καὶ τὴν τῶν ἀλόγων πραγματείαν καὶ τὴν τῶν κοσμικῶν σχημάτων σύστασιν ἀνεῦρεν.

Weights and Measures (D12)

D12 (14.12) Diog. Laert 8.14

καὶ πρῶτον εἰς τοὺς Ἕλληνας μέτρα καὶ σταθμὰ εἰσηγήσασθαι, καθά φησιν Ἀριστόξενος ὁ μουσικός [Frag. 24 Wehrli].

The Term 'Cosmos' (D13)

D13 (14. 21) Aët. 2.1.1 (Plut.) [περὶ κόσμου]

Πυθαγόρας πρῶτος ὠνόμασε τὴν τῶν ὅλων περιοχὴν κόσμον ἐκ τῆς ἐν αὐτῷ τάξεως.

PYTHAGORAS c

Geometry (D11)

D11 (< 58B.1) Eudemus in Proclus, *Commentary on Euclid's* Elements

After these [i.e. Thales and Mamercus (?)], Pythagoras transformed the kind of philosophy regarding this [i.e. geometry] by giving it the form of a free discipline, considering its principles from the origin and investigating its propositions independently of matter and in accordance with the intelligible—he who also discovered the study of the irrationals and the arrangement of the cosmic figures.

Weights and Measures (D12)

D12 (14.12) Aristoxenus in Diogenes Laertius

As Aristoxenus the writer on music says, he was the first to introduce measures and weights into Greece.

The Term 'Cosmos' (D13)

D13 (14.21) Aëtius

Pythagoras was the first to call what surrounds all things '*kosmos*' (i.e. a beautiful organized whole) because of the order (*taxis*) that is found there.

EARLY GREEK PHILOSOPHY IV

The Identity of the Morning Star and the Evening Star (D14)

D14 (< 28 A1) Diog. Laert. 8.14

πρῶτόν τε Ἕσπερον καὶ Φωσφόρον τὸν αὐτὸν εἰπεῖν [. . .].

'Symbols' (symbola) or 'Sayings' (akousmata) (D15–D25)
The Three Kinds of 'Sayings' (D15)

D15 (< 58C.4) Iambl. VP 82

πάντα δὲ τὰ οὕτως ‹καλούμενα›[1] ἀκούσματα διήρηται εἰς τρία εἴδη· τὰ μὲν γὰρ αὐτῶν τί ἐστι σημαίνει, τὰ δὲ τί μάλιστα, τὰ δὲ τί δεῖ πράττειν ἢ μὴ πράττειν.

[1] ‹καλούμενα› Nauck

PYTHAGORAS c

The Identity of the Morning Star and the Evening Star (D14)

D14 (< 28 A1) Diogenes Laertius

He was the first to say that the morning star and the evening star are one and the same [. . .].

See also **PARM. D22**

'Symbols' (symbola) or 'Sayings' (akousmata) (D15–D25)[1]
The Three Kinds of 'Sayings' (D15)

[1] A *symbolon* is originally a fragment of something permitting people who each possess a portion to recognize one another. This seems to be the original name for the statements that are also designated *akousmata* (a term that refers to the oral character of these statements: 'oral maxims,' 'sayings'), in relation with the distinction between two categories of Pythagoreans, the 'knowers' and the 'listeners' (see **PYTH b T15–T18**).

D15 (< 58C.4) Iamblichus, *Life of Pythagoras*

All of these sayings <called> 'acousmatic' are divided into three kinds: for some of them indicate what a thing is, others what something is most of all, and others what one should or should not do.[1]

[1] This indication may go back to Aristotle's treatise *On the Pythagoreans*.

EARLY GREEK PHILOSOPHY IV

Exegetical Traditions (D16–D19)

D16 (< 58C.6) *Suda* A.1987

Ἀναξίμανδρος, Ἀναξιμάνδρου, Μιλήσιος, ὁ νεώτερος, ἱστορικός. γέγονε δὲ κατὰ τοὺς Ἀρταξέρξου χρόνους τοῦ Μνήμονος[1] κληθέντος. ἔγραψε συμβόλων Πυθαγορείων ἐξήγησιν· οἷόν ἐστι τὸ ζυγὸν μὴ ὑπερβαίνειν, μαχαίρᾳ πῦρ μὴ σκαλεύειν, ἀπὸ ὁλοκλήρου ἄρτου μὴ ἐσθίειν· καὶ τὰ λοιπά.

[1] ἀμείνονος mss., corr. ed. Basil.

D17 (≠ DK) Iambl. *VP* 145

[. . .] τὰ ὑπὸ Ἀνδροκύδου ἐν τῷ περὶ Πυθαγορικῶν συμβόλων ἱστορούμενα περὶ Θυμαρίδου τοῦ Ταραντίνου, Πυθαγορικοῦ [. . .].

D18 (< 58C.4) Iambl. *VP* 86

ἐπ' ἐνίων μὲν οὖν ἐπιλέγεται ⟨διὰ⟩[1] τί δεῖ, οἷον ὅτι δεῖ τεκνοποιεῖσθαι ἕνεκα τοῦ καταλιπεῖν ἕτερον ἀνθ' ἑαυτοῦ θεῶν θεραπευτήν, τοῖς δὲ οὐδεὶς λόγος πρόσεστι. καὶ ἔνια μὲν τῶν ἐπιλεγομένων δόξει προσπεφυκέναι ἀπ' ἀρχῆς,[2] ἔνια δὲ πόρρω· οἷον περὶ τοῦ τὸν ἄρτον μὴ καταγνύναι, ὅτι πρὸς τὴν ἐν Ἅιδου κρίσιν οὐ συμφέρει. αἱ δὲ προστιθέμεναι εἰκοτολογίαι περὶ τῶν τοιούτων οὐκ εἰσὶ Πυθαγορικαί, ἀλλ' ἐνίων ἔξωθεν ἐπισοφιζομένων καὶ πειρωμένων προσάπτειν εἰκότα

PYTHAGORAS c

Exegetical Traditions (D16–D19)

D16 (< 58C.6) *Suda*

Anaximander the younger of Miletus, son of Anaximander, a historian. He lived in the time of Artaxerxes, called Mnemon [405–359 BC]. He wrote an *Exegesis of Pythagorean Symbols,* such as "do not step across a pair of scales," "do not stir up a fire with a knife," "do not eat from a bread that has not been cut," etc.

D17 (≠ DK) Iamblichus, *Life of Pythagoras*

[...] what Androcydes reports about Thymaridas of Tarentum, the Pythagorean, in his *On Pythagorean Symbols* [...].

D18 (< 58C.4) Iamblichus, *Life of Pythagoras*

In certain cases, the reason why one must [scil. do this] is added (for example, one must have children in order to leave behind another person in place of oneself to serve the gods), but in other cases no explanation has been added. And some of the added explanations seem to have been attached from the beginning, others later, for example, that one should not break a bread, for this is not helpful with regard to the judgment in Hades. But these added plausible explanations regarding these kinds of questions are not Pythagorean, but were devised additionally by certain outsiders who were trying to attach a plau-

---

¹ ‹διὰ› Kiessling   ² ἀπ' ἀρχῆς Deubner: ἅπερ ἂν ᾖ ms.: ἀπαρτί Diels

EARLY GREEK PHILOSOPHY IV

λόγον, οἷον καὶ περὶ τοῦ νῦν λεχθέντος, διὰ τί οὐ δεῖ καταγνύναι τὸν ἄρτον· οἱ μὲν γάρ φασιν ὅτι οὐ δεῖ τὸν συνάγοντα διαλύειν (τὸ δὲ ἀρχαῖον βαρβαρικῶς πάντες ἐπὶ ἕνα ἄρτον συνῄεσαν[3] οἱ φίλοι), οἱ δ᾽ ὅτι οὐ δεῖ οἰωνὸν ποιεῖσθαι τοιοῦτον ἀρχόμενον καταγνύντα καὶ συντρίβοντα.

[3] συνῄεσαν Rose: συνίεσαν ms.

D19 (≠ DK) Iambl. *Protr.* 21 (pp. 105.5–9, 106.9–12 Pistelli)

[. . .] τῶν γὰρ λεγομένων Πυθαγορικῶν συμβόλων ὅσα ἂν ἀξιομνημόνευτα ἡμῖν φαίνηται καὶ τὸ προτρεπτικὸν εἶδος παραδεικνύῃ ἐκθέμενοι, διεγνώκαμεν ἐξήγησιν ποιήσασθαι τὴν πρέπουσαν αὐτῶν εἰς παράκλησιν [. . .]. καὶ εἰ μή τις αὐτὰ τὰ σύμβολα[1] ἐκλέξας διαπτύξειε καὶ ἀμώκῳ ἐξηγήσει περιλάβοι, γελοῖα ἂν καὶ γραώδη δόξειε[2] τοῖς ἐντυγχάνουσι τὰ λεγόμενα λήρου μεστὰ καὶ ἀδολεσχίας.

[1] τὰ σύμβολα del. Nauck   [2] δόξειε Iambl. *VP* 105: δόξειαν ms.

Examples (D20–D25)
A List Transmitted by Iamblichus (D20)

D20 (< 58C.4) Iambl. *VP* 82–84

[82] [. . . = **D15**] τὰ μὲν οὖν τί ἐστι τοιαῦτα, οἷον

PYTHAGORAS c

sible explanation, as for example regarding what I have just said: why should one not break a bread? For some say that one should not undo what is similar (for in ancient times, friends met around a single bread in the manner of barbarians), while others say that one should not give an omen of this kind by making a beginning by breaking and shattering.

D19 (≠ DK) Iamblichus, *Protreptic*

[. . .] After having indicated all of those symbols called Pythagorean that seem to us worth mentioning and that present the protreptic genre, we have decided to provide the exegesis of them that is suitable for an exhortation [. . .]. For if one did not choose these symbols in order to explain them and to supply them with a serious exegesis, these statements would seem to readers to be full of stupidity and idle chatter, ridiculous and worthy of old women.

Examples (D20–D25)
A List Transmitted by Iamblichus (D20)

D20 (< 58C.4) Iamblichus, *Life of Pythagoras*

[82] [. . .] Those [scil. acousmatic statements that indicate] what a thing is are of this sort:

τί ἐστιν αἱ μακάρων νῆσοι; ἥλιος καὶ σελήνη.
τί ἐστι τὸ ἐν Δελφοῖς μαντεῖον; τετρακτύς· ὅπερ
ἐστὶν ἡ ἁρμονία, ἐν ᾗ αἱ Σειρῆνες.

τὰ δὲ τί μάλιστα, οἷον

τί τὸ δικαιότατον; θύειν.
τί τὸ σοφώτατον; ἀριθμός· δεύτερον δὲ τὸ τοῖς
πράγμασι τὰ ὀνόματα τιθέμενον.
τί σοφώτατον τῶν παρ' ἡμῖν; ἰατρική.
τί κάλλιστον; ἁρμονία.
τί κράτιστον; γνώμη.
τί ἄριστον; εὐδαιμονία.
τί δὲ ἀληθέστατον λέγεται; ὅτι πονηροὶ οἱ ἄνθρωποι. [. . .]

[83] [. . .] τὰ δὲ τί πρακτέον ἢ οὐ πρακτέον τῶν ἀκουσμάτων τοιαῦτά ἐστιν, οἷον

ὅτι δεῖ τεκνοποιεῖσθαι (δεῖ γὰρ ἀντικαταλιπεῖν
τοὺς θεραπεύοντας τὸν θεόν), ἢ
ὅτι δεῖ τὸν δεξιὸν ὑποδεῖσθαι πρότερον, ἢ
ὅτι οὐ δεῖ τὰς λεωφόρους βαδίζειν ὁδοὺς οὐδὲ εἰς
περιρραντήριον ἐμβάπτειν οὐδὲ ἐν βαλανείῳ
λούεσθαι· ἄδηλον γὰρ ἐν πᾶσι τούτοις εἰ καθαρεύουσιν οἱ κοινωνοῦντες.

[84] καὶ ἄλλα τάδε·

φορτίον μὴ συγκαθαιρεῖν (οὐ γὰρ δεῖ αἴτιον γίνεσθαι τοῦ μὴ πονεῖν), συνανατιθέναι δέ.

PYTHAGORAS c

What are the Islands of the Blessed?—The sun and the moon.
What is the oracle of Delphi?—The tetraktys, which is the harmony in which the Sirens [scil. sing].

Those that indicate what something is most of all, for example:

What is the most just thing?—To sacrifice.
What is the wisest thing?—Number, and secondly the man who gave things their names.
What is the wisest among us?—Medicine.
The most beautiful?—Harmony.
The strongest?—Intelligence.
The best?—Happiness.
What is the truest thing that is said?—That men are wicked. [. . .]

[83] [. . .] Those acousmatic statements that say what one should or should not do are of this kind, for example:

One must make children. For one must leave behind in place of oneself servants of god; or
One must put a shoe on one's right foot first; or
One must not use the main streets, nor soak oneself in a vessel of lustral water, nor bathe in a public bath. For in all these cases it is uncertain whether the people who are sharing them are pure.

[84] And here are some others:

Do not help someone put down a burden (for one should not be the reason for one's not exerting oneself), but help to lift it up.

EARLY GREEK PHILOSOPHY IV

χρυσὸν ἐχούσῃ μὴ πλησιάζειν ἐπὶ τεκνοποιίᾳ.
μὴ λέγειν ἄνευ φωτός.
σπένδειν τοῖς θεοῖς κατὰ τὸ οὖς τῆς κύλικος οἰωνοῦ
ἕνεκεν, καὶ ὅπως μὴ ἀπὸ τοῦ αὐτοῦ πίνηται.
ἐν δακτυλίῳ μὴ φέρειν σημεῖον θεοῦ εἰκόνα, ὅπως
μὴ μιαίνηται· ἄγαλμα γάρ, ὅπερ δεῖ φυτεῦσαι
ἐν τῷ οἴκῳ.
γυναῖκα οὐ δεῖ διώκειν τὴν αὑτοῦ, ἱκέτις γάρ· διὸ
καὶ ἀφ' ἑστίας ἀγόμεθα, καὶ ἡ λῆψις διὰ δεξιᾶς.
μηδὲ ἀλεκτρυόνα λευκὸν ‹θύειν›·[1] ἱκέτης γάρ, ἱερὸς[2] τοῦ Μηνός, διὸ καὶ σημαίνουσιν ὥραν. [. . .]

[1] ‹θύειν› suppl. Scaliger, cf. *Protr.* 107.18   [2] ‹καὶ› ἱερὸς Salmasius

Some Shorter Reports That Go Back to Aristotle (D21–D23)

D21 (58C.1) Arist. *An. Post.* 2.11 94b33–34

[. . .] καί, εἰ [scil. βροντᾷ] ὡς οἱ Πυθαγόρειοί φασιν,
ἀπειλῆς ἕνεκα τοῖς ἐν τῷ ταρτάρῳ, ὅπως φοβῶνται.

D22 (< 58C.3) Diog. Laert. 8.34–35.

φησὶ δ' Ἀριστοτέλης ἐν τῷ Περὶ τῶν Πυθαγορείων[1]
[Frag. 195 Rose] παραγγέλλειν αὐτὸν

[1] Πυθαγορείων Diels: κυάμων mss.

PYTHAGORAS c

Do not, in order to make children, sleep with a woman who is wearing gold.

Do not speak in darkness.

Pour libations to the gods from the side of the vase handle because of the good omen and in order not to drink from the same side.

Do not wear on your finger an image that is a sign of the god, lest it become dirty. For this is a holy image, which must be set up in the house.

Do not expel your wife, for she is a suppliant. That is why we lead her out from her hearth and take her by the right hand.

Do not ‹sacrifice› a white rooster, for it is a suppliant holy to the Month, and that is why they indicate the hour [. . .].[1]

[1] The list continues in the following paragraph. Iamblichus, *Protreptic* 21, gives thirty-nine maxims of the third type without exegesis, followed by a continuous exegetic block (58C.6).

Some Shorter Reports That Go Back to Aristotle (D21–D23)

D21 (58C.1) Aristotle, *Posterior Analytics*

[. . .] and if [scil. it thunders,] if it is as the Pythagoreans say, it is so as to threaten those in Tartarus, in order to make them afraid.

D22 (< 58C.3) Diogenes Laertius

Aristotle says in his *On the Pythagoreans* that he commands

ἀπέχεσθαι τῶν κυάμων ἤτοι ὅτι αἰδοίοις εἰσὶν
ὅμοιοι, ἢ ὅτι Ἅιδου πύλαις·² ἀγόνατον γὰρ μό-
νον· ἢ ὅτι φθείρει· ἢ ὅτι τῇ τοῦ ὅλου φύσει
ὅμοιον· ἢ ὅτι ⟨οὐκ⟩³ ὀλιγαρχικόν· κληροῦνται
γοῦν αὐτοῖς.
τὰ δὲ πεσόντα⁴ μὴ ἀναιρεῖσθαι, ὑπὲρ τοῦ ἐθίζεσθαι
μὴ ἀκολάστως ἐσθίειν, ἢ ὅτι ἐπὶ τελευτῇ τινος.
[. . .]
ἀλεκτρυόνος μὴ ἅπτεσθαι λευκοῦ, ὅτι ἱερὸς τοῦ
Μηνὸς⁵ καὶ ἱκέτης· τὸ δ' ἦν τῶν ἀγαθῶν.⁶ τῷ τε
Μηνὶ ἱερός· σημαίνει γὰρ τὰς ὥρας. καὶ τὸ μὲν
λευκὸν τῆς τἀγαθοῦ φύσεως, τὸ δὲ μέλαν τοῦ
κακοῦ.⁷
τῶν ἰχθύων μὴ ἅπτεσθαι ὅσοι ἱεροί· μὴ γὰρ δεῖν
τὰ αὐτὰ τετάχθαι θεοῖς καὶ ἀνθρώποις, ὥσπερ
οὐδὲ ἐλευθέροις καὶ δούλοις.
[35] ἄρτον μὴ καταγνύειν, ὅτι ἐπὶ ἕνα οἱ πάλαι τῶν
φίλων ἐφοίτων, καθάπερ ἔτι καὶ νῦν οἱ βάρβαροι·
μὴ δὴ⁸ διαιρεῖν ὃς συνάγει αὐτούς· οἱ δέ, πρὸς
τὴν ἐν Ἅιδου κρίσιν· οἱ δ', εἰς πόλεμον δειλίαν
ποιεῖν· οἱ δέ, ἐπεὶ ἀπὸ τούτου ἄρχεται τὸ ὅλον.
καὶ τῶν σχημάτων τὸ κάλλιστον σφαῖραν εἶναι
τῶν στερεῶν, τῶν δὲ ἐπιπέδων κύκλον.

---

² post πύλαις lac. indic. Diels   ³ ⟨οὐκ⟩ Richards
⁴ πεσόντα ⟨ἀπὸ τραπέζης⟩ Hübner   ⁵ μηνὸς mss.:
ἡλίου Suda   ⁶ τὸ . . . ἀγαθῶν secl. Menagius

PYTHAGORAS c

to abstain from beans, either because they resemble the testicles or the gates of Hades, for it is the only [scil. plant whose stem] has no knots; or because it is destructive; or because it resembles the nature of the whole; or because it is ⟨not⟩ oligarchic, in any case it is used for drawing lots.

not to pick up what has fallen, in order to become accustomed to not eating overmuch; or because it indicates someone's death. [...]

not to lay hands on a white rooster, because it is holy to the Month and a suppliant (which is one of the good things); and it is holy to the Month, for it indicates the hours; and white belongs to the nature of the good, black to that of evil.

not to lay hands on those fish that are sacred; for one must not assign the same things to gods and to humans, just as one must not do so to free men and to slaves.

[35] not to break bread, for in ancient times friends came together around one bread, just as even now the barbarians do; and one should not divide what unites them; others refer this to the judgment in Hades; others say that it causes cowardice in war; others, since it is from this (?) that the whole has its beginning.

And among figures, the most beautiful of the solid ones is the sphere, and of the plane ones the circle.

---

7 καὶ . . . τοῦ κακοῦ post δούλοις mss., huc transp. Diels   8 μὴ δὴ B² (δεῖ B¹) P¹: μὴ γοῦν Φ: μηδὲ FP²: καὶ μὴ Suda

123

γῆρας καὶ πᾶν τὸ μειούμενον[9] ὅμοιον· καὶ αὔξην καὶ νεότητα ταὐτόν.

ὑγίειαν τὴν τοῦ εἴδους διαμονήν, νόσον τὴν τούτου φθοράν.

περὶ τῶν ἁλῶν, ὅτι δεῖ παρατίθεσθαι πρὸς ὑπόμνησιν τοῦ δικαίου· οἱ γὰρ ἅλες πᾶν σῴζουσιν ὅ τι καὶ παραλάβωσι, καὶ γεγόνασιν ἐκ τῶν καθαρωτάτων ὑδάτων[10] καὶ[11] θαλάσσης.

[9] μειούμενον FP⁴: μιμούμενον BP¹Q   [10] ὑδάτων Suda: ὕδατος mss;: ἡλίου Cobet   [11] καὶ mss.: τῆς Marcovich

D23 (58C.2) Porph. *VP* 41

ἔλεγε δέ τινα καὶ μυστικῷ τρόπῳ συμβολικῶς, ἃ δὴ ἐπὶ πλέον Ἀριστοτέλης ἀνέγραψεν· οἷον ὅτι τὴν θάλατταν μὲν ἐκάλει εἶναι **δάκρυον**,[1] τὰς δ' ἄρκτους **Ῥέας χεῖρας,** τὴν δὲ Πλειάδα **Μουσῶν λύραν,** τοὺς δὲ πλανήτας **κύνας τῆς Φερσεφόνης.** τὸν δ' ἐκ χαλκοῦ κρουομένου γινόμενον ἦχον φωνὴν εἶναί τινος τῶν δαιμόνων ἐναπειλημμένου[2] τῷ χαλκῷ.

[1] ⟨Κρόνου⟩ δάκρυον Stanley, ⟨Ἰνοῦς⟩ δάκρυον Nauck   [2] ἐναπειλημμένου Nauck: -μένην mss.

Old age is similar to everything that diminishes; and growth and youth are the same thing.

Health is the persistence of the form, illness its destruction.

With regard to salt, it should be brought to the table as a reminder of justice: for salt preserves everything that it receives, and it comes from the purest waters and from the sea.

D23 (58C.2) Porphyry, *Life of Pythagoras*

Some things he said were expressed symbolically in the manner of the mysteries, and Aristotle has written down a great number of these, like the fact that he called the sea **'tear'** [i.e. probably ⟨**Cronus'**⟩], the constellations of the Bears **'Rhea's hands,'** the Pleiades **'the Muses' lyre,'** the planets **'Persephone's dogs,'** and the sound produced by bronze when it is struck **'the voice of one of the demons'** trapped in the bronze [. . .].[1]

[1] The examples continue until §45.

EARLY GREEK PHILOSOPHY IV

Two Other Reports (D24–D25)

D24 (< 58C.5) Ps.-Arist. *Oec.* 1.4 1344a8–12

[. . .] καθάπερ οἱ Πυθαγόρειοι λέγουσιν ὥσπερ ἱκέτιν καὶ ἀφ' ἑστίας ἠγμένην ὡς ἥκιστα δεῖν ἀδικεῖν.

D25 (58C.2) Ael. *Var. hist.* 4.17

ἔλεγε δὲ ἱερώτατον εἶναι τὸ τῆς μαλάχης φύλλον. ἔλεγε δὲ ὅτι πάντων σοφώτατον ὁ ἀριθμός, δεύτερος δὲ ὁ τοῖς πράγμασι τὰ ὀνόματα θέμενος. καὶ τὸν σεισμὸν ἐγενεαλόγει οὐδὲν ἄλλο εἶναι ἢ σύνοδον τῶν τεθνεώτων. ἡ δὲ ἶρις, ἔφασκεν, ὡς αὐγὴ[1] τοῦ ἡλίου ἐστί. καὶ ὁ πολλάκις ἐμπίπτων τοῖς ὠσὶν ἦχος φωνὴ τῶν κρειττόνων.

[1] ἡ γῆ mss., corr. Gessner

PYTHAGORAS c

Two Other Reports (D24–D25)

D24 (< 58C.5) Ps.-Aristotle, *Economics*

[. . .] as the Pythagoreans say, one must absolutely not commit injustice [scil. to one's wife], because she is like a suppliant who has been led away from her hearth.

D25 (58C.2) Aelian, *Historical Miscellany*

He said that the holiest thing is the leaf of the mallow; and he said that the wisest of all things is number, and second the man who gave things their names; and he explained that the origin of the earthquake was that it is nothing other than the assembly of the dead, and he said that the rainbow is like a ray of the sun and that the echo that often strikes the ears is the voice of those who are superior [i.e. the gods].

11. HIPPASUS [HIPPAS.]

We know very little about Hippasus, but he is interesting for two reasons connected with the question of the identity of Pythagoreanism, from both an institutional and a doctrinal perspective: with regard to the history of the school, his name is associated with the question of secrecy and the divulgation of doctrines; and the fact that, despite sharing an interest in numbers and musical ratios, he nonetheless adopted fire as a principle, is important evidence for the compatibility of diverse options and orientations with the designation as a 'Pythagorean.' Further evidence of this is provided by the case of Menestor, whom we have not included in our collection but whom we know to have been interested in plants (cf. 32.2–7 DK).

BIBLIOGRAPHY

K. von Fritz, "The Discovery of Incommensurability by Hippasus of Metapontum," in D. J. Furley and R. E. Allen, eds., *Studies in Presocratic Philosophy*, vol. 1, *The Beginnings of Philosophy* (London, 1970), pp. 242–64.

See also the titles listed in the General Introduction to Chapters 10–18.

HIPPASUS

OUTLINE OF THE CHAPTER

P

Origin (P1)
A Controversial Figure (P2–P3)

D

Writings? (D1–D2)
Fire as the Principle (D3–D4)
The Soul (D5)
The Means (D6)
Musical Theory (D7–D9)

HIPPASUS [18 DK]

P

Origin (P1)

P1 Iambl. VP

a (< 18.2) 81

τὸν δὲ Ἵππασον οἱ μὲν Κροτωνιάτην φασίν, οἱ δὲ Μεταποντῖνον.

b (18.2, 58A.) 267

Συβαρῖται [. . .] Ἵππασος [. . .].

A Controversial Figure (P2–P3)

P2 (< 18.4) Iambl. *Comm.* 25 (p. 77.18–23 Festa)

περὶ δ' Ἱππάσου λέγουσιν ὡς ἦν μὲν τῶν Πυθαγορείων, διὰ δὲ τὸ ἐξενεγκεῖν καὶ γράψασθαι πρῶτος σφαῖραν τὴν ἐκ τῶν δώδεκα πενταγώνων[1] ἀπώλετο

---

[1] πενταγώνων Iambl. VP 88: ἑξαγώνων mss.

HIPPASUS

P

Origin (P1)

P1 Iamblichus, *Life of Pythagoras*

a (< 18.2)

[. . .] Some say that Hippasus was from Croton, others from Metapontum.

b (18.2, 58A.)

From Sybaris [. . .] Hippasus [. . .] [cf. **PYTH. b T30[6]**].

A Controversial Figure (P2–P3)

P2 (< 18.4) Iamblichus, *On General Mathematical Science*

Regarding Hippasus in particular, [scil. the Pythagoreans called the 'knowers' (*mathêmatikoi*)] say that he was one of the Pythagoreans, but that, because he had for the first time revealed how to draw a sphere starting from twelve pentagons [i.e. the dodecahedron], he perished at sea be-

κατὰ θάλατταν ὡς ἀσεβήσας, δόξαν δὲ λάβοι ὡς εὑρών, εἶναι δὲ πάντα ἐκείνου τοῦ ἀνδρός.

P3 (17.3) Diog. Laert. 8.55

τὴν γὰρ περιφερομένην¹ πρὸς² ‹Φιλόλαον›³ Τηλαύγους ἐπιστολὴν ὅτι τε⁴ μετέσχεν Ἱππάσου καὶ Βροτίνου, μὴ εἶναι ἀξιόπιστον.

¹ περιφερομένην PF: προσφερομένην B   ² πρὸς mss.: ὡς Reiske   ³ ‹Φιλόλαον› Roeper (cf. 8.53)   ⁴ τε BP: μὲν F

cause of his impiety.[1] He acquired the reputation of having discovered it himself; but in fact everything came from the 'great man' [cf. **PYTH. b T8**].

[1] The name of Hippasus is also connected with the discovery—and the divulgation—of the irrational numbers, cf. **PYTH. b T20**.

P3 (17.3) Diogenes Laertius

The letter to ⟨Philolaus⟩ that is in circulation under the name of Telauges, in which he claims that he [i.e. Empedocles] participated [scil. in the teaching] of Hippasus and Brontinus, is not credible.

HIPPASUS [18 DK]

D

Writings? (D1–D2)

D1 (< 18.1) Diog. Laert. 8.84

φησὶ δ' αὐτὸν Δημήτριος ἐν Ὁμωνύμοις [Frag. 25 Mejer] μηδὲν καταλιπεῖν σύγγραμμα.

D2 (18.3) Diog. Laert. 8.7

τὸν δὲ Μυστικὸν λόγον Ἱππάσου φησὶν [scil. Ἡρακλείδης ὁ τοῦ Σαραπίωνος ἐν τῇ Σωτίωνος ἐπιτομῇ [Frag. 24 Wehrli]] εἶναι, γεγραμμένον ἐπὶ διαβολῇ Πυθαγόρου [. . .].

Fire as the Principle (D3–D4)

D3 (18.7) Arist. Metaph. A3 984a7

[. . .] Ἵππασος δὲ πῦρ ὁ Μεταποντῖνος καὶ Ἡράκλειτος ὁ Ἐφέσιος [. . .].

HIPPASUS

D

Writings? (D1–D2)

D1 (< 18.1) Demetrius of Magnesia in Diogenes Laertius

Demetrius says in his *Homonyms* that he [i.e. Hippasus] did not leave behind any written treatise.

D2 (18.3) Diogenes Laertius

He [i.e. Heraclides Lembos in his *Epitome of Sotion*] says that the *Mystic Discourse* was the work of Hippasus, and was written in order to defame Pythagoras [. . .].

Fire as the Principle (D3–D4)

D3 (18.7) Aristotle, *Metaphysics*

[. . .] Hippasus of Metapontum and Heraclitus of Ephesus [scil. say that the principle is] fire [. . .].

D4 (18.7) Simpl. *In Phys.*, pp. 23.33–24.4 (= Theophr. Frag. 225 FHS&G)

Ἵππασος δὲ ὁ Μεταποντῖνος καὶ Ἡράκλειτος ὁ Ἐφέσιος ἓν καὶ οὗτοι καὶ κινούμενον καὶ πεπερασμένον, ἀλλὰ πῦρ ἐποίησαν τὴν ἀρχὴν καὶ ἐκ πυρὸς ποιοῦσι τὰ ὄντα πυκνώσει καὶ μανώσει καὶ διαλύουσι πάλιν εἰς πῦρ, ὡς ταύτης μιᾶς οὔσης φύσεως τῆς ὑποκειμένης.

The Soul (D5)

D5 (18.9) Aët. 4.3.4 (Stob.; cf. Theod.) [εἰ σῶμα ἡ ψυχὴ καὶ τίς ἡ οὐσία αὐτῆς]

[. . .] Ἵππασος[1] πυρώδη.

[1] Ἵππασος καὶ Ἡράκλειτος Theod.

The Means (D6)

D6 (> 18.15) Iambl. *In Nic.*, pp. 100.19–101.1

μόναι δὲ τὸ παλαιὸν τρεῖς ἦσαν μεσότητες ἐπὶ Πυθαγόρου καὶ τῶν κατ᾽ αὐτὸν μαθηματικῶν, ἀριθμητική τε καὶ ἡ γεωμετρικὴ καὶ ἡ ποτὲ μὲν ὑπεναντία λεγομένη τῇ τάξει τρίτη,[1] ὑπὸ δὲ τῶν περὶ Ἀρχύταν αὖθις καὶ Ἵππασον ἁρμονικὴ μετακληθεῖσα, ὅτι τοὺς κατὰ

[1] τρίτῃ mss., corr. Pistelli

HIPPASUS

D4 (18.7) Theophrastus in Simplicius, *Commentary on Aristotle's* Physics

Hippasus of Metapontum and Heraclitus of Ephesus [scil. said] themselves too that it [i.e. the principle] is one, in motion, and limited, but they made fire the principle and explain the things that are as coming from fire by condensation and rarefaction, and they dissolve them once again into fire, on the supposition that this is the only nature that is a substrate.[1]

[1] It is from here that the Christian interpretation in the *Protreptic* of Clement of Alexandria arises: Hippasus of Metapontum and Heraclitus of Ephesus thought that fire was god (18.8 DK).

The Soul (D5)

D5 (18.9) Aëtius

[...] Hippasus: [scil. the soul is] made of fire.

The Means (D6)

D6 (> 18.15) Iamblichus, *Commentary on Nicomachus'* Introduction to Arithmetic

Formerly, at the time of Pythagoras and the mathematicians of his school, there were only three means: the arithmetic, the geometric, and, third in order, the one that used to be called 'subcontrary' [or: 'inverse' (*hupenantia*)] but which Archytas and Hippasus renamed 'harmonic,' since

τὸ ἡρμοσμένον καὶ ἐμμελὲς ἐφαίνετο λόγους περιέχουσα. ὑπεναντία δὲ πρότερον ἐκαλεῖτο, διότι ὑπεναντίον τι ἔπασχε τῇ ἀριθμητικῇ, ὡς δειχθήσεται.

Musical Theory (D7–D9)

D7 (18.12) Schol. in Plat. *Phaed.* 108d (< Aristox. Frag. 90 Wehrli)

Ἵππασος γάρ τις κατεσκεύασε χαλκοῦς τέτταρας δίσκους οὕτως ὥστε τὰς μὲν διαμέτρους αὐτῶν ἴσας ὑπάρχειν, τὸ δὲ τοῦ πρώτου δίσκου πάχος ἐπίτριτον μὲν εἶναι τοῦ δευτέρου, ἡμιόλιον δὲ τοῦ τρίτου, διπλάσιον δὲ τοῦ τετάρτου, κρουομένους δὲ τούτους ἐπιτελεῖν[1] συμφωνίαν τινά. καὶ λέγεται Γλαῦκον ἰδόντα τοὺς ἐπὶ τῶν δίσκων φθόγγους πρῶτον ἐγχειρῆσαι δι᾽ αὐτῶν χειρουργεῖν [. . .].

[1] κρουομένους . . . τούτους ἐπιτελεῖν T: κρινομένους . . . ἀποτελεῖν b

D8 (< 18.13) Theon Sm. *Exp.*, p. 59.7–21

Λᾶσος δὲ ὁ Ἑρμιονεύς, ὥς φασι, καὶ οἱ περὶ τὸν Μεταποντῖνον Ἵππασον Πυθαγορικὸν ἄνδρα συνέπε-

HIPPASUS

it manifestly contained the ratios that constitute harmony and melody. Earlier it was called 'subcontrary' because it manifested something 'contrary' to the arithmetic mean.[1]

[1] A little further, Iamblichus explains that, contrarily to the arithmetic mean, where the mean is exceeded and exceeds by one of its own parts, that is by an equal number [scil. in the two cases] or a unit, the middle term of the arithmetic mean exceeds and is exceeded by one of the parts of the extremes, that is by a number that is not equal [scil. in the two cases]. The harmonic mean is the subcontrary, or inverse, of the arithmetic mean because one can construct the octave by first ascending by a fourth then by a fifth, then descending by a fourth, then by a fifth (cf. Huffman, pp. 176–77).

Musical Theory (D7–D9)

D7 (18.12) Aristoxenus in Scholia on Plato's *Phaedo* [Regarding the expression 'Glaucus' art,' which suggests skill]

A certain Hippasus prepared four bronze disks in such a way that their diameters were equal, but the thickness of the first disk was epitritic with regard to the second one [= 4:3], hemiolic with regard to the third one [3:2], and the double of the fourth one, and when they were struck they produced a certain concord. And it is said that when Glaucus perceived the sounds coming from the disks, he was the first to try to make music with them [. . .].

D8 (< 18.13) Theon of Smyrna, *Aspects of Mathematics Useful for the Reading of Plato*

Lasus of Hermione, as they say, as well as the disciples of Hippasus of Metapontum, the Pythagorean, thinking that

σθαι τῶν κινήσεων τὰ τάχη καὶ τὰς βραδυτῆτας, δι᾽ ὧν αἱ συμφωνίαι[1] ἐν ἀριθμοῖς ἡγούμενος λόγους τοιούτους ἐλάμβανεν ἐπ᾽ ἀγγείων. ἴσων γὰρ ὄντων καὶ ὁμοίων πάντων τῶν ἀγγείων τὸ μὲν κενὸν ἐάσας, τὸ δὲ ἥμισυ ὑγροῦ ⟨πληρώσας⟩[2] ἐψόφει ἑκατέρῳ, καὶ αὐτῷ ἡ διὰ πασῶν ἀπεδίδοτο συμφωνία· θάτερον δὲ πάλιν τῶν ἀγγείων κενὸν ἐῶν εἰς θάτερον τῶν τεσσάρων μερῶν τὸ ἓν ἐνέχεε, καὶ κρούσαντι αὐτῷ ἡ διὰ τεσσάρων συμφωνία ἀπεδίδοτο, ἡ δὲ διὰ πέντε, ⟨ὅτε⟩[3] ἓν μέρος τῶν τριῶν συνεπλήρου οὔσης τῆς κενώσεως πρὸς τὴν ἑτέραν ἐν μὲν τῇ διὰ πασῶν ὡς β′ πρὸς ἕν, ἐν δὲ τῷ διὰ πέντε ὡς γ′ πρὸς β′, ἐν δὲ τῷ διὰ τεσσάρων ὡς δ′ πρὸς γ′.

[1] lac. post συμφωνίαι pos. Hiller   [2] ⟨πληρώσας⟩ Hiller   [3] ⟨ὅτε⟩ Hiller

D9 (18.14) Boeth. *Mus.* 2.19

sed Eubulides atque Hippasus alium consonantiarum ordinem ponunt. aiunt enim multiplicitatis augmenta superparticularitatis deminutioni rato ordine respondere. itaque non posse esse duplum praeter dimidium nec triplum praeter tertiam partem. quoniam igitur sit duplum, ex eo diapason consonantiam reddi, quoniam vero sit dimidium, ex eo quasi contrariam divisionem sesqualteram, id est diapente, effici proportionem. quibus mixtis, scilicet diapason ac diapente, triplicem procreari, quae utramque contineat symphoniam. sed rursus triplici partem tertiam

HIPPASUS

the quickness and slowness of the movements from which the concords [scil. arise] can be expressed in numbers, obtained these [scil. numerical] ratios by making use of vessels. For all the vessels being of the same size and shape, he left one empty and filled a second one half full with water; when he struck both of them, he obtained the concord of the octave. Then, again leaving one of the vases empty, he filled the other one a quarter full; and when he struck them he obtained the concord of the fourth; and the concord of a fifth, ⟨when⟩ he filled it one third full, the ratio between the emptiness of one vase and that of the other being as 2 to 1 in the concord of the octave, as 3 to 2 in the concord of the fifth, and as 4 to 3 in the concord of the fourth.[1]

[1] This alleged experiment does not correspond to the phenomena (see Barker, *Greek Musical Writings*, vol. 2, p. 32).

D9 (18.14) Boethius, *Fundamentals of Music*

But Eubulides and Hippasus posit a different order of concords. For they say that an increase of multiplicity corresponds to a decrease in superparticularity according to a fixed order. And thus there cannot be a double without a half, nor a triple without a third. Therefore, since there is the double, the concord of an octave (*diapasôn*) is produced; and since there is the half, the division that is as it were contrary, the ratio 3 to 2, i.e. the fifth (*dia pente*) is produced. When these, i.e. the octave and the fifth, are mixed together, this generates the triple, which contains within it both concords. But again the third is produced

contraria divisione partiri, ex qua rursus diatessaron symphonia nascetur. triplicem vero atque sesquitertium iunctos quadruplam comparationem proportionis efficere. unde fit, ut ex diapason ac diapente, quae est una consonantia, et diatessaron una concinentia coniungatur, quae in quadruplo consistens bis diapason nomen accepit. secundum hoc quoque hic ordo est: diapason, diapente, diapason ac diapente, diatessaron, bis diapason.

by the contrary division of the triple, out of which in turn the fourth (*diatessarôn*) is generated. When the triple and the 3 to 2 [scil. ratios] are combined, they produce a quadruple ratio. From this it comes about that from the octave and the fifth, which together form a consonance, as well as from the fourth, a concord is constructed, which, because it consists of a quadruple, has received the name 'double octave' (*bis diapasôn*). So according to this the order is the following: octave; fifth; octave and fifth; fourth; double octave.[1]

[1] It is very unlikely that these indications go back to Hippasus.

12. PHILOLAUS [PHILOL.]

Philolaus doubtless came from Croton (though Iamblichus' list speaks of Tarentum: **PYTH. b T30 [5]**); we lack any information to date his birth and death, but the indications that we do possess suggest that he was a contemporary of Socrates. He is the first Pythagorean whose doctrine we can really grasp, because he is the first one to have written a book, and of this book a certain number of fragments and a series of testimonia have survived. It is likely that Philolaus' book is Aristotle's principal source of doctrinal information on many aspects of Pythagorean thought; and if this is true, then he refers to it with a very revealing general formula, 'those whom people call the Pythagoreans,' suggesting that even if Philolaus is able to represent a 'school' that in several regards was surely already mysterious for Aristotle, nonetheless he could be sufficiently differentiated from the tutelary figure of Pythagoras that it was possible not to call him a 'Pythagorean' without further qualification. In fact, the degree of abstraction presupposed by Philolaus' doctrine of the principles (which he calls 'unlimited' and 'limiting') and the general function assigned to the notion of 'harmony' (or 'fitting together') give a new turn—one that will be important in determining the later development of Pythagorean

doctrine—to the original conception of numbers in Pythagoras himself and in the first generation of Pythagoreans (as difficult as this is to grasp). Indeed, Philolaus' thought is at least as close, and perhaps even closer, to the other great representatives of 'Presocratic' philosophy as it is to the singularities peculiar to the Pythagorean collectivity. But his transmission is disturbed by the existence—characteristic of the whole 'Pythagorean' problem—of a significant pseudepigraphic literature. Sometimes this can easily be identified (specimens are found in **PYTHS. R47–R51**), but this is not always the case. A certain number of fragments transmitted under the name of Philolaus are traditionally considered suspect: they are rejected by some interpreters and accepted by other ones. We have followed the edition of C. Huffman with regard to identifying the authentic fragments; but we have suggested the nature of the problem by providing as an appendix a selection of this type of fragments, about which readers will form their own opinion.

BIBLIOGRAPHY

Edition with Commentary

C. A. Huffman, ed. *Philolaus of Croton: Pythagorean and Presocratic* (Cambridge, 1993).

See also the titles listed in the General Introduction to Chapters 10–18.

PHILOLAUS

OUTLINE OF THE CHAPTER

P

Origin (P1)
Chronological Indications . . . (P2–P6)
   . . . Suggesting an Earlier Dating (P2–P3)
   . . . Suggesting a Later Dating (P4–P6)
Practice of the Aulos *(P7)*
Philolaus' Book as Plato's Source? (P8)

D

Philolaus' Book (D1)
The Principles (D2–D5)
Number and the Mathematical Sciences (D6–D12)
   Number in General (D6–D9)
   Noteworthy Numbers (D10–D12)
      The Monad (D10)
      The Hebdomad (D11)
      The Decad (?) (D12)
Means (D13)
Musical Harmony (D14)
Generation and Destruction of the Cosmos (D15–D18)
Cosmology (D19–D24)
   The Order of the World (D19)
   The Earth (D20–D21)
   The Sun and Moon (D22–D23)
   The Great Year (D24)
Embryology and Medicine (D25–D26)
Soul and Thought (D27–D28)
Appendix: Some Examples of Suspect Fragments and Reports (D29–D35)

PHILOLAUS [44 DK]

P

Origin (P1)

P1 (< A1) Diog. Laert. 8.84

Φιλόλαος Κροτωνιάτης [. . .].

Chronological Indications . . . (P2–P6)
. . . Suggesting an Earlier Dating (P2–P3)

P2 (cf. A1a) Schol. in Plat. *Phaed.* 61d

Φιλολάῳ] Πυθαγόρειος οὗτος ἦν, ἐξ Ἰταλίας πεφευγὼς διὰ τὸν ἐμπρησμὸν τούτων τὸν ὑπὸ Κύλωνος γεγονότα [. . .]. ἦλθεν οὗτος εἰς Θήβας, τεθνεῶτι τῷ διδασκάλῳ Λύσιδι χοὰς ποιήσασθαι ἐκεῖσε τεθαμμένῳ. Ἵππαρχος δὲ καὶ Φιλόλαος μόνοι τῆς εἰρημένης συμφορᾶς τῶν Πυθαγορείων διεσώθησαν.

PHILOLAUS

P

Origin (P1)

P1 (< A1) Diogenes Laertius

Philolaus of Croton [. . .].

See also **PYTH. b T30 [5]**

Chronological Indications . . . (P2–P6)
. . . Suggesting an Earlier Dating (P2–P3)

P2 (cf. A1a) Scholia on Plato's *Phaedo*

Philolaus: This was a Pythagorean who had fled from Italy because the burning of these men caused by Cylon [cf. **PYTH. b T25**] [. . .]. So he came to Thebes to make libations for his teacher Lysis, who had died and was buried there. Hipparchus[1] and Philolaus were the only Pythagoreans who escaped from the above-mentioned catastrophe.

[1] Often corrected to 'Archippos.'

EARLY GREEK PHILOSOPHY IV

P3 (A4a) Plut. *Gen. Socr.* 13 583A

ἐπεὶ γὰρ ἐξέπεσον αἱ κατὰ πόλεις ἑταιρεῖαι τῶν Πυθαγορικῶν στάσει κρατηθέντων, τοῖς δ' ἔτι συνεστῶσιν ἐν Μεταποντίῳ συνεδρεύουσιν ἐν οἰκίᾳ πῦρ οἱ Κυλώνειοι περιένησαν καὶ διέφθειραν ἐν ταὐτῷ[1] πάντας πλὴν Φιλολάου καὶ Λύσιδος νέων ὄντων ἔτι ῥώμῃ καὶ κουφότητι διωσαμένων τὸ πῦρ, Φιλόλαος μὲν εἰς Λευκανοὺς φυγὼν ἐκεῖθεν ἀνεσώθη πρὸς τοὺς ἄλλους φίλους ἤδη πάλιν ἀθροιζομένους καὶ κρατοῦντας τῶν Κυλωνείων [. . .].

[1] τούτῳ mss., corr. Wyttenbach

. . . *Suggesting a Later Dating (P4–P6)*

P4 (> A1a) Plat. *Phaed.* 61d–e

[ΣΩ.] τί δέ, ὦ Κέβης; οὐκ ἀκηκόατε σύ τε καὶ Σιμμίας περὶ τῶν τοιούτων Φιλολάῳ συγγεγονότες; [. . .]
[ΚΕ.] ἤδη γὰρ ἔγωγε [. . .] καὶ Φιλολάου ἤκουσα, ὅτε παρ' ἡμῖν διῃτᾶτο, ἤδη δὲ καὶ ἄλλων τινῶν, ὡς οὐ δέοι τοῦτο ποιεῖν.

P5 (A3) Cic. *De orat.* 3.34.139

[. . .] aut Philolaus Archytam Tarentinum?

PHILOLAUS

P3 (A4a) Plutarch, *On the Demon of Socrates*

For when the political associations of the Pythagoreans in the various cities, defeated in civil strife, had been expelled, and the Cylonians set fire to the house in which the survivors were meeting in Metapontum [cf. **PYTH. b T25**] and killed every one of them all together except for Philolaus and Lysis (who, being still young, managed to escape from the fire by their strength and agility), Philolaus fled to the Lucanians and from there found refuge among his other friends who had already gathered once again and defeated the Cylonians.

... Suggesting a Later Dating (P4–P6)

P4 (> A1a) Plato, *Phaedo*

[Socrates:] What is this, Cebes? Have you and Simmias, who have studied with Philolaus, not heard about such things? [. . .]
[Cebes:] I myself [. . .] heard Philolaus when he lived among us [scil. in Thebes], and certain other people earlier, saying that one must not do this [scil. kill oneself].

P5 (A3) Cicero, *On the Orator*

[. . .] and did not Philolaus [scil. teach] Archytas of Tarentum?

P6 (A2) Diog. Laert. 9.38

φησὶ δὲ καὶ Ἀπολλόδωρος ὁ Κυζικηνὸς [74 A2 DK] Φιλολάῳ αὐτὸν συγγεγονέναι.

Practice of the Aulos (P7)

P7 (A7) Athen. *Deipn.* 4 184d–e

καὶ τῶν Πυθαγορικῶν δὲ πολλοὶ τὴν αὐλητικὴν ἤσκησαν, ὡς Εὐφράνωρ τε καὶ Ἀρχύτας Φιλόλαός τε ἄλλοι τε οὐκ ὀλίγοι [. . . = **ARCHY. P14**].

Philolaus' Book as Plato's Source? (P8)

P8 (< A1) Diog. Laert. 8.85

[. . . = **D1b**] ὅ φησιν Ἕρμιππος [Frag. 40 Wehrli] λέγειν τινὰ τῶν συγγραφέων Πλάτωνα τὸν φιλόσοφον παραγενόμενον εἰς Σικελίαν πρὸς Διονύσιον ὠνήσασθαι παρὰ τῶν συγγενῶν τοῦ Φιλολάου ἀργυρίου Ἀλεξανδρείων[1] μνῶν τετταράκοντα καὶ ἐντεῦθεν μεταγεγραφέναι τὸν Τίμαιον. ἕτεροι δὲ λέγουσι τὸν Πλάτωνα λαβεῖν αὐτά, παρὰ Διονυσίου παραιτησάμενον ἐκ τῆς φυλακῆς νεανίσκον ἀπηγμένον τῶν τοῦ Φιλολάου μαθητῶν.

[1] ἀλεξανδρινῶν vel -ηνῶν mss., corr. Knoepfler

PHILOLAUS

P6 (A2) Diogenes Laertius

Apollodorus of Cyzicus too says that he [i.e. Democritus] studied with Philolaus [cf. **ATOM. P21**].

Practice of the Aulos *(P7)*

P7 (> 44 A7) Athenaeus, *Deipnosophists*

Many Pythagoreans practiced the art of the *aulos*, like Euphranor, Archytas, Philolaus, and many others [cf. **ARCHY. P14**].

Philolaus' Book as Plato's Source? (P8)

P8 (< A1) Diogenes Laertius

Hermippus says concerning this [i.e. Philolaus' book, cf. **D1**] that a certain author reports that when Plato the philosopher came to Sicily to Dionysius, he bought it from Philolaus' relatives for forty Alexandrian silver minas and from it transcribed his *Timaeus*. Others say that Plato received it for having asked Dionysius that a young man, who was one of Philolaus' disciples, be released from prison [cf. **PYTHS. R50**].

PHILOLAUS [44 DK]

D

Philolaus' Book (D1)

D1 (< A1) Diog. Laert. 8.85

a

τοῦτόν φησι Δημήτριος ἐν Ὁμωνύμοις [Frag. 26 Mejer] πρῶτον ἐκδοῦναι τῶν Πυθαγορικῶν[1] περὶ[2] φύσεως, ὧν ἀρχὴ ἥδε· [. . . = **D2**].

[1] post Πυθαγορικῶν ‹τὰ› Reiske, ‹βιβλία καὶ ἐπιγράψαι› Diels   [2] περὶ F: om. BP

b

γέγραφε δὲ βιβλίον ἕν [. . . = **P8**].

The Principles (D2–D5)

D2 (B1) Diog. Laert. 8.85

ἁ[1] φύσις δ' ἐν τῷ κόσμῳ ἁρμόχθη ἐξ ἀπείρων τε καὶ περαινόντων καὶ ὅλος ‹ὁ›[2] κόσμος καὶ τὰ ἐν αὐτῷ πάντα.

PHILOLAUS

D

Philolaus' Book (D1)

D1 (< A1) Diogenes Laertius

a

Demetrius in his *Homonyms* says that he [i.e. Philolaus] was the first of the Pythagoreans to publish on nature [or: an *On Nature*]; this is its beginning: [... = **D2**].

b

He wrote [scil. only] one book [...].

The Principles (D2–D5)

D2 (B1) Diogenes Laertius [The beginning of his book, cf. **D1a**]

Nature in the world was fitted together [*harmozein*] out of unlimited things and limiting ones, both the whole world and everything in it.

---

¹ ἁ Diels: α' BP¹: del P⁴: om. F   ² ⟨ὁ⟩ Cobet

D3 (B2) Stob. 1.21.7a [ἐκ τοῦ Φιλολάου Περὶ κόσμου]

ἀνάγκα τὰ ἐόντα εἶμεν πάντα ἢ περαίνοντα ἢ ἄπειρα ἢ περαίνοντά τε καὶ ἄπειρα, ἄπειρα δὲ μόνον[1] οὔ κα εἴη.[2] ἐπεὶ τοίνυν φαίνεται οὔτ᾽ ἐκ περαινόντων πάντων ἐόντα οὔτ᾽ ἐξ ἀπείρων πάντων, δῆλον τἆρα ὅτι ἐκ περαινόντων τε καὶ ἀπείρων ὅ τε κόσμος καὶ τὰ ἐν αὐτῷ συναρμόχθη. δηλοῖ δὲ καὶ τὰ ἐν τοῖς ἔργοις. τὰ μὲν γὰρ αὐτῶν ἐκ περαινόντων περαίνοντι,[3] τὰ δ᾽ ἐκ περαινόντων τε καὶ ἀπείρων περαίνοντί[4] τε καὶ οὐ περαίνοντι,[5] τὰ δ᾽ ἐξ ἀπείρων ἄπειρα φανέονται.[6]

[1] post μόνον lac. pos. edd., Diels ⟨ἢ περαίνοντα μόνον⟩   [2] οὐκ ἀεὶ mss., corr. Badham   [3] περαίνοντι mss.: περαίνοντα Canter   [4] περαίνοντί FP[1:] περαίνοντά P[2]   [5] περαίνοντι mss.: περαίνοντα Canter   [6] φανέονται Heeren: φαινέονται mss.: φαίνεται Usener

D4 (B3) Iambl. *In Nic.*, p. 7.24–25

ἀρχὰν γὰρ οὐδὲ τὸ γνωσούμενον ἐσσεῖται πάντων ἀπείρων ἐόντων.

D5 (< B6) Stob. 1.21.7d

περὶ δὲ φύσιος καὶ ἁρμονίας ὧδε ἔχει· ἁ μὲν ἐστὼ τῶν πραγμάτων ἀίδιος ἔσσα καὶ αὐτὰ μὰν[1] ἁ φύσις θείαν τε καὶ οὐκ ἀνθρωπίνην ἐνδέχεται γνῶσιν, πλάν[2] γα ἢ ὅτι οὐχ οἷον τ᾽ ἦν οὐθενὶ τῶν ἐόντων καὶ

PHILOLAUS

D3 (B2) Stobaeus, *Anthology* [From Philolaus, *On the World*]

It is necessary that the things that are be all either limiting, or unlimited, or limiting and unlimited: but only unlimited they could not be. Since therefore they manifestly did not come either from all the limiting things nor from all the unlimited ones, it is clear then that the world and the things in it were fitted together (*sunharmozein*) **out of both limiting things and unlimited ones. The effects make this clear too. For those things that come from limiting things limit, those that come from both limiting things and unlimited ones limit and do not limit, those that come from unlimited ones will show themselves to be unlimited.**

D4 (B3) Iamblichus, *Commentary on Nicomachus'* Introduction to Arithmetic

There will not be anything at all that is known if all things are unlimited.

D5 (< B6) Stobaeus, *Anthology*

With regard to nature and harmony (*harmonia*), **this is how things are: the being of things, which is eternal, and nature itself admit knowledge that is divine and not human, except that it would have been impossible for any of the things that exist and are**

---

varia orthographica corr. edd.   [1] μὲν ms., corr. Usener
[2] πλέον ms., corr. Badham

γιγνωσκομένων[3] ὑφ' ἁμῶν γενέσθαι,[4] μὴ ὑπαρχούσας τᾶς ἐστοῦς[5] τῶν πραγμάτων ἐξ ὧν συνέστα ὁ κόσμος καὶ τῶν περαινόντων καὶ τῶν ἀπείρων. ἐπεὶ δὲ ταὶ[6] ἀρχαὶ ὑπᾶρχον οὐχ ὁμοῖαι οὐδ' ὁμόφυλοι ἔσσαι, ἤδη ἀδύνατον ἦς κα[7] αὐταῖς[8] κοσμηθῆναι, εἰ μὴ ἁρμονία ἐπεγένετο ᾡτινιῶν ἂν τρόπῳ[9] ἐγένετο. τὰ μὲν ὦν ὁμοῖα καὶ ὁμόφυλα ἁρμονίας οὐδὲν ἐπεδέοντο, τὰ δὲ ἀνόμοια μηδὲ ὁμόφυλα μηδὲ †ἰσοταχῆ†[10] ἀνάγκα τᾷ τοιαύτᾳ[11] ἁρμονίᾳ[12] συγκεκλεῖσθαι, εἰ[13] μέλλοντι ἐν κόσμῳ κατέχεσθαι.

[3] γιγνωσκόμενον Usener [4] γενέσθαι E, Usener: γεγνέσθαι F.: γεγενῆσθαι Burkert [5] τὰς ἐντοὺς ms., corr. Badham [6] τε ms., corr. Badham [7] καὶ ms., corr. Badham [8] αὑτοῖς ms., corr. Boeckh [9] τρόπων ms.: corr. Meineke [10] ἰσολαχῆ (vel ἰσοπαλῆ) Meineke: ἰσοτελῆ Heeren [11] τὰ τοιαῦτα ms., corr. Badham [12] ἁρμονίαις ms., corr. Boeckh [13] ante εἰ hab. ms. ἢ, del. Huffman

Number and the Mathematical Sciences (D6–D12)
Number in General (D6–D9)

D6 (A7a) Plut. *Quaest. conv.* 8.2.1 718E

[. . .] μάλιστα δὲ γεωμετρία κατὰ τὸν Φιλόλαον[1] ἀρχὴ καὶ μητρόπολις οὖσα τῶν ἄλλων [scil. μαθημάτων] [. . .].

[1] φίλαον ms., corr. Hubert

PHILOLAUS

known by us to come to be if the being of the things out of which the world is constituted, both the limiting ones and the unlimited ones, did not exist. But since the principles existed, not being similar nor related as kindred, it would have been impossible for them to be arranged in a world if a harmony (*harmonia*) **had not supervened, in whatever way this came about. Therefore the things that are similar and related as kindred had no need at all of harmony, but as for the ones that are dissimilar and neither related as kindred nor** †as equally fast†**, it is necessary that these things be connected by this kind of harmony** (*harmonia*) **if they are going to maintain themselves in the world.**[1]

---

[1] Stobaeus' text continues with a passage that is also preserved by Nicomachus and that must be considered as independent (cf. **D14**), although the two texts are edited continuously as B6 DK.

Number and the Mathematical Sciences (D6–D12)
Number in General (D6–D9)

D6 (A7a) Plutarch, *Table Talk*

[...] geometry, which is, according to Philolaus, **the principle and mother city** of the other [scil. mathematical sciences] [...].

159

D7 (B4) Stob. 1.21.7b

καὶ πάντα γα μὰν τὰ γιγνωσκόμενα ἀριθμὸν ἔχοντι. οὐ γὰρ ὁτιῶν ‹οἷόν›[1] τε οὐδὲν οὔτε νοηθῆμεν οὔτε γνωσθῆμεν ἄνευ τούτου.

[1] ‹οἷόν› Boeckh

D8 (A29) Sext. Emp. *Adv. Math.* 7.92

οἱ δὲ Πυθαγορικοὶ τὸν λόγον μέν φασιν, οὐ κοινῶς δέ, τὸν δὲ ἀπὸ τῶν μαθημάτων περιγινόμενον, καθάπερ καὶ ὁ Φιλόλαος, θεωρητικόν τε ὄντα τῆς τῶν ὅλων φύσεως ἔχειν τινὰ συγγένειαν πρὸς ταύτην, ἐπείπερ ὑπὸ τοῦ ὁμοίου τὸ ὅμοιον καταλαμβάνεσθαι πέφυκεν [. . .].

D9 (B5) Stob. 1.21.7c

ὅ γα μὰν ἀριθμὸς ἔχει δύο μὲν ἴδια εἴδη, περισσὸν καὶ ἄρτιον, τρίτον δὲ ἀπ' ἀμφοτέρων μιχθέντων, ἀρτιοπέριττον. ἑκατέρω δὲ τῶ εἴδεος πολλαὶ μορφαί, ἃς ἕκαστον αὐτὸ[1] σημαίνει.[2]

[1] αὐτὸ Huffman: αὐτ' αὐτὸ ms. [2] δημαίνει ms., corr. Heeren

PHILOLAUS

D7 (B4) Stobaeus, *Anthology*

And certainly everything that is known possesses number. For it is not possible either to think or to know anything without this.

D8 (A29) Sextus Empiricus, *Against the Logicians*

The Pythagoreans say that it is reason [scil. that is the criterion], but not in general, but rather the one that comes from the mathematical sciences, as Philolaus too said; and since it studies the nature of the whole, it possesses a certain affinity with this latter, since by nature the similar is known by the similar [. . . = citation of **EMP. D207**].

D9 (B5) Stobaeus, *Anthology*

Number certainly possesses two proper species, odd and even, and a third species that comes from the mixture of both of these, even-odd. There are many forms of each of the two species, which each thing itself indicates.

Noteworthy Numbers (D10–D12)
The Monad (D10)

D10 (A10) Theon Sm. *Exp.*, p. 20.19–20

Ἀρχύτας δὲ καὶ Φιλόλαος ἀδιαφόρως τὸ ἓν καὶ μονάδα καλοῦσι καὶ τὴν μονάδα ἕν [= **ARCHY. D6**].

The Hebdomad (D11)

D11 (< B20) Io. Lyd. *Mens.* 2.12 (33.8–16 Wünsch)

οἵ γε μὴν Πυθαγόρειοι τῷ ἡγεμόνι τοῦ παντὸς τὴν ἑβδόμην ἀνατίθενται, τουτέστι τῷ ἑνί [. . .]. ὀρθῶς οὖν ἀμήτορα τὸν ἑπτὰ ἀριθμὸν ὁ Φιλόλαος προσηγόρευσε· μόνος γὰρ οὔτε γεννᾶν οὔτε γεννᾶσθαι πέφυκε. τὸ δὲ μήτε γεννῶν μήτε γεννώμενον ἀκίνητον.

The Decad (?) (D12)

D12 (ad B11) Theon Sm. *Exp.*, p. 106.10–11

[. . .] περὶ ἧς καὶ Ἀρχύτας ἐν τῷ Περὶ τῆς δεκάδος καὶ Φιλόλαος ἐν τῷ Περὶ φύσιος πολλὰ διεξίασιν.

Means (D13)

D13 (A24) Nicom. Geras. *Intr. arith.* 2.26.2 (135.10–17 Hoche)

τινὲς δὲ αὐτὴν ἁρμονικὴν καλεῖσθαι νομίζουσιν ἀκο-

PHILOLAUS

Noteworthy Numbers (D10–D12)
The Monad (D10)

D10 (A10) Theon of Smyrna, *Aspects of Mathematics Useful for Reading Plato*

But Archytas and Philolaus [scil. unlike other authors] call without distinction the one monad too and the monad one.

The Hebdomad (D11)

D11 (< B20) John Lydus, *On the Months*

The Pythagoreans dedicate the seventh day to the leader of the whole, that is, to the One [...]. So it was correct for Philolaus to call the number seven **'motherless.'** For this alone has the nature of not generating and of not being generated. But what does not generate and is not generated is immobile.

The Decad (?) (D12)

D12 (ad B11) Theon of Smyrna, *Aspects of Mathematics Useful for Reading Plato*

[...] both Archytas in his *On the Decad* and Philolaus in his *On Nature* have explained many things about it [scil. the decad].

Means (D13)

D13 (A24) Nicomachus, *Introduction to Arithmetic*

Some people think that it [i.e. the 'subcontrary' mean]

λούθως Φιλολάῳ ἀπὸ τοῦ παρέπεσθαι πάσῃ γεωμετρικῇ ἁρμονίᾳ, γεωμετρικὴν δὲ ἁρμονίαν φασὶ τὸν κύβον ἀπὸ τοῦ κατὰ τὰ τρία διαστήματα ἡρμόσθαι ἰσάκις ἴσα ἰσάκις· ἐν γὰρ παντὶ κύβῳ ἥδε ἡ μεσότης ἐνοπτρίζεται, πλευραὶ μὲν γὰρ παντὸς κύβου εἰσὶν ιβ΄, γωνίαι δὲ η΄, ἐπίπεδα δὲ ϛ΄· μεσότης ἄρα ὁ η΄ τῶν ϛ΄ καὶ τῶν ιβ΄ κατὰ τὴν ἁρμονικήν.

Musical Harmony (D14)

D14 (< B6) Nicom. *Harm.* 9 (p. 252.4–5, 13–14, 17–253.3 Jan)

ὅτι δὲ τοῖς ὑφ' ἡμῶν δηλωθεῖσιν ἀκόλουθα καὶ οἱ παλαιότατοι ἀπεφαίνοντο [. . .] δῆλον ποιεῖ Φιλόλαος ὁ Πυθαγόρου διάδοχος οὕτω πως ἐν τῷ πρώτῳ Φυσικῷ λέγων [. . .]. ἔχει δὲ οὕτως ἡ τοῦ Φιλολάου λέξις. "ἁρμονίας δὲ μέγεθος συλλαβὰ καὶ δι' ὀξειᾶν. τὸ δὲ δι' ὀξειᾶν μεῖζον τᾶς συλλαβᾶς ἐπογδόῳ. ἔστι γὰρ ἀπὸ ὑπάτας εἰς μέσαν συλλαβά, ἀπὸ δὲ μέσας πότι νεάταν δι' ὀξειᾶν, ἀπὸ δὲ νεάτας ἐς τρίταν συλλαβά, ἀπὸ δὲ τρίτας ἐς ὑπάταν δι' ὀξειᾶν. τὸ δ' ἐν μέσῳ τρίτας καὶ μέσας ἐπόγδοον, ἁ δὲ συλλαβὰ ἐπίτριτον, τὸ δὲ δι' ὀξειᾶν ἡμιόλιον, τὸ διὰ πασᾶν δὲ διπλόον. οὕτως ἁρμονία πέντε ἐπόγδοα καὶ δύο

PHILOLAUS

should be called 'harmonic,' following Philolaus, because it follows every geometrical harmony, and they call the cube a 'geometrical harmony' because it has been harmonized in the three dimensions, equal multiplied by equal multiplied by equal; for one sees this mean in every cube: in fact the sides are 12, the angles 8, and the surfaces 6. So 8 is the mean of 6 and 12 by virtue of the harmonic proportion.

See also **HIPPAS. D6; ARCHY. D8**

Musical Harmony (D14)

D14 (< B6) Nicomachus, *Harmonics*

The fact that the statements of the most ancient authors agree with what we have shown [. . .], is shown clearly by what Philolaus, the successor of Pythagoras, says in the first book of his *On Nature* [. . .]. This is what Philolaus says, quoted exactly: **The magnitude of harmony is the fourth** (*syllaba*) **and the fifth** (*di' oxeian*); **the fifth is greater than the fourth by a tone** [literally: by 9/8]. **For from the lowest string** (*hypatê*) **to the middle string** (*mesê*) **there is a fourth, from the middle string to the highest string** (*neatê*) **a fifth, from the highest string to the third string a fourth, and from the third string to the lowest string a fifth. What is in the middle between the highest string and the third string is a tone** [literally: 9/8], **the fourth is** [scil. the ratio] **4/3, the fifth** [scil. the ratio] **3/2, and the octave** [scil. the ratio] **2/1. And so the harmony is composed of five tones** [literally: 9/8] **and two semitones, the fifth**

διέσιες,[1] δι' ὀξειᾶν τρία ἐπόγδοα καὶ δίεσις, συλλαβὰ δὲ δύ' ἐπόγδοα καὶ δίεσις."

[1] ἐπόγδοα καὶ δύο διέσιες Nicom. p. 264.3–4: ἐπογδόων καὶ δυοῖν διέσεοιν Nicom. p. 253

Generation and Destruction of the Cosmos (D15–D18)

D15 (B7) Stob. 1.21.8

τὸ πρᾶτον ἁρμοσθέν, τὸ ἓν ἐν τῷ μέσῳ τᾶς σφαίρας, ἑστία καλεῖται.

D16 (< A9) Procl. *In Tim.* 1 ad 24e (vol. 1, p. 176.28–30 Diehl)

[. . .] καὶ εἷς ἀποτελεῖται κόσμος ἐξ ἐναντίων ἡρμοσμένος, ἐκ περαινόντων τε καὶ ἀπείρων ὑφεστηκὼς κατὰ τὸν Φιλόλαον.

D17 (B17) Stob. 1.15.7

[Φιλολάου Βάκχαι.]
ὁ κόσμος εἷς ἐστιν. ἤρξατο δὲ γίγνεσθαι ἄχρι[1] τοῦ μέσου, καὶ ἀπὸ τοῦ μέσου εἰς τὸ[2] ἄνω διὰ τῶν αὐτῶν τοῖς κάτω, ⟨καὶ⟩[3] ἐστὶ τὰ ἄνω τοῦ μέσου ὑπεναντίως κείμενα τοῖς κάτω. τοῖς γὰρ κάτω τὸ κατωτάτω

[1] ἄχρι mss.: ἀπὸ Meineke   [2] εἰς τὸ mss.: τὰ Boeckh
[3] ⟨καὶ⟩ Wachsmuth

PHILOLAUS

of three tones [literally: 9/8] **and one semitone, the fourth of two tones** [literally: 9/8] **and one semitone.**[1]

[1] The position assigned to the third cord in this fragment is anomalous (see Huffman, pp. 154–55).

Generation and Destruction of the Cosmos (D15–D18)

D15 (B7) Stobaeus, *Anthology*

The first thing fitted together (*harmozein*), **the one in the middle of the sphere, is called 'hearth'** (*hestia*).

D16 (< A9) Proclus, *Commentary on Plato's* Timaeus

[. . .] and according to Philolaus, the world, one only, is produced by being fitted together (*harmozein*) out of contraries, being constituted out of limiting things and unlimited ones.

D17 (B17) Stobaeus, *Anthology*

[The *Bacchants* of Philolaus:][1]
The world is one. It began to come to be just at (?) **the middle and from the middle upward in the same way as downward,** ⟨and⟩ **the things above the middle are arranged in a contrary way to those below it. For**

[1] The authenticity of this fragment has been contested, particularly because of what is thought to be a parallel passage in Plato's *Timaeus* (62c3), but it is defended by Huffman (pp. 215–19), who nonetheless acknowledges that the title of the work from which it is thought to derive is doubtless a forgery (p. 418).

μέγα⁴ ἐστὶν ὥσπερ τὸ ἀνωτάτω, καὶ τὰ ἄλλα ὡσαύτως. πρὸς γὰρ τὸ μέσον κατὰ ταὐτά ἐστιν ἑκάτερα, ὅσα μὴ μετενήνεκται.

⁴ μέγα mss.: μέρος Wachsmuth: τοῖς γὰρ κατωτάτω τὰ μέσα ἐστὶν Diels, alii alia

D18 (A18) Aët. 2.5.3 (Ps.-Plut., Stob.) [πόθεν τρέφεται ὁ κόσμος]

Φιλόλαος διττὴν εἶναι τὴν φθοράν, τὸ μὲν ἐξ οὐρανοῦ πυρὸς ῥυέντος, τὸ δ᾽¹ ἐξ ὕδατος σεληνιακοῦ περιστροφῇ τοῦ ἀέρος ἀποχυθέντος· καὶ τούτων εἶναι τὰς ἀναθυμιάσεις τροφὰς τοῦ κόσμου.

¹ τὸ μὲν . . . τὸ δ᾽ . . . Stob. 1.21.6d: τότε μὲν . . . τότε δ᾽ Plut., Stob. 1.20.1g

Cosmology (D19–D24)
The Order of the World (D19)

D19 (< A16) Aët. 2.7.7 (Stob.) [περὶ τάξεως τοῦ κόσμου]

Φιλόλαος πῦρ ἐν μέσῳ περὶ τὸ κέντρον, ὅπερ ἑστίαν τοῦ παντὸς καλεῖ καὶ Διὸς οἶκον [. . .]· καὶ πάλιν πῦρ ἕτερον ἀνωτάτω, τὸ περιέχον. πρῶτον δ᾽ εἶναι φύσει τὸ μέσον, περὶ δὲ τοῦτο δέκα σώματα θεῖα χορεύειν,

PHILOLAUS

below, the lowest part is large like [i.e. as large as?] **the highest one, and similarly for the other things. For with regard to the middle, both of them are identical, except that they are inverted.**

D18 (A18) Aëtius

Philolaus: there is a double destruction [scil. of the world], on the one hand coming from the heavens, when fire flows down, on the other coming from the lunar water, when air spreads out because of the rotation. And the exhalations of these are what the world is nourished with.[1]

[1] This testimonium, which is not free of obscurities (e.g. regarding the 'lunar water'), is sometimes considered suspect because the doctrine of a double destruction appears in Plato (cf. *Timaeus* 22a–d) and the theory of the two evaporations in Aristotle. It is defended by Huffman (pp. 215–19).

Cosmology (D19–D24)
The Order of the World (D19)

D19 (< A16) Aëtius

Philolaus: fire in the middle around the center, which he calls the **'hearth'** of the whole and **'Zeus' house'** [. . .]; and again there is another fire very high up, what surrounds [scil. the whole]. The first thing by nature is the middle, and around this ten divine bodies move as a cho-

οὐρανόν, τοὺς ἑ[1] πλανήτας, μεθ' οὓς ἥλιον, ὑφ' ᾧ σελήνην, ὑφ' ᾗ τὴν γῆν, ὑφ' ᾗ τὴν ἀντίχθονα, μεθ' ἃ σύμπαντα τὸ πῦρ, ἑστίας περὶ[2] τὰ κέντρα τάξιν ἐπέχον [. . .].

[1] τοὺς ἑ' Diels: τε F, om. P: ‹πέν›τε Mansfeld et Runia 2.7.6
[2] περὶ Meineke: ἐπὶ mss

The Earth (D20–D21)

D20 (A17) Aët. 3.11.3 (Ps.-Plut.) [περὶ θέσεως γῆς]

Φιλόλαος ὁ Πυθαγόρειος τὸ μὲν πῦρ μέσον, τοῦτο γὰρ εἶναι τοῦ παντὸς ἑστίαν· δευτέραν δὲ τὴν ἀντίχθονα, τρίτην δ' ἣν οἰκοῦμεν γῆν ἐξ ἐναντίας κειμένην τε καὶ περιφερομένην τῇ ἀντίχθονι· παρ' ὃ καὶ μὴ ὁρᾶσθαι ὑπὸ τῶν ἐν τῇδε τοὺς ἐν ἐκείνῃ.

D21 (A21) Aët. 3.13.2 (Ps.-Plut.) [περὶ κινήσεως γῆς]

Φιλόλαος δ' ὁ Πυθαγόρειος κύκλῳ περιφέρεσθαι περὶ τὸ πῦρ κατὰ κύκλον λοξόν[1] ὁμοιοτρόπως ἡλίῳ καὶ σελήνῃ.

[1] κύκλου λοξοῦ mss., corr. Reiske

PHILOLAUS

rus: the heavens, the five planets, after these the sun, under this the moon, under this the earth, under this the counter-earth, and after all of these the fire that occupies the position of the hearth around the center [. . .].[1]

[1] Together with Huffman (p. 237 and pp. 395–400), we omit those portions of this text that derive most probably from pseudo-Pythagorean insertions.

The Earth (D20–D21)

D20 (A17) Aëtius

Philolaus the Pythagorean: fire is in the middle (for this is the **hearth** of the whole), in second place the counter-earth, in third the earth we inhabit, which lies and revolves opposite to the counter-earth; and for this reason the people in that one are not seen by the ones in this one.

D21 (A21) Aëtius

Philolaus the Pythagorean: it [i.e. the earth] revolves in a circle around the fire following the ecliptic in the same way as the sun and moon.

EARLY GREEK PHILOSOPHY IV

The Sun and Moon (D22–D23)

D22 (< A19) Aët. 2.20.12 (Ps.-Plut.; cf. Stob.) [περὶ οὐσίας ἡλίου]

Φιλόλαος ὁ Πυθαγόρειος ὑαλοειδῆ, δεχόμενον μὲν τοῦ ἐν τῷ κόσμῳ πυρὸς τὴν ἀνταύγειαν, διηθοῦντα δὲ πρὸς ἡμᾶς τό τε φῶς καὶ τὴν ἀλέαν[1] [. . .].

[1] τό τε φῶς καὶ τὴν ἀλέαν Stob.: τό φῶς Plut.

D23 (A20) Aët. 2.30.1 (Stob.) [περὶ ἐμφάσεως αὐτῆς [scil. τῆς σελήνης] καὶ διὰ τί γεώδης φαίνεται]

τῶν Πυθαγορείων τινὲς μέν, ὧν ἐστι Φιλόλαος, τὸ γεωφανὲς αὐτῆς εἶναι διὰ τὸ περιοικεῖσθαι τὴν σελήνην, καθάπερ τὴν παρ' ἡμῖν γῆν, ζῴοις καὶ φυτοῖς μείζοσι καὶ καλλίοσιν. εἶναι γὰρ πεντεκαιδεκαπλάσια τὰ ἐπ' αὐτῆς ζῷα τῇ δυνάμει, μηδὲν περιττωματικὸν ἀποκρίνοντα, καὶ τὴν ἡμέραν τοσαύτην τῷ μήκει.

The Great Year (D24)

D24 (A22) Cens. *Die nat.* 18.8, 19.2

est et Philolai Pythagorici annus ex annis quinquaginta novem, in quo sunt menses intercalares viginti et unus [. . .]. Philolaus annum naturalem dies habere prodidit CCCLXIIII et dimidiatum.

PHILOLAUS

The Sun and Moon (D22–D23)

D22 (< A19) Aëtius

Philolaus the Pythagorean: the sun is like glass: on the one hand it receives the reflection of the fire that is in the world, on the other hand it filters light and heat toward us [. . .].[1]

[1] The continuation of this notice constitutes an exegesis of Philolaus' theory in terms that recall Empedocles' theory of the two suns (cf. **EMP. D126**).

D23 (A20) Aëtius

Some of the Pythagoreans, including Philolaus: the moon has the appearance of an earth because it is inhabited, just like our earth, by animals and plants that are larger and more beautiful. For the animals that live there are fifteen times greater in strength and do not produce any excrement; and the length of the day is corresponding [i.e. fifteen times longer].

The Great Year (D24)

D24 (A22) Censorinus, *The Birthday*

There is also a year of Philolaus the Pythagorean, consisting of fifty-nine years, which includes twenty-one intercalary months [. . .]. Philolaus declared that the natural year has 364 and a half days.

EARLY GREEK PHILOSOPHY IV

Embryology and Medicine (D25–D26)

D25 Anon. Lond.

a (A27) 18.8–19.1

Φιλόλαος | δὲ ὁ Κροτ[ωνιά]της συνεστάναι φησὶν τὰ ἡμέ|[10]τερα σώμ[ατα ἐκ] θερμοῦ. ἀμέτοχα γὰρ αὐτὰ εἶναι | ψυχροῦ[, ὑπομι]μνήσκων ἀπό τινων τοιούτων· | τὸ σπέρμ[α εἶναι θερ]μόν, κατασκευαστικὸν δὲ | τοῦτο τ[οῦ ζῴο]υ· καὶ ὁ τόπος δέ, εἰς ὃν | ἡ καταβολ[ή— μήτρ]α δὲ αὕτη—ἐστὶν θερμοτέρα | [15] καὶ ἐοικ[υῖα ἐκ]είνῳ· τὸ δὲ ἐοικός τινι ταὐτὸ δύναται ᾧ ἔοικεν· ἐπεὶ δὲ τὸ κατα|σκευάζ[ον ἀμέ]τοχόν ἐστιν ψυχροῦ καὶ ὁ τόπος | δέ, ἐν ᾧ [ἡ καταβολ]ή, ἀμέτοχός ἐστιν ψυχροῦ, | δῆλον [ὅτι καὶ τὸ] κατασκευαζόμενον ζῷον | τοιοῦτο[ν γίνε]ται. εἰς δὲ τούτου τὴν | [20] κατασκ[ευὴν ὑ]πομνήσει προσχρῆται τοιαύ|τῃ· με[τὰ γάρ], φησιν τὴν ἔκτεξιν εὐθέως | τὸ ζῷον ἐπισπᾶται τὸ ἐκτὸς πνεῦμα | ψυχρὸν ὄν· εἶτα πάλιν καθαπερεὶ χρέος | ἐκπέμπε[ι] αὐτό· διὰ τοῦτο δὴ καὶ ὄρεξις | [25] τοῦ ἐκτὸς πνεύματος, ἵνα τῇ | ἐπεισάκτῳ τοῦ πνεύματος ὁλκῇ θερμό|τερα ὑπάρχοντα τὰ ἡμέτερα σώματα πρὸς αὐτοῦ | καταψύχηται. καὶ τὴν μὲν σύστασιν | τῶν ἡμετέρων σωμάτων ἐν τούτοις φησίν. |

[30] λέγει δὲ γίνεσθαι τὰς νόσους διά τε χολὴν | καὶ αἷμα καὶ φλέγμα, ἀρχὴν δὲ γίνεσθαι | τῶν νόσων ταῦτα· ἀποτελεῖσθαι | δέ φησιν τὸ μὲν αἷμα παχὺ μὲν ἔσω παρα|θλιβομένης τῆς σαρκός, λεπτὸν | [35] δὲ

PHILOLAUS

Embryology and Medicine (D25–D26)

D25 Anonymous of London

a (A27)

Philolaus of Croton says that our [10] bodies are composed out of warmth, for they have no share in cold. He suggests this on the basis of the following considerations: that semen is warm, and it is this that produces the living being; and the place into which it is ejaculated (this is the uterus) is quite warm [15] and resembles this, and what resembles something has the same capacity as what it resembles. But since what produces has no share in cold, and since the place in which there is ejaculation has no share in cold, it is clear that the living being that is produced is of the same sort. But [20] to establish this, he also makes use of the following consideration: immediately after birth, the animal breathes in the air outside, which is cold; and then in turn it breathes it out, like a debt. For this reason there is also a desire [25] for the air outside: so that by the inhalation of air our bodies, which are too warm, are cooled down by it. And he says that the composition of our bodies depends upon these processes.

[30] As for illnesses, he says that they come about because of bile, blood, and phlegm, and that the origin of illnesses is the following: he says that the blood becomes thick when the flesh compresses it inward and becomes

γίνεσθαι διαιρουμένων τῶν ἐν τῇ σαρκὶ ἀγγείων· | τὸ
δὲ φλέγμα συνίστασθαι ἀπὸ τῶν ὄμ|βρων φησίν. λέ-
γει δὲ τὴν χολὴν ἰχῶρα | εἶναι τῆς σαρκός. παράδο-
ξόν τε αὐτὸς | ἀνὴρ ἐπὶ τούτου κινεῖ· λέγει γὰρ μηδὲ
τε||[40]τάχθα[ι] ἐ̣πὶ τ̣[ῷ] ἥπατι χολήν, ἰχῶρα μέν|τοι
τῆς σαρκὸς εἶναι τὴν χολήν. τό τ' αὖ | φλέγμα τῶν
πλείστων ψυχρὸν εἶναι λεγόν|των αὐτὸς θερμὸν τῇ
φύσει ὑπ[ο]τίθεται· ἀπὸ γὰρ τοῦ φλέγειν φλέγμα
εἰρῆσθαι. | [45] ταύτῃ δὲ καὶ τὰ φλεγμαῖνον[τα] | μετ-
οχῇ τοῦ φλέγματος φλεγμ[α]ί|νει. καὶ ταῦτα μὲν δὴ
ἀρχὰς τῶν νό[σ]ων | ὑπ[ο]τίθεται, [σ]υνεργὰ δὲ ὑπερ-
βολ[άς] | τε θερμασίας, τροφῆς, καταψύξεω[ς καὶ] |
[19.1] ἐνδείας τῶν τούτ[ο]ι̣ς [παραπλησίων].

plurima rest. et corr. Diels   18.48–19.1 ὑπερβολ[ας] τε
⟨καὶ ἐνδείας⟩ θερμασίας . . . {ἐνδείας} τ(ῶν) . . . coni. Manetti
19.1 ἐνδείας ⟨τούτων ἢ⟩ H. Fränkel apud Diels

b (A28) 20.21–23

καὶ σχεδὸν [οὕτω]ς | ὁ Φιλόλαος οἴεται μὴ εἶναι ἐν
ἡμῖν χο̣λὴ̣[ν] | ο̣ἰκείαν.

23 οἰκείαν legit Manetti: ἢ] | ἀ̣[χρ]είαν Diels

D26 (B13) Ps.-Iambl. *Theol.*, pp. 25.17–26.3

καὶ τέσσαρες ἀρχαὶ τοῦ ζῴου τοῦ λογικοῦ, ὥσπερ καὶ
Φιλόλαος ἐν τῷ Περὶ φύσεως λέγει, ἐγκέφαλος καρδία ὀμφαλὸς αἰδοῖον· **κεφαλὰ μὲν νόου, καρδία δὲ
ψυχᾶς καὶ αἰσθήσιος, ὀμφαλὸς δὲ ῥιζώσιος καὶ**

thin [35] when the vessels in the flesh are divided. He says that the phlegm is composed out of fluids (?).[1] He says that bile is a liquid that comes from the flesh. The same man says something paradoxical on this matter: for he says that bile is not [40] located in the liver, and yet that bile is a liquid that comes from the flesh. And again, while most people say that phlegm is cold, he himself posits that it is warm by nature. For the term 'phlegma' derives from *phlegein* [i.e., to burn]. [45] And inflammations (*ta phlegmainonta*) are inflamed (*phlegmainei*) because they have a share in phlegm. And this is what he indicates as the origin of illnesses, to which excesses of warmth, of nourishment, and of cold contribute, as well as [19.1] deficiencies of things similar to them.

[1] Diels understands the term to designate urine.

b (A28)

And in almost the same way [scil. as the medical writer Petronius of Aegina], Philolaus thinks that the bile in us is not inherent.

D26 (B13) Ps.-Iamblichus, *Theology of Arithmetic*

There are four principles of the animal endowed with reason, as Philolaus too says in his *On Nature,* the brain, the heart, the navel, the genitals: **the head** [scil. is the principle] **of intelligence, the heart of the soul and sensation, the navel of rootedness and first growth, the**

ἀναφύσιος τοῦ πρώτου, αἰδοῖον δὲ σπέρματος καταβολᾶς τε καὶ γεννήσιος. ἐγκέφαλος δὲ <ἔχει>[1] τὰν ἀνθρώπων ἀρχάν, καρδία δὲ τὰν ζῴων, ὀμφαλὸς δὲ τὰν φυτοῦ, αἰδοῖον δὲ τὰν ξυναπάντων· πάντα γὰρ ἀπὸ σπέρματος καὶ θάλλοντι καὶ βλαστάνοντι.

[1] <ἔχει> Huffman: <σαμαίνει> Boeckh

Soul and Thought (D27–D28)

D27 (A23) Macr. *In Somn.* 1.14.19

Pythagoras et Philolaus harmoniam [scil. animam esse dixerunt] [. . .].

D28 (B16) Arist. *EE* 2.8 1225a30–33

ὥστε καὶ διάνοιαί τινες καὶ πάθη οὐκ ἐφ' ἡμῖν εἰσιν, ἢ πράξεις αἱ κατὰ τὰς τοιαύτας διανοίας καὶ λογισμούς, ἀλλ' ὥσπερ Φιλόλαος ἔφη εἶναί τινας λόγους κρείττους ἡμῶν.

Appendix: Some Examples of Suspect Fragments and Reports (D29–D35)

D29 (A11) Luc. *Laps.* 5

εἰσὶ δὲ οἳ καὶ τὴν τετρακτύν, τὸν μέγιστον ὅρκον αὐτῶν, ἢ τὸν ἐντελῆ αὐτοῖς ἀριθμὸν ἀποτελεῖ, ἤδη καὶ[1] ὑγιείας ἀρχὴν ἐκάλεσαν· ὧν καὶ Φιλόλαός ἐστι.

genitals of the ejaculation of semen and of generation. The brain ⟨possesses⟩ **the principle of the human being, the heart that of the animal, the navel that of the plant, the genitals that of all of them. For all things flourish and develop out of seed.**

Soul and Thought (D27–D28)

D27 (A23) Macrobius, *Scipio's Dream*

Pythagoras and Philolaus [scil. said that the soul is] a harmony [. . .].

D28 (B16) Aristotle, *Eudemian Ethics*

So that some thoughts and passions are not in our power, nor the actions that are in conformity with such thoughts and reasonings, but, as Philolaus said, **"some reasons (*logoi*) are stronger than we are."**

Appendix: Some Examples of Suspect Fragments and Reports (D29–D35)[1]

[1] These texts are classified according to the chronological order of the sources.

D29 (A11) Lucian, *A Slip of the Tongue in Greeting*

*Some of them [i.e. of the Pythagoreans] also called the tetraktys—their greatest oath, which produces their perfect number—the **"principle of health"**; among them is Philolaus.*

---

[1] ἀποτελεῖν οἱ δὲ καὶ mss., corr. Marcilius: (ἣν . . .) ἀποτελεῖν οἴ⟨ονται τὸν⟩ δέκα Diels

D30 (B14) Clem. Alex. *Strom.* 3.17.1

ἄξιον δὲ καὶ τῆς Φιλολάου λέξεως μνημονεῦσαι· λέγει γὰρ ὁ Πυθαγόρειος ὧδε· "μαρτυρέονται δὲ καὶ οἱ παλαιοὶ θεολόγοι τε καὶ μάντιες, ὡς διά τινας τιμωρίας ἁ ψυχὰ τῷ σώματι συνέζευκται καὶ καθάπερ ἐν σήματι τούτῳ τέθαπται."

D31 (A14) Plut. *Is. et Os.* 30 363A

φαίνονται δὲ καὶ οἱ Πυθαγορικοὶ τὸν Τυφῶνα δαιμονικὴν ἡγούμενοι δύναμιν· λέγουσι γὰρ ἐν ἀρτίῳ μέτρῳ ἕκτῳ καὶ πεντηκοστῷ[1] γεγονέναι Τυφῶνα· καὶ πάλιν τὴν μὲν τοῦ τριγώνου ⟨γωνίαν⟩[2] Ἅιδου καὶ Διονύσου καὶ Ἄρεος εἶναι· τὴν δὲ τοῦ τετραγώνου Ῥέας καὶ Ἀφροδίτης καὶ Δήμητρος καὶ Ἑστίας καὶ Ἥρας· τὴν δὲ τοῦ δωδεκαγώνου Διός· τὴν δὲ ⟨τοῦ⟩[3] ἑκκαιπεντηκονταγωνίου[4] Τυφῶνος, ὡς Εὔδοξος ἱστόρηκεν [Frag. 293 Lasserre].

[1] ἐν ἀρτίῳ μέτρῳ ἕκτῳ καὶ πεντηκοστῷ] ἐν τετάρτῳ μέτρῳ ⟨τῶν⟩ ἓξ καὶ πεντήκοντα Holwerda   [2] ⟨γωνίαν⟩ Kranz   [3] ⟨τοῦ⟩ Reiske   [4] ὀκτωκαιπεντηκονταγωνίου mss., corr. Xylander

D32 (< A25) Porph. *In Ptol. Harm.* 5

[. . .] τινὲς τῶν μετ' αὐτὸν διάστημα ἐκάλεσαν εἶναι ὑπεροχήν, ὡς Αἰλιανὸς ὁ Πλατωνικός· καὶ Φιλόλαος δ' ἐπὶ πάντων τῶν διαστημάτων ⟨ταύτην εἴληφε τὴν⟩[1] προσηγορίαν [. . .].

PHILOLAUS

D30 (B14) Clement of Alexandria, *Stromata*

It is worth mentioning also what Philolaus said. For the Pythagorean speaks as follows: **"The ancient theologians and the seers too provide testimony that the soul is bound to the body because it suffers certain punishments and is buried in it as in a tomb."**

D31 (A14) Plutarch, *On Isis and Osiris*

The Pythagoreans evidently think that Typhon is a demonic power. For they say that Typhon was born in the even measure fifty-six. And in turn the ⟨angle⟩ of the triangle belongs to Hades, Dionysus, and Ares; that of the square to Rhea, Aphrodite, Demeter, Hestia, and Hera; that of the dodecagon to Zeus; and that of the fifty-six-sided polygon to Typhon, as Eudoxus has reported.

D32 (< A25) Porphyry, *Commentary on Ptolemy's* Harmonics

[. . .] some of those who came after him [i.e. Eratosthenes] gave to the interval the name of 'excess,' like Aelian the Platonist; and Philolaus ⟨applies this⟩ name to all the intervals [. . .].

---

¹ ⟨ταύτην εἴληφε τὴν⟩ Boeckh

D33 (cf. A14) Procl. *In Eucl.*

a p. 130.8–14

καὶ γὰρ παρὰ τοῖς Πυθαγορείοις εὑρήσομεν ἄλλας γωνίας ἄλλοις θεοῖς ἀνακειμένας, ὥσπερ καὶ ὁ Φιλόλαος πεποίηκε τοῖς μὲν τὴν τριγωνικὴν γωνίαν τοῖς δὲ τὴν τετραγωνικὴν ἀφιερώσας, καὶ ἄλλας ἄλλοις καὶ τὴν αὐτὴν πλείοσι θεοῖς καὶ τῷ αὐτῷ πλείους, κατὰ τὰς διαφόρους ἐν αὐτῷ δυνάμεις ἀνείς.

b p. 174.2–16

δεῖ δὲ μὴ λανθάνειν ὅπως τὴν μὲν τριγωνικὴν γωνίαν ὁ Φιλόλαος τέτταρσιν ἀνῆκεν θεοῖς, τὴν δὲ τετραγωνικὴν τρισίν, ἐνδεικνύμενος αὐτῶν τὴν δι' ἀλλήλων χώρησιν καὶ τὴν ἐν πᾶσι πάντων κοινωνίαν τῶν τε περισσῶν ἐν τοῖς ἀρτίοις καὶ τῶν ἀρτίων ἐν τοῖς περισσοῖς. τριὰς οὖν τετραδικὴ καὶ τετρὰς τριαδικὴ[1] τῶν τε γονίμων μετέχουσαι καὶ ποιητικῶν ἀγαθῶν τὴν ὅλην συνέχουσι τῶν γενητῶν διακόσμησιν. ἀφ' ὧν ἡ δυωδεκὰς εἰς μίαν μονάδα τὴν τοῦ Διὸς ἀρχὴν ἀνατείνεται. τὴν γὰρ τοῦ δωδεκαγώνου γωνίαν Διὸς εἶναί φησιν ὁ Φιλόλαος, ὡς κατὰ μίαν ἕνωσιν τοῦ Διὸς ὅλον συνέχοντος τὸν τῆς δυωδεκάδος ἀριθμόν. ἡγεῖται γὰρ καὶ παρὰ τῷ Πλάτωνι δυωδεκάδος ὁ Ζεὺς καὶ ἀπολύτως ἐπιτροπεύει τὸ πᾶν.

[1] καὶ τετρὰς τριαδικὴ om. MB₃G, secl. Heiberg

PHILOLAUS

D33 (cf. A14) Proclus, *Commentary on Euclid's Elements of Geometry*

a

For among the Pythagoreans we shall find that different angles are dedicated to different gods, as Philolaus has done in consecrating the angle of the triangle to some gods, the angle of the square to other ones, and others to other ones, and referring the same angle to a plurality of gods and a plurality of angles to the same god, according to the different powers that are in it.

b

It must be borne in mind that Philolaus dedicated the angle of the triangle to four gods, and the angle of the square to three, demonstrating their progression through one another and the participation of all in all, of the odd in the even as of the even in the odd. So a tetradic triad and a triadic tetrad, which participate in the generative and productive good things, hold together the whole cosmic organization of generated things. The number twelve, which is their product, extends all the way to the one monad, the reign of Zeus. For Philolaus says that the angle of the dodecagon belongs to Zeus, since he thinks that Zeus holds together in a single unity the totality of the number twelve. For in Plato too, Zeus is at the head of the twelve and governs the whole without hindrance [cf. Plato, Phaedrus 246e–247a].

D34 (A14) Dam. *In Parm.* 2.127.7, p. 100.7–21

διὰ τί γὰρ τῷ μὲν τὸν κύκλον ἀνιέρουν οἱ Πυθαγόρειοι, τῷ δὲ τρίγωνον, τῷ δὲ τετράγωνον, τῷ δὲ ἄλλο καὶ ἄλλο τῶν εὐθυγράμμων σχημάτων,[1] ὡς δὲ καὶ μικτῶν, ὡς τὰ ἡμικύκλια τοῖς Διοσκούροις; πολλάκις δὲ τῷ αὐτῷ ἄλλο καὶ ἄλλο ἀπονέμων κατ' ἄλλην ἰδιότητα καὶ ἄλλην, ὁ Φιλόλαος ἐν τούτοις σοφός. καὶ μήποτε, ὡς καθόλου εἰπεῖν, τὸ μὲν περιφερὲς κοινὸν σχῆμά ἐστιν πάντων τῶν νοερῶν θεῶν ᾗ νοεροί, τὰ δὲ εὐθύγραμμα ἴδια ἑκάστων ἄλλα ἄλλων κατὰ τὰς τῶν ἀριθμῶν, τῶν γωνιῶν καὶ τῶν πλευρῶν ἰδιότητας· οἷον Ἀθηνᾶς μὲν τὸ τρίγωνον, Ἑρμοῦ δὲ τὸ τετράγωνον· ἤδη δέ, φησὶν ὁ Φιλόλαος, καὶ τοῦ τετραγώνου ἥδε μὲν ἡ γωνία τῆς Ῥέας, ἥδε δὲ τῆς Ἥρας, ἄλλη δὲ ἄλλης θεοῦ· καὶ ὅλως[2] ἐστὶν θεολογικὸς ὁ[3] περὶ τῶν σχημάτων ἀφορισμός.

[1] τῶν ante σχημάτων secl. Diels   [2] ὅλος ms., corr. Schöne   [3] ὁ θεολογικὸς ms., corr. Schöne

D35 (< A26) Boeth. *Mus.* 3.5

Philolaus vero Pythagoricus alio modo tonum dividere temptavit, statuens scilicet primordium toni ab eo numero, qui primus cybum a primo inpari, quod maxime apud Pythagoricos honorabile fuit, efficeret [. . .].

PHILOLAUS

D34 (A14) Damascius, *Commentary on Plato's* Parmenides

For why did the Pythagoreans dedicate the circle to this one [scil. god], the triangle to that one, the square to that one, one or another rectilinear figure to that one, and likewise the mixed figures, like the semicircle to the Dioscuri? Inasmuch as he often attributes to the same one one figure or another, as a function of one individual property or another, Philolaus is wise in these matters. And perhaps, to put it more generally, the circle is the figure that is in common to all the intellectual gods insofar as they are intellectual, and the rectilinear figures are peculiar to each one, each one for another, as a function of the individual properties of the numbers, angles, and sides: for example, the triangle belongs to Athena, the square to Hermes; but, says Philolaus, this angle of the square belongs to Rhea, that one to Hera, another one to another god; and in general the determination regarding the figures is theological.

D35 (< A26) Boethius, *Fundamentals of Music*

But Philolaus the Pythagorean tried to divide the tone in a different way, positing as principle of the tone the number that produces the first cube of the first odd number [i.e. $27 = 3^3$], which was especially honored by the Pythagoreans [. . .].

13. EURYTUS [EUR.]

A disciple of Philolaus, whom Plato is said to have visited at the same time as he visited Archytas, Eurytus is known essentially from Aristotle's and Theophrastus' descriptions of a procedure of his that was intended to attribute a number to an object—a procedure that provokes a certain perplexity and surely underlines the very real difficulty of assigning a precise meaning to one of the fundamental tenets of early Pythagoreanism.

BIBLIOGRAPHY

See the titles listed in the General Introduction to Chapters 10–18.

OUTLINE OF THE CHAPTER

P

Origin (P1–P4)
    From Metapontum or from Tarentum . . . (P1–P3)
    . . . or from Croton (P4)
Chronology (P5)
His Teacher (P6)
Plato and Eurytus (P7)
An Anecdote (P8)

D

Eurytus' Procedure (D1–D2)

EURYTUS [45 DK]

P

Origin (P1–P4)
From Metapontum or Tarentum . . . (P1–P3)

P1 (< 58A.) Iambl. *VP* 267

a

Μεταποντῖνοι [. . .] Εὔρυτος [. . .] [cf. **PYTH. b T30[2]**].

b

Ταραντῖνοι [. . .] Εὔρυτος [. . .] [cf. **PYTH. b T30[5]**].

P2 (cf. 45.1) Iambl. *VP* 266

ζηλωτὰς δὲ γράφειν γενέσθαι τῶν ἀνδρῶν [. . .] ⟨ἐν⟩[1] Μεταποντίῳ δὲ [. . .] Εὔρυτον [. . .].

[1] ⟨ἐν⟩ Arcerius

EURYTUS

P

Origin (P1–P4)
From Metapontum or from Tarentum . . . (P1–P3)

P1 (< 58A.) Iamblichus, *Life of Pythagoras*

a

From Metapontum: [. . .] Eurytus [. . .].

b

From Tarentum: [. . .] Eurytus [. . .].

P2 (cf. 45.1) Iamblichus, *Life of Pythagoras*

He [scil. Diodorus of Aspendus] writes that disciples of these men [i.e. the Pythagoreans] were: [. . .] at Metapontum, [. . .] Eurytus.

EARLY GREEK PHILOSOPHY IV

P3 (< 14.10, 44 A4) Diog. Laert. 8.46

[. . . **PYTH. b T29**] ἦσαν δὲ ἀκροαταὶ Φιλολάου καὶ Εὐρύτου τῶν Ταραντίνων.

. . . *or from Croton (P4)*

P4 (< 45.1) Iambl. *VP* 148

[. . .] Εὔρυτος μὲν ὁ Κροτωνιάτης [. . . = **P8**].

Chronology (P5)

P5 (≠ DK) Iambl. *VP* 104

[. . .] οἱ ἐκ τοῦ διδασκαλείου τούτου, μάλιστα δὲ οἱ παλαιότατοι καὶ αὐτῷ συγχρονίσαντες καὶ μαθητεύσαντες τῷ Πυθαγόρᾳ πρεσβύτῃ νέοι, Φιλόλαός τε καὶ Εὔρυτος [. . .].

His Teacher (P6)

P6 (< 45.1) Iambl. *VP* 148

[. . .] Εὔρυτος [. . .] Φιλολάου ἀκουστής [. . . = **P8**].

EURYTUS

P3 (< 14.10, 44 A4) Diogenes Laertius

[...] they [i.e. the last Pythagoreans] had been the pupils of Philolaus and Eurytus, both of Tarentum.

... or from Croton (P4)

P4 (< 45.1) Iamblichus, *Life of Pythagoras*

[...] Eurytus of Croton [...].

Chronology (P5)

P5 (≠ DK) Iamblichus, *Life of Pythagoras*

[...] those who came from this school, and especially the most ancient ones, who lived at the same time as he [i.e. Pythagoras] did and who studied with Pythagoras when he was already old while they were young, Philolaus and Eurytus [...].

His Teacher (P6)

P6 (< 45.1) Iamblichus, *Life of Pythagoras*

[...] Eurytus [...] a pupil of Philolaus [...].

EARLY GREEK PHILOSOPHY IV

Plato and Eurytus (P7)

P7

a (< 44 A5, cf. 45.1) Diog. Laert. 3.6

[. . .] κἀκεῖθεν εἰς Ἰταλίαν πρὸς τοὺς Πυθαγορικοὺς Φιλόλαον καὶ Εὔρυτον.

b (cf. 45.1) Apul. *Plat.* 3

et ad Italiam iterum venit et Pythagoreos Eurytum Tarentinum et seniorem Archytam sectatus.

An Anecdote (P8)

P8 (45.1) Iambl. *VP* 148

[. . .] Εὔρυτος μὲν ὁ Κροτωνιάτης, Φιλολάου ἀκουστής, ποιμένος τινὸς ἀπαγγείλαντος αὐτῷ ὅτι μεσημβρίας ἀκούσειε Φιλολάου φωνῆς ἐκ τοῦ τάφου καὶ ταῦτα πρὸ πολλῶν ἐτῶν τεθνηκότος ὡσανεὶ ᾄδοντος, "καὶ τίνα πρὸς θεῶν" εἶπεν "ἁρμονίαν;"

EURYTUS

Plato and Eurytus (P7)

P7

a (< 44 A5, cf. 45.1) Diogenes Laertius

[. . .] and from there [scil. the home of Theodorus the mathematician, at Cyrene, Plato left] for Italy to meet Philolaus and Eurytus.

b (cf. 45.1) Apuleius, *Plato*

He [i.e. Plato] traveled to Italy again and sought out the Pythagoreans Eurytus of Tarentum and the aged Archytas.

An Anecdote (P8)

P8 (45.1) Iamblichus, *Life of Pythagoras*

[. . .] A shepherd announced to Eurytus of Croton, a pupil of Philolaus, that at noon he had heard Philolaus' voice rising up from his tomb—and this despite the fact that he had been dead for many years—as though he were singing; and he asked, "And in which harmony, by the gods?"

EURYTUS [45 DK]

D

Eurytus' Procedure (D1–D2)

D1 (< 45.3) Arist. *Metaph.* N5 1092b8–13

[. . .] ὡς Εὔρυτος ἔταττε τίς ἀριθμὸς τίνος, οἷον ὁδὶ μὲν ἀνθρώπου ὁδὶ δὲ ἵππου, ὥσπερ οἱ τοὺς ἀριθμοὺς ἄγοντες εἰς τὰ σχήματα τρίγωνον καὶ τετράγωνον, οὕτως ἀφομοιῶν ταῖς ψήφοις τὰς μορφὰς τῶν φυτῶν[1] [. . .].

[1] τῶν φυτῶν mss.: τούτων Zeller: ‹τῶν ζῴων καὶ› φυτῶν Christ

D2 (< 45.2) Theophr. *Metaph.* 6a15–22

ἀπὸ δ' οὖν ταύτης ἢ τούτων τῶν ἀρχῶν ἀξιώσειεν ἄν τις [. . .] τὰ ἐφεξῆς εὐθὺς ἀποδιδόναι καὶ μὴ μέχρι του προελθόντα παύεσθαι· τοῦτο γὰρ τελέου καὶ φρονοῦντος, ὅπερ Ἀρχύτας ποτ' ἔφη ποιεῖν Εὔρυτον διατιθέντα τινὰς ψήφους· λέγειν γὰρ ὡς ὅδε μὲν ἀνθρώπου ὁ ἀριθμός, ὅδε δὲ ἵππου, ὅδε δ' ἄλλου τινὸς τυγχάνει.

EURYTUS

D

Eurytus' Procedure (D1–D2)

D1 (< 45.3) Aristotle, *Metaphysics*

[. . .] the way in which Eurytus assigned what is the number of what, for example this one of man, and this one of horse, reproducing with pebbles the shapes of natural creatures (*phuta*),[1] like those people who put numbers into the figures, the triangle and square [. . .].[2]

[1] This term usually designates plants in particular. [2] The commentary by Michael of Ephesus (p. 827.9–26 Hayduck) explains the procedure in terms of a sort of mosaic, but it is unlikely that this comparison goes back to Eurytus.

D2 (< 45.2) Theophrastus, *Metaphysics*

On the basis of this or of these principles [. . .], it could be considered right that one give an account directly of those [scil. things] that come next and not stop once one has arrived at a certain point. For it belongs to an adult and intelligent man to proceed in this way, as Archytas once said that Eurytus did when he arranged certain pebbles. For he [i.e. Eurytus, according to Archytas] said that this is the number of man, and this of horse, and this of something else.

14. ARCHYTAS [ARCHY.]

Archytas of Tarentum was born ca. 435 BC and was still alive in 360, according to the testimony of the *Seventh Letter* attributed to Plato, of whom he was a friend. If he belongs therefore to the post-Socratic period in chronological terms, there is nonetheless good reason to connect him, as scholars have traditionally done, to the earlier Pythagorean tradition, of which his engagement in mathematical research, compounded with a sophisticated epistemological reflection, certainly makes him a representative of one of the principal orientations. Consideration of his scientific fragments makes it easy to understand the influence he was able to exert upon Plato's thought, visible in the classification of the sciences in Book 7 of his *Republic*. We have much more information about the personality of Archytas than about that of his predecessors. In particular, he was elected general seven times (between 367 and 361), and thus was involved in politics; this too belongs to the image of primitive Pythagoreanism, though in a rather different way. Even more than to Philolaus, very many pseudepigraphic writings are attributed to him. In most cases, the evidently Platonic and Aristotelian inspiration of these treatises makes it quite easy to recognize them as inauthentic (see **PYTHS. R52–R53**); but one treatise of a moral and political character entitled

ARCHYTAS

On Law and Justice has been defended as authentic by a number of scholars, and we provide some extracts from it in an appendix (**D25**).

BIBLIOGRAPHY

Edition with Commentary

C. Huffman, ed. *Archytas of Tarentum: Pythagorean, Philosopher and Mathematician King* (Cambridge, 2005).

Studies

On the Musical Theory

A. D. Barker. *Greek Musical Writings.* Vol. 2, *Harmonic and Acoustic Theory* (Cambridge, 1989).

On the Political Fragments Attributed to Archytas

J. Monte Ransome. "Sources for the Philosophy of Archytas" (review of Huffman 2005), *Ancient Philosophy* 28 (2008): 1–27.

See also the titles listed in the General Introduction to Chapters 10–18.

EARLY GREEK PHILOSOPHY IV

OUTLINE OF THE CHAPTER

P

Origin and Family (P1–P2)
Chronology (P3)
The General (P4–P5)
The Statesman (P6–P7)
Archytas as a Student of Philolaus (P8)
Archytas and Plato (P9–P12)
  Plato as a Student of Archytas (P9)
  Archytas as a Student of Plato (P10)
  The Sicilian Affair (P11–P12)
Eudoxus as a Student of Archytas (P13)
Practice and Theory of the Aulos *(P14)*
Dialect (P15)
Character and Apothegms (P16–P20)
A Caricature (P21)
A Meditation on His Death (P22)

D

Epistemological Considerations (D1–D2)
  Definition (D1)
  Resemblances (D2)
Archytas as a Mathematician (D3)
Calculation, Number, Arithmetic (D4–D8)
  Praise of Calculation (D4–D5)
  The One (D6–D7)
  The Means (D8)
Geometry: The Problem of Duplicating the Cube (D9–D12)
Mathematics Applicable to Music (D13)

ARCHYTAS

Music (D14–D19)
 The Production of Sounds (D14–D15)
 Concords and Tetrachord (D16–D17)
 Music and Other Sciences (D18–D19)
  Music and Grammar (D18)
  Music and Physics (D19)
Physics (D20–D22)
 Motion (D20)
 Cosmology (D21)
 Vision (D22)
The Geometry of Animal Physiology (D23)
Pleasure (D24)
Appendix: Some Fragments from a (Pseudepigraphic?) Treatise on Political Theory (D25)

ARCHYTAS [47 DK]

P

Origin and Family (P1–P2)

P1 (< A1) Diog. Laert. 8.79

Ἀρχύτας Μνησαγόρου Ταραντῖνος, ὡς δὲ Ἀριστόξενος [Frag. 47 Wehrli], Ἑστιαίου, Πυθαγορικὸς καὶ αὐτός.

P2 Iambl. *VP* 267

a (< A6b Huffman)

ζηλωτὰς δὲ γράφειν γενέσθαι τῶν ἀνδρῶν [. . .] ἐν Τάραντι δὲ Ἀρχύταν.

b (< 58A.)

[5] Ταραντῖνοι Φιλόλαος, Εὔρυτος, Ἀρχύτας [. . .].

ARCHYTAS

P

Origin and Family (P1–P2)

P1 (< A1) Diogenes Laertius

Archytas of Tarentum, son of Mnesagoras (or, according to Aristoxenus, of Hestiaeus), he too a Pythagorean.

P2 Iamblichus, *Life of Pythagoras*

a (≠ DK)

He [scil. Diodorus of Aspendus] writes that disciples of these men [i.e. the Pythagoreans] were: [. . .] at Tarentum, Archytas.

b (< 58A.)

[5] From Tarentum: Philolaus, Eurytus, Archytas, [. . .].

EARLY GREEK PHILOSOPHY IV

Chronology (P3)

P3 (< A6b Huffman) Iambl. *VP*

a 104

[. . .] οἱ ἐκ τοῦ διδασκαλείου τούτου, μάλιστα δὲ οἱ παλαιότατοι καὶ αὐτῷ συγχρονίσαντες καὶ μαθητεύσαντες τῷ Πυθαγόρᾳ πρεσβύτῃ νέοι, Φιλόλαός τε καὶ Εὔρυτος [. . .] Ἀρχύτας τε ὁ πρεσβύτερος [. . .].

b 250

οἱ δὲ λοιποὶ τῶν Πυθαγορείων ἀπέστησαν τῆς Ἰταλίας πλὴν Ἀρχύτου τοῦ Ταραντίνου.

The General (P4–P5)

P4 (< A1) Diog. Laert. 8.79, 82

[79] ἐθαυμάζετο δὲ καὶ παρὰ τοῖς πολλοῖς ἐπὶ πάσῃ ἀρετῇ· καὶ δὴ ἑπτάκις τῶν πολιτῶν ἐστρατήγησε, τῶν ἄλλων μὴ πλέον ἐνιαυτοῦ στρατηγούντων διὰ τὸ κωλύειν τὸν νόμον. [. . .] [82] τὸν δὲ Πυθαγορικὸν Ἀριστόξενός φησι μηδέποτε στρατηγοῦντα ἡττηθῆναι· φθονούμενον δ' ἅπαξ ἐκχωρῆσαι τῆς στρατηγίας καὶ τοὺς αὐτίκα ληφθῆναι.

P5 (A1d Huffman) Ael. *Var. hist.* 7.14

τί δέ; οὐκ ἦσαν καὶ οἱ φιλόσοφοι τὰ πολέμια ἀγαθοί;

ARCHYTAS

Chronology (P3)

P3 (≠ DK) Iamblichus, *Life of Pythagoras*

a

[...] those who came from this school, and especially the most ancient ones, who lived at the same time as he [i.e. Pythagoras] did and who studied with Pythagoras when he was already old while they were young, Philolaus and Eurytus [...] and the older Archytas [...].

b

The other Pythagoreans left Italy, except for Archytas of Tarentum [scil. after the anti-Pythagorean revolts, cf. **PYTH. b T25–T27**].

The General (P4–P5)

P4 (< A1) Diogenes Laertius

[79] He was admired by the people for every kind of excellence; indeed, he was made general of his fellow citizens seven times, while the others were not generals for more than one year because the law prohibited this. [...] [82] Aristoxenus says that this Pythagorean was never defeated while he was a general, but that one day he resigned the generalship because he was the object of ill will, and they [i.e. his soldiers] were immediately made prisoners.

P5 (≠ DK) Aelian, *Historical Miscellany*

What? Were philosophers not good at military matters

ἐμοὶ μὲν δοκοῦσιν· εἴ γε Ἀρχύταν μὲν εἵλοντο ἑξάκις στρατηγὸν Ταραντῖνοι [. . .].

The Statesman (P6–P7)

P6 (< A4) Strab. 6.3.4

ἀπεδέξαντο δὲ καὶ τὴν Πυθαγόρειον φιλοσοφίαν, διαφερόντως δ' Ἀρχύτας ὃς καί προέστη τῆς πόλεως πολὺν χρόνον.

P7 (A5c4 Huffman) Plut. *Lib. ed.* 8B

πειρατέον οὖν εἰς δύναμιν καὶ τὰ κοινὰ πράττειν καὶ τῆς φιλοσοφίας ἀντιλαμβάνεσθαι κατὰ τὸ παρεῖκον τῶν καιρῶν. οὕτως ἐπολιτεύσατο Περικλῆς, οὕτως Ἀρχύτας ὁ Ταραντῖνος [. . .].

Archytas as a Student of Philolaus (P8)

P8 (> 44 A3) Cic. *De orat.* 3.34.139

aliisne igitur artibus [. . .] instituit [. . .] Philolaus Archytam Tarentinum?

ARCHYTAS

too? It seems to me that they were, if the Tarentines chose Archytas as a general six times [. . .].

The Statesman (P6–P7)

P6 (< A4) Strabo, *Geography*

They [i.e. the Tarentines] also welcomed the Pythagorean philosophy, and this was especially the case with Archytas, who also governed the city for a long time.

P7 (≠ DK) Plutarch, *On the Education of Children*

Hence one must strive as far as lies within one's power both to participate in public life and to practice philosophy as far as circumstances permit. This is how Pericles engaged in politics, just like Archytas of Tarentum [. . .].

Archytas as a Student of Philolaus (P8)

P8 (> 44 A3) Cicero, *On the Orator*

Did Philolaus then teach Archytas of Tarentum other arts [scil. than philosophy]?

EARLY GREEK PHILOSOPHY IV

Archytas and Plato (P9–P12)
Plato as a Student of Archytas (P9)

P9

a (< A5b9 Huffman) Olymp. *In Alc.* 2.86–93

μετὰ δὲ τὴν τελευτὴν Σωκράτους διδασκάλῳ πάλιν ἐχρήσατο Κρατύλῳ τῷ Ἡρακλειτείῳ [. . .]. μετὰ τοῦτον δὲ πάλιν στέλλεται εἰς Ἰταλίαν καὶ διδασκαλεῖον εὑρὼν ἐκεῖ τῶν Πυθαγορείων συνιστάμενον Ἀρχύταν πάλιν ἔσχε διδάσκαλον τὸν Πυθαγόρειον.

b (A5b10 Huffman) Phot. *Bibl.* 2.49, p. 438b16–19 Bekker

ἀνεγνώσθη Πυθαγόρου βίος.

ὅτι ἔνατος ἀπὸ Πυθαγόρου διάδοχος γέγονε, φησί, Πλάτων, Ἀρχύτου τοῦ πρεσβυτέρου μαθητὴς γενόμενος [. . .].

Archytas as a Student of Plato (P10)

P10 (A5c3 Huffman) Philod. *Acad. Ind.* in P. Herc. 1021, V.32–VI.12 (pp. 134–35 Dorandi)

Πλάτωνος μ[αθητα]ὶ ἦσ[α]ν . . . Ἀρχύτας Ταραν[τῖ]νος . . .

ARCHYTAS

Archytas and Plato (P9–P12)
Plato as a Student of Archytas (P9)

P9

a (≠ DK) Olympiodorus, *Commentary on Plato's* First Alcibiades

After the death of Socrates, he [scil. Plato] in turn had Cratylus the Heraclitean as his teacher [. . .]. After him he traveled once again to Italy, and having found a school of Pythagoreans established there, in turn he had Archytas the Pythagorean as teacher.

b (≠ DK) Photius, *Library*

I have read a life of Pythagoras.
  It says that the ninth successor of Pythagoras was Plato, who had been the disciple of the older Archytas [. . .].

Archytas as a Student of Plato (P10)

P10 (≠ DK) Philodemus, *History of Philosophy: Index of the Members of the Academy*

Plato's students were . . . Archytas of Tarentum . . .

EARLY GREEK PHILOSOPHY IV

The Sicilian Affair (P11–P12)

P11 (< A5) (Ps.-?) Plat. *Epist.* 7

a 338c

ἔοικεν δὴ τὸ μετὰ τοῦτο Ἀρχύτης τε παρὰ Διονύσιον[1] ἀφικέσθαι—ἐγὼ γὰρ πρὶν ἀπιέναι ξενίαν καὶ φιλίαν Ἀρχύτῃ καὶ τοῖς ἐν Τάραντι καὶ Διονυσίῳ ποιήσας ἀπέπλεον [. . .].

[1] post Διονύσιον hab. AO πρὶν, in marg. O τὸ πρὶν ἀλλαχοῦ ὠβέλισται

b 339d

ἐπιστολαὶ δὲ ἄλλαι ἐφοίτων παρά τε Ἀρχύτου καὶ τῶν ἐν Τάραντι, τήν τε φιλοσοφίαν ἐγκωμιάζουσαι τὴν Διονυσίου, καὶ ὅτι, ἂν μὴ ἀφίκωμαι νῦν, τὴν πρὸς Διονύσιον αὐτοῖς γενομένην φιλίαν δι᾽ ἐμοῦ, οὐ σμικρὰν οὖσαν πρὸς τὰ πολιτικά, παντάπασιν διαβαλοίην.

c 350a

ᾤκουν δὴ τὸ μετὰ τοῦτο ἔξω τῆς ἀκροπόλεως ἐν τοῖς μισθοφόροις· προσιόντες δέ μοι ἄλλοι τε καὶ οἱ τῶν ὑπηρεσιῶν ὄντες Ἀθήνηθεν, ἐμοὶ πολῖται, ἀπήγγελλον ὅτι διαβεβλημένος εἴην ἐν τοῖς πελτασταῖς καί μοί τινες ἀπειλοῖεν, εἴ που λήψονταί με, διαφθερεῖν. μηχανῶμαι δή τινα τοιάνδε σωτηρίαν. πέμπω παρ᾽

ARCHYTAS

The Sicilian Affair (P11–P12)

P11 (< A5) (Ps.-?) Plato, *Letter* 7

a

After this Archytas seems to have gone to find Dionysius—for when I sailed away, before I left I had established bonds of hospitality and friendship between Archytas and the Tarentines on the one hand and Dionysius on the other [. . .].

b

Other letters reached me regularly from Archytas and from the men in Tarentum, who praised Dionysius' philosophical attitude and said that if I did not come immediately I would completely discredit the friendship between them and Dionysius that had been established thanks to me and that was no small matter from a political standpoint.

c

After this, I lived outside the acropolis among the mercenaries. Among other people, some attendants from Athens, fellow citizens of mine, arrived and announced to me that I had been slandered among the soldiers and that some were threatening that if they caught me they would kill me. This is the plan I devised to save myself: I sent

Ἀρχύτην καὶ τοὺς ἄλλους φίλους εἰς Τάραντα, φράζων ἐν οἷς ὢν τυγχάνω· οἱ δὲ πρόφασίν τινα πρεσβείας πορισάμενοι παρὰ τῆς πόλεως πέμπουσιν τριακόντορόν τε καὶ Λαμίσκον αὐτῶν ἕνα, ὃς ἐλθὼν ἐδεῖτο Διονυσίου περὶ ἐμοῦ, λέγων ὅτι βουλοίμην ἀπιέναι, καὶ μηδαμῶς ἄλλως ποιεῖν. ὁ δὲ συνωμολόγησεν καὶ ἀπέπεμψεν ἐφόδια δούς [. . .].

P12 (< A1) Diog. Laert. 8.79

οὗτός ἐστιν ὁ Πλάτωνα ῥυσάμενος δι' ἐπιστολῆς παρὰ Διονυσίου μέλλοντα ἀναιρεῖσθαι. [. . .] πρὸς τοῦτον καὶ Πλάτων γέγραφεν ἐπιστολὰς δύο, ἐπειδήπερ αὐτῷ πρότερος γεγράφει τοῦτον τὸν τρόπον· [. . .].

Eudoxus as a Student of Archytas (P13)

P13 (A6c Huffman) Diog. Laert. 8.86

οὗτος [sc. Εὔδοξος] τὰ μὲν γεωμετρικὰ Ἀρχύτα διήκουσε [. . .].

Practice and Theory of the Aulos *(P14)*

P14 (> 44 A7) Athen. *Deipn.* 4 184d–e

καὶ τῶν Πυθαγορικῶν δὲ πολλοὶ τὴν αὐλητικὴν ἤσκησαν, ὡς Εὐφράνωρ τε καὶ Ἀρχύτας Φιλόλαός τε ἄλλοι τε οὐκ ὀλίγοι. ὁ δ' Εὐφράνωρ καὶ σύγγραμμα περὶ αὐλῶν κατέλιπεν· ὁμοίως δὲ καὶ ὁ Ἀρχύτας.

emissaries to Tarentum, to Archytas and my other friends, explaining the situation in which I found myself. And they, providing as pretext some embassy from the city, sent a thirty-oared ship with Lamiscus, one of them. When he arrived he interceded with Dionysius on my behalf, saying that I wanted to leave, and asking him not to do anything at all to oppose this. He agreed and let me go after giving me provisions for my travel [. . .].

P12 (< A1) Diogenes Laertius

He is the one who saved Plato by means of a letter when he was going to be killed by Dionysius. [. . .] Plato also wrote two letters to him, since he had written first to him as follows: [. . .].[1]

[1] There follow two (apocryphal) letters from Archytas to Plato (Thesleff, p. 46.1–7) and from Plato to Archytas (Letter 12).

Eudoxus as a Student of Archytas (P13)

P13 (≠ DK) Diogenes Laertius

He [scil. Eudoxus] studied geometry with Archytas [. . .].

Practice and Theory of the Aulos *(P14)*

P14 (> 44 A7) Athenaeus, *Deipnosophists*

Many of the Pythagoreans practiced the art of the *aulos*, like Euphranor, Archytas, Philolaus, and many others. Euphranor also left behind a treatise on *auloi*, and so too Archytas.

EARLY GREEK PHILOSOPHY IV

Dialect (P15)

P15 (< A6g Huffman) Greg. Cor. *Dial.* Praef., pp. 5–6

αὐτοὶ τοίνυν [. . .] προθέμενοι [. . .] Δωρίδος δὲ τὸν Ταραντῖνον Ἀρχύταν καὶ Θεόκριτον [. . .], ἴσως ἂν περὶ τῶν διαλέκτων ἱκανῶς διαλάβοιμεν.

Character and Apothegms (P16–P20)

P16 (A7) Aristox. in Iambl. *VP* 197

Σπίνθαρος γοῦν διηγεῖτο πολλάκις περὶ Ἀρχύτου ⟨τοῦ⟩[1] Ταραντίνου, ὅτι διὰ χρόνου τινὸς εἰς ἀγρὸν ἀφικόμενος, ἐκ[2] στρατιᾶς[3] νεωστὶ παραγεγονώς, ἣν ἐστρατεύσατο ἡ πόλις εἰς Μεσσαπίους,[4] ὡς εἶδε τόν τε ἐπίτροπον καὶ τοὺς ἄλλους οἰκέτας οὐκ εὖ τῶν περὶ τὴν γεωργίαν ἐπιμελείας[5] πεποιημένους, ἀλλὰ μεγάλῃ τινὶ κεχρημένους ὀλιγωρίας ὑπερβολῇ, ὀργισθείς τε καὶ ἀγανακτήσας οὕτως, ὡς ἂν ἐκεῖνος, εἶπεν, ὡς ἔοικε, πρὸς τοὺς οἰκέτας ὅτι εὐτυχοῦσιν ὅτι αὐτοῖς ὤργισται· εἰ γὰρ μὴ τοῦτο συμβεβηκὸς ἦν, οὐκ ἄν ποτε αὐτοὺς ἀθῴους γενέσθαι τηλικαῦτα ἡμαρτηκότας.

[1] ⟨τοῦ⟩ Cobet   [2] ἐκ Scaliger: καὶ ms.   [3] στρατείας Mahne   [4] Μεσσαπίους Cobet: μεσανίους ms.: Μεσσηνίους Arcerius   [5] ἐπιμέλειαν Wakefield

ARCHYTAS

Dialect (P15)

P15 (≠ DK) Gregory of Corinth, *On Dialects*

If we establish as a canon [...] of the Doric dialect Archytas of Tarentum and Theocritus [...], then surely we shall have distinguished the dialects sufficiently.

Character and Apothegms (P16–P20)

P16 (A7) Aristoxenus in Iamblichus, *Life of Pythagoras*

Spintharus often told the story about Archytas of Tarentum, that when he arrived at his estate after some time, having just returned from the military campaign his city had waged against the Messapians, he saw that the administrator and the other slaves had not taken proper care of the farming, but had shown excessive neglect; becoming angry and annoyed, as he could be, he said, as it seems, to the slaves that they were lucky that he was angry; for if this had not been the case, they would not have gotten away without being punished for having made such terrible mistakes.

P17 (A7a Huffman) Cic. *Lael.* 88

verum ergo illud est, quod a Tarentino Archyta, ut opinor, dici solitum nostros senes commemorare audivi ab aliis senibus auditum: "si quis in caelum ascendisset naturamque mundi et pulchritudinem siderum perspexisset, insuavem illam admirationem ei fore; quae iucundissima fuisset, si aliquem,[1] cui narraret, habuisset."

[1] si aliquem] nisi aliquem *M*: nisi aliqui *B*

P18

a (A8) Athen. *Deipn.* 12 519b

καὶ Ἀθηνόδωρος δὲ ἐν τῷ Περὶ σπουδῆς καὶ παιδιᾶς[1] Ἀρχύταν φησὶ τὸν Ταραντῖνον πολιτικὸν ἅμα καὶ φιλόσοφον γενόμενον πλείστους οἰκέτας ἔχοντα αἰεὶ τούτ‹ων τοῖς παιδί›οις[2] παρὰ τὴν δίαιταν ἀφιεμένοις εἰς τὸ συμπόσιον ἥδεσθαι.

[1] παιδείας A, corr. Musurus
[2] ἀεὶ τούτοις ms., corr. Casaubon ex Ael. *Var. hist.* 12.15

b (A10) Arist. *Pol.* 8.6 1340b25–28

ἅμα δὲ καὶ δεῖ τοὺς παῖδας ἔχειν τινὰ διατριβήν, καὶ τὴν Ἀρχύτου πλαταγὴν οἴεσθαι γενέσθαι καλῶς, ἣν διδόασι τοῖς παιδίοις ὅπως χρώμενοι ταύτῃ μηδὲν καταγνύωσι τῶν κατὰ τὴν οἰκίαν.

ARCHYTAS

P17 (≠ DK) Cicero, *On Friendship*

What Archytas of Tarentum used to say, I believe, as our elders say they heard it from their own elders, is true: "If someone ascended into the heavens and saw the nature of the world and the beauty of the stars, his admiration would be without pleasure; but it would be extremely delightful, if he had someone to whom he could tell it."

P18 (A8)

a Athenaeus, *Deipnosophists*

Athenodorus says in his *On Seriousness and Play* that Archytas of Tarentum, who was both a statesman and a philosopher and had very many slaves, always took pleasure in their ‹little children› when, by his custom, they were admitted into his drinking party.

b Aristotle, *Politics*

At the same time it is also necessary that children have something to busy themselves with, and Archytas' rattle must be supposed to be a fine invention; they give it to children so that they play with this and so do not break anything in the house.

P19 (A11) Ael. *Var. hist.* 14.19

Ἀρχύτας τά τε ἄλλα ἦν σώφρων καὶ οὖν καὶ τὰ ἄκοσμα ἐφυλάττετο τῶν ὀνομάτων. ἐπεὶ δέ ποτε ἐβιάζετό τι εἰπεῖν τῶν ἀπρεπῶν, οὐκ ἐξενικήθη, ἀλλ᾽ ἐσιώπησε μὲν αὐτό, ἐπέγραψε δὲ κατὰ τοῦ τοίχου, δείξας μὲν ὃ εἰπεῖν ἐβιάζετο, οὐ μὴν βιασθεὶς εἰπεῖν.

P20 (A11a Huffman) Ael. *Var. hist.* 10.12

Ἀρχύτας ἔλεγεν "ὥσπερ ἔργον ἐστὶν ἰχθὺν εὑρεῖν ἄκανθαν μὴ ἔχοντα, οὕτω καὶ ἄνθρωπον μὴ κεκτημένον τι δολερὸν καὶ ἀκανθῶδες."

A Caricature (P21)

P21 (≠ DK) Bion Borysth. in Diog. Laert. 4.52 (= Frag. 227 SH)

ὦ πέπον Ἀρχύτα, ψαλληγενές, ὀλβιότυφε,
τῆς ὑπάτης ἔριδος πάντων ἐμπειρότατ᾽ ἀνδρῶν.

A Meditation on His Death (P22)

P22 (< A3) Hor. *Carm.* 1.28.1–6

te maris et terrae numeroque carentis harenae
    mensorem cohibent, Archyta,

ARCHYTAS

P19 (A11) Aelian, *Historical Miscellany*

Archytas was moderate in general and so he also avoided indecency in his speech. And one time when he was obliged to say something unseemly, he did not yield, but passed it over in silence and wrote it down on a wall, indicating what he was obliged to say but without being obliged to say it.

P20 (≠ DK) Aelian, *Historical Miscellany*

Archytas used to say, "It is just as difficult to find a fish that does not have bones (*akantha*), as a man who does not have something deceitful and prickly (*akanthôdes*) about him."

A Caricature (P21)

P21 (≠ DK) Bion of Borysthenes in Diogenes Laertius

Oh gentle Archytas, harp-born, happy in your own conceit,
Most expert of men in the bass tone of strife!

A Meditation on His Death (P22)

P22 (< A3) Horace, *Odes*

You who measured the sea and the earth and the numberless sands,
Archytas, the paltry funeral rites

pulveris exigui prope litus[1] parva Matinum
  munera, nec quidquam tibi prodest
aerias[2] temptasse domos animoque rotundum
  percurrisse polum morituro.
[. . .]

[1] litus Ψλ*l*: latus *E*: latum *ABR*   [2] aetherias *Meineke*

ARCHYTAS

Of a little heap of dust confine you near the Matine
    shore,
   Nor does it do you any good
That you made an attempt on the heavenly palaces
    and traversed
   The round sky with the aid of a mind that had to
    die.
[. . .]

ARCHYTAS [47 DK]

D

Epistemological Considerations (D1–D2)
Definition (D1)

D1 (< A22) Arist. *Metaph.* H2 1043a21–24

ὁμοίως δὲ καὶ οἵους Ἀρχύτας ἀπεδέχετο ὅρους· τοῦ συνάμφω γάρ εἰσιν. οἷον τί ἐστιν νηνεμία; ἠρεμία ἐν πλήθει ἀέρος· [. . .] τί ἐστι γαλήνη; ὁμαλότης θαλάττης.

Resemblances (D2)

D2 (> A12) Arist. *Rhet.* 3.11 1412a9–14

[. . .] καὶ ἐν φιλοσοφίᾳ ⟨τὸ⟩[1] τὸ ὅμοιον καὶ ἐν πολὺ διέχουσι θεωρεῖν εὐστόχου, ὥσπερ Ἀρχύτας ἔφη ταὐτὸν εἶναι διαιτητὴν καὶ βωμόν· ἐπ' ἄμφω γὰρ τὸ ἀδικούμενον καταφεύγει.

[1] ⟨τὸ⟩ Vahlen

ARCHYTAS

D

Epistemological Considerations (D1–D2)
Definition (D1)

D1 (< A22) Aristotle, *Metaphysics*

It is the same with the kinds of definitions that Archytas accepted: for they belong to both [scil. the matter and the form] at once. For example, what is windlessness? A stillness in a quantity of air [. . .]. What is an ocean calm? An evenness of the sea.

Resemblances (D2)

D2 (> A12) Aristotle, *Rhetoric*

[. . .] in philosophy too [scil. as in rhetoric], envisioning what is similar even in things that are very remote from one another is the mark of a shrewd person, as Archytas said that an arbitrator and an altar are the same thing: for the man who is suffering injustice seeks refuge at both of them.

EARLY GREEK PHILOSOPHY IV

Archytas as a Mathematician (D3)

D3 (< A1) Diog. Laert. 8.83

οὗτος πρῶτος τὰ μηχανικὰ ταῖς μαθηματικαῖς[1] προσχρησάμενος ἀρχαῖς μεθώδευσε καὶ πρῶτος κίνησιν ὀργανικὴν διαγράμματι γεωμετρικῷ προσήγαγε, διὰ τῆς τομῆς τοῦ ἡμικυλίνδρου δύο μέσας ἀνὰ λόγον λαβεῖν ζητῶν εἰς τὸν τοῦ κύβου διπλασιασμόν. κἂν[2] γεωμετρίᾳ πρῶτος κύβον[3] εὗρεν, ὥς φησι Πλάτων ἐν Πολιτείᾳ.

[1] μηχανικαῖς mss., corr. Kühn [2] κἂν Roeper: καὶ mss.
[3] ‹τὴν τῶν› κύβων ‹αὔξην› Huffman

Calculation, Number, Arithmetic (D4–D8)
Praise of Calculation (D4–D5)

D4 (B3) Stob. 4.1.139 (δεῖ γὰρ ... ἀδύνατον: cf. Iambl. *Comm.*, p. 44.10–17)

ἐκ τοῦ Ἀρχύτου Περὶ μαθημάτων

δεῖ γὰρ ἢ μαθόντα παρ' ἄλλω ἢ αὐτὸν ἐξευρόντα, ὧν ἀνεπιστάμων[1] ἦσθα, ἐπιστάμονα γενέσθαι. τὸ μὲν ὦν μαθὲν παρ' ἄλλω καὶ ἀλλότριον, τὸ δ' ἐξευρὲν αὐτὸν δι' αὐτοῦ καὶ ἴδιον. ἐξευρὲν δὲ μὴ[2] ζατοῦντα ἄπορον καὶ σπάνιον, ζατοῦντα δὲ[3] εὔπορον καὶ ῥᾴδιον· μὴ

ARCHYTAS

Archytas as a Mathematician (D3)

D3 (< A1) Diogenes Laertius

He was the first to systematize mechanics by making use of mathematical principles, and the first to apply the movement of an instrument to a geometrical proof, when he tried to find two mean proportionals by sectioning a half-cylinder in order to duplicate the cube. And in geometry he was the first to discover [scil. the dimensions of] the cube, as Plato says in his *Republic* [cf. *Rep.* 7 528b].

Calculation, Number, Arithmetic (D4–D8)
Praise of Calculation (D4–D5)

D4 (B3) Stobaeus, *Anthology*

From Archytas, *On the Sciences*:

For it is necessary to arrive at knowing what you did not know either by learning it from someone else or by discovering it yourself. Now what one learns from someone else also belongs to another, while what one discovers oneself belongs to oneself as one's own. But to discover without seeking is difficult and rare,

---

¹ ἀνεπιστάμων Blass: ἐπιστάμων Stob.: ἂν αὐτῶν ἐπιστάμων Iambl.   ² μὴ Iambl.: μὴν Stob.   ³ ἄπορον . . . δέ om. Stob., hab. Iambl.

ἐπιστάμενον δὲ ζητεῖν[4] ἀδύνατον. στάσιν μὲν
ἔπαυσεν, ὁμόνοιαν δὲ αὔξησεν λογισμὸς εὑρε-
θείς· πλεονεξία τε γὰρ οὐκ ἔστι τούτου γενομένου καὶ ἰσότας ἔστιν· τούτῳ γὰρ περὶ τῶν
συναλλαγμάτων διαλλασσόμεθα. διὰ τοῦτον
οὖν οἱ πένητες λαμβάνοντι παρὰ τῶν δυ-
ναμένων, οἵ τε πλούσιοι διδόντι[5] τοῖς δεομέ-
νοις, πιστεύοντες ἀμφότεροι διὰ τούτων[6] τὸ
ἶσον ἕξειν. κανὼν δὲ καὶ κωλυτὴρ τῶν ἀδικούν-
των ⟨ἐὼν⟩[7] τοὺς μὲν ἐπισταμένους λογίζεσθαι[8]
πρὶν ἀδικεῖν ἔπαυσε,[9] πείσας ὅτι οὐ δυνασοῦ-
νται λαθεῖν, ὅταν ἐπ' αὐτὸν ἔλθωντι, τοὺς δὲ
μὴ ἐπισταμένους, ἐν αὐτῷ δηλώσας ἀδικοῦ-
ντας, ἐκώλυσεν ἀδικῆσαι.

[4] ⟨λογίζεσθαι⟩ ζητεῖν Huffman   [5] διδόντες mss.,
corr. Canter   [6] τούτων mss.: τούτῳ Gesner   [7] ⟨ἐὼν⟩
Blass   [8] λογίζεσθαι Pflugk: ὀργίζεσθαι mss.: τῶ ὀργίζεσθαι Gesner   [9] παύσας mss., corr. Gesner

D5 (B4) Stob. 1 prooem. 4

ἐκ τῶν Ἀρχύτου διατριβῶν

καὶ δοκεῖ ἁ λογιστικὰ ποτὶ τὰν σοφίαν[1] τῶν
μὲν ἄλλων[2] τεχνῶν καὶ πολὺ διαφέρειν, ἀτὰρ
καὶ τᾶς γεωμετρικᾶς ἐναργεστέρω πράγμα-

[1] τὰν ἄλλαν σοφίαν ms., corr. Diels   [2] ἀλλᾶν Blass

ARCHYTAS

while to do so by seeking is practicable and easy; but if one does not know, then to seek is impossible.[1] **The discovery of calculation (*logismos*) puts an end to civil strife and increases concord. For when this is present, there is no desire to possess more (*pleonexia*), and there is equality. For it is thanks to this that we are in accord with one another in our mutual relations. Therefore it is thanks to this that the poor receive from the powerful, and that the rich give to the needy, both parties being convinced that they will thereby have equality. And being a rule and a hindrance for unjust men, it stops those who know how to calculate before they commit injustice by persuading them that they will not be able to remain undetected whenever they have recourse to it. As for those who do not know it, having shown them that they are unjust in this area, it prevents them from committing injustice.**

[1] Or, adopting Huffman's suggested supplement: "to seek without knowing ⟨how to calculate⟩ is impossible."

D5 (B4) Stobaeus, *Anthology*

From the *Discourses* (*Diatribes*) of Archytas:

And it seems that the art of calculation (*logistika*) is much superior to the other arts with regard to wisdom and that it investigates whatever it wishes more clearly than geometry

τεύεσθαι ἃ θέλει. καὶ ἃ ἐκλείπει αὖ ἁ γεωμετρία, καὶ ἀποδείξιας[3] ἁ λογιστικὰ ἐπιτελέει καὶ ὁμῶς,[4] εἰ μὲν εἰδέων τεὰ πραγματεία, καὶ τὰ περὶ τοῖς εἴδεσιν.[5]

[3] ἀπόδειξις ms., corr. Meineke [4] ὅμως ms., corr. Meineke [5] τὰ περὶ τοῖς εἰδέεσιν ‹πραγματεύεται› Meineke: τὰ ἐπὶ τοῖς εἴδεσιν ‹περιλαμβάνεν› Blass

The One (D6–D7)

D6 (A20) Theon Sm. *Exp.*, p. 20.19–20

Ἀρχύτας δὲ καὶ Φιλόλαος ἀδιαφόρως τὸ ἓν καὶ μονάδα καλοῦσι καὶ τὴν μονάδα ἕν.

D7 (A21) Arist. in Theon Sm. *Exp.*, p. 22.5–10

Ἀριστοτέλης δὲ ἐν τῷ Πυθαγορικῷ [Frag. 199 Rose] τὸ ἕν φησιν ἀμφοτέρων μετέχειν τῆς φύσεως [. . . = **PYTHS. ANON. D11**]· διὸ καὶ ἀρτιοπέριττον καλεῖσθαι τὸ ἕν. συμφέρεται δὲ τούτοις καὶ Ἀρχύτας.

The Means (D8)

D8 (< 18.15) Iambl. *In Nic.*, pp. 100.19–101.1

[. . . = **HIPPAS. D6**] ἡ ποτὲ μὲν ὑπεναντία λεγομένη τῇ τάξει τρίτη,[1] ὑπὸ δὲ τῶν περὶ Ἀρχύταν αὖθις καὶ Ἵππασον ἁρμονικὴ μετακληθεῖσα [. . .].

[1] τρίτῃ mss., corr. Pistelli

does; and for what, inversely, geometry lacks, calculation completes the proofs, and in the same way, if there is investigation of forms, for what concerns the forms.[1]

[1] The authenticity of this text is disputed.

The One (D6–D7)

D6 (A20) Theon of Smyrna, *Aspects of Mathematics Useful for Reading Plato*

Archytas and Philolaus [**PHILOL. D10**] call without distinction the one monad too and the monad one.

D7 (A21) Aristotle in Theon of Smyrna, *Aspects of Mathematics Useful for Reading Plato*

Aristotle in his book on Pythagoreans says that the one participates in the nature of both [scil. the even and the odd] [. . .]. That is why the one is called even-odd. Archytas too is in agreement with this.

The Means (D8)

D8 (< 18.15) Iamblichus, *Commentary on Nicomachus'* Introduction to Arithmetic

[. . . scil. the mean] that used to be called 'subcontrary,' the third in order, but that Archytas and Hippasus renamed 'harmonic' [. . .] [cf. **HIPPAS. D6**].

EARLY GREEK PHILOSOPHY IV

Geometry: The Problem of Duplicating the Cube (D9–D12)

D9 (< A15 Huffman) Erat. in Eutoc. *In Arch.*, p. 3.88.10–14

ἐζητεῖτο δὲ καὶ παρὰ τοῖς γεωμέτραις, τίνα ἄν τις τρόπον τὸ δοθὲν στερεὸν διαμένον ἐν τῷ αὐτῷ σχήματι διπλασιάσειεν. καὶ ἐκαλεῖτο τὸ τοιοῦτον πρόβλημα κύβου διπλασιασμός· [. . .] πάντων δὲ διαπορούντων ἐπὶ πολὺν χρόνον πρῶτος Ἱπποκράτης ὁ Χῖος ἐπενόησεν ὅτι, ἐὰν εὑρεθῇ δύο εὐθειῶν γραμμῶν, ὧν ἡ μείζων τῆς ἐλάσσονός ἐστι διπλασία, δύο μέσας ἀνάλογον λαβεῖν ἐν συνεχεῖ ἀναλογίᾳ, διπλασιασθήσεται ὁ κύβος, ὥστε τὸ ἀπόρημα αὐτοῦ εἰς ἕτερον οὐκ ἔλασσον ἀπόρημα κατέστρεφεν. [. . .] τῶν δὲ φιλοπόνως ἐπιδιδόντων ἑαυτοὺς καὶ ζητούντων δύο τῶν δοθεισῶν δύο μέσας λαβεῖν Ἀρχύτας μὲν ὁ Ταραντῖνος λέγεται διὰ τῶν ἡμικυλίνδρων εὑρηκέναι [. . .].

ARCHYTAS

Geometry: The Problem of Duplicating the Cube (D9–D12)[1]

[1] The texts relating to this question are numerous and the data are very controversial. The principal source for them was Eratosthenes' *Platonikos* (third century BC). The full documentation is commented in Huffman, pp. 342–401.

D9 (< A15 Huffman) Eratosthenes in Eutocius, *Commentary on Archimedes*' On Spheres and Cylinders[1]

Geometers tried to find a way to double a given solid while maintaining its shape. This kind of problem was called 'duplication of the cube.' [. . .] Everyone was at a loss for a long time. Then Hippocrates of Chios was the first to realize that if one found two mean proportionals in continued proportion between two straight lines, of which the larger is twice as big as the smaller, then the cube would be doubled. As a result he transformed that problem into another problem, which was not less difficult. [. . .] After they [i.e. geometers associated with Plato to whom the Delians had appealed in order to find out how to double their altars] had devoted themselves diligently to the question and had tried to find the two means of two given lines, Archytas of Tarentum is said to have discovered them by means of semicylinders [. . .].

[1] This is a letter addressed by Eratosthenes to Ptolemy III Euergetes (third century BC). Its authenticity is not absolutely certain (cf. Huffman, p. 373), but in any case the information it provides on the history of the problem of duplicating the cube is precious.

EARLY GREEK PHILOSOPHY IV

D10 (A15a Huffman) Plut. *Quaest. conv.* 8.2 718 E–F

διὸ καὶ Πλάτων αὐτὸς ἐμέμψατο τοὺς περὶ Εὔδοξον καὶ Ἀρχύταν καὶ Μέναιχμον εἰς ὀργανικὰς καὶ μηχανικὰς κατασκευὰς τὸν τοῦ στερεοῦ διπλασιασμὸν ἀπάγειν ἐπιχειροῦντας, ὥσπερ πειρωμένους δίχα λόγου δύο μέσας ἀνάλογον, ᾗ παρείκοι, λαβεῖν.

D11 (A14a Huffman) Procl. *In Tim.* 3 ad 32a–b (vol. 2, pp. 33.29–34.4 Diehl)

πῶς μὲν οὖν δύο δοθεισῶν εὐθειῶν δυνατὸν δύο μέσας ἀνάλογον λαβεῖν, ἡμεῖς ἐπὶ τέλει τῆς πραγματείας εὑρόντες τὴν Ἀρχύτειον δεῖξιν ἀναγράψομεν, ταύτην ἐκλεξάμενοι μᾶλλον ἢ τὴν Μεναίχμου, διότι ταῖς κωνικαῖς ἐκεῖνος χρῆται γραμμαῖς, καὶ τὴν Ἐρατοσθένους ὡσαύτως, διότι κανόνος χρῆται παραθέσει.

D12 (A14) Eudem. in Eutoc. *In Arch.*, pp. 3.84.12–88.2

Ἀρχύτου εὕρησις, ὡς Εὔδημος ἱστορεῖ. [Frag. 141 Wehrli]

ἔστωσαν αἱ δοθεῖσαι δύο εὐθεῖαι αἱ ΑΔ, Γ. δεῖ δὴ τῶν ΑΔ, Γ δύο μέσας ἀνάλογον εὑρεῖν. γεγράφθω περὶ τὴν μείζονα τὴν ΑΔ κύκλος ὁ ΑΒΔΖ, καὶ τῇ Γ ἴσῃ ἐνηρμόσθω ἡ ΑΒ καὶ ἐκβληθεῖσα συμπιπτέτω τῇ ἀπὸ τοῦ Δ ἐφαπτομένῃ τοῦ κύκλου κατὰ τὸ Π. παρὰ δὲ τὴν ΠΔΟ

ARCHYTAS

D10 (≠ DK) Plutarch, *Table Talk*

It is for this reason [scil. that geometry frees the intellect from the sensible] that Plato himself criticized Eudoxus, Archytas, Menaechmus, and their successors for trying to divert the problem of duplicating a solid towards constructions requiring the use of an instrument and possessing a mechanical nature, as though they were trying to discover two mean proportionals (*analogon*) independently of reason (*dikha logou*) [cf. Plato, *Republic* 7 531a–b].

D11 (≠ DK) Proclus, *Commentary on Plato's* Timaeus

How then it is possible to find two mean proportionals of two given straight lines I shall transcribe at the end of my treatise, because I have found Archytas' demonstration.[1] I chose this one rather than Menaechmus' because he uses conic lines [i.e. sections], and also rather than Eratosthenes' because he has recourse to apposing a ruler.

[1] This text has not been preserved.

D12 (A14) Eudemus in Eutocius, *Commentary on Archimedes'* On Spheres and Cylinders

Archytas' solution, as Eudemus reports it:

> Let there be two straight lines AΔ and Γ. Then one must find two mean proportionals of AΔ and Γ. Let the circle ABΔZ be drawn around the longer line AΔ, let AB equal to Γ be fitted inside [scil. the circle] and be extended it so that it meets the line, which is tangent to the circle and drawn from Δ, at Π. Let the line BEZ be drawn parallel to ΠΔO, and

ἤχθω ἡ ΒΕΖ, καὶ νενοήσθω ἡμικυλίνδριον ὀρθὸν ἐπὶ τοῦ ΑΒΔ ἡμικυκλίου, ἐπὶ δὲ τῆς ΑΔ ἡμικύκλιον ὀρθὸν ἐν τῷ τοῦ ἡμικυλινδρίου παραλληλογράμμῳ κείμενον. τοῦτο δὴ τὸ ἡμικύκλιον περιαγόμενον ὡς ἀπὸ τοῦ Δ ἐπὶ τὸ Β μένοντος τοῦ Α πέρατος τῆς διαμέτρου τεμεῖ τὴν κυλινδρικὴν ἐπιφάνειαν ἐν τῇ περιαγωγῇ καὶ γράψει ἐν αὐτῇ γραμμήν τινα. πάλιν δέ, ἐὰν τῆς ΑΔ μενούσης τὸ ΑΠΔ τρίγωνον περιενεχθῇ τὴν ἐναντίαν τῷ ἡμικυκλίῳ κίνησιν, κωνικὴν ποιήσει ἐπιφάνειαν τῇ ΑΠ εὐθείᾳ, ἣ δὴ περιαγομένη συμβαλεῖ τῇ κυλινδρικῇ γραμμῇ κατά τι σημεῖον· ἅμα δὲ καὶ τὸ Β περιγράψει ἡμικύκλιον ἐν τῇ τοῦ κώνου ἐπιφανείᾳ. ἐχέτω δὴ θέσιν κατὰ τὸν τόπον τῆς συμπτώσεως τῶν γραμμῶν τὸ μὲν κινούμενον ἡμικύκλιον ὡς τὴν τοῦ ΔΚΑ, τὸ δὲ ἀντιπεριαγόμενον τρίγωνον τὴν τοῦ ΔΛΑ, τὸ δὲ τῆς εἰρημένης συμπτώσεως σημεῖον ἔστω τὸ Κ· ἔστω δὲ καὶ τὸ διὰ τοῦ Β γραφόμενον ἡμικύκλιον τὸ ΒΜΖ, κοινὴ δὲ αὐτοῦ τομὴ καὶ τοῦ ΒΔΖΑ κύκλου ἔστω ἡ ΒΖ. καὶ ἀπὸ τοῦ Κ ἐπὶ τὸ τοῦ ΒΔΑ ἡμικυκλίου ἐπίπεδον κάθετος ἤχθω· πεσεῖται δὴ ἐπὶ τὴν τοῦ κύκλου περιφέρειαν διὰ τὸ ὀρθὸν ἑστάναι τὸν κύλινδρον. πιπτέτω καὶ ἔστω ἡ ΚΙ, καὶ ἡ ἀπὸ τοῦ Ι ἐπὶ τὸ Α ἐπιζευχθεῖσα συμβαλέτω τῇ ΒΖ κατὰ τὸ Θ, ἡ δὲ ΑΛ τῷ ΒΜΖ ἡμικυκλίῳ κατὰ τὸ Μ, ἐπεζεύχθωσαν δὲ καὶ αἱ ΚΔ, ΜΙ, ΜΘ.

let a right semicylinder be imagined on the semicircle ABΔ, and on AΔ a semicircle orthogonal lying in the parallelogram of the semicylinder. When this semicircle is rotated from Δ to B, while the extremity A of the diameter remains unmoved, it will cut the cylindrical surface during its rotation and will describe a certain line on it. And again, if, while AΔ remains unmoved, the triangle AΠΔ is rotated in the direction opposite to that of the semicircle, it will generate the surface of a cone with the line AΠ, which, as it is rotated, will meet the line on the cylinder in a point. At the same time, the point B will also describe a semicircle on the surface of the cone. Let ΔKA be the position of the moving semicircle where the lines meet, and let ΔΛA be the position of the triangle that is being rotated in the opposite direction, and let K be the point of intersection that is described above. Let BMZ be the semicircle described by B, and let BZ be the line of intersection between this and the circle BΔZA, and let a perpendicular be drawn from K to the plane of the semicircle BΔA. It will fall on the circumference of the circle, because the cylinder is a right cylinder. Let it fall and let it be KI, and let the line that connected I to A meet the line BZ in Θ and the line AΛ meet the semicircle BMZ in M. Let KΔ, MI, and MΘ be connected.

EARLY GREEK PHILOSOPHY IV

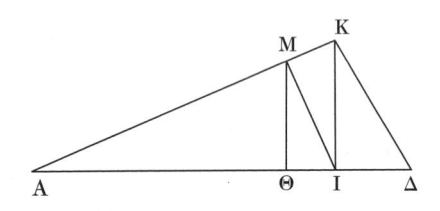

AΔ:AK :: AK:AI : : AI:AM

ἐπεὶ οὖν ἑκάτερον τῶν ΔΚΑ, ΒΜΖ ἡμικυκλίων ὀρθόν ἐστι πρὸς τὸ ὑποκείμενον ἐπίπεδον, καὶ ἡ κοινὴ ἄρα αὐτῶν τομὴ ἡ ΜΘ πρὸς ὀρθάς ἐστι τῷ τοῦ κύκλου ἐπιπέδῳ· ὥστε καὶ πρὸς τὴν ΒΖ ὀρθή ἐστιν ἡ ΜΘ. τὸ ἄρα ὑπὸ τῶν ΒΘΖ, τουτέστι τὸ ὑπὸ ΑΘΙ, ἴσον ἐστὶ τῷ ἀπὸ ΜΘ· ὅμοιον ἄρα ἐστὶ τὸ ΑΜΙ τρίγωνον ἑκατέρῳ τῶν ΜΙΘ, ΜΑΘ, καὶ ὀρθὴ ἡ ὑπὸ ΙΜΑ. ἔστιν δὲ καὶ ἡ ὑπὸ ΔΚΑ ὀρθή· παράλληλοι ἄρα εἰσὶν αἱ ΚΔ, ΜΙ, καὶ ἔσται ἀνάλογον, ὡς ἡ ΔΑ πρὸς ΑΚ, τουτέστιν ἡ ΚΑ πρὸς ΑΙ, οὕτως ἡ ΙΑ πρὸς ΑΜ, διὰ τὴν ὁμοιότητα τῶν τριγώνων. τέσσαρες ἄρα αἱ ΔΑ, ΑΚ, ΑΙ, ΑΜ ἑξῆς ἀνάλογόν εἰσιν. καί ἐστιν ἡ ΑΜ ἴση τῇ Γ, ἐπεὶ καὶ τῇ ΑΒ·

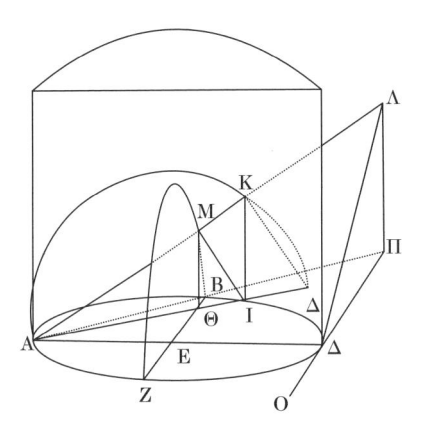

Since, then, each of the semicircles ΔKA and BMZ is orthogonal to the underlying plane, their line of intersection MΘ is also orthogonal to the plane of the circle, so that MΘ is also orthogonal to BZ. Therefore the rectangle contained by BΘZ, that is, the rectangle contained by AΘI, is equal to the square on MΘ. The triangle AMI therefore is similar to each of the triangles MIΘ and MAΘ. And the angle IMA is right. But the angle ΔKA is also right. Therefore the lines KΔ and MI are parallel and there will be a proportion: as ΔA is to AK, that is, as KA is to AI, so is IA to AM, in virtue of the similarity of the triangles. The four lines ΔA, AK, AI, AM are therefore in continued proportion. And AM is equal to Γ, since it is also equal to AB. There-

EARLY GREEK PHILOSOPHY IV

δύο ἄρα δοθεισῶν τῶν ΑΔ, Γ δύο μέσαι ἀνάλογον ηὕρηνται αἱ ΑΚ, ΑΙ.

Mathematics Applicable to Music (D13)

D13 (< A19) Boeth. *Mus.* 3.11

demonstratio Archytae superparticularem in aequa dividi non posse [. . .].

sit, inquit, superparticularis proportio A B, sumo in eadem proportione minimos C DE. quoniam igitur sunt minimi in eadem proportione C DE et sunt superparticulares, DE numerus[1] C numerum parte una sua eiusque transcendit. sit haec D. dico quoniam D non erit numerus, sed unitas. si enim est numerus D et pars est eius, qui est DE, metitur D numerus DE numerum; quocirca et E numerum metietur, quo fit, ut C quoque metiatur. utrumque igitur C et DE numeros metietur D numerus, quod est inpossibile. qui enim sunt minimi in eadem proportione quibuslibet aliis numeris, hi primi ad se invicem sunt.[2] unitas igitur est D. igitur DE numerus C numerum unitate transcendit. quocirca nullus incidit medius numerus, qui eam propor-

[1] superparticulares. DE numerus igitur *coni. Huffman*
[2] *post* sunt *hab. mss.* et solam differentiam retinent unitatem: *del. Tannery*

ARCHYTAS

fore for the two given lines AΔ and Γ, two mean proportionals AK and AI, have been found.[1]

[1] For a diagram of this solution (on which our own diagram is based), see Huffman p. 356. The specialists disagree about whether or not it goes back to Archytas. Huffman 2005 accepts this testimonium; for the opposite view, see Brisson 2013.

Mathematics Applicable to Music (D13)

D13 (< A19) Boethius, *Fundamentals of Music*

Archytas' demonstration that a superparticular [i.e. epimoric] ratio cannot be divided into equal parts [. . .]:

> Let there be, he says, an epimoric ratio A:B. I take C:D+E as the smallest numbers that are in the same ratio. Therefore, since C:D+E are the smallest numbers that are in the same ratio and since the ratio is epimoric, the number D+E exceeds the number C by one of its own parts and by a part of C. Let this be D. I say that D will not be a number but a unit. For if D is a number and it is a part of D+E, the number D measures the number D+E, so that it will also measure the number E, and from this it follows that it also measures C. Therefore, the number D will measure both the numbers C and D+E—which is impossible. For those numbers that are the smallest ones in the same ratio relatively to any other number at all are prime to one another. Therefore D is a unit. Therefore the number D+E exceeds the number C by a unit. From this it follows that no number falls in the middle in such a way as

tionem aequaliter scindat. quo fit, ut nec inter eos, qui eandem his proportionem tenent, medius possit numerus collocari, qui eandem proportionem aequaliter scindat.

Music (D14–D19)
The Production of Sounds (D14–D15)

D14 (B1) Porph. *In Ptol.* 1.3, pp. 55.32–57.27; cf. Nicom. *Intr. arith.* 1.3.3, p. 6 (καλῶς μοι . . . ἀδελφεά)

ὅτι μὲν τοίνυν ἡ τῆς τοιαύτης αἰτίας ἀπόδοσις παλαιά τις ἦν καὶ παρὰ τοῖς Πυθαγορείοις κυκλουμένη, καὶ διὰ τῶν ἔμπροσθεν μὲν ἀπεδείξαμεν. παρακείσθω δὲ καὶ νῦν τὰ Ἀρχύτα τοῦ Πυθαγορείου, οὗ μάλιστα καὶ γνήσια λέγεται εἶναι τὰ συγγράμματα. λέγει δ' ἐν τῷ Περὶ μαθηματικῆς εὐθὺς ἐναρχόμενος τοῦ λόγου τάδε·

καλῶς μοι δοκοῦντι τοὶ περὶ τὰ μαθήματα διαγνῶναι[1] καὶ οὐθὲν ἄτοπον ὀρθῶς αὐτοὺς οἷά ἐντι[2] περὶ ἑκάστου θεωρεῖν.[3] περὶ γὰρ τᾶς τῶν ὅλων φύσιος καλῶς διαγνόντες ἔμελλον καὶ περὶ τῶν κατὰ μέρος, οἷά ἐντι, ὄψεσθαι.[4] περί τε δὴ τᾶς τῶν ἄστρων ταχυτᾶτος καὶ ἐπιτολᾶν καὶ δυσίων παρέδωκαν ἁμὶν διάγνωσιν καὶ

---

[1] διαγνῶναι Porph.: διαγνώμεναι Nic.: διαγνώμεν Huffman
[2] οἷά ἐντι Nic.: om. Porph.   [3] θεωρεῖν] φρονέειν Nic.

ARCHYTAS

to divide the ratio into equal parts. From this it follows that in the case of those numbers that are in the same ratio as these, a number does not fall in the middle in such a way as to divide the ratio into equal parts.

Music (D14–D19)
The Production of Sounds (D14–D15)

D14 (B1) Porphyry, *Commentary on Ptolemy's* Harmonics

I showed earlier that the explanation of this cause [scil. the one given by Ptolemy for the production of high-pitched and low-pitched sounds] was ancient and was in circulation among the Pythagoreans. But now let us give a citation from Archytas the Pythagorean too, whose writings are said most of all to also be authentic. He says the following in his *On Mathematics*, right at the beginning of the text:

> **Those who concern themselves with the mathematical sciences seem to me to make distinctions well, and it is not surprising that they think correctly, about each thing, how they are. For, since they make distinctions well about the nature of the whole, they ought also to see well, about particular things, how they are. And certainly, about the speed of the heavenly bodies, their risings and settings, they have transmitted to us a clear distinction,**

---

[4] ὄψεσθαι Porph.: καλῶς ὀφεῖσθαι Nic.

περὶ γαμετρίας καὶ ἀριθμῶν καὶ οὐχ ἥκιστα περὶ μουσικᾶς.[5] ταῦτα γὰρ τὰ μαθήματα δοκοῦντι ἦμεν[6] ἀδελφεά.[7]

πρᾶτον μὲν οὖν ἐσκέψαντο ὅτι οὐ δυνατόν ἐστιν ἦμεν ψόφον μὴ γενηθείσας πλαγᾶς τινων ποτ' ἄλλαλα. πλαγὰν δ' ἔφαν γίνεσθαι, ὅκκα τὰ φερόμενα ἀπαντιάξαντα[8] ἀλλάλοις συμπέτῃ. τὰ μὲν οὖν ἀντίαν φορὰν φερόμενα ἀπαντιάζοντα αὐτὰ αὑτοῖς συγχαλᾶντα, ⟨τὰ⟩[9] δ' ὁμοίως φερόμενα, μὴ ἴσῳ δὲ τάχει, περικαταλαμβανόμενα παρὰ[10] τῶν ἐπιφερομένων τυπτόμενα ποιεῖν ψόφον.

πολλοὺς μὲν δὴ αὐτῶν οὐκ εἶναι[11] ἁμῶν τᾷ φύσει οἵους τε γινώσκεσθαι, τοὺς μὲν διὰ τὰν ἀσθένειαν τᾶς πλαγᾶς, τοὺς δὲ διὰ τὸ μᾶκος τᾶς ἀφ' ἁμῶν ἀποστάσιος, τινὰς δὲ καὶ διὰ τὰν ὑπερβολὰν τοῦ μεγέθεος. οὐ γὰρ παραδύεσθαι ἐς τὰν ἀκοὰν ἁμῖν τὼς μεγάλως τῶν ψόφων, ὥσπερ οὐδ' ἐς[12] τὰ σύστομα τῶν τευχέων, ὅκκα πολύ τις ἐκχέῃ, οὐδὲν ἐκχεῖται. τὰ

[5] περὶ τε δὴ ... μουσικᾶς] περί τε δὴ τὰς γεωμετρικᾶς καὶ ἀριθμητικᾶς καὶ σφαιρικᾶς παρέδωκαν ἄμμιν σαφῆ διάγνωσιν, οὐχ ἥκιστα δὲ καὶ περὶ μουσικᾶς Nic.   [6] εἶμεν g
[7] post ἀδελφεά hab. περὶ γὰρ ἀδελφεὰ τὰ τῶ ὄντος πρώτιστα δύο εἴδεα τὰν ἀναστροφὰν ἔχει Nic.: om. Porph.   [8] ἀπαντιάξαντα T² in marg.: ἄπαντ' ἄξαντα mss.   [9] ⟨τὰ⟩ Diels   [10] περί mss., corr. Stephanus   [11] ἔστιν mss., corr. Stephanus   [12] οὐδ' ἐς Blass: οὐδέ mss.

ARCHYTAS

and so too about geometry and numbers, and especially about music. For these sciences seem to be sisters.[1]

First then they observed that it is not possible for a sound to be produced unless there is a striking of some things against each other. And they said that a striking takes place when things in motion encounter one another and collide. Things that move in opposite directions produce a sound as they slow each other down when they meet, and those that move in the same direction, but not at the same speed, when they are overtaken and struck by the ones rushing upon them.

Certainly, many of these [i.e. sounds] cannot be perceived by our nature, some because of the weakness of the striking, others because of the distance separating them from us, some also because of their excessive magnitude. For those sounds that are great do not enter into our ear, just as nothing can be poured into the mouth of a vase, if someone pours out a lot. Among the things that strike sensation, those

---

[1] The version transmitted by Nicomachus continues as follows: "for they revolve around the first two forms of what exists [i.e. quantity (*plêthos*) and magnitude (*megethos*)], which are sisters." This phrase is generally considered a gloss, but Barker (*Greek Musical Writings*, vol. 2, p. 40, n. 40) thinks that it might go back to Archytas.

μὲν οὖν ποτιπίπτοντα ποτὶ τὰν αἴσθασιν, ἃ μὲν ἀπὸ τᾶν πλαγᾶν ταχὺ παραγίνεται καὶ ⟨ἰσχυρῶς⟩[13] ὀξέα φαίνεται· τὰ δὲ βραδέως καὶ ἀσθενῶς, βαρέα δοκοῦντι ἦμεν. αἰ γάρ τις ῥάβδον λαβὼν κινοῖ νωθρῶς τε καὶ ἀσθενέως, τᾷ πλαγᾷ βαρὺν ποιήσει τὸν ψόφον· αἰ δέ κα ταχύ τε καὶ ἰσχυρῶς, ὀξύν.

οὐ μόνον δέ κα τούτῳ[14] γνοίημεν, ἀλλὰ καὶ ὅκκα ἄμμες ἢ λέγοντες ἢ ἀείδοντες χρῄζομές τι[15] μέγα φθέγξασθαι καὶ ὀξύ, σφοδρῷ τῷ πνεύματι φθεγγόμενοι. ἔτι δὲ καὶ[16] τοῦτο συμβαίνει ὥσπερ ἐπὶ βελῶν· τὰ μὲν ἰσχυρῶς ἀφιέμενα πρόσω φέρεται, τὰ δ᾽ ἀσθενῶς ἐγγύς. τοῖς γὰρ ἰσχυρῶς φερομένοις μᾶλλον ὑπακούει ὁ ἀήρ, τοῖς δ᾽ ἀσθενέως ἧσσον. τωὐτὸ[17] δὲ καὶ ταῖς φωναῖς συμβήσεται· τᾷ μὲν ὑπὸ τῶ ἰσχυρῶ τῶ πνεύματος φερομένᾳ μεγάλᾳ τε ἦμεν καὶ ὀξέᾳ, τᾷ δ᾽ ὑπ᾽ ἀσθενέος μικρᾷ τε καὶ βαρέᾳ.

ἀλλὰ μὰν καὶ τούτῳ γά κα ἴδοιμες[18] ἰσχυροτάτῳ[19] σαμείῳ, ὅτι τῶ αὐτῶ φθεγξαμένω μέγα μὲν πόρσωθέν κ᾽ ἀκούσαιμες· μικκὸν δ᾽ οὐδ᾽ ἐγγύθεν. ἀλλὰ μὰν καὶ ἕν γα τοῖς αὐλοῖς τὸ ἐκ τῶ στόματος φερόμενον πνεῦμα ἐς[20] μὲν

---

[13] ⟨ἰσχυρῶς⟩ Blass [14] κα τούτῳ Blass: κατὰ τοῦτο mss.: τούτῳ ⟨τοῦτο⟩ Düring [15] τι Blass: εἰ mss. [16] φθεγγόμενοι. ἔτι δέ καὶ] φθεγγόμεθα· αἴ τι δέ ⟨κα μικκὸν καὶ βαρύ, ἀσθενεῖ.⟩ καὶ Düring cum Blass: lac. indic. Diels

that are produced quickly as the result of strikings manifest themselves as high-pitched, while those [scil. that are produced] **slowly and weakly seem to be low-pitched. For if someone takes a stick and moves it sluggishly and weakly, it will produce a low-pitched sound by striking; but if** [scil. one does this] **quickly and strongly, it will be high-pitched.**

And it is not only in this way that we can know this, but also whenever, speaking or singing, we must utter something loud and high-pitched, we utter it with a very strong breath. Furthermore, this happens as it does in the case of missiles: those that are hurled strongly land far, while those weakly, near. For the air yields more to those that move strongly, and less to those that do so weakly. The same thing will happen for the sounds of the voice: the one that is moved by a strong breath is loud and high-pitched, the one by a weak breath is soft and low-pitched.

What is more, we can also see this by the following very strong sign: the same thing, when it is uttered loudly, we hear from afar; but when softly, not even from nearby. What is more, in the case of *auloi* **too, the breath that moves from the mouth to the holes near the**

---

[17] τοῦτο mss., corr. Blass [18] κατίδοιμες mss., corr. Blass
[19] ἰσχυροτάτῳ Blass: ἰσχυρῷ τόπῳ mss. [20] ὡς mss., corr. Wallis

τὰ ἐγγὺς τῷ στόματος τρυπήματα ἐμπῖπτον
διὰ τὰν ἰσχὺν τὰν σφοδρὰν ὀξύτερον ἆχον
ἀφίησιν, ἐς δὲ τὰ πόρσω βαρύτερον, ὥστε
δῆλον ὅτι ἁ ταχεῖα κίνασις ὀξὺν ποιεῖ, ἁ δὲ
βραδεῖα βαρὺν τὸν ἆχον.

ἀλλὰ μὰν καὶ τοῖς ῥόμβοις τοῖς ἐν ταῖς
τελεταῖς κινουμένοις τὸ αὐτὸ συμβαίνει·
ἡσυχᾷ μὲν κινούμενοι βαρὺν ἀφίεντι ἆχον,
ἰσχυρῶς δ' ὀξύν.

ἀλλὰ μὰν καὶ ὅ γα[21] κάλαμος, αἴ κά τις[22]
αὐτῷ τὸ κάτω μέρος ἀποφράξας ἐμφυσῇ, ἀφή-
σει ⟨βαρέαν⟩[23] τινὰ ἁμῖν φωνάν· αἰ δέ κα ἐς
τὸ ἥμισυ ἢ ὁπόστον[24] μέρος αὐτῷ, ὀξὺ φθεγ-
ξεῖται. τὸ γὰρ αὐτὸ πνεῦμα διὰ μὲν τῷ μακρῷ
τόπῳ ἀσθενὲς ἐκφέρεται,[25] διὰ δὲ τῷ μείονος
σφοδρόν.

εἰπὼν δὲ καὶ ἄλλα περὶ τοῦ διαστηματικὴν εἶναι τὴν
τῆς φωνῆς κίνησιν συγκεφαλαιοῦται τὸν λόγον ὡς

ὅτι μὲν δὴ τοὶ ὀξεῖς φθόγγοι τάχιον κινέονται,
οἱ δὲ βαρεῖς βράδιον, φανερὸν ἁμῖν ἐκ πολλῶν γέγονεν.

[21] ὅ γα V: ὅσα T: ὅτου ἁ cett. [22] αἴ κά τις mG: ἕκατις cett. [23] ⟨βαρέαν⟩ Mullach [24] ὁπόστον ⟨ὢν⟩ Blass [25] ἐκφέρεται M: φέρεται cett.

> mouth makes a more high-pitched sound when it strikes because of its great force; but when [scil. it moves] to those further away, a more low-pitched one. So that it is clear that a quick motion produces a high-pitched sound, and a slow one a low-pitched one.
>
> What is more, the same thing happens with *rhomboi*[2] that are whirled around in the mystery initiations: when they are moved gently they emit a low-pitched sound, when strongly a high-pitched one.
>
> What is more, a reed too, if one blocks its lower part and blows into it, will emit for us a ⟨low-pitched⟩ sound; but if it is at the middle or any other place, it will emit a high-pitched one. For the same breath moves weakly when it traverses a long place, and forcefully when it is a smaller one.

After he has said other things too about the fact that the motion of the voice is a function of intervals, he summarizes his argument as follows:

> Thus it has become evident to us from many things that high-pitched sounds move more quickly, and low-pitched ones more slowly.

[2] Flat pieces of wood or metal fixed to a string and whirled around.

D15 (B2) Porph. *In Ptol.* 1.5, p. 93.5–17

Ἀρχύτας δὲ περὶ τῶν μεσοτήτων λέγων γράφει ταῦτα.

μέσαι δ' ἐντι τρῖς[1] τᾷ μουσικᾷ. μία μὲν ἀριθμητικά, δευτέρα δ' ἁ γεωμετρικά, τρίτα δ' ὑπεναντία, ἃν καλέοντι ἁρμονικάν.[2] ἀριθμητικὰ μέν, ὅκκα ἔωντι τρεῖς ὅροι κατὰ τὰν τοίαν[3] ὑπεροχὰν ἀνάλογον, ᾧ[4] πρᾶτος δευτέρου ὑπερέχει, τούτῳ[5] δεύτερος τρίτου ὑπερέχει. καὶ ἐν ταύτᾳ ⟨τᾷ⟩[6] ἀναλογίᾳ συμπίπτει εἶμεν τὸ τῶν μειζόνων ὅρων διάστημα μεῖον, τὸ δὲ τῶν μειόνων μεῖζον. ἁ[7] γεωμετρικὰ δὲ ὅκκα ἔωντι οἷος[8] ὁ πρᾶτος ποτὶ τὸν δεύτερον, καὶ ὁ δεύτερος ποτὶ τὸν τρίτον. τούτων δ' οἱ μείζονες ἴσον ποιοῦνται τὸ διάστημα καὶ οἱ μείους. ἁ δ' ὑπεναντία, ἃν καλοῦμεν ἁρμονικάν, ὅκκα ἔωντι ⟨τοῖοι, ᾧ⟩[9] ὁ πρᾶτος ὅρος ὑπερέχει τοῦ δευτέρου αὐταύτου[10] μέρει, τούτῳ ὁ μέσος τοῦ

---

[1] ἐντι τρῖς Wallis: ἐν τισι τρισί mss.
[2] ἃν ... ἁρμονικάν secl. Huffman
[3] τὰν τοίαν Blass: ταύτωιαν G: τὰν τωίαν p V: τὰν τῶ A
[4] ὧν mss., corr. Blass
[5] τούτου mss., corr. Blass
[6] ἐν ταύτᾳ ⟨τᾷ⟩ Mullach: ἐνταῦθα mss.
[7] τά mss.: corr. Blass
[8] οἷος Blass: οἷς GV: εἷς p
[9] ⟨τοῖοι ᾧ⟩ Diels
[10] αὐταύτου Blass: ἀνταύτου g V: αὐτὰν τοῦ A

ARCHYTAS

D15 (B2) Porphyry, *Commentary on Ptolemy's* Harmonics

Archytas, speaking about the means, writes the following [scil. in his *On Music,* cf. 92.29]:

> There are three means in music: the first is the arithmetic mean, the second is the geometric one, the third is the subcontrary one, which is called harmonic. It is arithmetic when three terms are in proportion according to the following kind of excess: that by which the first exceeds the second is the same as that by which the second exceeds the third. And in this proportion it turns out that the interval between the larger terms is smaller, while the one between the smaller terms is larger.[1] It is geometric when what the first term is to the second one, the second one is to the third one. Among these, the larger terms have an interval that is equal to the smaller ones.[2] The subcontrary one, which we call harmonic, is when they are ⟨such⟩ that, by that part of itself ⟨by which⟩ the first term exceeds the second one, by this part of the third term the middle term

---

[1] An example of an arithmetic proportion is the one between the numbers 12, 9, and 6. The arithmetic mean is 9 (arithmetic because $12 - 9 = 9 - 6$). The ratio 9/6 is equal to 3/2, which is that of the fifth (the larger interval), the ratio 12/9 is equal to 4/3, which is that of the fourth (the smaller interval). [2] An example of a geometric proportion is the one between the numbers 24, 12, and 6: $24/12 = 12/6$. The geometric mean is 12. In both cases the ration is equal to 2/1, which is that of the octave.

247

τρίτου ὑπερέχει τοῦ τρίτου μέρει. γίνεται δ' ἐν ταύτᾳ[11] τᾷ ἀναλογίᾳ τὸ τῶν μειζόνων ὅρων διάστημα μεῖζον, τὸ δὲ τῶν μειόνων μεῖον.

[11] ἐνταῦθα p

Concords and Tetrachord (D16–D17)

D16 (A18) Porph. *In Ptol.* 1.6, p. 104.12–13

ἔλεγον δ' οἱ περὶ τὸν Ἀρχύταν ἑνὸς φθόγγου γίνεσθαι κατὰ τὰς συμφωνίας τὴν ἀντίληψιν τῇ ἀκοῇ.

D17 (A16) Ptol. *Harm.* 1.13–14, pp. 30.3–31.17

περὶ τῆς κατὰ Ἀρχύταν τῶν γενῶν καὶ τῶν τετραχόρδων διαιρέσεως.

Ἀρχύτας δὲ ὁ Ταραντῖνος μάλιστα τῶν Πυθαγορείων ἐπιμεληθεὶς μουσικῆς πειρᾶται μὲν τὸ κατὰ τὸν λόγον ἀκόλουθον διασῴζειν οὐκ ἐν ταῖς συμφωνίαις μόνον ἀλλὰ καὶ ταῖς τῶν τετραχόρδων διαιρέσεσιν, ὡς οἰκείου τῇ φύσει τῶν ἐμμελῶν ὄντος τοῦ συμμέτρου τῶν ὑπεροχῶν [. . .] τρία μὲν τοίνυν οὗτος ὑφίσταται[1] γένη, τό τε ἐναρμόνιον καὶ τὸ χρωματικὸν καὶ τὸ διατονικόν· ἑκάστου δὲ αὐτῶν ποιεῖται τὴν

[1] ὑφίσταται (bis) MWEfg: ὑφιστᾳ W¹A: ὑφίστησι V ss. GAγρ

exceeds the third one. In this proportion it happens that the interval of the larger terms is larger, while that of the smaller terms is smaller.[3]

[3] An example of a harmonic proportion is the one between the numbers 12, 8, and 6. The harmonic mean is 8, because 12 − 8 = 4 (equal to one third of the first term, 12) and 8 − 6 = 2 (equal to one third of the last term, 6). Musically, one has the two ratios 12/8 (= 3/2), that is, again, the fifth (cf. n. 1), and 8/6 = 4/3, that is, the fourth (cf. ibid.). One also sees that if one inserts first the subcontrary (harmonic) mean and then the arithmetic mean between 12 and 6, one obtains the ratio corresponding to the tone, 9/8.

Concords and Tetrachord (D16–D17)

D16 (A18) Porphyry, *Commentary on Ptolemy's* Harmonics

Archytas and his followers used to say that what hearing perceives in the case of concords is a single sound.

D17 (A16) Ptolemy, *Harmonics* [On the classification of the genera and of the tetrachords according to Archytas]

Archytas of Tarentum, who of all the Pythagoreans studied music the most, tries to preserve what is in conformity with reason, not only in the concords, but also in the division of the tetrachord, on the idea that commensurability of excesses is by nature proper to what is harmonious [i.e. the intervals] [. . .]. So he establishes three genera: enharmonic, chromatic, and diatonic. He makes the division of

διαίρεσιν οὕτως· τὸν μὲν γὰρ ἑπόμενον λόγον
ἐπὶ τῶν τριῶν γενῶν τὸν αὐτὸν ὑφίσταται[1] καὶ
ἐπὶ κζ', τὸν δὲ μέσον ἐπὶ μὲν τοῦ ἐναρμονίου ἐπὶ
λε', ἐπὶ δὲ τοῦ διατονικοῦ ἐπὶ ζ', ὥστε καὶ τὸν
ἡγούμενον τοῦ μὲν ἐναρμονίου γένους συνάγε-
σθαι ἐπὶ δ', τοῦ δὲ διατονικοῦ ἐπὶ η'. τὸν δὲ ἐν
τῷ χρωματικῷ γένει δεύτερον ἀπὸ τοῦ ὀξυτάτου
φθόγγου λαμβάνει διὰ τοῦ τὴν αὐτὴν θέσιν
ἔχοντος ἐν τῷ διατονικῷ· φησὶ γὰρ λόγον ἔχειν
τὸν ἐν τῷ χρωματικῷ δεύτερον ἀπὸ τοῦ ὀξυτάτου πρὸς τὸν ὅμοιον τὸν ἐν τῷ διατονικῷ τὸν
τῶν σνϛ' πρὸς τὰ σμγ'. συνίσταται[2] δὴ τὰ
τοιαῦτα[3] τετράχορδα κατὰ τοὺς ἐκκειμένους λόγους ἐν πρώτοις ἀριθμοῖς τούτοις· ἐὰν γὰρ τοὺς
μὲν ὀξυτάτους τῶν τετραχόρδων ὑποστησώ-
μεθα, ͵αφιβ', τοὺς δὲ βαρυτάτους κατὰ τὸν
ἐπίτριτον λόγον τῶν αὐτῶν ͵βιϛ', ταῦτα μὲν
ποιήσει ἐπὶ κζ' πρὸς τὰ ͵αλμδ'· καὶ τοσούτων
ἔσονται πάλιν ἐν τοῖς τρισὶ γένεσιν οἱ δεύτεροι
ἀπὸ τῶν βαρυτάτων· τῶν δ' ἀπὸ τοῦ ὀξυτάτου
δευτέρων ὁ μὲν τοῦ ἐναρμονίου γένους ἔσται
͵αωͺ'. ταῦτα γὰρ πρὸς μὲν τὰ ͵αλμδ' ποιεῖ τὸν
ἐπὶ λε' λόγον, πρὸς δὲ τὰ ͵αφιβ' τὸν ἐπὶ δ'· ὁ δὲ
τοῦ διατονικοῦ γένους τῶν αὐτῶν ἔσται ͵αψα'·
καὶ ταῦτα γὰρ πρὸς μὲν τὰ ͵αλμδ' τὸν ἐπὶ ζ'

---

[1] ὑφίσταται (bis) MWEfg: ὑφιστᾷ W¹A: ὑφίστησι V ss.
GAγρ   [2] συνίσταται] συνίστησι ss. G

ARCHYTAS

each of them as follows: he posits that the 'following ratio [i.e. the one that corresponds to the lower interval of the tetrachord] is the same in the three genera, i.e. 28:27, but that the middle ratio [i.e. the one that corresponds to the middle interval] in the enharmonic genus is 36:35, in the diatonic genus 8:7, so that the 'leading ratio' [i.e. the one that corresponds to the higher interval] in the enharmonic genus becomes 5:4, and in the diatonic genus 9:8. In the chromatic genus he posits the note that comes second after the highest-pitched one by recurring to the note that has the same position in the diatonic genus. For he says that the note that comes second after the highest-pitched one in the chromatic genus stands in a ratio of 256:243 to the note that is similar to it in the diatonic genus. According to the ratios that I have set out, such tetrachords are constituted in the following way with regard to the lowest numbers: if we posit 1512 as the highest-pitched note in the tetrachords, and 2016 as the lowest-pitched one of the same [scil. probably tetrachords], in accordance with the epitrite ratio [i.e. 4:3], this latter number will make the ratio 28:27 in relation to 1944, and this will also be the quantity, in the three genera, of the second notes after the lowest-pitched one. As for the second notes after the highest-pitched one, the one in the enharmonic genus will be 1890. For this number gives the ratio 36:35 in relation to 1944, and the ratio 5:4 in relation to 1512. The equivalent note in the diatonic genus will be 1701, for this gives the ratio 8:7 in relation to 1944 and the ratio 9:8 in relation

---

³ τοιαῦτα τρία f ss. AV¹

EARLY GREEK PHILOSOPHY IV

ποιεῖ λόγον· πρὸς δὲ τὰ ͵αφιβ' τὸν ἐπὶ η'· ὁ δὲ τοῦ χρωματικοῦ καὶ αὐτὸς ἔσται τῶν αὐτῶν ͵αψϞβ'· ταῦτα γὰρ λόγον ἔχει πρὸς τὰ ͵αψα', ὃν τὰ σνϚ' πρὸς τὰ σμγ'.

Music and Other Sciences (D18–D19)
Music and Grammar (D18)

D18 (< A19c Huffman) Quintil. *Inst. or.* 1.10.17

[. . .] si quidem Archytas atque Evenus[1] etiam subiectam grammaticen musicae putaverunt [. . .].

[1] evenus B (. . . nus A): aristoxenus mss. plerique

Music and Physics (D19)

D19 (A19b) Ps.-Plut. *Mus.* 1147A

τὴν γὰρ τῶν ὄντων φορὰν καὶ τὴν τῶν ἀστέρων κίνησιν οἱ περὶ Πυθαγόραν καὶ Ἀρχύταν καὶ Πλάτωνα καὶ οἱ λοιποὶ τῶν ἀρχαίων φιλοσόφων οὐκ ἄνευ μουσικῆς γίγνεσθαι καὶ συνεστάναι ἔφασκον· πάντα γὰρ καθ' ἁρμονίαν ὑπὸ τοῦ θεοῦ κατεσκευάσθαι.

to 1512. The equivalent note in the chromatic genus will be 1792; for this has in relation to 1701 the ratio that 256 has in relation to 243.[1]

[1] There follows a table, not reproduced here (see Barker, *Greek Musical Writings*, vol. 2, p. 45).

See also **PYTHS. ANON. D26**

Music and Other Sciences (D18–D19)
Music and Grammar (D18)

D18 (< A19c Huffman) Quintilian, *Training in Oratory*

[. . .] if it is true that Archytas and Evenus thought that grammar was subordinated to music [. . .].

Music and Physics (D19)

D19 (≠ DK) Ps.-Plutarch, *On Music*

Pythagoras, Archytas, and Plato and the rest of the ancient philosophers frequently said that without music the motion of things and the movement of the heavenly bodies do not exist and do not come about. For they say that all things have been arranged by god in conformity with harmony.

EARLY GREEK PHILOSOPHY IV

Physics (D20–D22)
Motion (D20)

D20 (A23) Eudem. in Simpl. *In Phys.*, p. 431.12 (< Eudem. Frag. 60 Wehrli]

βέλτιον γὰρ αἴτια λέγειν ταῦτα ὥσπερ Ἀρχύτας [. . . = **PYTHS. R13**].

Cosmology (D21)

D21 (< A24) Eudem. in Simpl. *In Phys.*, p. 467.26–32

Ἀρχύτας δέ, ὥς φησιν Εὔδημος [Frag. 65 Wehrli], οὕτως ἠρώτα τὸν λόγον· ἐν τῷ ἐσχάτῳ[1] οὐρανῷ γενόμενος, πότερον ἐκτείναιμι ἂν τὴν χεῖρα ἢ τὴν ῥάβδον εἰς τὸ ἔξω, ἢ οὔ; καὶ τὸ[2] μὲν οὖν μὴ ἐκτείνειν ἄτοπον· [. . .] ἀεὶ οὖν βαδιεῖται τὸν αὐτὸν τρόπον ἐπὶ τὸ ἀεὶ λαμβανόμενον πέρας, καὶ ταὐτὸν ἐρωτήσει, καὶ εἰ ἀεὶ ἕτερον ἔσται ἐφ᾽ ὃ ἡ ῥάβδος, δῆλον ὅτι καὶ ἄπειρον.

[1] post ἐσχάτῳ hab. mss. οἷον τῷ ἀπλανεῖ quod ut glossema secl. Huffman
[2] ἢ οὔ. καὐτὸ F: ἢ οὐκ ἄν. τὸ E, corr. Diels

ARCHYTAS

Physics (D20–D22)
Motion (D20)

D20 (A23) Eudemus in Simplicius, *Commentary on Aristotle's* Physics

[Scil. instead of identifying motion with what is unequal, irregular, etc., as Plato does,] it is better to say, like Archytas, that these are its causes [. . .].

Cosmology (D21)

D21 (< A24) Eudemus in Simplicius, *Commentary on Aristotle's* Physics

As Eudemus says, Archytas asked the following question: "If I arrived at the furthest point of the heavens, could I stretch out my hand or a stick towards what was outside, or not?" Now, it would be very strange indeed not to be able to extend it. [. . .][1] Therefore each time he will go in the same way towards the limit that is chosen each time and will ask the same question, and if each time there is something else to which the stick can go, it is clear that it is an unlimited [scil. body].[2]

[1] The following sentence as well could go back to Archytas.
[2] In Archytas, the argument was surely intended to establish the existence of the void beyond the world, not that of an unlimited body.

Vision (D22)

D22 (< A25) Apul. *Apolog.* 15–16

[...] an [...] radii nostri [...] seu tantum oculis profecti sine ullo foris amminiculo, ut Archytas putat, [...] cum alicui corpori inciderunt spisso et splendido et levi, paribus angulis quibus inciderant resultent ad faciem suam reduces atque ita, quod extra tangant ac visant, id intra speculum imaginentur.

The Geometry of Animal Physiology (D23)

D23 (A23a) Ps.-Arist. *Probl.* 16.9 915a25–32

διὰ τί τὰ μόρια τῶν φυτῶν καὶ τῶν ζῴων, ὅσα μὴ ὀργανικά, πάντα περιφερῆ, τῶν μὲν φυτῶν τὸ στέλεχος καὶ οἱ πτόρθοι, τῶν δὲ ζῴων κνῆμαι, μηροί, βραχίονες, θώραξ· τρίγωνον δὲ οὐδὲ πολύγωνον οὔτε ὅλον οὔτε μόριόν ἐστιν; πότερον, ὥσπερ Ἀρχύτας ἔλεγεν, διὰ τὸ ἐν τῇ κινήσει τῇ φυσικῇ ἐνεῖναι τὴν τοῦ ἴσου ἀναλογίαν (κινεῖσθαι γὰρ ἀνάλογον πάντα), ταύτην δὲ μόνην εἰς αὑτὴν ἀνακάμπτειν, ὥστε κύκλους ποιεῖν καὶ στρογγύλα, ὅταν ἐγγένηται;

Pleasure (D24)

D24 (< A9) Cic. *Sen.* 12.39, 41

[Cato:] accipite enim, optimi adulescentes, veterem orationem Archytae Tarentini, magni in primis et praeclari

ARCHYTAS

Vision (D22)

D22 (< A25) Apuleius, *Apology*

[...] or else our [scil. visual] rays [...], only issuing forth from our eyes without any external support, as Archytas thinks, [...] are reflected at an angle equal to that of their incidence when they fall upon a body that is dense, shiny, and smooth, and then, returning towards the face from which they were emitted, they form in this way an internal image of what they touch and visit outside [...].

The Geometry of Animal Physiology (D23)

D23 (A23a) Ps.-Aristotle, *Problems*

Why are those parts of plants and animals that do not have an instrumental function all rounded (like the stem and shoots of plants, or the shanks, thighs, arms, and trunk of animals), while neither the whole nor any part [scil. of these parts] is triangular or polygonal? Is it, as Archytas said, because the proportion of equality is present in natural motion (because all things move in proportion), and this is the only one that turns back to itself, so that it produces circles and curves when it is in something?[1]

[1] For a tentative explanation of this difficult text, see Huffman, pp. 518–22.

Pleasure (D24)

D24 (< A9) Cicero, *Cato the Elder. On Old Age*

[Cato:] Listen, excellent young men, to an ancient speech of Archytas of Tarentum, an especially great and distin-

viri, quae mihi tradita est [. . .]. nullam capitaliorem pestem quam voluptatem corporis hominibus dicebat a natura datam, cuius voluptatis avidae libidines temere et ecfrenate ad potiendum incitarentur. [. . .] [41] quocirca nihil esse tam detestabile tamque pestiferum quam voluptatem, siquidem ea, cum maior esset atque longinquior, omne animi lumen exstingueret.

Appendix: Some Fragments from a (Pseudepigraphic?) Treatise on Political Theory (D25)

D25 (≠ DK) (Ps.-?) Archyt. *Leg.* in Stob.

a 4.1.135 (Frag. 1, p. 33.2–18 Thesleff)

Ἀρχύτα Πυθαγορείου ἐκ τοῦ Περὶ νόμου καὶ δικαιοσύνης.

νόμος ποτ' ἀνθρώπου ψυχάν τε καὶ βίον ὅπερ ἁρμονία ποτ' ἀκοάν τε καὶ φωνάν· ὅ τε γὰρ νό-

ARCHYTAS

guished man, which has been transmitted to me [. . .]. He used to say that no deadlier pestilence had been bestowed upon humans by nature than the pleasure of the body, since our desires, greedy for this pleasure, are spurred on to possess it rashly and without impediment. [. . .] [41] That is why there is nothing so detestable and pestilential as pleasure, since when it is too strong and lasts too long it extinguishes the whole light of the soul.[1]

[1] Huffman admits the possibility that the whole argument against bodily pleasures in Cicero might go back in the last instance to Archytas himself (see especially p. 331). Aristotle, *Nicomachean Ethics* 7.12 1152b16, also seems to preserve an echo.

Appendix: Some Fragments from a (Pseudepigraphic?) Treatise on Political Theory (D25)[1]

[1] Scholars are divided on whether this treatise is genuine or not (for most of the others that have been questioned, there is little doubt about their inauthenticity): see Huffman, pp. 599–606. The two passages that we include here as samples might also have been placed among the Pseudo-Pythagorean writings of which we provide samples (cf. **PYTHS. R53–R54**); this is why we print them here in italics.

D25 (≠ DK) (Ps.-?)Archytas, *On Law and Justice,* from Stobaeus, *Anthology*

a

From Archytas, Pythagorean, from his On Law and Justice:

Law is to a human being's soul and life what harmony (harmonia) *is to hearing and voice: for law*

μος παιδεύει μὲν τὰν ψυχάν, συνίστησι δὲ τὸν
βίον, ἅ τε ἁρμονία ἐπιστάμονα μὲν ποιεῖ τὰν
ἀκοάν, ὁμόλογον δὲ τὰν φωνάν. φαμὶ δ᾿ ἐγὼ
πᾶσαν κοινωνίαν ἐξ ἄρχοντος καὶ ἀρχομένω
συνεστάμεν καὶ τρίτον νόμων. νόμων δὲ ὁ μὲν
ἔμψυχος βασιλεύς, ὁ δὲ ἄψυχος γράμμα. πρᾶτος ὦν ὁ νόμος· τούτῳ γὰρ[1] ὁ μὲν βασιλεὺς νόμιμος, ὁ δ᾿ ἄρχων ἀκόλουθος, ὁ δ᾿ ἀρχόμενος
ἐλεύθερος, ἁ δ᾿ ὅλα κοινωνία εὐδαίμων· καὶ
τούτω[2] παραβάσει ‹ὁ›[3] μὲν βασιλεὺς τύραννος,
ὁ δ᾿ ἄρχων ἀνακόλουθος, ὁ δ᾿ ἀρχόμενος δοῦλος,
ὁ δ᾿ κοινωνία κακοδαίμων. συνείρονται μὲν γὰρ
ταὶ πράξιες ἐκ τοῦ ἄρχειν καὶ τοῦ ἄρχεσθαι καὶ
τρίτον ἐκ τοῦ κρατεῖν. τὸ μὲν οὖν ἄρχεν τῶ
κρείσσονος οἰκῆον, τὸ δ᾿ ἄρχεσθαι τῶ χερήο-
νος, τὸ δὲ κρατὲν ἀμφοτέρων· ἄρχει μὲν γὰρ τὸ
λόγον ἔχον τᾶς ψυχᾶς, ἄρχεται δὲ τὸ ἄλογον,
κρατοῦντι δὲ τῶν παθέων ἀμφότερα. γίνεται
γὰρ ἐκ τᾶς ἑκατέρων συναρμογᾶς[4] ἀρετά, αὗτα
δὲ καὶ ἀπὸ τᾶν ἁδονᾶν καὶ ἀπὸ τᾶν λυπᾶν εἰς
ἀρεμίαν καὶ ἀπάθειαν ἀπάγει τὰν ψυχάν.

[1] τούτων γὰρ mss., corr. Thesleff: τούτῳ γὰρ ‹ἐμμονᾷ› Hense   [2] τούτων mss., corr. Meineke   [3] ‹ὁ› Meineke   [4] συναρμογᾶς M: ἁρμογᾶς A

b 4.1.137 (Frag. 3, pp. 33.29–34.14 Thesleff)

ἐν ταὐτῷ.

ARCHYTAS

educates the soul and organizes life, and harmony makes hearing understandable and voice concordant (homologon). *I myself say that every community is constituted by someone who rules [i.e. a magistrate] and someone who is ruled, and thirdly by laws. Of laws, the one that is animate is a king, the one that is inanimate is what is written. What is primary, then, is the law: for by its means the king is law-abiding, he who rules [i.e. the magistrate] is in compliance, he who is ruled is free, and the whole community is fortunate; and by transgression of this the king is a tyrant, the man who rules [i.e. the magistrate] is not in compliance, the man who is ruled is a slave, and the whole community is unfortunate. For [scil. political] actions result from the conjunction of ruling, being ruled, and thirdly dominating* (kratein). *Therefore to rule is suitable for the better person, to be ruled for the worse one, and to dominate for both: for what rules is the part of the soul that has reason, what is ruled is the irrational part, but both of these conditions dominate over the affections* (pathê). *For out of the fitting together* (sunarmoga) *of both of these is produced excellence [or: virtue], and this leads the soul away from pleasures and away from pains towards tranquility and impassibility.*

b

In the same [scil. book]:

συμφέρων[1] δὲ τᾷ πολιτικᾷ κοινωνίᾳ, αἴκα μὴ μόναρχος ᾖ καὶ ἰδιωφελὴς ὁ νόμος, κοινωφελὴς δὲ καὶ διὰ πάντων διατείνων· δεῖ δὲ καὶ ποτὶ τὰν χώραν καὶ ποτὶ τὼς τόπως ἀποβλέπειν τὸν νόμον· οὔτε γὰρ γᾶ τὼς αὐτὼς καρπὼς οὔτε ψυχὰ ἀνθρώπων τὰν αὐτὰν ἀρετὰν παραδέξασθαι δύναται. διὸ τὸ δίκαιον τοὶ μὲν ἀριστοκρατικὸν τοὶ δὲ δημοκρατικὸν τοὶ δὲ ὀλιγαρχικὸν ποιοῦντι· καὶ τὸ ἀριστοκρατικὸν κατὰ τὰν ὑπεναντίαν μεσότατα· τοῖς μὲν γὰρ μέζοσι μέζονας τὼς[2] λόγως, τοῖς δὲ μείοσι μείονας διανέμει ἁ ἀναλογία αὔτα· τὸ δὲ δαμοκρατικὸν κατὰ τὰν γεωμετρικάν· ἐν γὰρ ταύτᾳ τοὶ λόγοι ἴσοι τῶν μειζόνων καὶ μειόνων μεγεθέων· τὸ δὲ ὀλιγαρχικὸν καὶ τυραννικὸν κατὰ τὰν ἀριθμητικάν· ἀντιάζει γὰρ αὔτα τᾷ ὑπεναντίᾳ· τοῖς γὰρ μείοσι μέζονας τοὺς λόγως, τοῖς δὲ μείζοσι μείονας. ταὶ μὲν ὦν ἰδέαι τᾶς διανομᾶς τοσαῦται, ταὶ δὲ εἰκόνες ἐν ταῖς πολιτείαις καὶ τοῖς οἴκοις θεωρέονται· τιμαί τε γὰρ καὶ κολάσεις καὶ ἀρχαὶ ⟨ἢ⟩[3] ἐξ ἴσω τοῖς μείζοσι καὶ μείοσι διανέμονται, ἢ ἐξ ἀνίσω ἢ τῷ ἀρετᾷ ὑπερέχεν ἢ τῷ πλούτῳ ἢ καὶ δυνάμει. τὸ μὲν ὦν ἐξ ἴσου δημοκρατικόν, τὸ δὲ ἐξ ἀνίσω ἀριστοκρατικὸν ἢ ὀλιγαρχικόν.

[1] συμφέροντα mss., corr. Halm [2] post τὼς hab. mss. δὲ, secl. Gaisford [3] ⟨ἢ⟩ Halm

ARCHYTAS

The law is beneficial for the political community if it is not monarchical and advantageous for a private person but is instead advantageous for the public and extends to everyone. And the law should have regard for the country [or: area] and for places: for neither can a [i.e. every] ground receive the same crops nor can men's soul [i.e. every one] receive the same excellence [or: virtue]. It is for this reason that some people adopt a justice that is aristocratic, some one that is democratic, and some one that is oligarchic. And the aristocratic one is in accordance with the subcontrary mean: for this proportion (analogia) *assigns greater ratios* (logoi) *to those that are greater and lesser ones to those that are lesser. The democratic one is in accordance with the geometric [scil. mean]: for in this one the ratios are equal for all the magnitudes, the greater and the lesser ones. The oligarchical and tyrannical one is in accordance with the arithmetic [scil. mean]: for this is opposed to the subcontrary [scil. mean], for [scil. it assigns] greater ratios to those that are lesser and lesser ones to those that are greater. These then are the various forms of distribution, and their manifestations are observed in polities and in households. For honors, punishments, and directive tasks are distributed ⟨either⟩ equally to the greater and the lesser, or unequally, by virtue of superiority in virtue, wealth, or else power. Thus democratic [scil. justice distributes] equally, aristocratic or oligarchic unequally.*

15. HICETAS [HIC.]

Nothing is known about Hicetas; he is generally considered to be, like Ecphantus, one of the later representatives of Pythagoreanism, dating from the end of the fifth or the beginning of the fourth century BC. Like Eurytus and Ecphantus, he is of interest for the contribution his doctrine makes to a specific point of the Pythagorean heritage. In the present case this is a point of astronomy, a crucial one to be sure, given that what is involved is nothing less than the rotation of the earth.

BIBLIOGRAPHY

See the titles listed in the General Introduction to Chapters 10–18.

OUTLINE OF THE CHAPTER

D
The Motion of Our Earth (D1)
Two Earths (D2)

HICETAS [50 DK]

D

The Motion of Our Earth (D1)

D1 (50.1) Cic. *Acad.* 2.39.123

Hicetas Syracosius, ut ait Theophrastus [Frag. 240 FHS&G] caelum solem lunam stellas supera denique omnia stare censet, neque praeter terram rem ullam in mundo moveri: quae cum circum axem se summa celeritate convertat et torqueat, eadem effici omnia quasi stante terra caelum moveretur.

Two Earths (D2)

D2 (50.2) Aët. 3.9.2 (Ps.-Plut.) [περὶ γῆς]

[. . .] Ἱκέτης ὁ Πυθαγόρειος δύο, ταύτην καὶ τὴν ἀντίχθονα.

HICETAS

D

The Motion of Our Earth (D1)

D1 (50.1) Theophrastus in Cicero, *Prior Academics*

Hicetas of Syracuse, as Theophrastus says, thinks that the heavens, the sun, the moon, the stars, in short everything on high, is at rest and that nothing in the world moves except the earth: because this turns and rotates on its axis at an extremely high speed, exactly the same effect is produced as if the heavens were moving while the earth was at rest.

Two Earths (D2)

D2 (50.2) Aëtius

[. . .] Hicetas the Pythagorean: [scil. that there are] two [scil. earths], this one and the counter-earth.

16. ECPHANTUS [ECPH.]

Nothing is known about Ecphantus, but scholars date him, like Hicetas, to the end of the fifth or the beginning of the fourth century BC. Ecphantus' interest, like Eurytus' and Hicetas', lies in his contribution to specific aspects of the Pythagorean heritage. In the present case this involves his materialistic interpretation in atomic terms (perhaps following Eurytus) of the Pythagorean monadic units, combined with a providential perspective, and an astronomical system in which the earth is in the center and rotates on its axis.

BIBLIOGRAPHY

See the titles listed in the General Introduction to Chapters 10–18.

OUTLINE OF THE CHAPTER

P

Origin (P1)

D

A General Summary (D1)
The Principles (D2)
The World (D3–D4)
The Motion of Our Earth (D5)

ECPHANTUS [51 DK]

P

Origin (P1)

P1 (< 58A.) Iambl. *VP* 267

[1]: Κροτωνιᾶται [. . .] Ἔκφαντος [. . .] [cf. **PYTH. b T30[1]**].

D

A General Summary (D1)

D1 (51.1) (Ps.-?) Hippol. *Ref.* 1.15

Ἔκφαντός τις Συρακούσιος ἔφη μὴ εἶναι ἀληθινὴν τῶν ὄντων λαβεῖν γνῶσιν· ὁρίζει δὲ ὡς νομίζει,[1] τὰ μὲν πρῶτα ἀδιαίρετα εἶναι σώματα καὶ παραλλαγὰς αὐτῶν τρεῖς ὑπάρχειν, μέγεθος σχῆμα δύναμιν, ἐξ ὧν τὰ αἰσθητὰ γίνεσθαι. εἶναι δὲ τὸ πλῆθος αὐτῶν, ὡρισμένων κατὰ[2] τοῦτο, ἄπειρον. κινεῖσθαι δὲ τὰ σώματα

[1] ὁρίζειν . . . νομίζειν Diels: ἀλλ' ἕκαστος ὁρίζει ὡς νομίζει τὰ πράγματα L i.m.

ECPHANTUS

P

Origin (P1)

P1 (< 58A.) Iamblichus, *Life of Pythagoras*
[1] From Croton: [...] Ecphantus [...].

D

A General Summary (D1)

D1 (51.1) (Ps.-?) Hippolytus, *Refutation of All the Heresies*

A certain Ecphantus of Syracuse said that it is not possible to acquire true knowledge of the things that are, and he makes definitions just as he supposes: the first things are indivisible bodies and their variations are of three kinds, size, form, and capability, and it is out of these that visible things come to be. The number of these, defined in this way (?), is unlimited. These bodies are moved neither by

---

² ὡρισμένον καὶ mss., corr. Duncker-Schneidewin

EARLY GREEK PHILOSOPHY IV

μήτε ὑπὸ βάρους μήτε πληγῆς, ἀλλ' ὑπὸ θείας δυνάμεως, ἣν νοῦν καὶ ψυχὴν προσαγορεύει. τού<του>[3] μὲν οὖν τὸν κόσμον εἶναι ἰδέαν,[4] δι' ὃ καὶ σφαιροειδῆ ὑπὸ θείας[5] δυνάμεως γεγονέναι. τὴν δὲ γῆν μέσον κόσμου κινεῖσθαι περὶ τὸ αὑτῆς κέντρον ὡς πρὸς ἀνατολήν.

[3] τοῦ mss., corr. Roeper   [4] εἶναι ἰδέαν Roeper: εἰδέναι ἰδεῖν mss.   [5] θείας Duncker-Schneidewin: μιᾶς mss.

The Principles (D2)

D2 (51.2) Aët. 1.3.19 (Stob.) [περὶ ἀρχῶν]

Ἔκφαντος Συρακούσιος, εἷς τῶν Πυθαγορείων, πάντων τὰ ἀδιαίρετα σώματα καὶ τὸ κενόν. τὰς γὰρ Πυθαγορικὰς μονάδας οὗτος πρῶτος ἀπεφήνατο σωματικάς.

The World (D3–D4)

D3 (51.3) Aët. 2.1.2 (Stob.) [περὶ κόσμου]

[. . .] Ἔκφαντος [. . .] ἕνα τὸν κόσμον.

D4 (51.4) Aët. 2.3.3 (Stob.) [εἰ ἔμψυχος [scil. ὁ κόσμος] καὶ προνοίᾳ διοικούμενος]

Ἔκφαντος ἐκ μὲν τῶν ἀτόμων συνεστάναι τὸν κόσμον, διοικεῖσθαι δὲ ὑπὸ[1] προνοίας.

[1] ὑπὸ cod. Monac. 396: ἀπὸ mss. optimi

ECPHANTUS

their weight nor by striking, but by a divine power, which he calls mind and soul. The world has the shape of this, and that is why it came into existence as spherical by divine power. The earth, the middle of the world, moves eastwards around its own center.

The Principles (D2)

D2 (51.2) Aëtius

Ecphantus of Syracuse, one of the Pythagoreans: indivisible bodies and the void [scil. are the principles] of all things. For he is the first to have declared that the Pythagorean monads are corporeal.

The World (D3–D4)

D3 (51.3) Aëtius

[. . .] Ecphantus [. . .]: there is [scil. only] one world.

D4 (51.4) Aëtius

Ecphantus: the world is composed out of atoms, but it is administered by providence.

EARLY GREEK PHILOSOPHY IV

The Motion of Our Earth (D5)

D5 (51.5) Aët. 3.13.3 (Ps.-Plut.; Eus.) [περὶ κινήσεως γῆς]

Ἡρακλείδης ὁ Ποντικὸς καὶ Ἔκφαντος ὁ Πυθαγόρειος κινοῦσι μὲν τὴν γῆν, οὐ μήν γε μεταβατικῶς, ἀλλὰ τρεπτικῶς[1] τροχοῦ δίκην ἐνηξονισμένην,[2] ἀπὸ δυσμῶν ἐπ' ἀνατολὰς περὶ τὸ ἴδιον αὐτῆς κέντρον.

[1] ἀλλὰ τρεπτικῶς Eus. *PE* 15.58.3: om. Plut. [2] ἐνηξονισμένην Reiske: ἐνιζωνισμένην M: ἐνι- et lac. 4 litt. m: ἐνιζομένην Π: ἐν ἄξονι στρεφομένην Eus.

ECPHANTUS

The Motion of Our Earth (D5)

D5 (A5) Aëtius

Heraclides Ponticus and Ecphantus the Pythagorean make the earth move, not by displacement, but by turning like a wheel on its axis, from west to east around its own center.

17. PYTHAGOREAN DOCTRINES NOT ATTRIBUTED BY NAME
[PYTHS. ANON.]

The reasons why many Pythagorean doctrines are not attributed to a specific author have to do with the particular history of this school (see the General Introduction to Chapters 10–18), and it would most often be futile to try to assign them to an individual or to date them: in many cases, it is quite possible, or indeed probable, that they were shared more or less in common by a number of thinkers; in others, a single author or a particular orientation might well be lurking behind the name of the school without our having any way of identifying it. Nonetheless a certain number of texts, especially ones deriving from Aristotle, overlap manifestly or probably with the doctrine of Philolaus, who seems indeed to have been one of his principal sources when he explains certain aspects—the most philosophical ones—of Pythagorean doctrine. We have marked these texts by cross-references from one chapter to the other.

EARLY GREEK PHILOSOPHY IV

BIBLIOGRAPHY

See the titles listed in the General Introduction to Chapters 10–18.

OUTLINE OF THE CHAPTER

D

A Representative Version of the Pythagorean Doctrine According to the First Book of Aristotle's Metaphysics *(D1–D2)*
    General Summary (D1)
    The Principles (D2)
Definition (D3–D4)
The Explanation of Nature (D5)
The Series of Contraries (D6–D9)
    Another Version of the Doctrine of Principles (D6)
    Examples of Classification (D7–D9)
Numbers (D10–D21)
    The Nature of Numbers and Noteworthy Numbers (D10–D17)
        The One, the Even, and the Odd (D10–D14)
        The Three (D15)
        The tetraktys *(D16–D17)*
    Numbers and Things (D18–D20)
        In General (D18–D19)
        Particular Examples (D20)
    The Discovery of Irrational Magnitudes (D21)
Geometry (D22–D23)
Theory of Music (D24–D26)
Cosmology (D27–D46)

PYTHAGOREAN DOCTRINES

The Formation of the World from the Originary One (D27–D30)
Right and Left (D31–D33)
Time and Eternal Return (D34–D35)
Astronomy (D36–D46)
   The Astronomical System (D36–D41)
   Astronomical Phenomena (D42–D46)
      Disappearance of the Moon (D42)
      Comets (D43)
      The Milky Way (D44–D45)
      The Harmony of the Spheres (D46)
Optics (D47–D48)
  Mirror Images (D47)
  Color (D48)
Life (D49–D53)
  The Soul (D49–D52)
  Zoological Particularities (D53)
Moral Precepts Reported by Aristoxenus (D54)

PYTHAGOREAN DOCTRINES NOT ATTRIBUTED BY NAME
[58 DK]

D

A Representative Version of the Pythagorean Doctrine According to the First Book of Aristotle's Metaphysics *(D1–D2)*
General Summary (D1)

D1 (> 58B.4) Arist. *Metaph.* A5 985b23–986a21

ἐν δὲ τούτοις καὶ πρὸ τούτων οἱ καλούμενοι Πυθαγόρειοι τῶν μαθημάτων ἁψάμενοι πρῶτοι ταῦτα[1] προήγαγον[2] καὶ ἐντραφέντες ἐν αὐτοῖς τὰς τούτων ἀρχὰς τῶν ὄντων ἀρχὰς[3] ᾠήθησαν εἶναι πάντων. ἐπεὶ δὲ τούτων οἱ ἀριθμοὶ φύσει πρῶτοι, ἐν δὲ τούτοις τοῖς ἀριθμοῖς[4] ἐδόκουν θεωρεῖν ὁμοιώματα πολλὰ τοῖς οὖσι καὶ γιγνομένοις, μᾶλλον ἢ ἐν πυρὶ καὶ γῇ καὶ ὕδατι, ὅτι τὸ μὲν τοιονδὶ τῶν ἀριθμῶν πάθος δικαιο-

[1] ταῦτά τε A[b] [2] προῆγον E [3] τῶν ὄντων ἀρχὰς om. A[b] [4] τοῖς ἀριθμοῖς, om. A[b]

PYTHAGOREAN DOCTRINES NOT ATTRIBUTED BY NAME

D

A Representative Version of the Pythagorean Doctrine According to the First Book of Aristotle's Metaphysics *(D1–D2)*
General Summary (D1)

D1 (> 58B.4) Aristotle, *Metaphysics*

Contemporary with these authors [scil. those natural philosophers who admit a plurality of causes, Empedocles, Anaxagoras, and Democritus] and before them, the people called Pythagoreans, who were the first ones to interest themselves in the mathematical disciplines (*mathêmata*), made them advance, and since they had been nourished by them they thought that the principles of these were the principles of all the things that are. But since, in the case of these [i.e. the mathematical disciplines], the numbers are first by nature, and since they thought that they could find (*theorein*) in them many similarities with the things that are and come to be—more than in fire, earth, and water, namely that [or: since] this attribute (*pathos*) of numbers is justice, that one is soul and intellect, that one

σύνη τὸ δὲ τοιονδὶ ψυχή τε[5] καὶ νοῦς ἕτερον δὲ καιρὸς καὶ τῶν ἄλλων ὡς εἰπεῖν ἕκαστον ὁμοίως, ἔτι δὲ τῶν ἁρμονιῶν ἐν ἀριθμοῖς ὁρῶντες τὰ πάθη καὶ τοὺς λόγους· ἐπεὶ δὴ[6] τὰ μὲν ἄλλα τοῖς ἀριθμοῖς ἐφαίνοντο[7] τὴν φύσιν ἀφωμοιῶσθαι[8] πᾶσαν,[9] οἱ [986a] δ᾽ ἀριθμοὶ πάσης τῆς φύσεως πρῶτοι, τὰ τῶν ἀριθμῶν στοιχεῖα τῶν ὄντων στοιχεῖα πάντων ὑπέλαβον εἶναι, καὶ τὸν ὅλον οὐρανὸν ἁρμονίαν εἶναι καὶ ἀριθμόν· καὶ ὅσα εἶχον[10] ὁμολογούμενα ἔν[11] τε τοῖς ἀριθμοῖς καὶ ταῖς ἁρμονίαις πρὸς τὰ τοῦ οὐρανοῦ πάθη καὶ μέρη καὶ πρὸς τὴν ὅλην διακόσμησιν, ταῦτα συνάγοντες ἐφήρμοττον. κἂν εἴ τί που[12] διέλειπε, προσεγλίχοντο[13] τοῦ συνειρομένην πᾶσαν αὐτοῖς εἶναι τὴν πραγματείαν· λέγω δ᾽ οἷον, ἐπειδὴ τέλειον ἡ δεκὰς εἶναι δοκεῖ καὶ πᾶσαν περιειληφέναι τὴν τῶν ἀριθμῶν φύσιν,[14] καὶ τὰ φερόμενα κατὰ τὸν οὐρανὸν δέκα μὲν εἶναί φασιν, ὄντων δὲ ἐννέα μόνον[15] τῶν φανερῶν διὰ τοῦτο δεκάτην τὴν ἀντίχθονα ποιοῦσιν. διώρισται δὲ περὶ τούτων ἐν ἑτέροις ἡμῖν ἀκριβέστερον. ἀλλ᾽ οὗ δὴ χάριν ἐπερχόμεθα, τοῦτό ἐστιν ὅπως λάβωμεν καὶ παρὰ τούτων τίνας εἶναι τιθέασι τὰς ἀρχὰς καὶ πῶς εἰς τὰς εἰρημένας ἐμπίπτουσιν αἰτίας. φαίνονται δὴ[16] καὶ οὗτοι τὸν ἀριθμὸν νομίζοντες ἀρχὴν εἶναι καὶ ὡς ὕλην τοῖς

[5] τε om. E   [6] ἐπειδὴ mss., corr. Christ   [7] ἐφαίνετο E   [8] ἀφωμοιῶσθαι recc.: ἀφομοιῶσθαι A[b]: ἀφομοιωθῆναι E   [9] πᾶσιν E: πάντα fort. Alex., coni. Bonitz   [10] εἶχεν A[b]   [11] ἕν A[b]: δεικνύναι ἕν E   [12] που E: πολὺ A[b]   [13] προεπεγλίχοντο E   [14] εἶναι ... φύσιν E: om. A[b]

PYTHAGOREAN DOCTRINES

is the right moment, and so too for almost each of the other things—and furthermore they saw that the attributes and the ratios of harmonies reside in numbers—since then all the other things seemed to resemble numbers in their whole nature and [986a] numbers are first in all of nature, they supposed that the elements of numbers are the elements of all the things that are and that the whole of the heavens is harmony and number; and everything that they were able to put into concord, both in numbers and in harmonies, with the attributes and parts of the heavens and with the whole organization of the world, all this they collected and fitted together (*epharmottein*). And if anything at all was missing, they did their very best to make sure that their whole theory would be coherent. I mean for example that, since the decad seems to be perfect and to contain the whole nature of numbers, they also say that the bodies moving in the heavens are ten, but given that there are only nine visible ones, for this reason they add the counter-earth as the tenth. I have discussed this subject more exactly elsewhere.[1] But the reason why we have discussed this is so that we can grasp, in the case of these people too, what the principles are that they posit and how they fall under the causes we have mentioned [i.e. the four causes]. Well, it is clear that these people too [scil. like other natural philosophers] think that number is a principle, both as the matter for the things

---

[1] Probably a reference to his lost work *On the Pythagoreans* (cf. **PYTHS. R6c**).

---

15 μόνον recc.: μόνων EA^b   16 δὴ E: δὲ A^b

οὖσι καὶ ὡς πάθη τε καὶ ἕξεις, τοῦ δὲ ἀριθμοῦ στοιχεῖα τό τε[17] ἄρτιον καὶ τὸ περιττόν, τούτων δὲ τὸ μὲν πεπερασμένον τὸ δὲ ἄπειρον,[18] τὸ δ' ἓν ἐξ ἀμφοτέρων εἶναι τούτων (καὶ γὰρ ἄρτιον εἶναι καὶ περιττόν[19]), τὸν δ' ἀριθμὸν ἐκ τοῦ ἑνός, ἀριθμοὺς δέ, καθάπερ εἴρηται, τὸν ὅλον οὐρανόν [. . . = **D6**].

[17] τε om. E [18] πεπερασμένον τὸ δ' ἄπειρον E: ἄπειρον τὸ δὲ πεπερασμένον A^b [19] καὶ . . . περιττόν E: om. A^b

The Principles (D2)

D2 (< 58B.8) Arist. *Metaph.* A5 987a9–20

μέχρι μὲν οὖν τῶν Ἰταλικῶν καὶ χωρὶς ἐκείνων μορυχώτερον[1] εἰρήκασιν οἱ ἄλλοι περὶ αὐτῶν[2] [. . .]. οἱ δὲ Πυθαγόρειοι δύο μὲν τὰς ἀρχὰς κατὰ τὸν αὐτὸν εἰρήκασι τρόπον, τοσοῦτον δὲ προσεπέθεσαν ὃ καὶ ἴδιον αὐτῶν ἐστίν, ὅτι τὸ πεπερασμένον καὶ τὸ ἄπειρον[3] οὐχ ἑτέρας τινὰς ᾠήθησαν εἶναι φύσεις, οἷον πῦρ ἢ γῆν ἤ τι τοιοῦτον ἕτερον, ἀλλ' αὐτὸ τὸ ἄπειρον καὶ αὐτὸ τὸ ἓν οὐσίαν εἶναι τούτων ὧν κατηγοροῦνται, διὸ καὶ ἀριθμὸν εἶναι τὴν οὐσίαν ἁπάντων. περί τε τούτων οὖν τοῦτον ἀπεφήναντο τὸν τρόπον [. . . = **D3**].

[1] μορυχώτερον vel μοναχώτερον legit Alex. *In Metaph.* p. 46.23–24: μαλακώτερον A^b (et Alex., p. 46.5 O, et p. 46.16 mss.): μετριώτερον E (et Alex., p. 46.5 A) [2] τῶν αὐτῶν E [3] post ἄπειρον hab. A^b καὶ τὸ ἕν: om. E

PYTHAGOREAN DOCTRINES

that are and as their attributes and states, that the elements of number are the even and the odd, that of these the one is limited and the other is unlimited, and that the One comes from both of these (for it is both even and odd) [cf. **PHILOL. D9**], and number comes from the one, and that the whole of the heavens, as I have said, is numbers.

The Principles (D2)

D2 (< 58B.8) Aristotle, *Metaphysics*

Until the Italians [i.e. the Pythagoreans], then, and except for them, the others have spoken about these [i.e. the causes] rather obscurely[1] [. . .]. The Pythagoreans said in the same way [scil. as the other philosophers in question] that there are two principles, but they also added something that was peculiar to them, in that they thought that the limited and the unlimited are not certain other natures like fire, earth, or something else of this sort, but that the unlimited itself and the One itself are the substance of those things of which they are predicated; and that is why number is the substance of all things. So this is how they spoke about these matters [. . .].

[1] The meaning of the term translated here as 'rather obscurely' (*moruchôteron*) was already uncertain in antiquity. Alexander of Aphrodisias mentions another interpretation, 'not very consistent'; and the manuscript tradition presents other terms.

EARLY GREEK PHILOSOPHY IV

Definition (D3–D4)

D3 (< 58B.8) Arist. *Metaph.* A5 987a20–21

[. . . = **D2**] καὶ περὶ τοῦ τί ἐστιν ἤρξαντο μὲν λέγειν καὶ ὁρίζεσθαι [. . . = **PYTHS. R15**].

D4 (58B.4) Arist. *EN* 5.8 1132b21–23

δοκεῖ δέ τισι καὶ τὸ ἀντιπεπονθὸς εἶναι ἁπλῶς δίκαιον, ὥσπερ οἱ Πυθαγόρειοι ἔφασαν· ὡρίζοντο γὰρ ἁπλῶς τὸ δίκαιον τὸ ἀντιπεπονθὸς ἄλλῳ.[1]

[1] ἄλλῳ om. L^{b}M^b

The Explanation of Nature (D5)

D5 (< 58B.22) Arist. *Metaph.* A8 989b29–990a5

οἱ μὲν οὖν καλούμενοι Πυθαγόρειοι ταῖς μὲν ἀρχαῖς καὶ τοῖς στοιχείοις ἐκτοπωτέρως χρῶνται τῶν φυσιολόγων [. . .], διαλέγονται μέντοι καὶ πραγματεύονται περὶ φύσεως πάντα· γεννῶσί τε γὰρ τὸν οὐρανόν, [990a] καὶ περὶ τὰ τούτου μέρη καὶ τὰ πάθη καὶ τὰ ἔργα διατηροῦσι τὸ συμβαῖνον, καὶ τὰς ἀρχὰς καὶ τὰ αἴτια εἰς ταῦτα καταναλίσκουσιν, ὡς ὁμολογοῦντες τοῖς ἄλλοις φυσιολόγοις ὅτι τό γε ὂν τοῦτ' ἐστὶν ὅσον αἰσθητόν ἐστι καὶ περιείληφεν ὁ καλούμενος οὐρανός [. . . cf. **PYTHS. R18, R19**].

PYTHAGOREAN DOCTRINES

Definition (D3–D4)

D3 (< 58B.8) Aristotle, *Metaphysics*

[...] they also began to speak about what a thing is and to give definitions [...].

D4 (58B.4) Aristotle, *Nicomachean Ethics*

It seems to some people that suffering in return (*to antipeponthos*) is simply what is just, as the Pythagoreans said. For they defined justice simply as "suffering in return with someone else."

The Explanation of Nature (D5)

D5 (< 58B.22) Aristotle, *Metaphysics*

The people called Pythagoreans use principles and elements in a stranger way than the natural philosophers do [...] even though their discussion and study is entirely about nature. For they generate the heavens [990a] and they observe what happens regarding its parts and the effects it undergoes and produces. And they expend the principles and causes for [scil. explaining] these questions, which indicates that they agree with the other natural philosophers that what exists is only what is perceptible and is contained within the so-called heavens [...].

EARLY GREEK PHILOSOPHY IV

The Series of Contraries (D6–D9)
Another Version of the Doctrine of Principles (D6)

D6 (< 58B.5) Arist. *Metaph.* A5 986a22–27

[... = **D1**] ἕτεροι δὲ τῶν αὐτῶν τούτων τὰς ἀρχὰς δέκα λέγουσιν εἶναι τὰς 'κατὰ συστοιχίαν' λεγομένας, πέρας ἄπειρον, περιττὸν ἄρτιον, ἓν πλῆθος, δεξιὸν ἀριστερόν, ἄρρεν θῆλυ, ἠρεμοῦν κινούμενον, εὐθὺ καμπύλον, φῶς σκότος, ἀγαθὸν κακόν, τετράγωνον ἑτερόμηκες [... = **ALCM. D5**].

Examples of Classification (D7–D9)

D7 (58B.6) Arist. *EN* 1.4 1096b5

πιθανώτερον δ' ἐοίκασιν οἱ Πυθαγόρειοι λέγειν περὶ αὐτοῦ, τιθέντες ἐν τῇ τῶν ἀγαθῶν συστοιχίᾳ τὸ ἕν.

D8 (58B.7) Arist. *EN* 2.5 1106b29

τὸ γὰρ κακὸν τοῦ ἀπείρου, ὡς οἱ Πυθαγόρειοι εἴκαζον, τὸ δ' ἀγαθὸν τοῦ πεπερασμένου.

D9 (58B.30) Simpl. *In Cael.*, p. 386.20–23 (= Arist. Frag. 200 Rose)

τὸ γοῦν δεξιὸν καὶ ἄνω καὶ ἔμπροσθεν καὶ ἀγαθὸν ἐκάλουν, τὸ δὲ ἀριστερὸν καὶ κάτω καὶ ὄπισθεν καὶ κακὸν ἔλεγον, ὡς αὐτὸς Ἀριστοτέλης ἱστόρησεν ἐν τῇ τῶν Πυθαγορείοις ἀρεσκόντων συναγωγῇ.

PYTHAGOREAN DOCTRINES

The Series of Contraries (D6–D9)
Another Version of the Doctrine of Principles (D6)

D6 (< 58B.5) Aristotle, *Metaphysics*

[. . .] Others among these same people [i.e. the Pythagoreans] say that the principles are ten, those that are called the ones 'in series' (*sustoikhia*): limit unlimited, odd even, one multiple, right left, male female, resting moving, straight curved, light darkness, good bad, square rectangle [. . .].

Examples of Classification (D7–D9)

D7 (58B.6) Aristotle, *Nicomachean Ethics*

The Pythagoreans seem to have spoken about it [i.e. the good] more convincingly [scil. than the Platonists who posit the Forms], in placing the one in the series of good things.

D8 (58B.7) Aristotle, *Nicomachean Ethics*

For evil belongs to what is unlimited, as the Pythagoreans represented it, and good to what is limited.

D9 (58B.30) Aristotle in Simplicius, *Commentary on Aristotle's* On the Heavens

They also called the right the higher, and the front 'good,' and the left the lower, and behind 'bad,' as Aristotle has reported in his *Collection of the Opinions of the Pythagoreans*.

EARLY GREEK PHILOSOPHY IV

Numbers (D10–D21)
The Nature of Numbers and
Noteworthy Numbers (D10–D17)
The One, the Even, and the Odd (D10–D14)

D10 (58B.9) Arist. *Metaph.* M6 1080b16–18

καὶ οἱ Πυθαγόρειοι δ' ἕνα, τὸν μαθηματικόν, πλὴν οὐ κεχωρισμένον ἀλλ' ἐκ τούτου τὰς αἰσθητὰς οὐσίας συνεστάναι φασίν [. . . = **PYTHS. R23**].

D11 (< 47 A21) Arist. in Theon Sm. *Exp.*, p. 22.5–9

Ἀριστοτέλης δὲ ἐν τῷ Πυθαγορικῷ τὸ ἕν φησιν [Frag. 199 Rose] ἀμφοτέρων μετέχειν τῆς φύσεως· ἀρτίῳ μὲν γὰρ προστεθὲν περιττὸν ποιεῖ, περιττῷ δὲ ἄρτιον, ὃ οὐκ ἂν ἠδύνατο, εἰ μὴ ἀμφοῖν τοῖν φυσέοιν μετεῖχε· διὸ καὶ ἀρτιοπέριττον καλεῖσθαι τὸ ἕν.

D12

a (< 58B.28) Arist. *Phys.* 3.4 203a10–15

καὶ οἱ μὲν τὸ ἄπειρον εἶναι τὸ ἄρτιον (τοῦτο γὰρ ἐναπολαμβανόμενον καὶ ὑπὸ τοῦ περιττοῦ περαινόμενον παρέχειν τοῖς οὖσι τὴν ἀπειρίαν· σημεῖον δ' εἶναι τούτου τὸ συμβαῖνον ἐπὶ τῶν ἀριθμῶν· περιτιθεμένων γὰρ τῶν γνωμόνων περὶ τὸ ἓν καὶ χωρὶς ὁτὲ μὲν ἄλλο ἀεὶ γίγνεσθαι τὸ εἶδος, ὁτὲ δὲ ἕν).

PYTHAGOREAN DOCTRINES

Numbers (D10–D21)
The Nature of Numbers and
Noteworthy Numbers (D10–D17)
The One, the Even, and the Odd (D10–D14)

D10 (< 58B.9) Aristotle, *Metaphysics*

And the Pythagoreans say that it is the One, the mathematical number, [scil. that is the principle], except that it is not separated but that it is out of this that the perceptible substances are constituted [. . .].

D11 (< 47 A21) Aristotle in Theon of Smyrna, *Aspects of Mathematics Useful for Reading Plato*

Aristotle in his Pythagorean book says that the unit has a share in the nature of both [scil. of the even and the odd]. For when it is added to the even it makes the odd, and when to the odd the even, and this would not be possible if it did not have a share in both natures. That is why the unit is called even-odd [cf. **PHILOL. D9; ARCHY. D7**].

D12

a (< 58B.28) Aristotle, *Physics*

And they [i.e. the Pythagoreans] said that the unlimited is the even. For when this is cut off, enclosed, and limited by the odd, it provides the things that are with the element of infinity. A sign of this is what happens to numbers: the gnomons being placed around the one and separately, now the species becomes continuously different, now it is one [. . .].[1]

[1] A notoriously obscure passage.

EARLY GREEK PHILOSOPHY IV

b (≠ DK) Simpl. *In Phys.*, p. 457.12–16

καλῶς δὲ καὶ οὕτως ἐπέβαλε τῇ ἐξηγήσει ὁ Ἀλέξανδρος, ὅτι τὸ μὲν "περιτιθεμένων τῶν γνωμόνων" τὴν κατὰ τοὺς περιττοὺς ἀριθμοὺς σχηματογραφίαν ἐνδείκνυται, τὸ δὲ "καὶ χωρὶς" τὴν ἀριθμητικὴν προσθήκην χωρὶς περιθέσεως σχηματικῆς γινομένην ἐπὶ τῶν ἀρτίων.

c (58B.28) Stob. 1 *Proem.* 10 (p. 22.16–19 Wachsmuth)

τῇ μονάδι τῶν ἐφεξῆς περισσῶν γνωμόνων περιτιθεμένων ὁ γινόμενος ἀεὶ τετράγωνός ἐστι· τῶν δὲ ἀρτίων ὁμοίως περιτιθεμένων ἑτερομήκεις καὶ ἄνισοι πάντες ἀποβαίνουσιν, ἴσος δὲ ἰσάκις οὐδείς [. . . = **D14**].

D13 (< 58B.26) Arist. *Metaph.* N3 1091a23–24

τοῦ μὲν οὖν περιττοῦ γένεσιν οὔ φασιν, ὡς δηλονότι τοῦ ἀρτίου οὔσης γενέσεως.

D14 (43 Mansfeld/Primavesi) Stob. 1 *Proem.* 10 (p. 22.19–23 Wachsmuth)

[. . . = **D11c**] καὶ μὴν εἰς δύο διαιρουμένων ἴσα τοῦ μὲν περισσοῦ μονὰς ἐν μέσῳ περίεστι, τοῦ δὲ ἀρτίου κενὴ λείπεται χώρα καὶ ἀδέσποτος καὶ ἀνάριθμος, ὡς ἂν ἐνδεοῦς καὶ ἀτελοῦς ὄντος.

PYTHAGOREAN DOCTRINES

b (≠ DK) Simplicius, *Commentary on Aristotle's* Physics

Alexander has correctly remarked in his interpretation that "when the gnomons are placed around" refers to the figure that is traced for odd numbers, and "and separately" to the arithmetical addition, which in the case of even numbers is produced separately from the disposition in a figure.

c (58B.28) Stobaeus, *Anthology*

When a series of odd gnomons are arranged around the unit, then what is produced is always a square; but when even ones are arranged in the same way, they all turn out to be rectangles with sides that are unequal and different lengths, and none is an equal multiplied by an equal.

D13 (< 58B.26) Aristotle, *Metaphysics*

They [i.e. the Pythagoreans] say that there is no generation of the odd, which evidently presupposes that there is a generation of the even.

D14 (≠ DK) Stobaeus, *Anthology*

[. . .] If they are divided, in the case of the odd a unit remains in the middle, while in the case of the even an empty place remains, without owner and without number, as though it were something lacking and incomplete.

EARLY GREEK PHILOSOPHY IV

The Three (D15)

D15 (58B.17) Arist. *Cael.* 1.1 268a10–13

καθάπερ γάρ φασι καὶ οἱ Πυθαγόρειοι, τὸ πᾶν καὶ τὰ πάντα τοῖς τρισὶν ὥρισται· τελευτὴ γὰρ καὶ μέσον καὶ ἀρχὴ τὸν ἀριθμὸν ἔχει τὸν τοῦ παντός, ταῦτα δὲ τὸν τῆς τριάδος.

The tetraktys *(D16–D17)*

D16 (cf. 58B.15) Sext. Emp. *Adv. Math.* 7.94

[. . . = **D19**] ὁτὲ δὲ τὸν φυσικώτατον ὀμνύναι ὅρκον οὑτωσί,

οὐ μὰ τὸν ἁμετέρᾳ κεφαλᾷ παραδόντα τετρακτύν,
παγὰν ἀενάου φύσεως ῥιζώματ' ἔχουσαν. [. . . =
PYTH. c D10]

D17 (58B.16) Ps.-Arist. *Probl.* 15.3 910b36 [διὰ τί πάντες ἄνθρωποι, καὶ βάρβαροι καὶ Ἕλληνες, εἰς τὰ δέκα καταριθμοῦσι]

ἢ ὅτι ἐν δέκα ἀναλογίαις τέτταρες κυβικοὶ ἀριθμοὶ ἀποτελοῦνται, ἐξ ὧν φασιν ἀριθμῶν οἱ Πυθαγόρειοι τὸ πᾶν συνεστάναι;

PYTHAGOREAN DOCTRINES

The Three (D15)

D15 (58B.17) Aristotle, *On the Heavens*

For as the Pythagoreans too say, the whole and all things are defined by the three. For the end, the middle, and the beginning give the number of the whole, and what they give is that of the triad.

The tetraktys *(D16–D17)*

D16 (cf. 58B.15) Sextus Empiricus, *Against the Logicians*

[... = **D19**] at other times [scil. the Pythagoreans had the custom] of swearing this oath, which was in the greatest conformity with nature:

> No, by the man who bequeathed to our very self the tetraktys,
> The source that holds the roots of ever-flowing nature.

D17 (58B.16) Ps.-Aristotle, *Problems* [Why do all humans, both barbarians and Greeks, count by tens?]

Is it because in ten proportions (*analogiai*), four cubic numbers are produced, from which the Pythagoreans say the whole is constituted?[1]

---

[1] The first proportion is $n : n^2 = n^2 : n^3$; the second one is $n^2 : n^3 = n^3 : n^4$; and so on, until the tenth one $n^{10} : n^{11} = n^{11} : n^{12}$. In this way, among the terms $n, n^2, n^3 \ldots n^{12}$ we have four cubes: n^3, n^6, n^9, and n^{12}.

EARLY GREEK PHILOSOPHY IV

Numbers and Things (D18–D22)
In General (D18–D19)

D18 (< 58B.12) Arist. *Metaph.* A6 987b11–12

οἱ μὲν γὰρ Πυθαγόρειοι μιμήσει τὰ ὄντα φασὶν εἶναι τῶν ἀριθμῶν [. . .].

D19 (cf. 58B.15) Sext. Emp. *Adv. Math.* 7.94

καὶ τοῦτο ἐμφαίνοντες οἱ Πυθαγορικοὶ ποτὲ μὲν εἰώθασι λέγειν τὸ

– ⏑ ⏑ | – ⏑ ⏑ | – ἀριθμῷ δέ τε πάντ' ἐπέοικεν

ὁτὲ δὲ [. . . = **D16**].

Particular Examples (D20)

D20

a (< 58B.4) Arist. *Metaph.* M4 1078b21–23

οἱ δὲ Πυθαγόρειοι πρότερον περί τινων ὀλίγων, ὧν τοὺς λόγους εἰς τοὺς ἀριθμοὺς ἀνῆπτον, οἷον τί ἐστι καιρὸς ἢ τὸ δίκαιον ἢ γάμος [. . .].

b (≠ DK) Alex. *In Metaph.*, p. 75.21–28

οἷον ἣν ᾤοντο τάξιν ἔχειν τὴν δυάδα, ταύτην ἔλεγον ἔχειν τὴν τάξιν ἐν τῷ κόσμῳ τὴν δόξαν, ἐπειδὴ δυὰς δόξα ἦν αὐτοῖς. πάλιν ἣν τάξιν ἡ ἑπτάς, ταύτην ἀπ-

PYTHAGOREAN DOCTRINES

Numbers and Things (D18–D20)
In General (D18–D19)

D18 (< 58B.12) Aristotle, *Metaphysics*

The Pythagoreans say that the things that are exist by imitation of the numbers [. . .].

D19 (cf. 58B.15) Sextus Empiricus, *Against the Logicians*

To indicate this [scil. that the criterion of all things is number], the Pythagoreans had the habit of saying sometimes,

all things resemble number,

at other times [. . . = **D16**].

See also **D1**

Particular Examples (D20)

D20

a (< 58B.4) Aristotle, *Metaphysics*

The Pythagoreans earlier [scil. than Democritus] [scil. had proposed definitions] concerning a small number of things, whose definitions they attached to numbers, like what is the right moment, or what is just, or marriage [. . .].

b (≠ DK) Alexander of Aphrodisias, *Commentary on Aristotle's* Metaphysics

Thus they said that opinion had the position in the world that they thought was the position that the dyad had, since for them opinion was the dyad. So too the position that

ἐδίδοσαν ἐν τῷ κόσμῳ τῷ καιρῷ, ἐπεὶ καὶ τὸν ἑπτὰ
ἀριθμὸν[1] καιρὸν ἡγοῦντο εἶναι. μικρὸν δὲ ἄνωθεν τοῦ
καιροῦ ἢ κάτωθεν ἐποίουν, εἴ ἔτυχεν, ἀδικίαν ἢ κρίσιν, ὅτι καὶ ἡ τῶν αὐτῶν τούτοις ἀριθμῶν τάξις ἡ
αὐτὴ ἦν. γράφεται δὲ ἔν τισιν ἀντιγράφοις ἀντὶ τοῦ
ἀδικίαν 'ἀνικίαν'· ἀνικίαν δέ φασιν ὑπὸ τῶν Πυθαγορείων λέγεσθαι τὴν πεντάδα.

[1] post ἀριθμὸν hab. mss. καὶ, del. Bonitz

The Discovery of Irrational Magnitudes (D21)

D21 (63 Mansfeld/Primavesi) Schol. in Eucl. 10.1 (vol. 5.2, p. 415.7–11 Heiberg)

ἦλθον δὲ τὴν ἀρχὴν ἐπὶ τὴν τῆς συμμετρίας ζήτησιν
οἱ Πυθαγόρειοι πρῶτοι αὐτὴν ἐξευρόντες ἐκ τῆς τῶν
ἀριθμῶν κατανοήσεως. κοινοῦ γὰρ ἁπάντων ὄντος
μέτρου τῆς μονάδος καὶ ἐπὶ τῶν μεγεθῶν κοινὸν
μέτρον εὑρεῖν οὐκ ἠδυνήθησαν.

Geometry (D22–D23)

D22 (< 58B.21) Eudem. in Procl. *In Eucl.* Prop. 32, theor. 22, p. 379.2–16 (< Eudem. Frag. 136 Wehrli)

Εὔδημος δὲ ὁ Περιπατητικὸς εἰς τοὺς Πυθαγορείους
ἀναπέμπει τὴν τοῦδε τοῦ θεω-
ρήματος εὕρεσιν, ὅτι τρίγωνον
ἅπαν δυσὶν ὀρθαῖς ἴσας ἔχει
τὰς ἐντὸς γωνίας. καὶ δεικνύναι
φησὶν αὐτοὺς οὕτως τὸ προκεί-

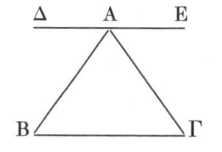

seven had they assigned in the world to the right moment, because they thought that the right moment was the number seven too. And they put a little above or below the right moment, for example, injustice or judgment, because the order of the numbers that are identical to these things was the same; in some manuscripts, 'nonvictory' (*anikia*) is found written instead of 'injustice' (*adikia*); and they say that the pentad was called nonvictory by the Pythagoreans.

The Discovery of Irrational Magnitudes (D21)

D21 (≠ DK) Scholia on Euclid's *Elements*

It was the Pythagoreans who in the beginning were the first to come upon the study of commensurability, which they discovered on the basis of their reflection on numbers. For while the monad is the common measure of all of these, they were not able to discover a common measure of magnitudes too.

See also **PYTH. b T20**

Geometry (D22–D23)

D22 (< 58B.21) Eudemus in Proclus, *Commentary on Euclid's* Elements of Geometry

Eudemus the Peripatetic attributes to the Pythagoreans the discovery of this theorem, according to which every triangle has its internal angles equal to two straight lines. And he says that they demonstrated it as follows: Let there

μενον. ἔστω τρίγωνον τὸ ΑΒΓ, καὶ ἤχθω διὰ τοῦ Α τῇ ΒΓ παράλληλος ἡ ΔΕ. ἐπεὶ οὖν παράλληλοί εἰσιν αἱ ΒΓ ΔΕ, καὶ αἱ ἐναλλὰξ ἴσαι εἰσίν, ἴση ἄρα ἡ μὲν ὑπὸ ΔΑΒ τῇ ὑπὸ ΑΒΓ, ἡ δὲ ὑπὸ ΕΑΓ τῇ ὑπὸ ΑΓΒ. κοινὴ προσκείσθω ἡ ΒΑΓ. αἱ ἄρα ὑπὸ ΔΑΒ ΒΑΓ ΓΑΕ τουτέστιν αἱ ὑπὸ ΔΑΒ ΒΑΕ, τουτέστιν αἱ δύο ὀρθαὶ ἴσαι εἰσὶ ταῖς τοῦ ΑΒΓ τριγώνου τρισὶ γωνίαις. αἱ ἄρα τρεῖς τοῦ τριγώνου δύο ὀρθαῖς εἰσιν ἴσαι.

D23 (< 58B.20) Eudem. in Procl. *In Eucl.* 1.44, p. 419.15–18 (< Eudem. Frag. 137 Wehrli)

ἔστι μὲν ἀρχαῖα, φασὶν οἱ περὶ τὸν Εὔδημον, καὶ τῆς τῶν Πυθαγορείων μούσης εὑρήματα ταῦτα, ἥ τε παραβολὴ τῶν χωρίων καὶ ἡ ὑπερβολὴ καὶ ἡ ἔλλειψις.

Theory of Music (D24–D26)

D24 (58B.18) Porph. *In Ptol. Harm.*, p. 115.4–9 (< Eudem. Frag. 142 Wehrli)

[. . .] Εὔδημος ἐν τῷ πρώτῳ τῆς Ἀριθμητικῆς ἱστορίας, λέγων περὶ τῶν Πυθαγορείων ταυτὶ κατὰ λέξιν· "ἔτι δὲ τοὺς τῶν τριῶν συμφωνιῶν λόγους τοῦ τε διὰ τεσσάρων καὶ τοῦ διὰ πέντε καὶ τοῦ διὰ πασῶν ὅτι συμβέβηκεν ἐν πρώτοις ὑπάρχειν τοῖς ἐννέα· β' γὰρ καὶ γ' καὶ δ' γίνεται ἐννέα."

PYTHAGOREAN DOCTRINES

be a triangle ABC, and let the straight line DE be drawn parallel to BC through A. Since BC and DE are parallel, the alternating angles are equal. Therefore the angle DAB is equal to the angel ABC, and the angle EAC is equal to the angle ACB. Let the angle BAC be added to both. Therefore the angles DAB, BAC, and CAE, that is, the angles DAB and BAE, that is, two straight lines, are equal to the three angles of the triangle ABC. Therefore the three angles of a triangle are equal to two straight lines.

D23 (< 58B.20) Eudemus in Proclus, *Commentary on Euclid's* Elements of Geometry

Those who follow Eudemus say that the following discoveries are ancient and belong to the Muse of the Pythagoreans: the application of areas, the hyperbola, and the ellipse.

Theory of Music (D24–D26)

D24 (58B.18) Eudemus in Porphyry, *Commentary on Ptolemy's* Harmonics

Eudemus in the first book of his *History of Arithmetic*, saying the following about the Pythagoreans, quoted exactly: "[scil. they say] moreover that the ratio of the three concords, of the fourth (*diatessarôn*), the fifth (*diapente*), and the octave (*diapasôn*), are within the nine first numbers. For two plus three plus four make nine."

D25 (≠ DK) Porph. *In Ptol. Harm.*, p. 96.21–23 (= Theophr. Frag. 717 FHS&G)

οἱ μὲν Πυθαγόρειοι τὴν μὲν διὰ τεσσάρων συμφωνίαν '**συλλαβὴν**' ἐκάλουν, τὴν δὲ διὰ πέντε '**δι' ὀξειᾶν**,' τὴν δὲ διὰ πασῶν τῷ συστήματι, ὡς καὶ Θεόφραστος ἔφη, ἔθεντο ἁρμονίαν.

D26 (> 47 A17) Porph. *In Ptol. Harm.*, p. 107.15–108.21

τῶν Πυθαγορικῶν τινες, ὡς Ἀρχύτας καὶ Δίδυμος ἱστοροῦσι, μετὰ τὸ καταστήσασθαι τοὺς λογους τῶν συμφωνιῶν συγκρίνοντες αὐτοὺς πρὸς ἀλλήλους καὶ τοὺς συμφώνους μᾶλλον ἐπιδεικνύναι βουλόμενοι τοιοῦτόν τι ἐποίουν. πρώτους λαβόντες ἀριθμοὺς, οὓς ἐκάλουν '**πυθμένας**,' τῶν τοὺς λόγους τῶν συμφωνιῶν ἀποτελούντων—τουτέστιν ἐν οἷς ἐλαχίστοις ἀριθμοῖς συμφωνίαι ἀποτελοῦνται, ὡς λόγου χάριν ἡ μὲν διὰ πασῶν ἐν πρώτοις θεωρεῖται ἀριθμοῖς τοῖς β΄ καὶ α΄· πρῶτος γὰρ διπλάσιος ὁ δύο τοῦ ἑνὸς καὶ πυθμὴν τῶν ἄλλων διπλασίων· ἡ δὲ διὰ τεσσάρων ἐν ἐπιτρίτοις τοῖς τέσσαρσι καὶ τρισί· πρῶτος γὰρ ἐπίτριτος καὶ πυθμὴν ὁ δ΄ τῶν γ΄. ὁ δὲ διὰ πέντε ἐν τρισὶ καὶ δύο· πρῶτος γὰρ ἡμιόλιος καὶ πυθμὴν ὁ γ΄ τοῦ β΄[1]—τούτους οὖν τοὺς ἀριθμοὺς ἀποδόντες ταῖς συμφωνίαις ἐσκόπουν καθ' ἕκαστον λόγον—τῶν τοὺς ὅρους περι-

[1] ὁ δὲ . . . τοῦ β΄ om. G

PYTHAGOREAN DOCTRINES

D25 (≠ DK) Theophrastus in Porphyry, *Commentary on Ptolemy's* Harmonics

The Pythagoreans called the concord of the fourth (*diatessarôn*) **'syllabê'** [literally: 'holding together'], the concord of the fifth (*diapente*) **'di oxeian'** [literally: 'by the high-pitched'], and they made the concord of the octave (*diapasôn*) the harmony (*harmonia*) of the whole, as Theophrastus too says [cf. **PHILOL. D14**].

D26 (> 47 A17) Porphyry, *Commentary on Ptolemy's* Harmonics

Certain Pythagoreans, as Archytas and Didymus report, after having established the ratios of the concords, compared them with one another and, wishing to indicate those that were more concordant, they proceeded as follows. Of the numbers that produce the ratios of the concords, they took the first ones, which they called **'foundations'** (*pythmenes*), that is, the smallest numbers productive of the concord; for example, the numbers 2 and 1 are the first ones in which the octave (*diapasôn*) is observed, since 2 of 1 is the first double and is the foundation of the other doubles; the epitritic 4 and 3 [scil. are the first ones in which] the fourth (*diatessarôn*) [scil. is observed], since 4 of 3 is the first epitritic and is the foundation [scil. of the other epitritics]; and 3 and 2 [scil. are the first ones in which] the fifth (*diapente*) [scil. is observed], since 3 of 2 is the first hemiolic and is the foundation [scil. of the other hemiolics]. Then, having assigned these numbers to the concords, they examined for each ratio of the numbers

εχόντων ἀριθμῶν ἀφελόντες ἀφ' ἑκατέρων τῶν ὅρων
ἀνὰ μονάδα—τοὺς ἀπολειπομένους ἀριθμοὺς μετὰ
τὴν ἀφαίρεσιν, οἵτινες εἶεν, οἷον τῶν β' <καὶ>[2] α', οἵ-
περ ἦσαν τῆς διὰ πασῶν, ἀφελόντες ἀνὰ μονάδα
ἐσκόπουν τὸ καταλειπόμενον· ἦν δ' ἕν· τῶν δὲ δ' καὶ
γ', οἵτινες ἦσαν τῆς διὰ τεσσάρων, ἀφελόντες ἀνὰ
μονάδα εἶχον ἐκ μὲν οὖν τῶν τεσσάρων ὑπολειπόμε-
νον τὸν τρία, ἐκ δὲ τῶν τριῶν τὸν δύο· ὥστ' ἀπὸ συν-
αμφοτέρων τῶν ὅρων μετὰ τὴν ἀφαίρεσιν τὸ ὑπολει-
πόμενον ἦν πέντε. τῶν δὲ γ' καὶ β', οἵτινες ἦσαν τῆς
διὰ πέντε, ἀφελόντες ἀνὰ μονάδα εἶχον ἐκ μὲν τῶν
τριῶν ὑπολειπόμενα δύο, ἐκ δὲ τῶν δύο ὑπολειπόμε-
νον ἕν, ὥστε τὸ συναμφότερον λειπόμενον[3] εἶναι τρία.
ἐκάλουν δὲ τὰς μὲν ἀφαιρουμένας μονάδας 'ὅμοια,' τὰ
δὲ λειπόμενα μετὰ τὴν ἀφαίρεσιν 'ἀνόμοια,' διὰ δύο
αἰτίας, ὅτι ἐξ ἀμφοῖν τῶν ὅρων ὁμοία ἡ ἀφαίρεσις
ἐγίνετο καὶ ἴση· ἴση γὰρ ἡ μονὰς τῇ μονάδι· ὧν ἀφαιρουμένων ἐξ ἀνάγκης τὰ ὑπολειπόμενα ἀνόμοια καὶ
ἄνισα. ἐὰν γὰρ ἀπ' ἀνίσων ἴσα ἀφαιρεθῇ, τὰ λοιπὰ
ἔσται ἄνισα. οἱ δὲ πολλαπλάσιοι λόγοι καὶ ἐπιμόριοι,
ἐν οἷς θεωροῦνται αἱ συμφωνίαι, ἐν ἀνίσοις ὅροις
ὑφεστήκασιν, ἀφ' ὧν ἴσων ἀφαιρουμένων τὰ λοιπὰ
πάντως ἄνισα. γίνεται οὖν τὰ ἀνόμοια τῶν συμφωνιῶν 'συμμιγέντα'· 'συμμίσγειν' δὲ λέγουσιν οἱ Πυθαγόρειοι τὸ ἕνα ἐξ ἀμφοτέρων ἀριθμὸν λαβεῖν.
ἔσται οὖν τὰ ἀνόμοια συντεθέντα καθ' ἑκάστην τῶν
συμφωνιῶν τοιαῦτα· τῆς μὲν διὰ πασῶν ἕν, τῆς δὲ διὰ
τεσσάρων πέντε, τῆς δὲ διὰ πέντε τρία. ἐφ' ὧν δ' ἂν

PYTHAGOREAN DOCTRINES

comprising (?) the two terms, having subtracted a unit from each term, the numbers remaining after the subtraction. For example, having subtracted 1 from 2 ⟨and⟩ 1, which are the numbers of the octave, they examined the remainder, which is 1; having subtracted 1 from 4 and 3, which are those of the fourth, they obtained 3 as the remainder of 4 and 2 as the remainder of 3, so that the remainder of the sum of the two terms after subtraction was 5; and having subtracted 1 from 3 and 2, which are those of the fifth, they obtained 2 as the remainder of 3 and 1 as the remainder of 2, so that the combined remainder was 3. And they called the units that were subtracted **'similars'** and the remainders resulting from the subtraction **'dissimilars,'** for two reasons, since the subtraction from both terms was similar and equal (for one unit is equal to another unit), and if these are subtracted, then of necessity the remainders are dissimilar and unequal; for if equals are subtracted from unequals, the remainders will be unequal. But multiple ratios and epimoric ratios, which are the ones in which the concords are observed, are composed of unequal terms, and if equal ones are subtracted from them, the remainders are always unequal. Therefore, among the concords, the dissimilars are produced when there is a **'mixture.' 'Performing a mixture'** is the term the Pythagoreans use for deriving one number from two. The dissimilars constructed for each of the concords are the following: for the octave, 1; for the fourth, 5; for the fifth, 3. And they say that those concords whose dis-

---

² ⟨καὶ⟩ Diels   ³ ὥστε συναμφότερον ⟨τὸ ὑπὸ⟩λειπόμενον ἦν Diels

φασι τὰ ἀνόμοια ἐλάσσονα ᾖ, ἐκεῖνα τῶν ἄλλων εἰσὶ συμφωνότερα. σύμφωνον μέν ἐστιν ἡ διὰ πασῶν, ὅτι ταύτης τὰ ἀνόμοια ἕν· μεθ' ἣν ἡ διὰ πέντε, ὅτι ταύτης τὰ ἀνόμοια τρία· τελευταία δ' ἡ διὰ τεσσάρων, ὅτι ταύτης τὰ ἀνόμοια πέντε.

Cosmology (D27–D46)
The Formation of the World from the
Originary One (D27–D30)

D27 (< 58B.9) Arist. *Metaph.* M6 1080b17–20

[. . .] ἐκ τούτου τὰς αἰσθητὰς οὐσίας συνεστάναι φασίν· τὸν γὰρ ὅλον οὐρανὸν κατασκευάζουσιν ἐξ ἀριθμῶν, πλὴν οὐ μοναδικῶν, ἀλλὰ τὰς μονάδας ὑπολαμβάνουσιν ἔχειν μέγεθος.

D28 (< 58B.26) Arist. *Metaph.* N3 1091a13–18

οἱ μὲν οὖν Πυθαγόρειοι πότερον οὐ ποιοῦσιν ἢ ποιοῦσι γένεσιν οὐδὲν δεῖ διστάζειν· φανερῶς γὰρ λέγουσιν ὡς τοῦ ἑνὸς συσταθέντος, εἴτ' ἐξ ἐπιπέδων εἴτ' ἐκ χροιᾶς εἴτ' ἐκ σπέρματος εἴτ' ἐξ ὧν ἀποροῦσιν εἰπεῖν, εὐθὺς τὸ ἔγγιστα τοῦ ἀπείρου ὅτι εἵλκετο καὶ ἐπεραίνετο ὑπὸ τοῦ πέρατος.

D29 (58B.30) Arist. *Phys.* 4.6 213b22–27

εἶναι δ' ἔφασαν καὶ οἱ Πυθαγόρειοι κενόν, καὶ ἐπεισι-

PYTHAGOREAN DOCTRINES

similars are smaller are more concordant than the others. The octave is concordant because its dissimilars are 1; then comes the fifth, because its dissimilars are 3; and last of all comes the fourth, because its dissimilars are 5.

Cosmology (D27–D46)
The Formation of the World from the
Originary One (D27–D30)

D27 (< 58B.9) Aristotle, *Metaphysics*

[. . .] it is from this [i.e. the One], they say, that the perceptible substances are constituted. For they construct the whole heavens out of numbers, except that these are not monadic, but they suppose that the monads have a magnitude.

D28 (< 58B.26) Aristotle, *Metaphysics*

There can be no disagreement about whether the Pythagoreans do or do not accept a generation. For they say clearly that once the One had been formed, whether out of planes, out of a surface (*khroia*), out of a seed, or out of something that they have difficulty in naming, the nearest part of the unlimited was immediately breathed in and limited by the limit.

D29 (58B.30) Aristotle, *Physics*

The Pythagoreans also said that there is a void, and that it

ἔναι αὐτὸ τῷ οὐρανῷ ἐκ τοῦ ἀπείρου πνεύματος[1] ὡς ἀναπνέοντι καὶ τὸ κενόν, ὃ διορίζει τὰς φύσεις, ὡς ὄντος τοῦ κενοῦ χωρισμοῦ τινὸς τῶν ἐφεξῆς καὶ[2] διορίσεως· καὶ τοῦτ' εἶναι πρῶτον ἐν τοῖς ἀριθμοῖς· τὸ γὰρ κενὸν διορίζειν τὴν φύσιν αὐτῶν.

[1] πνεύματος E²Λ: πνεῦμα Tennemann: πνεῦμά τε fort. E, Diels [2] post καὶ hab. mss. τῆς, secl. Bonitz

D30 (58B.30) Aët. 1.18.6 (Stob.) (= Arist. Frag. 201 Rose) [περὶ κενοῦ]

ἐν δὲ τῷ Περὶ τῆς Πυθαγόρου φιλοσοφίας πρώτῳ γράφει, τὸν μὲν[1] οὐρανὸν εἶναι ἕνα, ἐπεισάγεσθαι δὲ ἐκ τοῦ ἀπείρου χρόνον τε καὶ πνοὴν καὶ τὸ κενόν, ὃ διορίζει ἑκάστων τὰς χώρας ἀεί.

[1] τὸν μὲν Heeren: τὸ δὲ mss.

Right and Left (D31–D33)

D31 (58B.30) Arist. *Cael.* 2.2 284b6–8

ἐπειδὴ δέ τινές εἰσιν οἵ φασιν εἶναί τι δεξιὸν καὶ ἀριστερὸν τοῦ οὐρανοῦ, καθάπερ οἱ καλούμενοι Πυθαγόρειοι (ἐκείνων γὰρ οὗτος ὁ λόγος ἐστίν) [. . .].

PYTHAGOREAN DOCTRINES

is introduced into the heavens from the unlimited breath as though it [i.e. the heavens] were inhaling the void too, which produces a distinction in the natures of things, on the idea that the void is some kind of separation between the elements of a series and a distinction. And this happens first of all in numbers. For the void produces a distinction in their nature.

D30 (58B.30) Aristotle in Aëtius

In the first book of his *On the Philosophy of Pythagoras,* he [i.e. Aristotle] writes that the heavens are one, but that into them, coming from the unlimited, were introduced time, breath, and also the void, which always produces a distinction in [or: defines] the places of each thing.

See also **PHILOL. D15, D17**

Right and Left (D31–D33)

D31 (58B.30) Aristotle, *On the Heavens*

Since there are some people who say that there is a right and a left of the heavens, like the people called Pythagoreans (for this assertion is theirs) [. . .].

D32 (< 58B.31) Arist. *Cael.* 2.2 285a10–13

διὸ καὶ τῶν Πυθαγορείων ἄν τις θαυμάσειεν ὅτι δύο μόνας ταύτας ἀρχὰς ἔλεγον, τὸ δεξιὸν καὶ τὸ ἀριστερόν, τὰς δὲ τέτταρας παρέλιπον οὐθὲν ἧττον κυρίας οὔσας.

D33 (< 58B.31) Arist. *Cael.* 2.2 285b23–27

καὶ οἱ μὲν ἐκεῖ οἰκοῦντες ἐν τῷ ἄνω εἰσὶν ἡμισφαιρίῳ καὶ πρὸς τοῖς δεξιοῖς, ἡμεῖς δ' ἐν τῷ κάτω καὶ πρὸς τοῖς ἀριστεροῖς, ἐναντίως ἢ ὡς οἱ Πυθαγόρειοι λέγουσιν· ἐκεῖνοι γὰρ ἡμᾶς ἄνω ποιοῦσι καὶ ἐν τῷ δεξιῷ μέρει, τοὺς δ' ἐκεῖ κάτω καὶ ἐν τῷ ἀριστερῷ.

Time and Eternal Return (D34–D35)

D34 (58B.33) Arist. *Phys.* 4.10 218a33–b1

οἱ μὲν γὰρ τὴν τοῦ ὅλου κίνησιν εἶναί φασιν, οἱ δὲ τὴν σφαῖραν αὐτήν.

D35 (cf. 58B.34) Simpl. *In Phys.*, p. 732.23–24

οὕτω καὶ οἱ Πυθαγόρειοι τὰ αὐτά πως καὶ τῷ ἀριθμῷ τῷ πάλιν καὶ πάλιν ἔλεγον γίνεσθαι [. . . = **PYTHS. R27**].

PYTHAGOREAN DOCTRINES

D32 (< 58B.31) Aristotle, *On the Heavens*

And this is why one might well be astonished at the Pythagoreans, that they posited only these two principles, the right and the left, and neglected the other four [i.e. up, down, in front, behind], which are not less decisive.

D33 (< 58B.31) Aristotle, *On the Heavens*

Those who live there [scil. at the invisible pole] are located in the upper hemisphere and on the right, while we are in the lower one and on the left, contrary to what the Pythagoreans say: for they place us up high and on the right, and those who live there down below and on the left.

Time and Eternal Return (D34–D35)

D34 (58B.33) Aristotle, *Physics*

For some say that it [i.e. time] is the movement of the whole, others the sphere itself.[1]

[1] This last position is attributed to Pythagoras himself by Aëtius 1.21.1.

D35 (cf. 58B.34) Eudemus in Simplicius, *Commentary on Aristotle's* Physics

Thus the Pythagoreans said that things are also numerically identical because they happen over and over again [. . .].

EARLY GREEK PHILOSOPHY IV

Astronomy (D36–D46)
The Astronomical System (D36–D41)

D36 (< 58B.37) Arist. *Cael.* 2.13 293a20–24 et b1–4

ἐναντίως οἱ περὶ τὴν Ἰταλίαν, καλούμενοι δὲ Πυθαγόρειοι λέγουσιν· ἐπὶ μὲν γὰρ τοῦ μέσου πῦρ εἶναί φασι, τὴν δὲ γῆν, ἓν τῶν ἄστρων οὖσαν, κύκλῳ φερομένην περὶ τὸ μέσον νύκτα τε καὶ ἡμέραν ποιεῖν. ἔτι δ' ἐναντίαν ἄλλην ταύτῃ κατασκευάζουσι γῆν, ἣν 'ἀντίχθονα' ὄνομα[1] καλοῦσιν [. . . = **PYTHS. R16**]. ἔτι δ' οἵ γε Πυθαγόρειοι καὶ[2] διὰ τὸ μάλιστα προσήκειν φυλάττεσθαι τὸ κυριώτατον τοῦ παντός, τὸ δὲ μέσον εἶναι τοιοῦτον,[3] 'Διὸς φυλακὴν' ὀνομάζουσι τὸ ταύτην ἔχον τὴν χώραν πῦρ[4] [. . . = **PYTHS. R24**].

[1] ὄνομα E: om. JHE[2]   [2] καὶ] om. E   [3] post τοιοῦτον hab. mss. ὅ, secl. Allan   [4] πῦρ EH: om. J

D37 (≠ DK) Schol. (*Laur.* 87.20) ad Arist. *Cael.* 293b20; cf. 293a24 (p. 239 Rashed)

αἰνιγματωδῶς οἱ Πυθαγόρειοι 'γῆν' ἐκάλουν καὶ τὴν ἀπλανῆ ὡς παντοίων ζῴων θείων μεστήν· ἐκάλουν δὲ 'γῆν' καὶ τὴν σελήνην καὶ ⟨τὴν⟩[1] ἀντίχθονα [. . .].

[1] ⟨τὴν⟩ prop. Rashed

PYTHAGOREAN DOCTRINES

Astronomy (D36–D46)
The Astronomical System (D36–D41)

D36 (< 58B.37) Aristotle, *On the Heavens*

The people in Italy who are called Pythagoreans say the contrary [scil. to those who say that the earth rests in the middle]. For they say that it is fire that is in the middle, while the earth, which is one of the heavenly bodies, produces night and day by moving in a circle around the middle. Moreover, they posit another earth opposite to this one, which they call by the name **'counter-earth'** [. . .]. Moreover, the Pythagoreans, because it is most imperative of all to preserve what in the whole is the most important thing of all—and the middle is like that—call the fire that occupies this place **'Zeus' guardian'** [. . .].

D37 (≠ DK) Scholia to Aristotle's *On the Heavens*

The Pythagoreans enigmatically called the fixed [scil. sphere] too **'earth,'** as it is full of divine animate beings of all kinds; they also called the moon and ⟨the⟩ counter-earth **'earth.'**

D38 (58B.35) Alex. *In Metaph.*, p. 75.15–17 (= Arist. Frag. 202 Rose)

τῆς δὲ τάξεως τῆς ἐν τῷ οὐρανῷ, ἣν ἐποιοῦντο τῶν ἀριθμῶν οἱ Πυθαγόρειοι, μνημονεύει ἐν τῷ δευτέρῳ περὶ τῆς Πυθαγορικῶν δόξης.

D39 (< 12 A19) Simpl. *In Cael.*, p. 471.5–6 (< Eudem. Frag. 146 Wehrli)

[. . .] τὴν τῆς θέσεως τάξιν εἰς τοὺς Πυθαγορείους πρώτους ἀναφέρων [cf. **ANAXIMAND. R17**].

D40 Alex. *In Metaph.*

a (cf. 44 A16) pp. 38.20–39.3

καὶ τὸν ἥλιον δέ, ἐπεὶ αὐτὸς αἴτιος εἶναι τῶν καιρῶν,[1] φησί,[2] δοκεῖ, ἐνταῦθά φασιν ἱδρῦσθαι καθ' ὃ ὁ ἕβδομος ἀριθμός ἐστιν, ὃν 'καιρὸν' λέγουσιν· ἑβδόμην γὰρ αὐτὸν τάξιν ἔχειν τῶν περὶ τὸ μέσον καὶ τὴν ἑστίαν κινουμένων δέκα σωμάτων· κινεῖσθαι γὰρ μετὰ τὴν τῶν ἀπλανῶν σφαῖραν καὶ τὰς πέντε τὰς τῶν πλανήτων· μεθ' ὃν ὀγδόην τὴν σελήνην, καὶ τὴν γῆν ἐννάτην, μεθ' ἣν τὴν ἀντίχθονα [. . .].

[1] καιρῶν Asclep. *In Metaph.* p. 36.11: καρπῶν mss.
[2] φύσει Bonitz

PYTHAGOREAN DOCTRINES

D38 (58B.35) Alexander of Aphrodisias, *Commentary on Aristotle's* Metaphysics

He [i.e. Aristotle] mentions in the second book of his *On the Opinion of the Pythagoreans* the order in the heavens that the Pythagoreans attribute to the numbers.

D39 (< 12 A19) Simplicius, *Commentary on Aristotle's* On the Heavens

[. . .] while he [i.e. Eudemus] attributes to the Pythagoreans to have been the first to have indicated the order in which they [i.e. the planets] are arranged.

D40 Aristotle in Alexander of Aphrodisias, *Commentary on Aristotle's* Metaphysics

a (cf. 44 A16)

And since, he [i.e. Aristotle] says, the sun itself seems to be the cause of the seasons (*kairoi*), they [i.e. the Pythagoreans] say that it is located where the seventh number, which they call **'the right moment'** (*kairos*), is located. For it occupies the seventh position of the ten bodies that move around the middle and the hearth. For its movement is located after the sphere of the fixed stars and the five spheres of the planets. After it comes in the eighth position the moon, and the earth in the ninth, and after this the counter-earth [. . .].

b (> 58B.4) pp. 40.27–41.2

αὐτίκα γοῦν τέλειον ἀριθμὸν ἡγούμενοι τὴν δεκάδα, ὁρῶντες δὲ ἐν τοῖς φαινομένοις ἐννέα τὰς κινουμένας σφαίρας, ἑπτὰ μὲν τὰς τῶν πλανωμένων, ὀγδόην δὲ τὴν τῶν ἀπλανῶν, ἐννάτην δὲ τὴν γῆν (καὶ γὰρ καὶ ταύτην ἡγοῦντο κινεῖσθαι κύκλῳ περὶ μένουσαν τὴν ἑστίαν, ὃ πῦρ ἐστι κατ' αὐτούς), αὐτοὶ προσέθεσαν ἐν τοῖς δόγμασι καὶ τὴν ἀντίχθονά τινα, ἣν ἀντικινεῖσθαι ὑπέθεντο τῇ γῇ καὶ διὰ τοῦτο τοῖς ἐπὶ τῆς γῆς ἀόρατον εἶναι. λέγει δὲ περὶ τούτων καὶ ἐν τοῖς Περὶ οὐρανοῦ [293a23, b20] καὶ ἐν ταῖς τῶν Πυθαγορικῶν δόξαις ἀκριβέστερον [= Frag. 203 Rose].

D41 (cf. ad 58B.22, 36) Alex. *In Metaph.*, pp. 74.6–75.2

ἔλεγον γὰρ ἐν τινὶ μὲν μέρει τοῦ κόσμου δόξαν συνίστασθαι, ἐν ἄλλῳ δὲ καιρόν, πάλιν δ' αὖ ἐν ἄλλῳ ἢ κάτωθεν τούτων ἢ ἄνωθεν ἢ ἀδικίαν[1] ἢ κρίσιν ἢ μῖξιν ἢ ἄλλο τι τῶν ἐν τῷ οὐρανῷ. τῆς δὲ τούτων κατὰ τὴν τάξιν τὴν τοιαύτην συστάσεως ἀπόδειξιν ἔφερον ὅτι τούτων μὲν ἕκαστον τοῦ ἀριθμοῦ ἐστιν, ἑκάστῳ δὲ τόπῳ ἐν τῷ κόσμῳ οἰκεῖός τίς ἐστιν ἀριθμός. τῷ μὲν γὰρ μέσῳ τὸ ἕν (πρῶτον γάρ ἐστιν ἐνταῦθα), μετὰ δὲ τὸ μέσον τὰ δύο, ἃ δόξαν τε ἔλεγον καὶ τόλμαν· καὶ οὕτως ἀεὶ ἀφισταμένων ἀπὸ τοῦ μέσου πλείονα τὸν ἀριθμὸν γίγνεσθαι τῶν συνισταμένων διὰ τὸ καὶ τοὺς

[1] ἀνικίαν Asclep. *In Metaph.* p. 68.19

PYTHAGOREAN DOCTRINES

b (> 58B.4)

Thinking at first that the decad was the perfect number, but seeing in the phenomena that the moving spheres were nine, seven those of the planets, the eighth that of the fixed stars, and the ninth the earth (for they thought that this too moves in a circle around the motionless hearth, which according to them is fire), they added in their doctrines a counter-earth, of which they supposed that it moved opposite to the earth and for this reason was invisible to the people who live on the earth. He [i.e. Aristotle] speaks about these matters in greater detail in his *On the Heavens* and in his *The Doctrines of the Pythagoreans*.

D41 (cf. ad 58B.22, 36) Alexander of Aphrodisias, *Commentary on Aristotle's* Metaphysics

For they said that opinion is constituted in a certain part of the world, in another one the right moment, in another one, below or above these, injustice or judgment or mixture or one of the other things that exist in the world. And they brought as proof of the formation of these things according to this order the claim that each of them belongs to a number and that there is an appropriate number for each place in the world. For in the middle there is the one (for what is first is located there), after the middle comes the two, which they said were opinion and audacity; and in this way, moving further and further away from the middle, the things that are constituted come to be ever more in number, because the numbers out of which they

ἀριθμοὺς ἐξ ὧν συνίστανται, μᾶλλον δὲ οἷς ἔστι ταὐτά,[2] τοιούτους εἶναι· τὰ γὰρ τῶν ἀριθμῶν πάθη καὶ τοὺς ἀριθμοὺς τοῖς τόποις ἀκολουθεῖν τοῖς ἐν τῷ οὐρανῷ καὶ οἰκείους αὐτοῖς εἶναι· διὸ καὶ τὰ μεγέθη ἐκ τούτων ἐπισυμβαίνειν.

[2] ταῦτα mss., corr. Dooley

Astronomical Phenomena (D42–D46)
Disappearance of the Moon (D42)

D42 (58B.36) Aët. 2.29.4 (Stob., cf. Ps.-Plut.) [περὶ ἐκλείψεως σελήνης]

τῶν Πυθαγορείων τινὲς κατὰ τὴν Ἀριστοτέλειον ἱστορίαν [≠ Rose, Frag. 16 Ross, cf. *Cael.* 293a18–b2] καὶ τὴν Φιλίππου τοῦ Ὀπουντίου ἀπόφασιν ἀντιφράξει τοτὲ μὲν τῆς γῆς, τοτὲ δὲ τῆς ἀντίχθονος. τῶν δὲ νεωτέρων[1] εἰσί τινες οἷς ἔδοξε κατ' ἐπινέμησιν φλογὸς κατὰ μικρὸν ἐξαπτομένης τεταγμένως, ἕως ἂν[2] τὴν τελείαν πανσέληνον ἀποδῷ, καὶ πάλιν ἀναλόγως μειουμένης μέχρι τῆς συνόδου καθ' ἣν τελείως σβέννυται.

[1] μεθ' ἑτέρων ms., corr. Canter   [2] ἂν Plut.: om. Stob.

Comets (D43)

D43 (< 42.5) Arist. *Meteor.* 1.6 342b29–33

τῶν δ' Ἰταλικῶν τινες καλουμένων Πυθαγορείων ἕνα

PYTHAGOREAN DOCTRINES

are constituted, or rather with which they are identical, are like this too. For the attributes of numbers and the numbers follow the locations in the heavens and are appropriate for them. And that is why magnitudes are produced out of these later.

Astronomical Phenomena (D42–D46)
Disappearance of the Moon (D42)

D42 (58B.36) Aëtius

Some of the Pythagoreans, according to the report of Aristotle and the statement of Philip of Opus: [scil. the eclipse of the moon is caused] by the interposition sometimes of the earth, sometimes of the counter-earth. But among the more recent ones, there are some who thought that it was caused by the spreading outward of a flame which burns little by little in a regular manner until it produces the full moon, and analogously diminishes in turn until the conjunction [scil. with the sun], when it is completely extinguished.

Comets (D43)

D43 (< 42.5) Aristotle, *Meteorology*

Some of the Italians who are called Pythagoreans say that

λέγουσιν αὐτὸν εἶναι τῶν πλανήτων ἀστέρων, ἀλλὰ διὰ πολλοῦ τε χρόνου τὴν φαντασίαν αὐτοῦ εἶναι καὶ τὴν ὑπερβολὴν ἐπὶ μικρόν, ὅπερ συμβαίνει καὶ περὶ τὸν τοῦ Ἑρμοῦ ἀστέρα [. . .].

The Milky Way (D44–D45)

D44 (41.10) Arist. *Meteor.* 1.8 345a13–18

τῶν μὲν οὖν καλουμένων Πυθαγορείων φασί τινες ὁδὸν εἶναι ταύτην οἱ μὲν τῶν ἐκπεσόντων τινὸς ἀστέρων κατὰ τὴν λεγομένην ἐπὶ Φαέθοντος φθοράν, οἱ δὲ τὸν ἥλιον τοῦτον τὸν κύκλον φέρεσθαί ποτέ φασιν· οἷον οὖν διακεκαῦσθαι τὸν τόπον τοῦτον ἤ τι τοιοῦτον ἄλλο πεπονθέναι πάθος ὑπὸ τῆς φορᾶς αὐτῶν.

D45 (58B.37c) Aët. 3.1.2 (Ps.-Plut.) [περὶ τοῦ γαλαξίου κύκλου]

τῶν Πυθαγορείων οἱ μὲν ἔφασαν ἀστέρος εἶναι διάκαυσιν, ἐκπεσόντος μὲν ἀπὸ τῆς ἰδίας[1] ἕδρας, δι' οὗ δὲ ἐπέδραμε[2] χωρίου κυκλοτερῶς αὐτὸ καταφλέξαντος ἐπὶ τοῦ κατὰ Φαέθοντα ἐμπρησμοῦ· οἱ δὲ τὸν ἡλιακὸν ταύτῃ φασὶ κατ' ἀρχὰς γεγονέναι δρόμον. τινὲς δὲ κατοπτρικὴν εἶναι φαντασίαν τοῦ ἡλίου τὰς αὐγὰς πρὸς τὸν οὐρανὸν ἀνακλῶντος, ὅπερ καὶ ἐπὶ τῆς ἴριδος καὶ ἐπὶ τῶν νεφῶν συμβαίνει.

[1] ἰδίας ΜΠ: οἰκείας m   [2] ἐπέδραμε Mm: περι- E

PYTHAGOREAN DOCTRINES

it [i.e. a comet] is one of the wandering heavenly bodies [i.e. planets] but that it only makes an appearance at great intervals and at a low altitude, which is the case with Mercury too [. . .].

The Milky Way (D44–D45)

D44 (41.10) Aristotle, *Meteorology*

Some of the people who are called Pythagoreans say that it [i.e. the Milky Way] is a path; some say it is that of one of the heavenly bodies that fell at the destruction said to have occurred at the time of Phaethon, while the others say that the sun formerly moved along this circle, and so this region was burned as it were or was affected in some other way because of their passage.

D45 (58B.37c) Aëtius

Among the Pythagoreans, some said that it [i.e. the Milky Way] was the combustion of a heavenly body which fell from its place during the conflagration caused by Phaethon and set on fire the area through which it moved in a circle; others say that it was here that in the beginning the sun had its course; and some say that it is a mirror image of the sun whose rays are reflected on the heavens, which also happens in the case of the rainbow and clouds.

EARLY GREEK PHILOSOPHY IV

The Harmony of the Spheres (D46)

D46 (58B.35) Arist. *Cael.* 2.9 290b12–29

φανερὸν δ' ἐκ τούτων ὅτι καὶ τὸ φάναι γίνεσθαι φερομένων ἁρμονίαν, ὡς συμφώνων γινομένων τῶν ψόφων, κομψῶς μὲν εἴρηται καὶ περιττῶς ὑπὸ τῶν εἰπόντων, οὐ μὴν οὕτως ἔχει τἀληθές. δοκεῖ γάρ τισιν ἀναγκαῖον εἶναι τηλικούτων φερομένων σωμάτων γίγνεσθαι ψόφον, ἐπεὶ καὶ τῶν παρ' ἡμῖν οὔτε τοὺς ὄγκους ἐχόντων ἴσους οὔτε τοιούτῳ τάχει φερομένων· ἡλίου δὲ[1] καὶ σελήνης, ἔτι τε τοσούτων τὸ πλῆθος ἄστρων καὶ τὸ μέγεθος φερομένων τῷ[2] τάχει τοιαύτην φορὰν ἀδύνατον μὴ γίγνεσθαι ψόφον ἀμήχανόν τινα τὸ μέγεθος. ὑποθέμενοι δὲ ταῦτα καὶ τὰς ταχυτῆτας ἐκ τῶν ἀποστάσεων ἔχειν τοὺς τῶν συμφωνιῶν λόγους, ἐναρμόνιον γίγνεσθαί φασι τὴν φωνὴν φερομένων κύκλῳ τῶν ἄστρων. ἐπεὶ δ' ἄλογον δοκεῖ τὸ μὴ συνακούειν ἡμᾶς τῆς φωνῆς ταύτης, αἴτιον τούτου φασὶν εἶναι τὸ γιγνομένων εὐθὺς ὑπάρχειν τὸν ψόφον, ὥστε μὴ διάδηλον εἶναι πρὸς τὴν ἐναντίαν σιγήν· πρὸς ἄλληλα γὰρ φωνῆς καὶ σιγῆς εἶναι τὴν διάγνωσιν· ὥστε καθάπερ τοῖς χαλκοτύποις διὰ συνήθειαν οὐθὲν δοκεῖ διαφέρειν, καὶ τοῖς ἀνθρώποις ταὐτὸ συμβαίνειν [. . . = **PYTHS. R25**].

[1] τε mss., corr. Bekker   [2] τῷ] τοιούτῳ coni. Moraux

PYTHAGOREAN DOCTRINES

The Harmony of the Spheres (D46)

D46 (58B.35) Aristotle, *On the Heavens*

This shows clearly that the statement that the movement [scil. of the heavenly bodies] produces a harmony, on the idea that the sounds emitted form a chord, has been made by its proponents in a subtle and refined manner, but that nonetheless it is not true. For some people think that it is necessary that the movement of such large bodies produce a sound, since this is also the case of bodies among us too, which have a smaller mass and move with less rapidity. And since the sun and moon, and furthermore such a great number of heavenly bodies of such a large size, are moving with rapidity along such a course, it would be impossible that there not be produced a sound of an immense magnitude. Taking this as a hypothesis, and supposing that their speeds, on the basis of their distances, had the proportions of concords, they said that the sound emitted by the heavenly bodies moving in a circle was harmonious. And since it seemed inexplicable that we do not hear this sound, they said that the reason for this was that the sound exists beginning with the moment of our birth, so that it never becomes noticeable by a contrast with silence; for sound and silence are distinguished by their relation to one another, so that just as for coppersmiths it [i.e. the noise in their workshop] seems to make no difference because of their habituation, so too the same thing happens for humans [. . .].

Optics (D47–D48)
Mirror Images (D47)

D47 (≠ DK) Aët. 4.14.3 (Ps.-Plut.) [περὶ κατοπτρικῶν ἐμφάσεων]

οἱ ἀπὸ Πυθαγόρου κατ' ἀνάκλασεις τῆς ὄψεως. φέρεσθαι μὲν γὰρ τὴν ὄψιν τεταμένην ὡς ἐπὶ τὸν χαλκόν, ἐντυχοῦσαν δὲ πυκνῷ καὶ λείῳ πληχθεῖσαν ὑποστρέφειν αὐτὴν ἐφ' ἑαυτήν, ὅμοιόν τι πάσχουσαν τῇ ἐκτάσει τῆς χειρὸς καὶ τῇ ἐπὶ τὸν ὦμον ἀντεπιστροφῇ.

Color (D48)

D48 (58B.42) Arist. *Sens.* 3 439a30–31

τὸ γὰρ χρῶμα ἢ ἐν τῷ πέρατί ἐστιν ἢ πέρας (διὸ καὶ οἱ Πυθαγόρειοι τὴν ἐπιφάνειαν 'χρόαν' ἐκάλουν).

Life (D49–D53)
The Soul (D49–D52)

D49 (< 58B.40) Arist. *An.* 1.2 404a16–20

[. . .] ἔφασαν γάρ τινες αὐτῶν ψυχὴν εἶναι τὰ ἐν τῷ ἀέρι ξύσματα, οἱ δὲ τὸ ταῦτα κινοῦν, περὶ δὲ τούτων εἴρηται ὅτι συνεχῶς φαίνεται κινούμενα, κἂν ᾖ νηνεμία παντελής.

PYTHAGOREAN DOCTRINES

Optics (D47–D48)
Mirror Images (D47)

D47 (≠ DK) Aëtius

The followers of Pythagoras: [scil. the images in mirrors are produced] by reflection of the visual ray. For when the visual ray is tensed and directed toward the bronze, and it encounters a compact and smooth object, it undergoes a striking and turns back toward itself, undergoing something similar to the extension of a hand and its return to the shoulder [cf. **ARCHY. D22**].

Color (D48)

D48 (58B.42) Aristotle, *On Sensation*

For color (*khrôma*) is either at the limit or is a limit. And it is for this reason that the Pythagoreans called the surface **'complexion'** (*khroa*).

Life (D49–D53)
The Soul (D49–D52)

D49 (< 58B.40) Aristotle, *On the Soul*

[...] For some of them [scil. of the Pythagoreans] said that the soul is motes (*xusmata*) in the air, others that it is what moves these. People say about these that they are seen to be in constant motion, even if there is a total lack of a breeze.

D50 (44 A23) Arist. *An.* 1.4 407b27–32

καὶ ἄλλη δέ τις δόξα παραδέδοται περὶ ψυχῆς [. . .]. ἁρμονίαν γάρ τινα αὐτὴν λέγουσι· καὶ γὰρ τὴν ἁρμονίαν κρᾶσιν καὶ σύνθεσιν ἐναντίων εἶναι, καὶ τὸ σῶμα συγκεῖσθαι ἐξ ἐναντίων.

D51 (58B.41) Arist. *Pol.* 8.5 1340b18

διὸ πολλοί φασι τῶν σοφῶν οἱ μὲν ἁρμονίαν εἶναι τὴν ψυχήν, οἱ δ' ἔχειν ἁρμονίαν.

D52 (< 58B.39) Arist. *An.* 1.3 407b21–23

[. . .] ὥσπερ ἐνδεχόμενον κατὰ τοὺς Πυθαγορικοὺς μύθους τὴν τυχοῦσαν ψυχὴν εἰς τὸ τυχὸν ἐνδύεσθαι σῶμα.

Zoological Particularities (D53)

D53 (< 58B.43) Arist. *Sens.* 5 445a16–17

[. . .] τρέφεσθαι γάρ φασιν ἔνια ζῷα ταῖς ὀσμαῖς.

Moral Precepts Reported by Aristoxenus (D54)

D54 Aristox. in Stob. [ἐκ τῶν Ἀριστοξένου Πυθαγορικῶν ἀποφάσεων]

PYTHAGOREAN DOCTRINES

D50 (44 A23) Aristotle, *On the Soul*

Another opinion is transmitted about the soul [. . .]. For they [i.e. its proponents] say that it is a kind of harmony. For harmony is a mixture and conjunction of contraries, and the body is composed out of contraries.

D51 (58B.41) Aristotle, *Politics*

That is why many sages say, some that the soul is a harmony, others that it possesses a harmony.

D52 (< 58B.39) Aristotle, *On the Soul*

[. . .] as though it were possible, in conformity with the Pythagorean myths, for any given soul to enter into any given body.

Zoological Particularities (D53)

D53 (< 58B.43) Aristotle, *On Sensation*

[. . .] They [i.e. some of the Pythagoreans] say [. . .] that some animals are nourished by odors.

Moral Precepts Reported by Aristoxenus (D54)

D54 Aristoxenus, *Pythagorean Precepts* in Stobaeus, *Anthology*[1]

[1] Iamblichus' *Life of Pythagoras* 137, 163–66, 174–76, 180–83, 196–98, 200–13, 230–33, 233–39 provides a parallel transmission to Stobaeus' excerpts from Aristoxenus' book, but Iamblichus has evidently freely elaborated his source (see 58D.1, 2, 3, 5–9 DK).

a (58D.4) 4.25.45 (Frag. 34 Wehrli)

μετὰ τὸ θεῖον καὶ δαιμόνιον πλεῖστον ποιεῖσθαι λόγον γονέων τε καὶ νόμων μὴ πλαστῶς ἀλλὰ πεπιστευμένως ἑαυτὸν πρὸς ταῦτα παρασκευάζοντα. τὸ μένειν ⟨ἐν⟩[1] τοῖς πατρίοις ἔθεσί τε καὶ νόμοις ἐδοκίμαζον, εἰ καὶ μικρῷ[2] χείρω τῶν ἑτέρων εἴη.

[1] ⟨ἐν⟩ Hense   [2] μακρῷ Wehrli post Deubner

b (58D.4) 4.1.49 (Frag. 35 Wehrli)

καθόλου δὲ ᾤοντο δεῖν ὑπολαμβάνειν μηδὲν εἶναι μεῖζον κακὸν ἀναρχίας· οὐ γὰρ πεφυκέναι τὸν ἄνθρωπον διασῴζεσθαι μηδενὸς ἐπιστατοῦντος. περὶ δὲ ἀρχόντων καὶ ἀρχομένων οὕτως ἐφρόνουν, τοὺς μὲν γὰρ ἄρχοντας ἔφασκον οὐ μόνον ἐπιστήμονας ἀλλὰ καὶ φιλανθρώπους δεῖν εἶναι, καὶ τοὺς ἀρχομένους οὐ μόνον πειθηνίους ἀλλὰ καὶ φιλάρχοντας. ἐπιμελητέον δὲ πάσης ἡλικίας ἡγοῦντο, καὶ τοὺς μὲν παῖδας ἐν γράμμασι καὶ τοῖς ἄλλοις μαθήμασιν ἀσκεῖσθαι, τοὺς δὲ νεανίσκους τοῖς τῆς πόλεως ἔθεσί τε καὶ νόμοις γυμνάζεσθαι, τοὺς δὲ ἄνδρας ταῖς πράξεσί τε καὶ δημοσίαις λειτουργίαις προσέχειν. τοὺς δὲ πρεσβύτας ἐνθυμήσεσι καὶ κριτηρίοις καὶ συμβουλίαις δεῖν ἐναναστρέφεσθαι μετὰ πάσης ἐπιστήμης ὑπελάμβανον, ὅπως μήτε οἱ παῖδες νηπιάζοιεν, μήτε οἱ νεανίσκοι παιδαριεύοιντο, μήτε οἱ ἄνδρες νεανιεύοιντο, μήτε οἱ γέροντες παραφρονοῖεν. δεῖν δὲ ἔφασκον εὐθὺς ἐκ παίδων καὶ τὴν τροφὴν τεταγμένως

PYTHAGOREAN DOCTRINES

a (58D.4)

After the divinity and the *daimones,* one must attribute the highest value to one's parents and the laws, preparing oneself with regard to these things without dissimulation, but on the contrary with full conviction. And they thought it right to abide by the ancestral customs and laws, even if these were a little worse than the others.

b (58D.4)

In general they thought that one must suppose that there is no greater evil than lack of rule (*anarkhia*): for by nature a human being cannot preserve himself when there is no one directing him. And this is what they thought about those who rule and those who are ruled: they said that those who rule must not only possess knowledge but must also love human beings; and those who are ruled must not only be obedient but must also love their rulers. And they thought that it belongs to every age to exercise oneself: children practice reading, writing, and the other kinds of knowledge; young men are trained in the customs and laws of the city; adult men devote themselves to the affairs and liturgies of the community. And they thought that old men must occupy themselves with encouragement, rules, and advice using all their knowledge, so that children would not act like babies, nor young people like children, nor would adult men act like adolescents, nor old men like madmen. And they said that already beginning in childhood one must eat one's food in an orderly way: they

προσφέρεσθαι, διδάσκοντες[1] ὡς ἡ μὲν τάξις καὶ συμμετρία καλὰ καὶ σύμφορα, ἡ δ' ἀταξία καὶ ἀσυμμετρία αἰσχρά τε καὶ ἀσύμφορα.

[1] διδάσκουσα A, διδάσκουσαν SM: corr. Gesner

c (58D.10) 3.1.101 (Frag. 40 Wehrli)

τὴν ἀληθῆ φιλοκαλίαν ἐν τοῖς ἐπιτηδεύμασι καὶ ἐν ταῖς ἐπιστήμαις ἔλεγεν εἶναι. τὸ γὰρ ἀγαπᾶν καὶ στέργειν τῶν καλῶν ἐθῶν τε καὶ ἐπιτηδευμάτων ὑπάρχειν,[1] ὡσαύτως δὲ καὶ τῶν ἐπιστημῶν τε καὶ ἐμπειριῶν τὰς καλὰς καὶ εὐσχήμονας ἀληθῶς εἶναι φιλοκάλους, τὴν δὲ λεγομένην ὑπὸ τῶν πολλῶν φιλοκαλίαν, οἷον ⟨ἐν⟩[2] τοῖς ἀναγκαίοις καὶ χρησίμοις πρὸς τὸν βίον γινομένην, λάφυρά που τῆς ἀληθινῆς κεῖσθαι φιλοκαλίας.

[1] ὑπάρχει mss., corr. Meineke [2] ⟨ἐν⟩ Hense, ⟨τὴν ἐν⟩ Diels

d (58D.11) 1.6.18 (Frag. 41 Wehrli)

περὶ δὲ τύχης τάδ' ἔφασκον· εἶναι μέν τι[1] καὶ δαιμόνιον μέρος αὐτῆς, γενέσθαι γὰρ ἐπίπνοιάν τινα παρὰ τοῦ δαιμονίου τῶν ἀνθρώπων ἐνίοις ἐπὶ τὸ βέλτιον ἢ ἐπὶ τὸ χεῖρον, καὶ εἶναι φανερῶς κατ' αὐτὸ τοῦτο τοὺς μὲν εὐτυχεῖς, τοὺς δὲ ἀτυχεῖς. καταφανέστατον δὲ εἶναι τοῦτο ⟨τῷ⟩[2] τοὺς μὲν ἀπροβουλεύτως καὶ εἰκῇ τι πράττοντας πολλάκις κατατυγχάνειν, τοὺς δὲ προ-

PYTHAGOREAN DOCTRINES

taught that order and proportion are fine and useful things, while disorder and disproportion are unseemly and harmful ones.

c (58D.10)

He said that the true love of beauty resides in actions and forms of knowledge. For to love and to like belong to fine customs and activities. In the same way, those forms of science and of practical knowledge that are fine and graceful are truly lovers of beauty; but what most people call love of beauty, residing in what is necessary and useful for life, is as it were the spoils of the true love of beauty.

d (58D.11)

About fortune they said the following: One part of it is also divine (*daimonios*). For some people receive a certain inspiration, deriving from the divinity, toward what is better or what is worse, and it is clearly because of this that some people are fortunate and others unfortunate. What makes this most evident is the fact that often those people who act without reflecting beforehand and at random are successful, while those who reflect beforehand and plan

---

¹ μέντοι mss., corr. Usener ² ⟨τῷ⟩ Usener

βουλευομένους καὶ προνοουμένους ὀρθῶς τι πράττειν
ἀποτυγχάνειν. εἶναι δὲ καὶ ἕτερον τύχης εἶδος, καθ' ὃ
οἱ μὲν εὐφυεῖς καὶ εὔστοχοι, οἱ δὲ ἀφυεῖς τε καὶ ἐναντίαν ἔχοντες φύσιν βλάστοιεν,[3] ὧν οἱ μὲν εὐθυβο-
λοῖεν[4] ἐφ' ὅ τι ἂν ἐπιβάλωνται, οἱ δὲ ἀποπίπτοιεν τοῦ
σκοποῦ, μηδέποτε τῆς διανοίας αὐτῶν εὐστόχως φε-
ρομένης, ἀλλὰ ἀεὶ[5] ταρασσομένης. ταύτην δὲ τὴν ἀτυ-
χίαν σύμφυτον εἶναι καὶ οὐκ ἐπείσακτον.

[3] βλάπτοιεν mss., corr. Wyttenbach [4] εὐθύβουλοι εἶεν
F, εὐθύβουλοι εἶναι P, corr. Jacobs [5] καὶ mss., corr.
Wachsmuth

e (58D.5) 2.31.119 (Frag. 36 Wehrli)

ἔφασκον δὲ καὶ τὰς μαθήσεις πάσας τῶν τε ἐπιστημῶν καὶ τῶν τεχνῶν τὰς μὲν ἑκουσίους ὀρθάς τε εἶναι
καὶ εἰς τέλος ἀφικνεῖσθαι, τὰς δὲ ἀκουσίους φαύλους
τε καὶ ἀτελεῖς γίνεσθαι.

f (58D.8) 3.10.66 (Frag. 37 Wehrli)

περὶ δὲ ἐπιθυμίας τάδε ἔλεγον.[1] εἶναι τὸ πάθος τοῦτο
ποικίλον καὶ πολυειδέστατον. εἶναι δὲ τῶν ἐπιθυμιῶν
τὰς μὲν ἐπικτήτους τε καὶ παρασκευαστάς, τὰς δὲ
συμφύτους. αὐτὴν μέντοι τὴν ἐπιθυμίαν ἐπιφοράν
τινα τῆς ψυχῆς καὶ ὁρμὴν καὶ ὄρεξιν εἶναι πληρώ-
σεως ἢ παρουσίας αἰσθήσεως, ἢ κενώσεως καὶ ἀπου-
σίας καὶ τοῦ μὴ αἰσθανέσθαι. ἐπιθυμίας δὲ ἡμαρτη-
μένης τε καὶ φαύλης τρία εἶναι εἴδη τὰ γνωριμώτατα,

PYTHAGOREAN DOCTRINES

beforehand to do something correctly are unsuccessful. But there is another kind of chance, because of which some people develop in such a way that they possess a good nature and hit the target, while others have a bad nature and the opposite kind of natural disposition—the ones hitting the mark, whatever they aim at, while the others miss the mark, their plan never reaching its goal but always being disturbed. This kind of misfortune is innate and is not introduced from outside.

e (58D.5)

And they said that all forms of knowledge, and those sciences and arts that are practiced voluntarily, are correct and arrive at their goal, while those that are done against one's will turn out to be inferior and ineffectual.

f (58D.8)

About desire they said the following: This affection (*pathos*) is variegated and has very many species. For some desires are adventitious and are acquired, while others are innate. And as for desire itself, it is a kind of movement, impulse, and drive of the soul for a state of fullness or the presence of a sensation, or for a state of emptiness, an absence and the lack of a sensation. The most familiar kinds of mistaken and inferior desire are three: ungrace-

---

1 ἔλεγον M^dA: ἔλεγεν S

ἀσχημοσύνην, ἀσυμμετρίαν, ἀκαιρίαν. ἢ γὰρ αὐτόθεν εἶναι τὴν ἐπιθυμίαν ἀσχήμονά τε καὶ φορτικὴν καὶ ἀνελεύθερον, ἢ τοῦτο μὲν οὔ, σφοδρότερον δὲ καὶ χρονιώτερον τοῦ προσήκοντος, ἢ τρίτον πρός ταῦτα, ὅτε οὐ δεῖ καὶ πρὸς ἃ οὐ δεῖ.

g (58D.8) 4.37.4 (Frag. 39 Wehrli)

περὶ δὲ γενέσεως παίδων τάδε ἔλεγε· καθόλου μὲν φυλάττεσθαι τὸ καλούμενον προφερές, οὔτε γὰρ τῶν φυτῶν οὔτε τῶν ζῴων εὔκαρπα τὰ προφερῆ γίγνεσθαι, ἀλλὰ χρόνον τινὰ προπαρασκευάζεσθαι τῆς καρποφορίας, ἐν ᾧ ἐξισχύσαντα καὶ τετελειωμένα τὰ σώματα παρέχειν τά τε σπέρματα καὶ τοὺς καρποὺς δεδύνηται. πολλὰ δὲ εἶναι ἐν τῷ <βίῳ>,[1] ἐν οἷς ἡ ὀψιμαθία ἐστὶ βελτίων, οἷον καὶ τὸ τοῦ ἀφροδισιάζειν πρᾶγμα. δέον οὖν ἐστι[2] παῖδας οὕτως ἄγεσθαι διὰ τῶν ἀσκημάτων ἀσχόλους, ὥστε μὴ μόνον μὴ ζητεῖν, ἀλλ' εἰ δυνατὸν μηδὲ εἰδέναι[3] τὴν τοιαύτην συνουσίαν ἐντὸς τῶν εἴκοσι ἐτῶν. ὅταν δὲ καὶ εἰς τοῦτο ἀφίκηται, σπανίοις εἶναι χρηστέον τοῖς ἀφροδισίοις. τοῦτο γὰρ πρός τε τὴν τῶν γεννώντων καὶ γεννησομένων εὐεξίαν πολύ τι συμβάλλεσθαι. ἔλεγε δὲ καὶ μήτε τροφῆς[4] μήτε μέθης πλήρη ταῖς γυναιξὶν εἰς τὸ γεννᾶν ὁμιλεῖν, οὐ γὰρ οἴεται[5] ἐκ φαύλης καὶ ἀσυμφώνου καὶ ταραχώδους κράσεως εὔρυθμα καὶ καλά, ἀλλ' οὐδὲ ἀγαθὰ τὴν ἀρχὴν γίγνεσθαι.[6]

[1] <βίῳ> Koën   [2] δεῖν οὖν ἔτι Wehrli

PYTHAGOREAN DOCTRINES

fulness, disproportion, and inopportuneness. For either the desire is in itself ungraceful, vulgar, and illiberal, or else it is not this, but it is more intense and lasts longer than what is suitable, or third besides these, it occurs when it should not and with regard to objects that it should not.

g (58D.8)

About the begetting of children he said the following: In general one should avoid what is called 'premature,' for neither in plants nor in animals is what is premature fruitful, but it needs to be prepared before bearing fruit for a certain period of time, during which the bodies are strengthened and matured, and become capable of producing seed and fruits. There are many things in ⟨life⟩ in which it is better to learn late; and this applies to the activity of sexual intercourse as well. Therefore one must make children occupied by exercises when they are busy in such a way that they not only do not seek this kind of sexual activity, but even, if possible, do not even know anything about it before they are twenty years old. And when they reach this age, it is only seldom that they should engage in sexual intercourse. For this contributes greatly to the good health of parents and of those who will be born. He also said that one should not approach women for the sake of reproduction when one is full of food or wine, for he thinks that from an inferior, unharmonious, and disturbed mixture things cannot be produced that are rhythmical and fine, or even good at all.

---

[3] εἶναι mss., corr. Koën   [4] τρυφῆς ed. Trincavelli   [5] οἱ ταῖς mss., corr. Diels   [6] γίγνεται mss., corr. Wyttenbach

18. PYTHAGORAS, PYTHAGOREANS, PYTHAGOREANISM: RECEPTION [PYTHS. R]

The conditions that make the Pythagorean writings unique in the history of Greek philosophy have to do not only with the particularities of the Pythagorean 'school' and the relations between the tutelary figure of Pythagoras and those people who were able to lay claim to him in the first generations (see the General Introduction to Chapters 10–18), but also and above all with the fact that the guiding principles of ancient Pythagoreanism were entirely absorbed by Platonism: on the theoretical side, number, limit, the unlimited, harmony, as they are found especially in Philolaus; on the practical side, the care for the soul and the rules of life, as these can be grasped in the functioning of the Pythagorean communities and in an abundant corpus of precepts. This absorption already begins to a certain degree in Plato, who pays anonymous but transparent homage to Philolaus in the *Philebus,* chooses a Pythagorean, Timaeus, to expound a cosmology mathematized in its principles by the harmonic structuring of the soul of the world, and uses the transmigration of souls as the foundation for several eschatological narratives; Plato's immediate successors (Speusippus in particular) seem indeed to

have begun a process of directly retrojecting Platonic doctrines onto Pythagoras; but it is among the Neoplatonists, especially beginning with Iamblichus, that this process attains its full culmination. A mythical Pythagoras becomes the ancestor of Plato, adulated for himself and in a certain manner superior to him—closer to the gods, to put it in the terms Plato himself used, but without the irony with which Plato had colored it (cf. **R3**). The portion of authentic information regarding Pythagoras and his Preplatonic disciples gradually diminishes as projection, syncretism, amalgamation, and fantasy increase, providing room for the creation of an abundant pseudepigraphic corpus, which is difficult to date and is doubtless even more interesting for the sociology of philosophy than it is for the doctrines it transmits.

The present chapter illustrates the principal stages and the most important aspects of this unparalleled reception process, which had considerable effects on the history of Platonism itself, notably during the Renaissance: indeed, Pythagoras is one of the constitutive figures of the *'prisca philosophia,'* that primeval philosophy thought to derive from the depths of human wisdom, where not only Plato and Pythagoras but also Moses, Hermes Trismegistus, and the Chaldaean oracles live happily together. Given the mass (and the dispersal) of the pertinent materials and the complexity of the traditions involved, the texts presented here can have nothing more than an indicative value. Many texts have been simply omitted, and interested readers will often have to complete the few sentences included by using specialized editions and collections. Orientation can be derived from the complete texts of the *Lives* of Pythagoras by Porphyry and Iamblichus, and from the collection by K. S. Guthrie indicated below.

PYTHAGOREAN RECEPTION

BIBLIOGRAPHY

Editions and Translations

Pseudopythagorean Literature

L. Delatte. *Les traités de la royauté d'Ecphante, Diotogène et Sthénidas* (Paris, 1942).

H. Thesleff. *The Pythagorean Texts of the Hellenistic Period* (Abo, 1965).

Translations of many Pseudopythagorean texts can be found in:

The Pythagorean Sourcebook and Library: An Anthology of Ancient Writings which Relate to Pythagoras and Pythagorean Philosophy. Compiled and translated by K. S. Guthrie, with additional translations by T. Taylor and A. Fairbanks Jr. Introduced and edited by D. R. Fideler, with a foreword by J. Godwin (Grand Rapids, MI, 1987, 1920^1).

Studies

D. J. O'Meara. *Pythagoras Revived, Mathematics and Philosophy in Late Antiquity* (Oxford, 1989).

H. Thesleff. *An Introduction to the Pythagorean Writings of the Hellenistic Period* (Abo, 1961).

See also the titles listed in the General Introduction to Chapters 10–18.

EARLY GREEK PHILOSOPHY IV

OUTLINE OF THE CHAPTER

R

Pre-Platonic Reports and Allusions Regarding Pythagoras (Heraclitus, Ion of Chios, Herodotus, Democritus; Xenophanes, Empedocles?) (PYTH. a P27–P33)
References and Allusions in Plato (R1–R5)
    A Reference by Name to Pythagoras (PYTH. b T1)
    A Reference by Name to Philolaus (PHILOL. P4)
    An Explicit Reference to the Pythagoreans (R1)
    Allusions to the Pythagoreans (R2–R4)
    A Reference That Perhaps Also Concerns the Pythagoreans (R5)
    References by Name to Archytas in (Ps.-?) Plato's Seventh Letter (ARCHY. P1)
The Pythagoreans in the Old Academy and Peripatos (R6–R32)
    Works Dedicated to the Pythagoreans (R6–R8)
    Aristotle and the Peripatetics on Plato and the Pythagoreans: Similarities and Differences (R9–R13)
    Aristotle on Speusippus and the Pythagoreans (R14)
    Aristotelian Criticisms (R15–R26)
        On Definition (R15)
        On the Delimitation between Mathematics, Physics, and First Philosophy (R16–R18)
        On the Recourse to Numbers as Principles in Explanations of Natural Phenomena (R19–R21)
        On the Unlimited Principle (R22)
        On Cosmology (R23–R24)
        On the Harmony of the Spheres (R25)
        On the Soul (R26)

PYTHAGOREAN RECEPTION

Eudemus on the Eternal Return (R27)
The Platonization of Older Pythagoreanism (R28–R32)
    The Appropriation of Pythagoreanism by the Older Academy (R28)
    Characteristic Attributions of Platonic and Academic Doctrines to Pythagoras (R29–R31)
        Pythagoras, Inventor of the Terms 'Philosophy' and 'Philosopher'? (R29)
        Pythagoras and the Xenocratean Definition of the Soul (R30)
        Pythagoras as the Source of Plato's and Aristotle's Theory of Emotions (R31)
    The Construction of a Line of Descent by Instruction: Pythagoras-Archytas-Plato-Aristotle (R32)
Aspects of Hellenistic and Later Pythagoreanism (R33–R72)
    An Attempted Syncretic Systematization (R33)
    Pythagoras as Moralizer (R34–R37)
        The Interpretation of the Acousmatic Formulas (R34)
        Moral Education According to The Golden Verses *(R35)*
        Pythagorean Maxims (R36)
        Speeches to the Crotonians Attributed to Pythagoras (R37)
        Recommendations Attributed to Pythagoreans (cf. R63–R66)
    Representations of Pythagoreans in Middle Comedy (DRAM. T35–T39)
    Some Testimonia about Pythagoras' Presence in Rome (R38–R44)

Pythagoras' Statue in Rome at the Beginning of the 3rd Century BC (R38)
The Legend of Numa as a Pupil of Pythagoras (R39–R41)
A Renewal of Pythagoreanism in the 1st Century BC? Nigidius Figulus (R42)
The Vanity of Archytas' Science (Horace)
Aspects of Pythagoreanism at Rome: Cosmology, Way of Life, and Vegetarianism (R43–R44)
Pseudo-Pythagorean Literature (R45–R66)
Examples of Writings Attributed to Pythagoras (R45–R46)
    The Three Treatises (R45)
    The "Sacred Discourse" in Doric Prose (R46)
Examples of Writings Attributed to Philolaus (R47–R51)
    A Late Testimonium on the Existence of Numerous Writings of Philolaus (R47)
    Two Examples of Pseudepigraphic Texts Constructed on the Basis of Philolaus' Theory of Principles (R48–R49)
    Philolaus as the Source of Plato's Timaeus (R50)
    An Aristotelian Philolaus (R51)
Examples of Writings Attributed to Archytas (R52–R53)
Other Themes That Feature in the Pseudepigraphic Writings (R54–R66)
    On the Divulgation of the Pythagorean Doctrine (R54)
    On the Universe (R55–R56)

PYTHAGOREAN RECEPTION

    A Pseudepigraphic Summary of Plato's Timaeus: *Timaeus of Locri (R55)*
    A Pseudepigraphic Text of an Aristotelian Tendency: Ocellus of Lucania (R56)
  Political Theory (R57–R62)
    The King (R57–R60)
    Preambles to the Laws of Zaleucus and Charondas (R61–R62)
  The Virtue of Women (R63–R66)
Some Neopythagorean Presentations of 'Pythagorean' Doctrines Concerning the Principles (R67–R71)
  Eudorus of Alexandria (R67)
  Moderatus of Gades (R68)
  Numenius (R69)
  Longinus (R70)
  The Variety of Pythagorean Doctrines According to a (Neopythagorean) Report in Sextus Empiricus (R71)
An Example of Doxographic Syncretism (R72)
Pythagoras in The Assembly of Philosophers *(R73)*

PYTHAGORAS AND THE PYTHAGOREANS: RECEPTION

R

Pre-Platonic Reports and Allusions Regarding Pythagoras (Heraclitus, Ion of Chios, Herodotus, Democritus; Xenophanes, Empedocles?)

See **PYTH. a P27–P33**

References and Allusions in Plato (R1–R5)
A Reference by Name to Pythagoras

Cf. **PYTH. b T1**

A Reference by Name to Philolaus

Cf. **PHILOL. P4**

An Explicit Reference to the Pythagoreans (R1)

R1 (cf. ad 47 B1) Plat. *Rep.* 7.530d

[ΣΩ.] κινδυνεύει [. . .] ὡς πρὸς ἀστρονομίαν ὄμματα

PYTHAGORAS AND THE PYTHAGOREANS: RECEPTION

R

Pre-Platonic Reports and Allusions Regarding Pythagoras (Heraclitus, Ion of Chios, Herodotus, Democritus; Xenophanes, Empedocles?)

See **PYTH. a P27–P33**

References and Allusions in Plato (R1–R5)
A Reference by Name to Pythagoras

Cf. **PYTH. b T1**

A Reference by Name to Philolaus

Cf. **PHILOL. P4**

An Explicit Reference to the Pythagoreans (R1)

R1 (cf. ad 47 B1) Plato, *Republic*

[Socrates:] It is quite possible [. . .] that just as the eyes

πέπηγεν ὡς πρὸς ἐναρμόνιον φορὰν ὦτα παγῆναι, καὶ αὗται ἀλλήλων ἀδελφαί τινες αἱ ἐπιστῆμαι εἶναι, ὥς οἵ τε Πυθαγόρειοί φασι καὶ ἡμεῖς, ὦ Γλαύκων, συγχωροῦμεν.

Allusions to the Pythagoreans (R2–R4)

R2 (≠ DK) Plat. *Rep.* 7.531c

[ΣΩ.] τοὺς γὰρ ἐν ταύταις ταῖς συμφωνίαις ταῖς ἀκουομέναις ἀριθμοὺς ζητοῦσιν, ἀλλ᾽ οὐκ εἰς προβλήματα ἀνίασιν, ἐπισκοπεῖν τίνες σύμφωνοι ἀριθμοὶ καὶ τίνες οὔ, καὶ διὰ τί ἑκάτεροι.

R3 (≠ DK) Plat. *Phil.* 16c

[ΣΩ.] [. . .] καὶ οἱ μὲν παλαιοί, κρείττονες ἡμῶν καὶ ἐγγυτέρω θεῶν οἰκοῦντες, ταύτην φήμην παρέδοσαν, ὡς ἐξ ἑνὸς μὲν καὶ πολλῶν ὄντων τῶν ἀεὶ λεγομένων εἶναι, πέρας δὲ καὶ ἀπειρίαν ἐν αὑτοῖς σύμφυτον ἐχόντων.

R4 (< 44 B14) Plat. *Gorg.* 493a–b

[ΣΩ.] ἤδη γάρ του ἔγωγε καὶ ἤκουσα τῶν σοφῶν ὡς νῦν ἡμεῖς τέθναμεν καὶ τὸ μὲν σῶμά ἐστιν ἡμῖν σῆμα, τῆς δὲ ψυχῆς τοῦτο ἐν ᾧ αἱ ἐπιθυμίαι εἰσὶ τυγχάνει ὂν οἷον ἀναπείθεσθαι καὶ μεταπίπτειν ἄνω κάτω, καὶ τοῦτο ἄρα τις μυθολογῶν κομψὸς ἀνήρ, ἴσως Σικελός

have been constructed for the purpose of astronomy, so too the ears have been constructed for harmonic movement, and that these sciences are as it were sisters of one another, as at the same time the Pythagoreans say [cf. **ARCHY. D14**] and as we ourselves agree, Glaucon [. . .].

Allusions to the Pythagoreans (R2–R4)

R2 (≠ DK) Plato, *Republic*

[Socrates:] They look for the numbers found in these concords that are audible, but they do not ascend to the problems that consist in investigating which numbers are in accord with one another and which ones are not, and why this is so in both cases.

R3 (≠ DK) Plato, *Philebus*

[Socrates:] [. . .] and the ancients, who were better than we are and who dwelt closer to the gods, have passed down to us this tradition, that the things that are said always to exist come from one and many, and that they possess limit and unlimitedness within their own nature [cf. **PHILOL. D2–D3**].

R4 (< 44 B14) Plato, *Gorgias*

[Socrates:] [. . .] I myself once heard one of the sages say that at present we are dead, and our body (*sôma*) is our tomb (*sêma*), and that the part of the soul in which desires are located is capable of being persuaded and of being tossed now upward, now downward; and so some smart

EARLY GREEK PHILOSOPHY IV

τις ἢ Ἰταλικός, παράγων τῷ ὀνόματι διὰ τὸ πιθανόν
τε καὶ πειστικὸν ὠνόμασε πίθον, τοὺς δὲ ἀνοήτους
ἀμυήτους, τῶν δ' ἀνοήτων[1] τοῦτο τῆς ψυχῆς οὗ αἱ ἐπιθυμίαι εἰσί, τὸ[2] ἀκόλαστον αὐτοῦ[3] καὶ οὐ στεγανόν,
ὡς τετρημένος εἴη πίθος διὰ τὴν ἀπληστίαν ἀπεικά-
σας.

[1] ἀνοήτων F: ἀμυήτων BTWf [2] ⟨συνεὶς⟩ τὸ Dodds
[3] αὐτοῦ secl. Sauppe

*A Reference That Perhaps Also
Concerns the Pythagoreans (R5)*

R5 (≠ DK) Plat. *Men.* 81b

[ΣΩ.] φασὶ γὰρ τὴν ψυχὴν τοῦ ἀνθρώπου εἶναι ἀθάνατον, καὶ τοτὲ μὲν τελευτᾶν—ὃ δὴ ἀποθνῄσκειν καλοῦσι—τοτὲ δὲ πάλιν γίγνεσθαι, ἀπόλλυσθαι δ' οὐ-
δέποτε· δεῖν δὴ διὰ ταῦτα ὡς ὁσιώτατα διαβιῶναι τὸν
βίον [. . .].

*References by Name to Archytas in (Ps.-?)
Plato's Seventh Letter*

Cf. **ARCHY. P11**

man, perhaps a Sicilian or an Italian,[1] speaking in the form of a myth, called this part, slightly modifying the word, a 'jar' (*pithos*) because it is capable of being persuaded (*pithanos*) and influenced (*peistikos*), while those who are unintelligent he called 'uninitiated'—making an image for this part of the soul of the unintelligent, where the desires are located, the uncontrolled and leaky part, as though it were a cracked jar, because it cannot be filled.

[1] Perhaps Philolaus?

A Reference That Perhaps Also Concerns the Pythagoreans (R5)

R5 (≠ DK) Plato, *Meno*

[Socrates:] They [i.e. certain priests and priestesses, as well as divine poets like Pindar] say that the soul [i.e. the life] of a human being is immortal, and at one time comes to an end (what they call dying), and at another time is born again, without ever being destroyed. And this is why one must live one's life in as holy a fashion as possible [. . . citation of Pindar = **MOR. T32d**].

References by Name to Archytas in (Ps.-?) Plato's Seventh Letter

Cf. **ARCHY. P11**

EARLY GREEK PHILOSOPHY IV

The Pythagoreans in the Old Academy and Peripatos (R6–R32)
Works Dedicated to the Pythagoreans (R6–R8)

R6

a (< 44 A13) Ps.-Iambl. *Theol.*, p. 82.10–20

Σπεύσιππος [. . .] Περὶ Πυθαγορικῶν ἀριθμῶν [Frag. 28 Tarán, 122 Isnardi-Parente]

b (≠ DK) Diog. Laert. 4.13

Ξενοκράτης [. . .] Πυθαγόρεια αʹ [p. 158 Heinze]

c (47 A13, 49.2) Diog. Laert. 5.25

Ἀριστοτέλης [. . .] Περὶ τῆς Ἀρχυτείου φιλοσοφίας αʹ βʹ γʹ [. . .] Πρὸς τοὺς Πυθαγορείους αʹ [. . .] Περὶ τῶν Πυθαγορείων αʹ [. . .] Τὰ ἐκ τοῦ Τιμαίου καὶ Ἀρχυτείων αʹ [pp. 6–7 Rose]

d (≠ DK) Diog. Laert. 5.86 et 88

Ἡρακλείδης [. . .] Περὶ τῶν Πυθαγορείων [Frag. 22.40–41 Wehrli]

PYTHAGOREAN RECEPTION

*The Pythagoreans in the Old
Academy and Peripatos (R6–R32)
Works Dedicated to the Pythagoreans (R6–R8)*

R6

a (< 44 A13) Ps.-Iamblichus, *Theology of Arithmetic*

Speusippus, [. . .] *On the Pythagorean Numbers*

b (≠ DK) Diogenes Laertius

Xenocrates, [. . .] *Pythagorean Subjects* (one book)

c (47 A13, 49.2) Diogenes Laertius

Aristotle, [. . .] *On the Philosophy of Archytas* (three books), *On* [or: *Against*] *the Pythagoreans* (one book), *On the Pythagoreans* (one book), *Extracts from the* Timaeus *and the Writings of Archytas* (one book)

d (≠ DK) Diogenes Laertius

Heraclides [scil. of Pontus], [. . .] *On the Pythagoreans*[1]

---

[1] Heraclides also spoke about Pythagoras in his *Abaris* (Frag. 73–75 Wehrli) and in *On the Woman Who Stopped Breathing* (Frag. 76–89 Wehrli).

e Aristoxenus (cf. Frag. 11–41 et 47–50 Wehrli)

Ἀριστόξενος [. . .]
(< 14.8) Περὶ Πυθαγόρου καὶ τῶν γνωρίμων αὐτοῦ (Diog. Laert. 1.118)
(≠ DK) Πυθαγόρεια αʹ (Diog. Laert. 4.13)
(≠ DK) Πυθαγόρου βίος (Porph. *VP* 59)
(58D., cf. D.11) Πυθαγορικαὶ ἀποφάσεις (Stob. 1.6.18 et al.)
(cf. 47 A9) Ἀρχύτα βίος (Athen. *Deipn.* 12.545A)

R7 (< 44 A13) Ps.-Iambl. *Theol.*, pp. 82.10–83.5 (= Speus. Frag. 28 Tarán, 122 Isnardi-Parente)

Σπεύσιππος [. . .] διάδοχος δὲ Ἀκαδημίας πρὸ[1] Ξενοκράτου, ἐκ τῶν ἐξαιρέτως σπουδασθεισῶν ἀεὶ Πυθαγορικῶν ἀκροάσεων, μάλιστα δὲ τῶν Φιλολάου συγγραμμάτων, βιβλίδιόν τι συντάξας γλαφυρὸν ἐπέγραψε μὲν αὐτὸ Περὶ Πυθαγορικῶν ἀριθμῶν, ἀπ' ἀρχῆς δὲ μέχρι ἡμίσους περὶ τῶν ἐν αὐτοῖς[2] γραμμικῶν ἐμμελέστατα διεξελθὼν πολυγωνίων τε καὶ παντοίων τῶν ἐν ἀριθμοῖς ἐπιπέδων ἅμα καὶ στερεῶν,[3] περί τε[4] τῶν πέντε σχημάτων, ἃ τοῖς κοσμικοῖς ἀποδίδοται στοιχείοις, ἰδιότητός <τε>[5] αὐτῶν καὶ πρὸς ἄλληλα[6] κοινότητος, <περὶ>[7] ἀναλογίας τε καὶ ἀντακολουθίας,[8] μετὰ ταῦτα λοιπὸν θάτερον τὸ[9] τοῦ βιβλίου ἥμισυ περὶ δεκάδος ἄντικρυς ποιεῖται, φυσικωτάτην αὐτὴν ἀποφαίνων καὶ τελεστικωτάτην τῶν ὄντων, οἷον

[1] παρὰ mss., corr. Boeckh   [2] αὐτῶ mss., corr. edd.

PYTHAGOREAN RECEPTION

- **e** Diogenes Laertius, Porphyry, Stobaeus, Athenaeus

  Aristoxenus,
  - (< 14.8) *On Pythagoras and His Companions* (Diogenes Laertius)
  - (≠ DK) *Pythagorean Subjects* (one book: Diogenes Laertius)
  - (≠ DK) *Life of Pythagoras* (Porphyry)
  - (58D., cf. D.11) *Pythagorean Precepts* (Stobaeus)
  - (cf. 47 A9) *Life of Archytas* (Athenaeus)

R7 (< 44 A13) Ps.-Iamblichus, *Theology of Arithmetic*

Speusippus [...], who was the successor as head of the Academy before Xenocrates, composed on the basis of the Pythagoreans' teachings (for which he always demonstrated a particular zeal), and most of all on that of Philolaus' writings, a refined little book that he entitled *On the Pythagorean Numbers*. In the first half of this book, he provides a very elegant explanation for linear numbers, polygonal numbers, and all kinds of plane and solid numbers, and for the five figures that are attributed to the cosmic elements, their individual properties and the ones they share with each other, their analogies and correspondences. After this, he dedicates the second half of the book directly to the decad, stating that it is the most natural and the most effective among the things that exist, like the

---

³ πολυγωνίοις ... παντοίοις τοῖς ... ἐπιπέδοις ... στερεοῖς mss., corr. Ast ⁴ τι mss., corr. edd. ⁵ ⟨τε⟩ Diels post Lang ⁶ πρὸς ἄλληλα καὶ mss., transp. Tannery ⁷ ⟨περὶ⟩ De Falco post Tannery ⁸ ἀνακολουθίας Ast ⁹ τὸ secl. Diels

εἶδός τι τοῖς κοσμικοῖς ἀποτελέσμασι τεχνικὸν ἀφ'
ἑαυτῆς (ἀλλ' οὐχ ἡμῶν νομισάντων ἢ ὡς ἔτυχε) θεμέ-
λιον[10] ὑπάρχουσαν καὶ παράδειγμα παντελέστατον
τῷ τοῦ παντὸς ποιητῇ θεῷ προεκκειμένην.[11]

[10] θεμένων MLNBF, θέλλων P: corr. Diels   [11] ὑπάρ-
χουσα ... προεκκειμένη (vel προσ-) mss., corr. Diels

R8 (≠ DK) Heracl. Pont. in Clem. Alex. *Strom.* 2.130.3
(Frag. 44 Wehrli)

Πυθαγόραν δὲ ὁ Ποντικὸς Ἡρακλείδης ἱστορεῖ τὴν
ἐπιστήμην τῆς τελειότητος[1] τῶν ἀριθμῶν[2] τῆς ψυχῆς
εὐδαιμονίαν εἶναι παραδεδωκέναι.

[1] τὴν τελεωτάτην Hoyer   [2] ἀριθμῶν Potter ex Theod.
Cur. 11.6: ἀρετῶν ms.

*Aristotle and the Peripatetics on Plato and the
Pythagoreans: Similarities and
Differences (R9–R13)*

R9 (< 58B.13) Arist. *Metaph.* A6 987b22–29

[...] τὸ μέντοι γε ἓν οὐσίαν εἶναι, καὶ μὴ ἕτερόν τι ὂν
λέγεσθαι ἕν, παραπλησίως τοῖς Πυθαγορείοις ἔλεγε,
καὶ τὸ τοὺς ἀριθμοὺς αἰτίους εἶναι τοῖς ἄλλοις τῆς
οὐσίας ὡσαύτως ἐκείνοις· τὸ δὲ ἀντὶ τοῦ ἀπείρου ὡς
ἑνὸς δυάδα ποιῆσαι, τὸ δ' ἄπειρον ἐκ μεγάλου καὶ
μικροῦ, τοῦτ' ἴδιον· καὶ ἔτι ὁ μὲν τοὺς ἀριθμοὺς παρὰ

artisanal form of the events that take place in the universe, that it exists by itself as a foundation and not because of our own thoughts or arbitrary conventions, and that it presents itself as the most perfect paradigm to the god that has created everything.

R8 (≠ DK) Heraclides of Pontus in Clement of Alexandria, *Stromata*

Heraclides of Pontus reports that Pythagoras teaches that knowledge of the perfection of numbers is the happiness of the soul.

Aristotle and the Peripatetics on Plato and the Pythagoreans: Similarities and Differences (R9–R13)

R9 (< 58B.13) Aristotle, *Metaphysics*

[. . .] that the one is a substance, and that no other thing is said to be one, he [i.e. Plato] said this in a way very similar to the Pythagoreans, and also that the numbers are causes for the other things for their being, [scil. he said] just like them. As for positing the dyad instead of the unlimited, in the idea that it is one, and deriving the unlimited from the large and the small, this is peculiar to him. Furthermore, he posits the numbers apart from the per-

τὰ αἰσθητά, οἱ δ' ἀριθμοὺς εἶναί φασιν αὐτὰ τὰ πράγματα, καὶ τὰ μαθηματικὰ μεταξὺ τούτων οὐ τιθέασιν.

R10 (58B.12) Arist. *Metaph.* A6 987b10–14

τὴν δὲ μέθεξιν τοὔνομα μόνον μετέβαλεν· οἱ μὲν γὰρ Πυθαγόρειοι μιμήσει τὰ ὄντα φασὶν εἶναι τῶν ἀριθμῶν, Πλάτων δὲ μεθέξει, τοὔνομα μεταβαλών. τὴν μέντοι γε μέθεξιν ἢ τὴν μίμησιν ἥτις ἂν εἴη τῶν εἰδῶν ἀφεῖσαν ἐν κοινῷ ζητεῖν.

R11 (47 A13) Arist. in Dam. *In Parm.* vol. 3, p. 74.19–21

Ἀριστοτέλης δὲ ἐν τοῖς Ἀρχυτείοις ἱστορεῖ [Frag. 207 Rose] καὶ Πυθαγόραν 'ἄλλο' τὴν ὕλην καλεῖν ὡς ῥευστὴν καὶ ἀεὶ ἄλλο καὶ ἄλλο γιγνόμενον.

R12 (< 58B.14) Theophr. *Metaph.* 11a27–b3

Πλάτων δὲ καὶ οἱ Πυθαγόρειοι μακρὰν τὴν ἀπόστασιν, ἐπεὶ μιμεῖσθαί[1] γ' ἐθέλειν ἅπαντα· καίτοι καθάπερ ἀντίθεσίν τινα ποιοῦσιν τῆς ἀορίστου δυάδος καὶ τοῦ ἑνός [. . .].

[1] ἐπεὶ μιμεῖσθαί Allan: ἐπιμιμεῖσθαι mss.: alii alia

ceptibles, while they say that the things themselves are numbers, and they do not make the mathematical objects intermediaries between the two.

R10 (58B.12) Aristotle, *Metaphysics*

He [i.e. Plato] did nothing more than change the name to 'participation' (*methexis*). For the Pythagoreans say that the things that are exist by 'imitation' (*mimesis*) of numbers, Plato by 'participation': he changes the name. But they left open the question what participation in the forms or imitation of them might be.

R11 (47 A13) Aristotle in Damascius, *Commentary on Plato's* Parmenides

Aristotle reports in his writings *On Archytas* that Pythagoras too called matter 'other' since it is fluid and is always becoming something other.

R12 (< 58B.14) Theophrastus, *Metaphysics*

Plato and the Pythagoreans [scil. say that] the distance is great, if it is true that everything has a desire to imitate; and yet they admit a kind of opposition between the unlimited dyad and the one [. . .].

R13 (58B.32) Eudem. in Simpl. *In Phys.*, p. 431.13–16 (= Frag. 27 Wehrli)

[... cf. **ARCHY. D20**] τὸ δὲ ἀόριστον, φησί, καλῶς ἐπὶ τὴν κίνησιν οἱ Πυθαγόρειοι καὶ ὁ Πλάτων ἐπιφέρουσιν (οὐ γὰρ δὴ ἄλλος γε οὐδεὶς περὶ αὐτῆς εἴρηκεν)· ἀλλὰ γὰρ ὁριστὴ[1] οὐκ[2] ἔστι, καὶ τὸ ἀτελὲς δὴ καὶ τὸ μὴ ὄν· γίνεται γάρ, γινόμενον δὲ οὐκ ἔστι.

[1] ὥρισται mss., corr. Diels   [2] οὐκ E: καὶ οὐκ F

Aristotle on Speusippus and the Pythagoreans (R14)

R14 (58B.11) Arist. *Metaph.* Λ7 1072b30–34

ὅσοι δὲ ὑπολαμβάνουσιν, ὥσπερ οἱ Πυθαγόρειοι καὶ Σπεύσιππος [Frag. 42a Tarán], τὸ κάλλιστον καὶ ἄριστον μὴ ἐν ἀρχῇ εἶναι, διὰ τὸ καὶ τῶν φυτῶν καὶ τῶν ζῴων τὰς ἀρχὰς αἴτια μὲν εἶναι, τὸ δὲ καλὸν καὶ τέλειον ἐν τοῖς ἐκ τούτων, οὐκ ὀρθῶς οἴονται.

Aristotelian Criticisms (R15–R26)
On Definition (R15)

R15 (< 58B.8) Arist. *Metaph.* A5 987a19–27

[... = **PYTHS. ANON. D3**] λίαν δ' ἁπλῶς ἐπραγματεύθησαν. ὡρίζοντό τε γὰρ ἐπιπολαίως, καὶ ᾧ πρώτῳ ὑπάρξειεν ὁ λεχθεὶς ὅρος, τοῦτ' εἶναι τὴν οὐσίαν τοῦ

PYTHAGOREAN RECEPTION

R13 (58B.32) Eudemus in Simplicius, *Commentary on Aristotle's* Physics

[. . .] The indefinite (*aoriston*), he [i.e. Eudemus] says, is referred correctly by the Pythagoreans and Plato to movement (for no one else has spoken about this latter). For this is not definite (?), and so too what is incomplete and what does not exist; for it becomes and, becoming, it does not exist.

*Aristotle on Speusippus and the
Pythagoreans (R14)*

R14 (58B.11) Aristotle, *Metaphysics*

All those who suppose, like the Pythagoreans and Speusippus, that the most beautiful and the best are not located in the principle, because the principles of plants and animals are causes, while the beautiful and the perfect are located in the things that derive from them, do not think correctly.

*Aristotelian Criticisms (R15–R26)
On Definition (R15)*

R15 (< 58B.8) Aristotle, *Metaphysics*

[. . .] but they studied this subject in too simple a manner. For at the same time their definitions were superficial and they thought that what the stated definition applied to first

πράγματος ἐνόμισαν, ὥσπερ εἴ τις οἴοιτο ταὐτὸν εἶναι διπλάσιον καὶ τὴν δυάδα διότι πρῶτον ὑπάρχει τοῖς δυσὶ τὸ διπλάσιον. ἀλλ' οὐ ταὐτὸν ἴσως ἐστὶ τὸ εἶναι διπλασίῳ καὶ δυάδι· εἰ δὲ μή, πολλὰ τὸ ἓν ἔσται, ὃ κἀκείνοις συνέβαινεν.

On the Delimitation between Mathematics, Physics, and First Philosophy (R16–R18)

R16 (< 58B.37) Arist. *Cael.* 2.13 293a25–27

[... **PYTHS. ANON. D36**] οὐ πρὸς τὰ φαινόμενα τοὺς λόγους καὶ τὰς αἰτίας ζητοῦντες, ἀλλὰ πρός τινας λόγους καὶ δόξας αὑτῶν τὰ φαινόμενα προσέλκοντες καὶ πειρώμενοι συγκοσμεῖν.

R17 (< 58B.26) Arist. *Metaph.* N3 1091a18–20

ἀλλ' ἐπειδὴ κοσμοποιοῦσι καὶ φυσικῶς βούλονται λέγειν, δίκαιον αὐτοὺς ἐξετάζειν τι περὶ φύσεως, ἐκ δὲ τῆς νῦν ἀφεῖναι μεθόδου.

R18 (< 58B.22) Arist. *Metaph.* A8 989b29–34, 990a5–8

οἱ μὲν οὖν καλούμενοι Πυθαγόρειοι ταῖς μὲν ἀρχαῖς καὶ τοῖς στοιχείοις ἐκτοπωτέρως χρῶνται τῶν φυσιολόγων (τὸ δ' αἴτιον ὅτι παρέλαβον αὐτὰς οὐκ ἐξ αἰσθητῶν· τὰ γὰρ μαθηματικὰ τῶν ὄντων ἄνευ κινήσεώς ἐστιν ἔξω τῶν περὶ τὴν ἀστρολογίαν) διαλέγον-

of all was the substance of the thing, as though one thought that the double and the dyad are the same thing because 'double' is applied first of all to dualities. But surely the essence of the double and that of the dyad are not identical; for otherwise the one will be many—which also happened to them.

On the Delimitation between Mathematics, Physics, and First Philosophy (R16–R18)

R16 (< 58B.37) Aristotle, *On the Heavens*

[...] they [i.e. "those who are called Pythagoreans"] do not seek explanations and causes that would be adapted to the phenomena, but they drag the phenomena in the direction of some of their own explanations and opinions and try to adjust them.

R17 (< 58B.26) Aristotle, *Metaphysics*

Since they are generating the world and want to speak as natural philosophers do, it is fair to examine them also with regard to nature, but to dismiss them from the present inquiry [scil. first philosophy or 'metaphysics'].

R18 (< 58B.22) Aristotle, *Metaphysics*

The people called Pythagoreans use principles and elements in a stranger way than the natural philosophers do (the reason for this is that they did not derive them from the perceptibles; for, among the things that are, mathematical entities are without movement, except for those that belong to astronomy): and yet everything that they

ται μέντοι καὶ πραγματεύονται περὶ φύσεως πάντα·
[... = **PYTHS. ANON. D5**] [990a5] τὰς δ' αἰτίας καὶ
τὰς ἀρχάς, [...] ἱκανὰς λέγουσιν ἐπαναβῆναι καὶ ἐπὶ
τὰ ἀνωτέρω τῶν ὄντων, καὶ μᾶλλον ἢ τοῖς περὶ φύ
σεως λόγοις ἁρμοττούσας [= ... **R19**].

On the Recourse to Numbers as Principles in Explanations of Natural Phenomena (R19–R21)

R19 (58B.22) Arist. *Metaph.* A8 990a8–29

[... = **R18**] ἐκ τίνος μέντοι τρόπου κίνησις ἔσται
πέρατος καὶ ἀπείρου μόνων ὑποκειμένων καὶ περιττοῦ
καὶ ἀρτίου, οὐθὲν λέγουσιν, ἢ πῶς δυνατὸν ἄνευ κι
νήσεως καὶ μεταβολῆς γένεσιν εἶναι καὶ φθορὰν ἢ τὰ
τῶν φερομένων ἔργα κατὰ τὸν οὐρανόν.

ἔτι δὲ εἴτε δοίη τις αὐτοῖς ἐκ τούτων εἶναι μέγεθος
εἴτε δειχθείη τοῦτο, ὅμως τίνα τρόπον ἔσται τὰ μὲν
κοῦφα τὰ δὲ βάρος ἔχοντα τῶν σωμάτων; ἐξ ὧν γὰρ
ὑποτίθενται [990a15] καὶ λέγουσιν, οὐθὲν μᾶλλον περὶ
τῶν μαθηματικῶν λέγουσι σωμάτων ἢ περὶ τῶν αἰ
σθητῶν· διὸ περὶ πυρὸς ἢ γῆς ἢ τῶν ἄλλων τῶν
τοιούτων σωμάτων οὐδ' ὁτιοῦν εἰρήκασιν, ἅτε οὐθὲν
περὶ τῶν αἰσθητῶν οἶμαι λέγοντες ἴδιον.

ἔτι δὲ πῶς δεῖ λαβεῖν αἴτια μὲν εἶναι τὰ τοῦ ἀριθ
μοῦ πάθη καὶ τὸν ἀριθμὸν [990a20] τῶν κατὰ τὸν
οὐρανὸν ὄντων καὶ γιγνομένων καὶ ἐξ ἀρχῆς καὶ νῦν,
ἀριθμὸν δ' ἄλλον μηθένα εἶναι παρὰ τὸν ἀριθμὸν

discuss and consider bears upon nature. [. . .] As for the causes and principles [. . .], the ones they discuss are sufficient for progressing in the direction of the highest beings as well, and they agree more [scil. with these] than with reasonings about nature [. . .].

On the Recourse to Numbers as Principles in Explanations of Natural Phenomena (R19–R21)

R19 (58B.22) Aristotle, *Metaphysics*

[. . .] But in what way there will be motion if one only posits the limit and the unlimited, and the odd and the even—they do not say anything at all about this, nor how generation and destruction are possible without motion or transformation, or the behavior of bodies that move in the heavens.

Moreover, if one granted to them that magnitude is constituted out of these [scil. principles] or this had been demonstrated, all the same in what way will some bodies be light and others heavy? For on the basis of what they posit [990a15] and say, they do not speak more about the mathematical bodies than about the perceptible ones. And this is why they have not said anything at all about fire or earth or the other bodies of this sort, because, I suppose, they say nothing of their own about the perceptibles.

Moreover, how should we understand it that the affections of number and number are causes [990a20] of the things that exist and come to be in the heavens, both from the beginning and now, and that no other number exists

τοῦτον ἐξ οὗ συνέστηκεν ὁ κόσμος; ὅταν γὰρ ἐν τῳδὶ
μὲν τῷ μέρει δόξα καὶ καιρὸς αὐτοῖς ᾖ, μικρὸν δὲ
ἄνωθεν ἢ κάτωθεν ἀδικία καὶ κρίσις[1] ἢ μῖξις, ἀπόδειξιν δὲ λέγωσιν ὅτι [990a25] τούτων ἓν[2] ἕκαστον ἀριθμός ἐστι, συμβαίνῃ[3] δὲ κατὰ τὸν τόπον τοῦτον ἤδη
πλῆθος εἶναι τῶν συνισταμένων μεγεθῶν διὰ τὸ τὰ
πάθη ταῦτα ἀκολουθεῖν τοῖς τόποις ἑκάστοις, πότερον
οὗτος ὁ αὐτός ἐστιν ἀριθμός, ὁ ἐν τῷ οὐρανῷ, ὃν δεῖ
λαβεῖν ὅτι τούτων ἕκαστόν ἐστιν, ἢ παρὰ τοῦτον ἄλλος;

[1] κρίσις A[b]: διάκρισις E   [2] ἓν A[b]: μὲν ἕν E   [3] συμβαίνει mss., corr. Bonitz

R20 (58B.10) Arist. *Metaph.* M8 1083b8–19

ὁ δὲ τῶν Πυθαγορείων τρόπος τῇ μὲν ἐλάττους ἔχει
δυσχερείας τῶν πρότερον εἰρημένων, τῇ δὲ ἰδίας
ἑτέρας. τὸ μὲν γὰρ μὴ χωριστὸν ποιεῖν τὸν ἀριθμὸν
ἀφαιρεῖται πολλὰ τῶν ἀδυνάτων· τὸ δὲ τὰ σώματα ἐξ
ἀριθμῶν εἶναι συγκείμενα, καὶ τὸν ἀριθμὸν τοῦτον
εἶναι μαθηματικόν, ἀδύνατόν ἐστιν. οὔτε γὰρ ἄτομα
μεγέθη λέγειν ἀληθές, εἴ θ' ὅτι μάλιστα τοῦτον ἔχει
τὸν τρόπον, οὐχ αἵ γε μονάδες μέγεθος ἔχουσιν· μέγεθος δὲ ἐξ ἀδιαιρέτων συγκεῖσθαι πῶς δυνατόν;
ἀλλὰ μὴν ὅ γ' ἀριθμητικὸς ἀριθμὸς μοναδικός ἐστιν.
ἐκεῖνοι δὲ τὸν ἀριθμὸν τὰ ὄντα λέγουσιν· τὰ γοῦν
θεωρήματα προσάπτουσι τοῖς σώμασιν ὡς ἐξ ἐκείνων
ὄντων τῶν ἀριθμῶν.

besides this number out of which the world is constituted? For when opinion and occasion are located for them in this region, and a little lower or higher injustice, judgment, or mixture, and they say as a proof for this that [990a25] each of these things is a number [cf. **PYTHS. ANON. D19**], and it happens that in this place there is already a multitude of constituted magnitudes because these affections follow each of the places: is this the same number, the one that is located in the heavens, of which we must understand that it is each of these things, or some other one besides this?

R20 (58B.10) Aristotle, *Metaphysics*

In one regard the method of the Pythagoreans encounters fewer difficulties than the ones we spoke of earlier [scil. the various theories about ideas and numbers of Platonic allegiance], but in another it encounters others that are peculiar to it. For not to separate number removes many impossibilities; but that bodies be composed out of numbers, and that this number be the mathematical number—this is impossible. For it is not true to speak of indivisible magnitudes, and even if there were magnitudes of this sort, the units at least do not have magnitude; and how can a magnitude be constituted out of indivisibles? But certainly arithmetical number, at least, is constituted out of unities. But these people say that the things that are are number. At any rate they apply their theoretical conceptions to bodies as though they consisted of those numbers.

EARLY GREEK PHILOSOPHY IV

R21 (58B.38) Arist. *Cael.* 3.1 300a14–19

τὸ δ' αὐτὸ συμβαίνει καὶ τοῖς ἐξ ἀριθμῶν συντιθεῖσι τὸν οὐρανόν· ἔνιοι γὰρ τὴν φύσιν ἐξ ἀριθμῶν συνιστᾶσιν, ὥσπερ τῶν Πυθαγορείων τινές· τὰ μὲν γὰρ φυσικὰ σώματα φαίνεται βάρος ἔχοντα καὶ κουφότητα, τὰς δὲ μονάδας οὔτε σώματα ποιεῖν οἷόν τε συντιθεμένας οὔτε βάρος ἔχειν.

On the Unlimited Principle (R22)

R22 (58B.29) Arist. *Phys.* 3.5 204a29–34

κατὰ συμβεβηκὸς ἄρα ὑπάρχει τὸ ἄπειρον· ἀλλ' εἰ οὕτως, εἴρηται ὅτι οὐκ ἐνδέχεται αὐτὸ λέγειν ἀρχήν, ἀλλ' ᾧ συμβέβηκε, τὸν ἀέρα ἢ τὸ ἄρτιον. ὥστε ἀτόπως ἂν ἀποφαίνοιντο οἱ λέγοντες οὕτως ὥσπερ οἱ Πυθαγόρειοί φασιν· ἅμα γὰρ οὐσίαν ποιοῦσι τὸ ἄπειρον καὶ μερίζουσιν.

On Cosmology (R23–R24)

R23 (< 58B.9) Arist. *Metaph.* M6 1080b20–21

[. . . **PYTHS. ANON. D21**] ὅπως δὲ τὸ πρῶτον ἓν συνέστη ἔχον μέγεθος, ἀπορεῖν ἐοίκασιν.

R24 (< 58B.37) Arist. *Cael.* 2.13 293b4–10

[. . . **PYTHS. ANON. D10**] ὥσπερ τὸ μέσον ἁπλῶς

PYTHAGOREAN RECEPTION

R21 (58B.38) Aristotle, *On the Heavens*

The same difficulty [scil. as the one encountered by the Platonic theory of the generation of bodies starting from elementary surfaces] comes about for those who compose the heavens out of numbers (for some people compose nature out of numbers, like some of the Pythagoreans). For it is evident that natural bodies possess weight and lightness, whereas monads, when they are composed, are not capable either of forming a body or of possessing weight.

On the Unlimited Principle (R22)

R22 (58B.29) Aristotle, *Physics*

So the unlimited is predicated contingently. But if this is so, as I have said, it is not possible to say that it is a principle, but [scil. the principle is] that of which it is predicated, the air or the even. So that the statement of those who speak as the Pythagoreans do might seem to be absurd: for at one and the same time they make the unlimited a substance and divide it into parts.

On Cosmology (R23–R24)

R23 (< 58B.9) Aristotle, *Metaphysics*

[. . .] How the first One, which possesses a magnitude, was formed, they seem to have difficulties explaining.

R24 (< 58B.37) Aristotle, *On the Heavens*

[. . .], as though the center were spoken of in a simple way,

EARLY GREEK PHILOSOPHY IV

λεγόμενον, καὶ τὸ τοῦ μεγέθους μέσον καὶ τοῦ πράγματος ὂν μέσον καὶ τῆς φύσεως. καίτοι καθάπερ ἐν τοῖς ζῴοις οὐ ταὐτὸν τοῦ ζῴου καὶ τοῦ σώματος μέσον, οὕτως ὑποληπτέον μᾶλλον καὶ περὶ τὸν ὅλον οὐρανόν. διὰ μὲν οὖν ταύτην τὴν αἰτίαν οὐθὲν αὐτοὺς δεῖ θορυβεῖσθαι περὶ τὸ πᾶν, οὐδ' εἰσάγειν φυλακὴν ἐπὶ τὸ κέντρον, ἀλλ' ἐκεῖνο ζητεῖν τὸ μέσον, ποῖόν τι καὶ ποῦ πέφυκεν.

On the Harmony of the Spheres (R25)

R25 (≠ DK)

a Arist. *Cael.* 2.9 290b30–291a6

[. . . = **PYTHS. ANON. D46**] ταῦτα δή [. . .] ἐμμελῶς μὲν λέγεται καὶ μουσικῶς, ἀδύνατον δὲ τοῦτον ἔχειν τὸν τρόπον. οὐ γὰρ μόνον τὸ μηθὲν ἀκούειν ἄτοπον, περὶ οὗ λέγειν ἐγχειροῦσι[1] τὴν αἰτίαν,[2] ἀλλὰ καὶ τὸ μηδὲν πάσχειν χωρὶς αἰσθήσεως. οἱ γὰρ ὑπερβάλλοντες ψόφοι διακναίουσι καὶ τῶν ἀψύχων σωμάτων τοὺς ὄγκους, οἷον ὁ τῆς βροντῆς διίστησι λίθους καὶ τὰ καρτερώτατα τῶν σωμάτων. τοσούτων δὲ φερομένων, καὶ τοῦ ψόφου διιόντος πρὸς τὸ φερόμενον μέγεθος, πολλαπλάσιον μέγεθος ἀναγκαῖον ἀφικνεῖσθαί τε δεῦρο καὶ τὴν ἰσχὺν ἀμήχανον εἶναι τῆς βίας. ἀλλ' εὐλόγως οὔτ' ἀκούομεν οὔτε πάσχοντα φαίνεται τὰ σώματα βίαιον οὐδὲν πάθος, διὰ τὸ μὴ ψοφεῖν.

[1] ἐγχειροῦσι EH: ἐπιχειροῦσι J

whether it is the center of a magnitude or the center of a thing or of nature. But just as in animals the center of the animal is not that of the body, so too and even more one must think that this is how it is with regard to the totality of the heavens. This is the reason why these people [i.e. the Pythagoreans] should not be disturbed with regard to the whole, nor introduce a guard in the center, but instead should seek what kind this center is and where it is located.

On the Harmony of the Spheres (R25)

R25 (≠ DK)

a Aristotle, *On the Heavens*

[...] These things [...] are said harmoniously and musically, but it is impossible that matters be this way. For it is not only strange that we do not hear anything—a fact for which they undertake to indicate the reason—but also, independently even of sensation, we do not suffer any effect. For excessive noises also tear apart the masses of inanimate bodies, like that of thunder, which splits apart stones and the hardest bodies. But given the size of the bodies that are moving and the fact that the sound that is transmitted is in proportion to the magnitude that is displaced, it follows of necessity that the magnitude [scil. of the sound] that arrives here must be many times superior and that the force of its intensity be overwhelming. But it is reasonable that we do not hear anything and that our bodies evidently do not suffer anything violent, given that no sound is produced.

---

² λέγειν ... τὴν αἰτίαν (vel λύειν ... τὴν ἀπορίαν) Bonitz: λύειν ... τὴν αἰτίαν mss.

b Porph. *In Ptol. Harm.*, pp. 80.28–81.5

εἰ μέντοι, ὥς φασιν οἱ Πυθαγόρειοι, ἡ τοῦ παντὸς ἁρμονία διὰ μέγεθος ψόφων ὑπερβάλλει ἡμῶν τὴν ἀκοήν, μείζων ἂν εἴη ὁ ὅρος τῶν ψόφων τῶν τῆς ἀκοῆς. ἔχοι γὰρ ἂν καὶ ὀξυτάτους καὶ βαρυτάτους φθόγγους ἡ τοῦ παντὸς ἁρμονία, ὧν ἡμῶν ἡ ἀκοὴ ἀπολείπεται.

On the Soul (R26)

R26 (58B.39) Arist. *An.* 1.3 407b20–24

οἱ δὲ μόνον ἐπιχειροῦσι λέγειν ποῖόν τι ἡ ψυχή, περὶ δὲ τοῦ δεξομένου σώματος οὐθὲν ἔτι προσδιορίζουσιν, ὥσπερ ἐνδεχόμενον κατὰ τοὺς Πυθαγορικοὺς μύθους τὴν τυχοῦσαν ψυχὴν εἰς τὸ τυχὸν ἐνδύεσθαι σῶμα.

Eudemus on the Eternal Return (R27)

R27 (> 58B.34) Simpl. *In Phys.*, p. 732.24–26, 732.30–733.1

[. . . = **PYTHS. ANON. D35**] οὐδὲν δὲ ἴσως χεῖρον καὶ τῆς Εὐδήμου ῥήσεως ἐκ τοῦ τρίτου τῶν Φυσικῶν τὰ ἐνταῦθα λεγόμενα παραφραζούσης ἀκούειν· [Frag. 88 Wehrli] "ὁ δὲ αὐτὸς χρόνος πότερον γίνεται ὥσπερ ἔνιοί φασιν ἢ οὔ, ἀπορήσειεν ἄν τις [. . .]. εἰ δέ τις πιστεύσειε τοῖς Πυθαγορείοις, ὥστε πάλιν τὰ αὐτὰ[1] ἀριθμῷ,[2] κἀγὼ μυθολογήσω τὸ ῥαβδίον ἔχων ὑμῖν

b Porphyry, *Commentary on Ptolemy's* Harmonics

But if, as the Pythagoreans say, the harmony of the whole exceeds our hearing by reason of the magnitude of its sounds, its limit [i.e. that of the harmony of the whole] would be larger than that of the sounds of hearing. For the harmony of the whole would include very high-pitched sounds and very low-pitched ones which our hearing fails [scil. to perceive].

On the Soul (R26)

R26 (58B.39) Aristotle, *On the Soul*

Some try to say only what kind of thing the soul is, and make no further definition regarding the body that will receive it, as if it were possible, according to the Pythagorean myths, for just any soul to enter into just any body.

Eudemus on the Eternal Return (R27)

R27 (> 58B.34) Eudemus in Simplicius, *Commentary on Aristotle's* Physics

[...] But perhaps it is not worse to listen to what Eudemus says in the third book of his *Physics* when he paraphrases what is said in this passage [i.e. Arist. *Phys.* 4.12 220b12–14]: "One might well pose the difficulty of knowing whether the time can return as identical, as some say, or not [...]. If one believes, following the Pythagoreans, that things will happen again as numerically identical, that I

---

¹ τὰ αὐτὰ F: om. E   ² ἀριθμῷ om. F

καθημένοις οὕτω, καὶ τὰ ἄλλα πάντα ὁμοίως ἕξει, καὶ τὸν χρόνον εὔλογόν ἐστι τὸν αὐτὸν εἶναι. μιᾶς γὰρ καὶ τῆς αὐτῆς κινήσεως, ὁμοίως δὲ καὶ πολλῶν τῶν αὐτῶν τὸ πρότερον καὶ ὕστερον ἓν καὶ ταὐτόν, καὶ ὁ τούτων δὴ ἀριθμός· πάντα ἄρα τὰ αὐτά, ὥστε καὶ ὁ χρόνος."

*The Platonization of Older
Pythagoreanism (R28–R32)
The Appropriation of Pythagoreanism
by the Older Academy (R28)*

R28 (≠ DK) Porph. *VP* 53

ἡ μὲν δὴ περὶ τῶν ἀριθμῶν πραγματεία τοιαύτη τοῖς Πυθαγορείοις. καὶ διὰ ταύτην πρωτίστην οὖσαν[1] τὴν φιλοσοφίαν ταύτην συνέβη σβεσθῆναι, πρῶτον μὲν διὰ τὸ αἰνιγματῶδες, ἔπειτα διὰ τὸ καὶ τὰ γεγραμμένα δωριστὶ[2] γεγράφθαι, ἐχούσης τι καὶ ἀσαφὲς τῆς διαλέκτου, καὶ μὴν[3] διὰ τοῦτο ὑπονοεῖσθαι καὶ τὰ ὑπ' αὐτῆς ἀνιστορούμενα δόγματα ὡς νόθα καὶ παρηκουσμένα τῷ μὴ ἄντικρυς Πυθαγορικοὺς εἶναι τοὺς ἐκφέροντας ταῦτα. πρὸς δὲ τούτοις τὸν Πλάτωνα καὶ Ἀριστοτέλη Σπεύσιππόν τε καὶ Ἀριστόξενον καὶ Ξενοκράτη, ὥς φασιν οἱ Πυθαγόρειοι, τὰ μὲν κάρπιμα σφετερίσασθαι διὰ βραχείας ἐπισκευῆς, τὰ δ' ἐπιπόλαια καὶ ἐλαφρὰ καὶ ὅσα πρὸς ἀνασκευὴν[4] καὶ

[1] αἰτίαν coni. Zeller

will speak, holding this staff as I am, to you who will be seated as you are, and that all other things will be in the same way, it is also reasonable that the time will be identical. For if there is one and the same motion, in the same way, if there are many of them that are identical, the earlier and the later will be one and the same, and so too certainly their number; hence all things will be identical, including time as well."

*The Platonization of Older
Pythagoreanism (R28–R32)
The Appropriation of Pythagoreanism
by the Older Academy (R28)*

R28 (≠ DK) Porphyry, *Life of Pythagoras*

Such is the Pythagoreans' theory with regard to numbers. And it is because of this [scil. theory], which was the principal [scil. part of their philosophy], that it came about that this philosophy became extinguished, first because of its enigmatic quality, and second because its writings were written in Doric (a dialect that is somewhat obscure), and, what is more, the doctrines that were investigated by it fell under suspicion of being spurious and misunderstood because of this, that it was not genuine Pythagoreans who divulged them. What is more, Plato and Aristotle, Speusippus and Aristoxenus and Xenocrates, as the Pythagoreans say, appropriated the fruitful parts with slight modifications, while they gathered together the superficial and

---

² δωριστὶ Rittershusius: δωρίδι mss.   ³ μηδὲν mss., corr. Shorey   ⁴ διασκευὴν mss., corr. Burkert

χλευασμὸν τοῦ διδασκαλείου ὑπὸ τῶν βασκάνως
ὕστερον συκοφαντούντων προβάλλεται συναγαγεῖν
καὶ ὡς ἴδια τῆς αἱρέσεως καταχωρίσαι.

*Characteristic Attributions of Platonic and
Academic Doctrines to Pythagoras (R29–R31)
Pythagoras, Inventor of the Terms 'Philosophy'
and 'Philosopher'? (R29, cf. PYTH. c D9)*

R29 (≠ DK)

a Diog. Laert. 1.12

φιλοσοφίαν δὲ πρῶτος ὠνόμασε Πυθαγόρας καὶ ἑαυτὸν φιλόσοφον, ἐν Σικυῶνι διαλεγόμενος Λέοντι τῷ Σικυωνίων τυράννῳ ἢ Φλιασίων, καθά φησιν Ἡρακλείδης ὁ Ποντικὸς ἐν τῇ Περὶ τῆς ἄπνου [Frag. 84 Schorn = 87 Wehrli]· μηδένα γὰρ εἶναι σοφὸν[1] ἀλλ᾽ ἢ θεόν.

[1] post σοφὸν hab. mss. ἄνθρωπον, secl. Cobet

b Diog. Laert. 8.8

Σωσικράτης[1] δὲ ἐν Διαδοχαῖς φησιν [Frag. 17 Giannattasio Andria] αὐτὸν ἐρωτηθέντα ὑπὸ Λέοντος τοῦ Φλιασίων τυράννου τίς εἴη, 'φιλόσοφον' εἰπεῖν. καὶ τὸν βίον ἐοικέναι πανηγύρει· ὡς οὖν εἰς ταύτην οἱ μὲν ἀγωνιούμενοι, οἱ δὲ κατ᾽ ἐμπόριαν, οἱ δέ γε βέλτιστοι

trivial parts, and those that were put forward later as aspersions by envious slanderers in order to refute and deride the doctrine, and they separated these out as peculiar to that sect.

Characteristic Attributions of Platonic and Academic Doctrines to Pythagoras (R29–R31) Pythagoras, Inventor of the Terms 'Philosophy' and 'Philosopher'? (R29, cf. PYTH. c D9)

R29 (≠ DK)

a Diogenes Laertius

Pythagoras was the first to use the term 'philosophy' and to call himself a 'philosopher,' when he was conversing in Sicyon with Leon the tyrant of Sicyon (or of Phlius, as Heraclides of Pontus says in his *On the Woman Who Stopped Breathing*). For no one is wise except for god.[1]

[1] The interpretation of the term 'philosopher' as 'lover of wisdom' as opposed to 'sage, wise man' derives from Plato (cf. e.g. *Symp.* 204a1–2). It is not certain that it is part of Heraclides' original explanation.

b Diogenes Laertius

Sosicrates says in his *Successions* that when he [i.e. Pythagoras] was asked by Leon the tyrant of Phlius who he was, he said, "A philosopher," and that life resembles a festal assembly: just as some people go there in order to compete, others in order to sell their wares, but the best

---

[1] σωσικράτης rec.: σωκράτης BPF

ἔρχονται θεαταί, οὕτως ἐν τῷ βίῳ οἱ μὲν ἀνδραποδώδεις, ἔφη, φύονται δόξης καὶ πλεονεξίας θηραταί, οἱ δὲ φιλόσοφοι τῆς ἀληθείας.

c Cic. *Tusc.* 5.8–9

[. . .] admiratum Leontem novitatem nominis quaesivisse, quinam essent philosophi, et quid inter eos et reliquos interesset; [9] Pythagoram autem respondisse [. . .] raros esse quosdam, qui ceteris omnibus pro nihilo habitis rerum naturam studiose intuerentur; hos se appellare sapientiae studiosos, id est enim philosophos [. . .].

Pythagoras and the Xenocratean
Definition of the Soul (R30)

R30 (≠ DK) Aët. 4.2.3–4 (Stob.) [περὶ ψυχῆς]

[3] Πυθαγόρας ἀριθμὸν αὐτὸν κινοῦντα, τὸν δὲ ἀριθμὸν ἀντὶ τοῦ νοῦ παραλαμβάνει.
[4] ὁμοίως δὲ καὶ Ξενοκράτης [Frag. 60 Heinze].

Pythagoras as the Source of Plato's and Aristotle's
Theory of Emotions (R31)

R31 (≠ DK) Gal. *Plac. Hipp. Plat.* 4.7.38

οὐ γὰρ Ἀριστοτέλης μόνον ἢ Πλάτων ἐδόξαζον οὕτως ἀλλ' ἔτι πρόσθεν ἄλλοι τέ τινες καὶ Πυθαγόρας, ὡς

ones go in order to be spectators, so too in life slaves, he said, are born as people who hunt for reputation or increased acquisition, and philosophers for the truth.[1]

[1] There are many ancient references to this comparison, which must go back to Heraclides.

c Cicero, *Tusculan Disputations*

[...] Leon marveled at the novelty of the term and asked who the philosophers were and what the difference was between them and the rest of mankind. [9] Pythagoras answered [...] that it was a small number of men who, considering everything else worthless, studied closely the nature of things; and these called themselves lovers of wisdom, that is, philosophers [...].

*Pythagoras and the Xenocratean
Definition of the Soul (R30)*

R30 (≠ DK) Aëtius

[3] Pythagoras: it [i.e. the soul] is a number that moves itself; he understands number instead of the mind.
[4] So too Xenocrates.

*Pythagoras as the Source of Plato's and Aristotle's
Theory of Emotions (R31)*

R31 (≠ DK) Galen, *On the Opinions of Hippocrates and Plato*

Aristotle and Plato were not the only people who had this opinion [scil. that there is a conflict between reason and

καὶ Ποσειδώνιός φησι [Frag. T95 Edelstein-Kidd], ἐκείνου πρῶτον μὲν εἶναι λέγων τὸ δόγμα, Πλάτωνα δ' ἐξεργάσασθαι καὶ κατασκευάσαι τελεώτερον αὐτό.

*The Construction of a Line of
Descent by Instruction:
Pythagoras-Archytas-Plato-Aristotle (R32)*

R32 (p. 237 Thesleff) Anon. *VP*, in Phot. *Bibl.* (cod. 249, 438b)

ὅτι ἔνατος ἀπὸ Πυθαγόρου διάδοχος γέγονέ φησι Πλάτων Ἀρχύτου τοῦ πρεσβυτέρου μαθητὴς γενόμενος, δέκατος δὲ Ἀριστοτέλης [= **ARCHY. P9b**].

*Aspects of Hellenistic and Later
Pythagoreanism (R33–R72)*

An Attempted Syncretic Systematization (R33)

R33 (58B.1a) Alex. Poly. *Mem. Pyth.* in Diog. Laert. 8.24–33

---

[1] It is difficult to date this eclectic presentation, unique in its genre, of the doctrine of Pythagoras. Alexander Polyhistor, who lived at Rome at the beginning of the first century BC, provides a *terminus ante quem*. The summary probably dates from the second century, but other, earlier dates (even the end of the fourth century) have been proposed.

the emotions], but there were others even earlier, and in particular Pythagoras, as Posidonius states as well, saying that he was the first to assert this thesis and that Plato elaborated it and rendered it more complete.

The Construction of a Line of Descent by Instruction: Pythagoras-Archytas-Plato-Aristotle (R32)

R32 (≠ DK) Anonymous, *Life of Pythagoras*, in Photius, *Library*

He [i.e. the author of the anonymous *Life*] says that the ninth successor of Pythagoras was Plato, who had been the disciple of the older Archytas, and that the tenth was Aristotle.

Aspects of Hellenistic and later Pythagoreanism (R33–R72)[1]

[1] Given the considerable uncertainty of dating the Pythagorean texts, it is not impossible that some of the texts collected in this section antedate the Hellenistic period (for example, the interpretation of the Pythagorean *sumbola*, **R34**). Moreover, it is certain or probable that some extracts belong to the corpus of Pseudo-Pythagorica, to which we have dedicated a specific rubric (**R45–R66**). The cross-references are indicated.

An Attempted Syncretic Systematization (R33)[1]

R33 (58.B1a) *Pythagorean Memoirs* quoted by Alexander Polyhistor in Diogenes Laertius

[24] φησὶ δὲ ὁ Ἀλέξανδρος ἐν ταῖς τῶν Φιλοσόφων διαδοχαῖς καὶ ταῦτα εὑρηκέναι ἐν Πυθαγορικοῖς ὑπομνήμασιν.

[25] ἀρχὴν μὲν τῶν ἁπάντων μονάδα· ἐκ δὲ τῆς μονάδος ἀόριστον δυάδα ὡς ἂν ὕλην τῇ μονάδι αἰτίῳ ὄντι[1] ὑποστῆναι· ἐκ δὲ τῆς μονάδος καὶ τῆς ἀορίστου δυάδος τοὺς ἀριθμούς· ἐκ δὲ τῶν ἀριθμῶν τὰ σημεῖα· ἐκ δὲ τούτων τὰς γραμμάς, ἐξ ὧν τὰ ἐπίπεδα σχήματα· ἐκ δὲ τῶν ἐπιπέδων τὰ στερεὰ σχήματα· ἐκ δὲ τούτων τὰ αἰσθητὰ σώματα, ὧν καὶ τὰ στοιχεῖα εἶναι τέτταρα, πῦρ, ὕδωρ, γῆν, ἀέρα· ἃ μεταβάλλειν καὶ τρέπεσθαι δι' ὅλων, καὶ γίγνεσθαι ἐξ αὐτῶν κόσμον ἔμψυχον, νοερόν, σφαιροειδῆ, μέσην περιέχοντα τὴν γῆν καὶ αὐτὴν σφαιροειδῆ καὶ περιοικουμένην. εἶναι δὲ καὶ ἀντίποδας καὶ τὰ ἡμῖν κάτω ἐκείνοις ἄνω.

[26] ἰσόμοιρά τε εἶναι ἐν τῷ κόσμῳ φῶς καὶ σκότος, καὶ θερμὸν καὶ ψυχρόν, καὶ ξηρὸν καὶ ὑγρόν· ὧν κατ' ἐπικράτειαν θερμοῦ μὲν θέρος γίγνεσθαι, ψυχροῦ δὲ χειμῶνα· ἐὰν δὲ ἰσομοιρῇ, τὰ κάλλιστα εἶναι τοῦ ἔτους, οὗ τὸ μὲν θάλλον ἔαρ ὑγιεινόν, τὸ δὲ φθίνον φθινόπωρον νοσερόν. ἀλλὰ καὶ τῆς ἡμέρας θάλλειν μὲν τὴν ἕω, φθίνειν δὲ τὴν ἑσπέραν· ὅθεν καὶ νοσερώτερον εἶναι. τόν τε περὶ τὴν γῆν αἰθέρα[2] ἄσειστον[3] καὶ νοσερὸν καὶ τὰ ἐν αὐτῷ πάντα θνητά· τὸν δὲ ἀνωτάτω ἀεικίνητόν τε εἶναι καὶ καθαρὸν καὶ ὑγιᾶ καὶ πάντα τὰ ἐν αὐτῷ ἀθάνατα καὶ διὰ τοῦτο θεῖα.

PYTHAGOREAN RECEPTION

[24] This is what Alexander in his *Successions of the Philosophers* says that he also found in *Pythagorean Memoirs*.
[25] The principle of all things is the monad [or: the unit]; from the monad has come the unlimited dyad [i.e. duality], as so to speak a matter for the monad, which is the cause; and from the monad and the unlimited dyad have come the numbers; from the numbers, the points; from these, the lines; from which, the plane figures; from the planes, the solid figures; from these, the perceptible bodies, of which there are four elements, fire, water, earth, and air: these change and are transformed in totality. And from these there has come to be [scil. the vault of] the world, which is animated, intelligent, spherical, and surrounds the earth located in the middle, which is itself also spherical and inhabited all around. There are antipodes, and what is down for us is up for them.
[26] There is the same portion of light and darkness in the world, of heat and cold, and of dry and moist; when, among these, heat dominates, there is summer; when cold, winter; when dry, spring; when moist, autumn. If they are in equilibrium, this is the finest part of the year, of which the flowering, in the spring, is healthy while the declining, in the autumn, is unhealthy. So too, in the day, there is flowering, in the morning, and declining, in the evening; which is why this is also more unhealthy. The air around the earth is stagnant and unhealthy and everything that is in it is mortal; but the one that is higher is always in motion, pure, and healthy, and everything that is in it is immortal and for this reason divine.

---

¹ οὔσῃ Reiske   ² αἰθέρα BP¹ F: ἀέρα P⁴   ³ ἄσειστον ⟨καὶ θολερὸν⟩ Reiske

[27] ἥλιόν τε καὶ σελήνην καὶ τοὺς ἄλλους ἀστέρας εἶναι θεούς· ἐπικρατεῖ γὰρ τὸ θερμὸν ἐν αὐτοῖς, ὅπερ ἐστὶ ζωῆς αἴτιον. τήν τε σελήνην λάμπεσθαι ὑφ' ἡλίου. καὶ ἀνθρώπων εἶναι πρὸς θεοὺς συγγένειαν, κατὰ τὸ μετέχειν ἄνθρωπον θερμοῦ· διὸ καὶ προνοεῖσθαι τὸν θεὸν ἡμῶν. εἱμαρμένην τε τῶν ὅλων καὶ κατὰ μέρος αἰτίαν εἶναι τῆς διοικήσεως. διήκειν τε ἀπὸ τοῦ ἡλίου ἀκτῖνα διὰ τοῦ αἰθέρος τοῦ τε ψυχροῦ καὶ παχέος. καλοῦσι δὲ τὸν μὲν ἀέρα ψυχρὸν αἰθέρα, τὴν δὲ θάλασσαν καὶ τὸ ὑγρὸν παχὺν[1] αἰθέρα. ταύτην δὲ τὴν ἀκτῖνα καὶ εἰς τὰ βένθη[2] δύεσθαι καὶ διὰ τοῦτο ζωοποιεῖν πάντα.

[28] καὶ ζῆν μὲν πάνθ' ὅσα μετέχει τοῦ θερμοῦ· διὸ καὶ τὰ φυτὰ ζῷα εἶναι· ψυχὴν μέντοι μὴ ἔχειν πάντα. εἶναι δὲ τὴν ψυχὴν ἀπόσπασμα αἰθέρος καὶ τοῦ θερμοῦ καὶ τοῦ ψυχροῦ τῷ <τε>[3] συμμετέχειν ψυχροῦ αἰθέρος διαφέρειν ψυχὴν ζωῆς· ἀθάνατόν τε εἶναι αὐτήν, ἐπειδήπερ καὶ τὸ ἀφ' οὗπερ ἀπέσπασται ἀθάνατόν ἐστι. τὰ δὲ ζῷα γεννᾶσθαι ἐξ ἀλλήλων ἀπὸ σπερμάτων, τὴν δὲ ἐκ γῆς γένεσιν ἀδύνατον ὑφίστασθαι. τὸ δὲ σπέρμα εἶναι σταγόνα ἐγκεφάλου περιέχουσαν ἐν ἑαυτῇ ἀτμὸν θερμόν· ταύτην δὲ προσφερομένην τῇ μήτρᾳ ἀπὸ μὲν τοῦ ἐγκεφάλου ἰχῶρα καὶ ὑγρὸν καὶ αἷμα προΐεσθαι, ἐξ ὧν σάρκας τε καὶ νεῦρα καὶ ὀστᾶ καὶ τρίχας καὶ τὸ ὅλον συνίστασθαι[4] σῶμα· ἀπὸ δὲ τοῦ ἀτμοῦ ψυχὴν καὶ αἴσθησιν.

[29] μορφοῦσθαι δὲ τὸ μὲν πρῶτον παγὲν ἐν ἡμέραις τεσσαράκοντα, κατὰ δὲ τοὺς τῆς ἁρμονίας λόγους ἐν

PYTHAGOREAN RECEPTION

[27] The sun, the moon, and the other heavenly bodies are gods; for in them heat dominates, which is the cause of life; and the moon is illuminated by the sun. And there is a consanguinity between humans and gods, because humans have a share in heat: and that is why god exercises his providence for us. Fate is the cause of the administration both of the whole and of its parts. The ray of the sun penetrates through the cold and dense aether. And they call the air 'cold aether,' the sea and the moist 'thick aether.' This ray goes down into the depths and that is why it gives life to everything.

[28] All those things are alive that have a share of heat; and that is why plants too are living beings. But not all things possess a soul. The soul is a piece detached from the aether, from both the warm aether and the cold one, and since it has a share in the cold aether the soul differs from life; and it is immortal, since what it has been detached from is immortal too. Animals are generated by one another from semen, and it is impossible for generation to come about from the earth. The semen is a drop of the brain which surrounds within itself a hot vapor; when it is conveyed to the womb it emits lymph, fluid, and blood that come from the brain; from these are formed flesh, muscles, bones, hair, and the whole body; and from the vapor, the soul and sensation.

[29] After it has first congealed, the embryo acquires its form in forty days, and, according to harmonic ratios, the

---

¹ παχὺν BP¹: ψυχρὸν F, γρ P⁴   ² βένθη P¹F: βάθη BP⁴
³ τῷ <τε> Diels: τῷ P: τὸ BF   ⁴ συνίστασθαι BP: ὑφίστασθαι F

ἑπτὰ ἢ ἐννέα ἢ δέκα τὸ πλεῖστον μησὶ τελειωθὲν ἀποκυΐσκεσθαι τὸ βρέφος· ἔχειν δὲ ἐν αὐτῷ πάντας τοὺς λόγους τῆς ζωῆς, ὧν εἰρομένων συνέχεσθαι κατὰ τοὺς τῆς ἁρμονίας λόγους, ἑκάστων ἐν τεταγμένοις καιροῖς ἐπιγινομένων. τήν τε αἴσθησιν κοινῶς καὶ κατ' εἶδος τὴν ὅρασιν[1] ἀτμόν τινα ἄγαν εἶναι[2] θερμόν. καὶ[3] διὰ τοῦτον[4] λέγεται[5] δι' ἀέρος ὁρᾶν καὶ δι' ὕδατος· ἀντερείδεσθαι γὰρ τὸ θερμὸν ἀπὸ[6] τοῦ ψυχροῦ. ἐπεί τοι εἰ ψυχρὸς ἦν ὁ ἐν τοῖς ὄμμασιν ἀτμός, διειστήκει ἂν[7] πρὸς τὸν ὅμοιον ἀέρα· νῦν δὲ[8] ἔστιν ἐν οἷς 'ἡλίου πύλας' καλεῖ τοὺς ὀφθαλμούς. τὰ δ' αὐτὰ καὶ περὶ τῆς ἀκοῆς καὶ τῶν λοιπῶν αἰσθήσεων δογματίζει.[9]

[30] τὴν δὲ ἀνθρώπου ψυχὴν διῃρῆσθαι[10] τριχῆ, εἴς τε νοῦν καὶ φρένας[11] καὶ θυμόν. νοῦν μὲν οὖν καὶ θυμὸν εἶναι καὶ ἐν τοῖς ἄλλοις ζῴοις, φρένας δὲ μόνον ἐν ἀνθρώπῳ. εἶναι δὲ τὴν ἀρχὴν τῆς ψυχῆς ἀπὸ καρδίας μέχρις ἐγκεφάλου· καὶ τὸ μὲν ἐν τῇ καρδίᾳ μέρος αὐτῆς ὑπάρχειν θυμόν, φρένας δὲ καὶ νοῦν τὰ ἐν τῷ ἐγκεφάλῳ· σταγόνας δὲ εἶναι[12] ἀπὸ[13] τούτων τὰς αἰσθήσεις. καὶ τὸ μὲν φρόνιμον ἀθάνατον, τὰ δὲ λοιπὰ θνητά. τρέφεσθαί τε τὴν ψυχὴν ἀπὸ τοῦ αἵματος· τοὺς δὲ λόγους ψυχῆς ἀνέμους[14] εἶναι. ἀόρατόν τ' εἶναι αὐτὴν καὶ τοὺς λόγους, ἐπεὶ καὶ ὁ αἰθὴρ ἀόρατος.

---

[1] ὅρασιν BP¹: κρᾶσιν F   [2] ἄγαν εἶναι B: εἶναι P: εἶναι ἄγαν F   [3] καὶ om. F   [4] τοῦτον BP¹: τοῦτο F
[5] λέγεται mss.: λέγει καὶ Bywater: λέγει Reiske

completed child is born in seven, nine, or most often ten [scil. lunar] months. It has within itself all the ratios suitable for life, and these form a series, maintaining it according to harmonic ratios, every feature being produced at the established moment. Sensation in general, and in particular vision, is a certain very hot vapor. And it is said that this is why one sees through air and through water. For heat is repelled far away from the cold, since if the vapor in the eyes were cold, it would differ (?) with regard to the air, which would be similar to it. But as it is, there are passages in which he calls the eyes **'the gates of the sun.'** He teaches the same doctrine also about hearing and the other sensations.

[30] The soul of the human being is divided into three parts: discrimination (*nous*), intelligence (*phrenes*), and the vital spirit (*thumos*). Discrimination and the vital spirit are also found in the other animals, intelligence only in the human being. The principle of the soul extends from the heart to the brain. And the part of it that is located in the heart is the vital spirit; intelligence and discrimination are those located in the brain. Sensations are drops coming from these. The intelligent part is immortal, the others mortal. The soul is nourished by blood. The 'reasons' (*logoi*) of the soul are winds. It is invisible, as are the 'reasons,' since the aether is invisible too.

---

6 ἀπὸ rec.: ἐπὶ mss.   7 ἂν ⟨οὐδὲν⟩ Diels   8 lac. post δὲ ind. Reiske   9 δογματίζει rec.: -ζειν mss.   10 διηρῆσθαι BP: διαι- F: διαιρεῖ- rec.   11 φρένα FP[4]   12 εἶναι rec.: εἰδέναι BPF: ἰέναι Kuhn   13 ἀπὸ B: ὑπὸ PF   14 ἀναίμους Janda

[31] δεσμά τε εἶναι τῆς ψυχῆς τὰς φλέβας καὶ τὰς ἀρτηρίας καὶ τὰ νεῦρα· ὅταν δὲ ἰσχύῃ καὶ καθ' αὑτὴν γενομένη ἠρεμῇ, δεσμὰ[1] γίνεσθαι αὐτῆς τοὺς λόγους καὶ τὰ ἔργα. ἐκριφθεῖσάν[2] τε[3] αὐτὴν ἐπὶ γῆς πλάζεσθαι ἐν τῷ ἀέρι ὁμοίαν τῷ σώματι. τὸν δὲ Ἑρμῆν ταμίαν εἶναι τῶν ψυχῶν καὶ διὰ τοῦτο πομπέα λέγεσθαι καὶ πυλαῖον[4] καὶ χθόνιον, ἐπειδήπερ οὗτος καὶ εἰσπέμπει ἀπὸ τῶν σωμάτων τὰς ψυχὰς ἀπό τε γῆς καὶ ἐκ θαλάττης· καὶ ἄγεσθαι τὰς μὲν[5] καθαρὰς ἐπὶ τὸν ὕψιστον,[6] τὰς δὲ ἀκαθάρτους μήτε ἐκείναις πελάζειν μήτε ἀλλήλαις, δεῖσθαι δ' ἐν ἀρρήκτοις δεσμοῖς ὑπὸ Ἐρινύων.

[32] εἶναί τε πάντα τὸν ἀέρα ψυχῶν ἔμπλεων· καὶ τούτους τοὺς[7] δαίμονάς τε καὶ ἥρωας νομίζεσθαι·[8] καὶ ὑπὸ τούτων πέμπεσθαι ἀνθρώποις τούς τ' ὀνείρους καὶ τὰ σημεῖα νόσους τε,[9] καὶ οὐ μόνον ἀνθρώποις, ἀλλὰ καὶ προβάτοις καὶ τοῖς ἄλλοις κτήνεσιν· εἴς τε τούτους γίνεσθαι τούς τε καθαρμοὺς καὶ ἀποτροπιασμοὺς μαντικήν τε πᾶσαν καὶ κληδόνας καὶ τὰ ὅμοια. μέγιστον δέ φησιν τῶν[10] ἐν ἀνθρώποις εἶναι τὴν ψυχὴν πεῖσαι ἐπὶ τὸ ἀγαθὸν ἢ ἐπὶ τὸ κακόν.[11] εὐδαιμονεῖν τε ἀνθρώπους ὅταν ἀγαθὴ ψυχὴ προσγένηται, μηδέποτε δὲ ἠρεμεῖν μηδὲ τὸν αὐτὸν[12] ῥόον[13] κρατεῖν.[14]

[1] δεῖγμα Wiersma   [2] ἐκριφθεῖσαν P: κρυφθεῖσαν B: ἐξελθοῦσαν F   [3] τε BP: δὲ F   [4] ἐμπολαῖον Lobeck
[5] τὰς μὲν Cobet: μὲν τὰς BP: τὰς F   [6] ὕψιστον ⟨τόπον⟩ Cobet: ὕψιστον ⟨κύκλον⟩ vel τὸ ὕψιστον Rohde

PYTHAGOREAN RECEPTION

[31] What binds the soul are the veins, arteries, and tendons; but when it is strong and, having become independent, is at rest, it is its 'reasons' and activities that bind it. But when it is expelled onto the earth, it wanders in the air, similar to the body. Hermes is the administrator of the souls and that is why he is called 'escorter,' 'guardian of the gates,' and 'subterranean' (*khthonios*), since it is he who sends the souls away from their bodies, both from the earth and out of the sea. The pure ones are led into the highest region, while the impure ones approach neither them nor each other, but are bound in unbreakable bonds by the Erinyes.

[32] All the air is filled with souls, and these are called demons (*daimones*) and heroes. And it is by these that dreams and signs of sickness and health are sent to humans, and not only to humans, but also to sheep and other domestic animals. And it is to them that purifications, expiations, all forms of divination, incantations, and similar practices are directed. He says that the most important thing for human beings is the persuasion of the soul toward good or toward evil. Humans are happy when a good soul falls to their lot, but they can never be at rest nor master the same course (?).

---

^{7} τούς om. F ^{8} ὀνομάζεσθαι Cobet ^{9} νόσους τε PF: νόσου τε B: νόσου τε καὶ ὑγείας rec.: νόσου τε ⟨καὶ θανάτου⟩ von der Mühll ^{10} τῶν PF: τὸν B: αὐτῶν (scil. τῶν δαιμόνων) Wiersma ^{11} ἢ ἐπὶ τὸ κακόν secl. Reiske ^{12} post αὐτὸν lac. ind. Cobet: ⟨ῥεύματος⟩ Wellmann ^{13} ῥόον BPF: νόον Kuhn ^{14} κρατεῖν ⟨αὐτοὺς ὅταν κακὴ ψυχὴ προσγένηται⟩ Gigante

[33] ὅρκιόν τε εἶναι τὸ δίκαιον καὶ διὰ τοῦτο Δία ὅρκιον λέγεσθαι. τήν τε ἀρετὴν ἁρμονίαν εἶναι καὶ τὴν ὑγίειαν καὶ τὸ ἀγαθὸν ἅπαν καὶ τὸν θεόν· διὸ καὶ καθ' ἁρμονίαν συνεστάναι τὰ ὅλα. φιλίαν τε εἶναι ἐναρμόνιον ἰσότητα. τιμὰς θεοῖς δεῖν νομίζειν καὶ ἥρωσιν μὴ τὰς ἴσας, ἀλλὰ θεοῖς μὲν ἀεὶ μετ' εὐφημίας λευχειμονοῦντας καὶ ἁγνεύοντας, ἥρωσι δὲ ἀπὸ μέσου ἡμέρας. τὴν δὲ ἁγνείαν εἶναι διὰ καθαρμῶν καὶ λουτρῶν καὶ περιρραντηρίων καὶ διὰ τοῦ αὐτὸν καθαρεύειν ἀπό τε κήδους καὶ λεχοῦς[1] καὶ μιάσματος παντὸς καὶ ἀπέχεσθαι βρωτῶν θνησειδίων τε κρεῶν καὶ τριγλῶν καὶ μελανούρων καὶ ᾠῶν καὶ τῶν ᾠοτόκων[2] ζῴων καὶ κυάμων καὶ τῶν ἄλλων ὧν παρακελεύονται καὶ οἱ τὰς τελετὰς ἐν τοῖς ἱεροῖς ἐπιτελοῦντες [. . . = **PYTH. c D22**].

[1] λέχους mss., corr. Cobet   [2] post ᾠοτόκων hab. ἢ BP^{ac}, om. F: ἢ ζῴων secl. Diels

Pythagoras as Moralizer (R34–R37)
The Interpretation of the Acousmatic Formulas (R34)

R34 (< 58C.6) Porph. *VP* 42

'ζυγὸν μὴ ὑπερβαίνειν,' τουτέστι μὴ πλεονεκτεῖν, 'μὴ τὸ πῦρ τῇ μαχαίρᾳ σκαλεύειν,' ὅπερ ἦν μὴ τὸν ἀνοιδοῦντα καὶ ὀργιζόμενον κινεῖν λόγοις παρατεθηγμέ-

PYTHAGOREAN RECEPTION

[33] What is just is like an oath (*horkion*), and for this reason Zeus is called 'of the oath' (*horkios*). Virtue is a harmony, as are health, all that is good, and god. And that is why the whole (*ta hola*) is constituted in conformity with harmony. Friendship is an equality in conformity with harmony. We must think that the honors rendered to gods and to heroes are not identical: for the gods these are performed always, avoiding any blasphemous utterance, dressed in white and purified, but for the heroes it is only starting at midday. Purity is obtained by purifications, ablutions, lustrations, and by remaining uncontaminated by death, birth, and all pollution, and by abstaining from the meat and flesh of animals that have died, red mullets, gray mullets, eggs, oviparous animals, beans, and the other foods that are forbidden by those too who perform initiations in the temples [. . .].

Pythagoras as Moralizer (R34–R37)
The Interpretation of the Acousmatic
Formulas (R34)[1]

[1] Cf. **PYTH. c D16–D19**

R34 (< 58C.6) Porphyry, *Life of Pythagoras*

"Do not step across a pair of scales," i.e. "do not desire more"; "do not stir up a fire with a knife," which means "do not stir up with cutting words someone who is swollen

EARLY GREEK PHILOSOPHY IV

νοις, 'στέφανόν τε μὴ τίλλειν,' τουτέστι τοὺς νόμους μὴ λυμαίνεσθαι· στέφανοι γὰρ πόλεων οὗτοι. [. . .] 'μὴ καρδίαν ἐσθίειν,' οἷον μὴ λυπεῖν ἑαυτὸν ἀνίαις, 'μηδ' ἐπὶ χοίνικος καθέζεσθαι,' οἷον μὴ ἀργὸν ζῆν [. . .].

Moral Education According to
The Golden Verses (R35)

R35 (≠ DK) *Carm. Aur.*

a vv. 40–42

μὴ δ' ὕπνον μαλακοῖσιν ἐπ' ὄμμασι
    προσδέξασθαι,
πρὶν τῶν ἡμερινῶν ἔργων τρὶς ἕκαστον ἐπελθεῖν·
"πῇ παρέβην; τί δ' ἔρεξα; τί μοι δέον οὐκ
    ἐτελέσθη;"

b vv. 45–49

ταῦτα πόνει, ταῦτ' ἐκμελέτα, τούτων χρὴ ἐρᾶν σε·
ταῦτά σε τῆς θείης Ἀρετῆς εἰς ἴχνια θήσει
ναὶ μὰ τὸν ἁμετέρᾳ ψυχᾷ παραδόντα τετρακτύν,
παγὰν ἀενάου φύσεως. ἀλλ' ἔρχευ ἐπ' ἔργον
θεοῖσιν ἐπευξάμενος τελέσαι.

c vv. 61–64, 70–71

Ζεῦ πάτερ, ἦ πολλῶν κε[1] κακῶν λύσειας ἅπαντας,
εἰ πᾶσιν δείξαις, οἵῳ τῷ δαίμονι χρῶνται.

with anger"; "do not pluck apart a garland," i.e. "do not destroy the laws," for they are the garlands of cities. [...] "Do not eat the heart," for "do not afflict yourself by grief." "Do not sit on a loaf of bread," for "do not live idly" [...].

Moral Education According to
The Golden Verses *(R35)*

R35 (≠ DK) *The Golden Verses*

a [Examination of one's conscience:]

Do not welcome sleep into your languid eyes
Before you have gone three times through each of your deeds that day:
"Where did I go astray? What did I accomplish? What duty did I neglect?"

b [Effort:]

Labor at these things [scil. precepts], practice them, you must love them:
These will set you in the footsteps of divine Virtue,
Yes indeed, by him who transmitted to our soul the *tetraktys*,
Fountain of ever-flowing nature. But get to work,
Praying to the gods for their fulfillment.

c [The promise of immortality:]

Father Zeus, you would certainly free all men from their many evils,

---

[1] κε ex vers. Arab. edd.: γε Diehl: τε mss. plerique

ἀλλὰ σὺ θάρσει, ἐπεὶ θεῖον γένος ἐστὶ βροτοῖσιν,
οἷς ἱερὰ προφέρουσα φύσις δείκνυσιν ἕκαστα.
[. . .]
ἢν δ' ἀπολείψας σῶμα ἐς αἰθέρ' ἐλεύθερον ἔλθῃς,
ἔσσεαι ἀθάνατος, θεὸς ἄμβροτος, οὐκέτι θνητός.

Pythagorean Maxims (R36)

R36 (≠DK) Stob. 3.1.30–44

[30] ἀνανεούσθω σοι ὁ περὶ τῶν ἀγαθῶν λόγος καθ'
ἡμέραν μᾶλλον ἢ τὰ σιτία.
[31] ἄγρυπνος ἔσο κατὰ νοῦν· συγγενὴς γὰρ τοῦ ἀληθινοῦ θανάτου ὁ περὶ τοῦτον ὕπνος.
[32] ἃ μὴ δεῖ ποιεῖν, μηδὲ ὑπονοοῦ ποιεῖν.
[33] ζητεῖν δεῖ καὶ ἄνδρα καὶ τέκνα καὶ φίλους τοὺς
μετὰ τὴν ἀπαλλαγὴν τοῦ βίου παραμένοντας.
[34] ζῆν κρεῖττόν ἐστιν ἐπὶ στιβάδος κατακείμενον
καὶ θαρρεῖν ἢ ταράττεσθαι χρυσῆν ἔχοντα κλίνην.
[35] ἰσχύειν τῇ ψυχῇ αἱροῦ μᾶλλον ἢ τῷ σώματι.

---

[1] These fifteen maxims, like many others cited by Stobaeus in different chapters of his *Anthology*, are also found in the collection of 123 Pythagorean maxims arranged alphabetically that is preserved in a manuscript in Vienna (see H. Chadwick, *The Sentences of Sextus: A Contribution to the History of Early Christian*

PYTHAGOREAN RECEPTION

If you showed them all what kind of divinity they possess.
But you, be courageous, since their race is divine, those mortals
To whom nature bestows and displays each of the holy things.
[...]
If you leave the body and come to the free aether,
You will be deathless, an undying god, no longer mortal. [cf. **EMP. D4.4**]

Pythagorean Maxims (R36)

R36 (≠ DK) Fifteen Pythagorean maxims in Stobaeus, *Anthology* ("On virtue")[1]

[30] Renew your doctrine about good things every day, rather than your food.
[31] May you remain awake in your intelligence. For its sleep is akin to a real death.
[32] What you should not do, do not even think of doing it.
[33] One must look for a man, children, and friends who remain after the end of life.
[34] It is better to live sleeping on straw and fearing nothing, than to be troubled and possess a golden bed.
[35] Choose to be strong in your soul rather than in your body.

Ethics, Cambridge, 1959, pp. 84–94). Some of them are also found in the collection of the 411 maxims of Sextus, in which Pythagoreanism and Christianity come together (ed. Chadwick, pp. 12–61; cf. pp. 140–41).

[36] πέπεισο μὴ εἶναι σὸν κτῆμα, ὅπερ μὴ ἐντὸς διανοίας ἔχεις.

[37] πρᾶττε μεγάλα μὴ ὑπισχνούμενος μεγάλα.

[38] τέκνα μάθε τίκτειν οὐ τὰ γηροβοσκήσοντα τὸ σῶμα, τὰ δὲ τὴν ψυχὴν θρέψοντα τῇ ἀιδίῳ τροφῇ.

[39] τὰ ἐπίπονα τῶν ἡδέων μᾶλλον ἡγοῦ συντελεῖν εἰς ἀρετήν.

[40] χαλεπὸν πολλὰς ὁδοὺς ἅμα τοῦ βίου βαδίζειν.

[41] ψυχῆς πᾶν πάθος εἰς σωτηρίαν αὐτῆς πολεμιώτατον.

[42] ὧν ἡ τύχη κυρία καὶ δοῦναι καὶ ἀφελέσθαι, οὐ δεήσῃ οὐδενός.

[43] ὧν τοῦ σώματος ἀπαλλαγεὶς οὐ δεήσῃ, ἐκείνων καταφρόνει πάντων· καὶ ὧν ἀπαλλαγεὶς δεήσῃ, πρὸς ταῦτά σοι ἀσκουμένῳ τοὺς θεοὺς παρακάλει γίνεσθαι συλλήπτορας.

[44] ὧν ἕνεκα ζῆν ἐθέλεις, τούτων χάριν καὶ ἀποθανεῖν μὴ κατόκνει.

Speeches to the Crotonians Attributed to Pythagoras (R37)

R37 (≠DK) Iambl. *VP* 37–42

[37] περιχυθέντων δὲ τῶν νεανίσκων παραδέδοται λόγους τινὰς διαλεχθῆναι πρὸς αὐτούς, ἐξ ὧν εἰς τὴν σπουδὴν παρεκάλει τὴν περὶ τοὺς πρεσβυτέρους, ἀποφαίνων ἔν τε τῷ κόσμῳ καὶ τῷ βίῳ καὶ ταῖς

PYTHAGOREAN RECEPTION

[36] Be convinced that what you do not have within your thought is not a possession of yours.

[37] Perform great actions without promising great things.

[38] Learn to create children who will not take care of the body when it is old but who will nourish the soul by an eternal sustenance.

[39] Think that what requires effort contributes more to virtue than what provides pleasure.

[40] It is difficult to follow many paths at once in life.

[41] Every affection (*pathos*) of the soul is most inimical to its salvation.

[42] You will need nothing of what fortune has the power to give and to take away.

[43] Despise all the things you will not need once you have left the body; and train yourself in those you will need once you have left it, praying the gods to help you.

[44] Do not hesitate to die too for the things for which you wish to live.

Speeches to the Crotonians Attributed to Pythagoras (R37)

R37 (≠ DK) Iamblichus, *Life of Pythagoras*

[37] It is reported that he [i.e. Pythagoras] delivered certain speeches to crowds of youths in which he exhorted them to take care of their elders, showing that, in the world just as in life or in cities or nature, what precedes is

395

πόλεσι καὶ τῇ φύσει μᾶλλον τιμώμενον τὸ προηγούμενον ἢ τὸ τῷ χρόνῳ ἑπόμενον [. . .]. [41] ἐφεξῆς δὲ ἔλεγε περὶ σωφροσύνης, φάσκων τὴν τῶν νεανίσκων ἡλικίαν πεῖραν τῆς φύσεως λαμβάνειν, καθ' ὃν καιρὸν ἀκμαζούσας ἔχουσι τὰς ἐπιθυμίας [. . .]. [42] παρεκάλει δὲ τοὺς νεανίσκους καὶ πρὸς τὴν παιδείαν, ἐνθυμεῖσθαι κελεύων ὡς ἄτοπον ἂν εἴη πάντων μὲν σπουδαιότατον κρίνειν τὴν διάνοιαν καὶ ταύτῃ βουλεύεσθαι περὶ τῶν ἄλλων, εἰς δὲ τὴν ἄσκησιν τὴν ταύτης μηδένα χρόνον μηδὲ πόνον ἀνηλωκέναι [. . .].

Recommendations Attributed to Pythagoreans

See **R63–R66**

Representations of Pythagoreans in Middle Comedy

See **DRAM. T35–T39**

Some Testimonia about Pythagoras' Presence in Rome (R38–R44)
Pythagoras' Statue in Rome at the Beginning of the 3rd Century BC (R38)

R38 (≠DK) Plin. *Nat. hist.* 34.12.26

invenio et Pythagorae et Alcibiadi in cornibus Comitii positas, cum bello Samniti Apollo Pythius iussisset for-

more honored than what follows in time [. . .]. [41] He then spoke about self-control, saying that adolescence provides a good indication of people's nature, since at this age their passions are at a maximum [. . .]. [42] He also exhorted the youths to study, telling them to consider that it would be absurd to judge that thought is the most serious thing of all and to deliberate by its means about everything else, and yet not to dedicate any time or effort to training oneself in it [. . .].[1]

[1] In what follows, Iamblichus quotes other speeches addressed to different groups: men engaged in politics (*VP* 45–50), children (*VP* 51–53), women (*VP* 54–57).

Recommendations Attributed to Pythagoreans

See **R63–R66**

Representations of Pythagoreans in Middle Comedy

See **DRAM. T35–T39**

Some Testimonia about Pythagoras' Presence in Rome (R38–R44) Pythagoras' Statue in Rome at the Beginning of the 3rd Century BC (R38)

R38 (≠ DK) Pliny, *Natural History*

I also find that [scil. statues] of Pythagoras and Alcibiades were placed in the corners of the Comitium, when during

tissimo Graiae gentis et alteri sapientissimo simulacra celebri loco dicari. eae stetere, donec Sulla dictator ibi curiam faceret. mirumque est, illos patres Socrati cunctis ab eodem deo sapientia praelato Pythagoran praetulisse [. . .].

The Legend of Numa as a Pupil of Pythagoras (R39–R41)

R39 (≠DK) Cic. *Tusc.* 4.1.2–3

Pythagorae autem doctrina cum longe lateque flueret, permanavisse mihi videtur in hanc civitatem, idque cum coniectura probabile est, tum quibusdam etiam vestigiis indicatur. quis enim est qui putet, cum floreret in Italia Graecia potentissimis et maximis urbibus, ea quae magna dicta est, in iisque primum ipsius Pythagorae, deinde postea Pythagoreorum tantum nomen esset, nostrorum hominum ad eorum doctissimas voces aures clausas fuisse? quin etiam arbitror propter Pythagoreorum admirationem Numam quoque regem Pythagoreum a posterioribus existimatum. nam cum Pythagorae disciplinam et instituta cognoscerent regisque eius aequitatem et sapientiam a maioribus suis accepissent, aetates autem et tempora ignorarent propter vetustatem, eum, qui sapientia excelleret, Pythagorae auditorem crediderunt fuisse.

the Samnite War [i.e. between 343 and 290 BC, probably ca. 300] Pythian Apollo ordered that one effigy of the bravest of the Greeks and another of the wisest be dedicated in a public place; and they remained there until Sulla the dictator had the Senate built in that place [i.e. in 80 BC]. It is surprising that those senators preferred Pythagoras to Socrates, who on account of his wisdom had been preferred by that same god [i.e. Apollo] to all other men [...].

The Legend of Numa as a Pupil of Pythagoras (R39–R41)

R39 (≠ DK) Cicero, *Tusculan Disputations*

Given that the doctrine of Pythagoras was disseminated far and wide, it seems likely to me that it reached this city of ours; and this is not only probable as a conjecture, but it is also indicated by various traces. For who could suppose that—although what was called Magna Graecia flourished in Italy with such large and powerful cities and in these first the name of Pythagoras, and then that of the Pythagoreans, were held in such high regard—the ears of our people remained closed to their very learned voices? On the contrary, I think that it is because of their admiration for the Pythagoreans that posterity thought that King Numa too was a Pythagorean. For since they knew of Pythagoras' doctrine and institutions and had heard from their ancestors of this king's justice and wisdom, but were ignorant of the ages and dates because of their antiquity, they believed that that man, who was distinguished for his wisdom, had been a student of Pythagoras.

R40 (≠ DK) Liv. 40.29

[8] adicit Antias Valerius Pythagoricos fuisse, vulgatae opinioni, qua creditur Pythagorae auditorem fuisse Numam, mendacio probabili adcommodata fide [. . .]. [14] libri in comitio [. . .] in conspectu populi cremati sunt.

R41 (≠DK) Plut. *Numa*

a 1.3–4

λεγομένου δὲ οὖν ὡς Νομᾶς γένοιτο Πυθαγόρου συνήθης, οἱ μὲν ὅλως ἀξιοῦσι μηδὲν Ἑλληνικῆς παιδεύσεως Νομᾷ μετεῖναι, καθάπερ ἢ φύσει δυνατὸν[1] καὶ αὐτάρκη γενέσθαι πρὸς ἀρετὴν ἢ βελτίονι Πυθαγόρου βαρβάρῳ τινὶ τὴν τοῦ βασιλέως ἀποδοῦναι ⟨δέον⟩[2] παίδευσιν· οἱ δὲ Πυθαγόραν μὲν ὀψὲ γενέσθαι τῶν Νομᾶ χρόνων ὁμοῦ τι πέντε γενεαῖς ἀπολειπόμενον [. . .].

[1] δυνατὸν ⟨ὄντα⟩ Flacelière   [2] ⟨δέον⟩ Flacelière

b 8.4–7

ἔστι δ' ὅτε καὶ φόβους τινὰς ἀπαγγέλλων παρὰ τοῦ θεοῦ καὶ φάσματα δαιμόνων ἀλλόκοτα καὶ φωνὰς οὐκ εὐμενεῖς, ἐδούλου καὶ ταπεινὴν ἐποίει τὴν διάνοιαν αὐτῶν ὑπὸ δεισιδαιμονίας. ἐξ ὧν καὶ μάλιστα λόγον ἔσχεν ἡ σοφία καὶ ἡ παίδευσις τοῦ ἀνδρός, ὡς Πυθαγόρᾳ συγγεγονότος. μέγα γὰρ ἦν μέρος, ὡς ἐκείνῳ

PYTHAGOREAN RECEPTION

R40 (≠ DK) Livy, *Roman History*

[8] Valerius Antias adds that they [scil. the seven Greek books of philosophy discovered in the tomb of Numa in 181 BC] were Pythagorean, providing credibility by a plausible fiction to the widespread opinion according to which Numa is believed to have been a student of Pythagoras [. . .]. [14] The books were burned in the Comitium in the sight of the people [. . .].

R41 (≠ DK) Plutarch, *Numa*

a

It is reported that Numa associated with Pythagoras; but some people think that Numa did not partake in Greek education at all (either because he was able by nature to attain virtue on his own or because the king's education ⟨had to be⟩ entrusted to a non-Greek greater than Pythagoras), others that Pythagoras was born later, by a difference of five generations from the time of Numa [. . .].

b

Sometimes he [i.e. Numa] announced terrifying events sent by god, prodigious apparitions of demonic beings and threatening voices, and in this way he enslaved them [i.e. the people] and used fear of the gods to humble their thought. It is above all this that gave rise to the story that his wisdom and education were due to his associating with Pythagoras: for intimacy and familiarity with divinity were

τῆς φιλοσοφίας, καὶ τούτῳ τῆς πολιτείας ἡ περὶ τὸ θεῖον ἀγχιστεία καὶ διατριβή. λέγεται δὲ καὶ τὸν ἔξωθεν ὄγκον καὶ σχηματισμὸν ἀπὸ τῆς αὐτῆς Πυθαγόρᾳ διανοίας περιβαλέσθαι.

*A Renewal of Pythagoreanism in the
1st Century BC? Nigidius Figulus (R42)*

R42 (≠DK) Cic. *Tim.* 1.1–2

fuit enim vir ille cum ceteris artibus, quae quidem dignae libero essent, ornatus omnibus, tum acer investigator et diligens earum rerum, quae a natura involutae videntur; denique sic iudico, post illos nobiles Pythagoreos, quorum disciplina extincta est quodam modo, cum aliquot saecla in Italia Siciliaque viguisset, hunc extitisse, qui illam renovaret.

The Vanity of Archytas' Science (Horace)

See **ARCHY. P22**

*Aspects of Pythagoreanism at Rome: Cosmology,
Way of Life, and Vegetarianism (R43–R44)*

R43 (≠ DK) Ovid. *Met.* 15.60–74

60   vir fuit hic ortu Samius, sed fugerat una
     et Samon et dominos odioque tyrannidis exul

PYTHAGOREAN RECEPTION

a large part of the latter's philosophy, as of the former's politics. And it is reported that he cloaked himself in an external solemnity and bearing with the same intention as Pythagoras.

*A Renewal of Pythagoreanism in the
1st Century BC? Nigidius Figulus (R42)*

R42 (≠ DK) Cicero, *Timaeus*

That man [i.e. P. Nigidius, whom Cicero attacks in various passages of his *Academics*] was not only embellished by all the other arts worthy of a free man but was also a keen and zealous explorer of those things that seem to have been concealed by nature. In short I consider that, after those illustrious Pythagoreans whose school was extinguished in some way after it had flourished for several centuries in Italy and Sicily, this man arose to renew it.

The Vanity of Archytas' Science (Horace)

See **ARCHY. P22**

*Aspects of Pythagoreanism at Rome: Cosmology,
Way of Life, and Vegetarianism (R43–R44)*

R43 (≠ DK) Ovid, *Metamorphoses*

> Here [i.e. at Croton] there was a man who came from Samos but had fled
> Both Samos and its rulers, and who because of his hatred for tyranny was a voluntary

> sponte erat, isque licet caeli regione remotos
> mente deos adiit et quae natura negabat
> visibus humanis, oculis ea pectoris hausit.
> 65 cumque animo et vigili perspexerat omnia cura,
> in medium discenda dabat coetusque silentum
> dictaque mirantum magni primordia mundi
> et rerum causas et quid natura docebat,
> quid deus, unde nives, quae fulminis esset origo,
> 70 Iuppiter an venti discussa nube tonarent,
> quid quateret terras, qua sidera lege mearent,
> et quodcumque latet. primusque animalia mensis
> arguit imponi, primus quoque talibus ora
> docta quidem soluit, sed non et credita, verbis:
> [. . .]

62 remotos $B^{v}FG$: remotus $UB^{c^{?}}P$

R44 (≠DK) Sen. *Epist.* 108.17–19

[17] quoniam coepi tibi exponere, quanto maiore impetu ad philosophiam iuvenis accesserim quam senex pergam,

Exile; and to the gods, remote though they were in
   their heavenly domain,
He traveled by his mind, and what nature denied
To human sight, this he drank in with the eyes of the
   mind,
And when he had examined everything with his spirit
   and wakeful zeal [cf. **EMP. D38**],
He made them learn it publicly, and he taught to the
   assemblies of silent
Admirers of his sayings the origins of the great world,
And the causes of things, and what nature is,
What god is, what the snows come from, what the
   origin of lightning is,
Whether it is Jupiter that thunders or the winds from
   a shattered cloud,
What causes earthquakes, what law regulates the
   motion of the stars—
And everything that is hidden; and he was the first to
   denounce serving animals for meals,
And the first too to unlock his mouth, learned but not
   believed, with the following words:
[. . .][1]

[1] The approximately four hundred verses that follow put into Pythagoras' mouth a long eclectic doctrinal presentation whose purpose is to provide both a justification for vegetarianism and a philosophical foundation for metamorphoses.

R44 (≠ DK) Seneca, *Letters to Lucilius*

[17] Since I have begun to explain to you with how much more eagerness I approached philosophy as a young man than I continue with it as an old one, I shall not be ashamed

non pudebit fateri quem mihi amorem Pythagoras iniecerit. Sotion dicebat quare ille animalibus abstinuisset, quare postea Sextius. dissimilis utrique causa erat, sed utrique magnifica. [18] hic homini satis alimentorum citra sanguinem esse credebat et crudelitatis consuetudinem fieri ubi in voluptatem esset adducta laceratio. [. . .] [19] at Pythagoras omnium inter omnia cognationem esse dicebat et animorum commercium in alias atque alias formas transeuntium. nulla, si illi credas, anima interit, ne cessat quidem nisi tempore exiguo, dum in aliud corpus transfunditur. videbimus per quas temporum vices et quando pererratis pluribus domiciliis in hominem revertatur: interim sceleris hominibus ac parricidii metum fecit, cum possent[1] in parentis animam inscii incurrere et ferro morsuve violare, si in quo[2] cognatus aliqui spiritus hospitaretur.

[1] possint *mss., corr. Buecheler*   [2] quo ‹corpore› *Axelson*

Pseudo-Pythagorean Literature (R45–R66)
Examples of Writings Attributed to Pythagoras (R45–R46)
The Three Treatises (R45)

R45 Diog. Laert.

a (< 14.19) 8.6–7

γέγραπται δὲ τῷ Πυθαγόρᾳ συγγράμματα τρία, Παι-

to confess to you what love Pythagoras inspired in me. Sotion used to say why Pythagoras abstained from eating animals, and why Sextius did so later. The reason was different in each case, but in each case it was noble. [18] The latter believed that man had enough kinds of food without needing blood and that a habit of cruelty is produced whenever butchery is performed for the sake of pleasure. [...] [19] But Pythagoras stated that there is a consanguinity of all things with one another and an exchange of souls that transmigrate from one form into another. If you believe him, no soul perishes or even stops, except for a brief time, while it is being transferred into another body. We shall see after what periods of time and at what time it returns to man after it has wandered through many domiciles; but in the meantime, he made men afraid of crimes and parricide, given that they might encounter a parent's soul without knowing it and commit violence against it with a knife or with their teeth, if there were any relative's spirit lodging there [cf. **EMP. D29**].

Pseudo-Pythagorean Literature (R45–R66)[1]
Examples of Writings Attributed to
Pythagoras (R45–R46)
The Three Treatises (R45)

[1] Pseudo-Pythagorean literature forms a very large corpus (see the collections of H. Thesleff and K. S. Guthrie indicated in the introduction to this chapter); here it is merely evoked.

R45 Diogenes Laertius

a (< 14.19)

Pythagoras wrote three treatises, on education, on politics,

δευτικόν, Πολιτικόν, Φυσικόν· τὸ δὲ[1] φερόμενον ὡς
Πυθαγόρου Λύσιδός ἐστι τοῦ Ταραντίνου Πυθαγορικοῦ.

[1] δὲ ‹τέταρτον› Nauck

b (< 14.19) 8.6

οὕτω δ᾽ εἶπεν, ἐπειδήπερ ἐναρχόμενος ὁ Πυθαγόρας
τοῦ Φυσικοῦ συγγράμματος λέγει ὧδε· "οὐ μὰ τὸν
ἀέρα, τὸν ἀναπνέω, οὐ μὰ τὸ ὕδωρ, τὸ πίνω, οὔ κοτ᾽
οἴσω[1] ψόγον περὶ τοῦ λόγου τοῦδε."

[1] οὐ κατοίσω mss., corr. Diels

c (≠ DK) 8.9–10

ἐν δὲ τοῖς τρισὶ συγγράμμασι τοῖς προειρημένοις
φέρεται Πυθαγόρου τάδε καθολικῶς. οὐκ ἐᾷ εὔχεσθαι
ὑπὲρ αὑτῶν διὰ τὸ μὴ εἰδέναι τὸ συμφέρον. τὴν μέθην
ἓν ἀνθ᾽ ἑνὸς 'βλάβην' καλεῖ καὶ πλησμονὴν πᾶσαν
ἀποδοκιμάζει, λέγων μὴ παραβαίνειν μήτε τῶν πο-
τῶν[1] μήτε τῶν σιτίων μηδένα τὴν συμμετρίαν. καὶ
περὶ ἀφροδισίων δέ φησιν οὕτως· "ἀφροδίσια χειμῶ-
νος ποιέεσθαι, μὴ θέρεος· φθινοπώρου δὲ καὶ ἦρος
κουφότερα, βαρέα δὲ πᾶσαν ὥρην καὶ ἐς ὑγιείην οὐκ
ἀγαθά." [. . .] [10] διαιρεῖται δὲ καὶ τὸν τοῦ ἀνθρώπου
βίον οὕτως· "παῖς εἴκοσι ἔτεα, νεηνίσκος εἴκοσι, νεη-
νίης εἴκοσι, γέρων εἴκοσι. αἱ δὲ ἡλικίαι πρὸς τὰς
ὥρας ὧδε σύμμετροι· παῖς ἔαρ, νεηνίσκος θέρος, νεη-
νίης φθινόπωρον, γέρων χειμών."

and on nature. But the one that circulates under the name of Pythagoras is in fact the work of Lysis of Tarentum, a Pythagorean [. . . cf. **PYTH. b T36**].

b (< 14.19)

He [i.e. Heraclitus] says this [= **HER. D26**], because Pythagoras says at the beginning of his treatise on nature, "No, by the air I breathe, no, by the water I drink, never will I receive blame for this discourse."

c (≠ DK)

In the three treatises mentioned above, what is transmitted of Pythagoras in general is the following: he does not permit people to pray for themselves because they do not know what is beneficial; he calls drunkenness 'damage,' substituting the one word for the other, and he condemns all satiety, saying that no one should transgress proportion either in drink or in food. And with regard to sexual relations he says, "One must have sexual relations in the winter, not in the summer; in the fall and spring they are easier, but they are grievous in every season and not good for health." [. . .] [10] And the life of man is divided as follows: "twenty years a child, twenty years an adolescent, twenty years a young man, twenty years an old man; and the ages of life have the following proportion with the seasons: child and spring, adolescent and summer, young man and autumn, old man and winter."

---

¹ πόνων mss. corr. Casaubon (ex Iambl. *VP* 244)

EARLY GREEK PHILOSOPHY IV

d (≠ DK) 8.14

ἀλλὰ καὶ αὐτὸς ἐν τῇ γραφῇ φησι δι' ἑκκαίδεκα[1] καὶ διηκοσίων ἐτέων ἐξ ἀΐδεω παραγεγενῆσθαι ἐς ἀνθρώπους.

[1] ἑκκαίδεκα Rohde e Ps.-Iambl. *Theol.* 53.6 (σιϛ'): ἑπτὰ mss.

The "Sacred Discourse" in Doric Prose (R46)

R46 (p. 164 Thesleff)

a Iambl. *VP* 146

οὐκέτι δὴ οὖν ἀμφίβολον γέγονε τὸ τὰς ἀφορμὰς παρὰ Ὀρφέως λαβόντα Πυθαγόραν συντάξαι τὸν περὶ θεῶν λόγον, ὃν καὶ ἱερὸν διὰ τοῦτο ἐπέγραψεν [. . .] εἴτε ὄντως τοῦ ἀνδρός, ὡς οἱ πλεῖστοι λέγουσι, σύγγραμμά ἐστιν, εἴτε Τηλαύγους [. . .]. λέγει γάρ· "<λόγος>[1] ὅδε περὶ θεῶν Πυθαγόρα τῶ Μνημάρχω, τὸν ἐξέμαθον ὀργιασθεὶς ἐν Λιβήθροις τοῖς Θρακίοις, Ἀγλαοφάμω τελεστᾶ[2] μεταδόντος, ὡς ἄρα Ὀρφεὺς ὁ Καλλιόπας κατὰ τὸ Πάγγαιον ὄρος ὑπὸ τᾶς ματρὸς πινυσθεὶς ἔφα, τὰν ἀριθμῶ οὐσίαν ἀΐδιον ἔμμεν[3] ἀρχὰν προμαθεστάταν τῶ παντὸς ὠρανῶ καὶ γᾶς καὶ τᾶς μεταξὺ φύσιος, ἔτι δὲ καὶ θείων[4] καὶ θεῶν καὶ δαιμόνων διαμονᾶς ῥίζαν."

[1] <λόγος> Lobeck, post Μνημάρχῳ Holstenius [2] τελεύτα mss., corr. Schneider e Proclo *In Tim.* 3.168.9–14: τελετὰς Lobeck [3] εἶναι μὲν mss. corr. Vahlen [4] θείων <ἀνθρώπων> Deubner

PYTHAGOREAN RECEPTION

d (≠ DK)

And he himself says in his text that he returned to mankind from Hades after 216 (?) years.

The "Sacred Discourse" in Doric Prose (R46)

R46 (≠ DK)

a Iamblichus, *Life of Pythagoras*

So it can no longer be doubted that it was by taking his starting point from Orpheus that Pythagoras composed his discourse about the gods, which for this reason he entitled 'sacred' [. . .], whether the treatise was really by that man, as most people say, or by Telauges [. . .]. For he says: "This ⟨discourse⟩ about the gods is by Pythagoras son of Mnemarchus, and I learned it when I was initiated in Leibethra in Thrace, with Aglaophamus performing the initiatory ritual, namely that Orpheus, son of Calliope, whom his mother had taught on Mount Pangaeus, said that the essence of number is the eternal and most providential principle of all the heavens, the earth, and the nature in between, and furthermore that it is the root of the permanency of divine things, gods, and demons."

b Syr. *In Met.*, p. 123.1–6

πῶς δ' ἂν αὐτὸς μὲν Πυθαγόρας ἐν τῷ Ἱερῷ λόγῳ διαρρήδην μορφῶν καὶ ἰδεῶν κράντορα τὸν ἀριθμὸν ἔλεγεν εἶναι, καὶ θεῶν <καὶ>[1] δαιμόνων αἴτιον καὶ τῷ πρεσβίστῳ καὶ κρατιστεύοντι τεχνίτᾳ θεῷ κανόνα καὶ λόγον τεχνικόν, "νοῦν τε καὶ στάθμαν ἀκλινεστάταν τὸν ἀριθμὸν ὑπεῖμεν συστάσιός τε καὶ γενέσιος τῶν πάντων";

[1] <καὶ> Kroll

Examples of Writings Attributed to
Philolaus (R47–R51)
A Late Testimonium on the Existence of
Numerous Writings of Philolaus (R47)

R47 (< 44 B22) Claud. Mam. *Stat. an.*

a 2.3, p. 105.7–20

[. . . = **PYTH. c D3**] in quibus vel potissimum floruisse Philolaum reperio Tarentinum, qui multis voluminibus de intelligendis rebus et qui quaeque significent oppido obscure dissertans, priusque de animae substantia decernat, de mensuris ponderibus et numeris iuxta geometricam musicam atque arithmeticam mirifice disputat per haec omne universum extitisse confirmans [. . .].

b Syrianus, *Commentary on Aristotle's* Metaphysics

How [scil. if the Pythagoreans had spoken only of perceptible numbers] could Pythagoras himself have explicitly said in his *Sacred Discourse* that number is the master (*krantôr*) of the forms and ideas, and the cause of the gods ⟨and⟩ demons, the rule and the technical reason for the most ancient and powerful craftsman god, that "number is the intellect (*nous*) and most unswerving plumb line of the organization and birth of all things"?

Examples of Writings Attributed to
Philolaus (R47–R51)
A Late Testimonium on the Existence of
Numerous Writings of Philolaus (R47)

R47 (< 44 B22) Claudianus Mamertus, *On the State of the Soul*

a

[. . .] Among these [scil. those from among whom Pythagoras' opinion must be sought, since he himself wrote nothing] I find that the most illustrious was Philolaus of Tarentum, who, writing very obscurely in numerous volumes about the understanding of things and what each one signifies, discusses marvelously, before he defines the substance of the soul, about measures, weights, and numbers, together with geometry, music, and arithmetic, confirming that the whole universe has come about thanks to these [. . .].

b 2.7, p. 120.12–20

nunc ad Philolaum redeo [. . .] qui in tertio voluminum, quae περὶ ῥυθμῶν καὶ μέτρων[1] praenotat, de anima sic loquitur: "anima inditur corpori per numerum et inmortalem eandemque incorporalem convenentiam." item post alia: "diligitur corpus ab anima, quia sine eo non potest uti sensibus, a quo postquam morte deducta est, agit in mundo incorporalem vitam."

[1] περὶ . . . μέτρων rest. edd. e lectionibus lingua Latina scriptis discrepantibus

Two Examples of Pseudepigraphic Texts Constructed on the Basis of Philolaus' Theory of Principles (R48–R49)

R48 (> 44 B11) Stob. 1 *Proem. cor.* 3

Φιλολάου· θεωρὲν δεῖ τὰ ἔργα καὶ τὰν ἐσσίαν τῶ ἀριθμῶ[1] καττὰν δύναμιν ἅ τις ἐντὶ ἐν τᾷ δεκάδι. μεγάλα γὰρ καὶ παντελὴς καὶ παντοεργὸς καὶ θείω καὶ ὠρανίω βίω καὶ ἀνθρωπίνω ἀρχὰ καὶ ἀγεμὼν κοινωνοῦσα ⟨. . .⟩[2] δύναμις ἁ[3] τᾶς δεκάδος. ἄνευ δὲ ταύτας πάντ' ἄπειρα[4] καὶ ἄδηλα καὶ ἀφανῆ. κανονικὰ[5] γὰρ ἁ φύσις ἁ τῶ ἀριθμῶ καὶ ἁγεμονικὰ καὶ διδασκαλικὰ τῶ ἀπορουμένω παντὸς καὶ ἀγνοουμένω παντί. οὐ γὰρ

[1] τῶν ἀριθμῶν ms., corr. Boeckh   [2] lac. 12 litt. ms.: ⟨κοινῶς ἐοῦσα φαίνεται⟩ Heeren, alii alia

b

Now I come back to Philolaus [. . .], who in the third volume of the work entitled *On Rhythms and Measures,* speaks about the human soul as follows: "The soul is introduced into the body by number and by a harmony that is immortal and hence also incorporeal." And later: "The body is loved by the soul, because without the body the soul cannot make use of the senses. And later when the soul has been removed from the body by death, it enjoys an incorporeal life in the world."

Two Examples of Pseudepigraphic Texts Constructed on the Basis of Philolaus' Theory of Principles (R48–R49)

R48 (> 44 B11) Stobaeus, *Anthology*

From Philolaus: "It is necessary to observe the operations and the essence of number according to the power that is present in the decad. For it is great, perfect, all-accomplishing, the principle and director of divine and heavenly life and of human as well, sharing <. . .> the power of the decad. Without this, all things are unlimited, unclear, and uncertain. For the nature of number is to measure, direct, and teach all that causes difficulty and is not known by anyone. For things would not be clear to

---

³ ἁ Heeren: καὶ ms.   ⁴ ἄπορα Iacobs   ⁵ γνωμικὰ ms., cor. Meineke: νομικὰ D'Orville, γνωμονικὰ Iacobs

ἧς[6] δῆλον οὐδενὶ οὐδὲν τῶν πραγμάτων, οὔτε αὐτῶν[7] ποθ' αὐτά, οὔτε ἄλλω ποτ' ἄλλο, αἰ μὴ ἧς[8] ἀριθμὸς καὶ ἁ τούτω[9] ἐσσία. νῦν δὲ οὗτος καττὰν ψυχὰν ἁρμόσδων αἰσθήσι πάντα γνωστὰ καὶ ποτάγορα ἀλλάλοις κατὰ γνώμονος φύσιν ἀπεργάζεται, σωματῶν[10] καὶ σχίζων τὼς λόγως χωρὶς ἑκάστως τῶν πραγμάτων, τῶν τε ἀπείρων καὶ τῶν περαινόντων. ἴδοις δέ κα[11] οὐ μόνον ἐν τοῖς δαιμονίοις καὶ θείοις πράγμασι τὰν τῶ ἀριθμῶ φύσιν καὶ τὰν δύναμιν ἰσχύουσαν, ἀλλὰ καὶ ἐν τοῖς ἀνθρωπικοῖς ἔργοις καὶ λόγοις πᾶσι παντᾶ καὶ καττὰς δαμιουργίας τὰς τεχνικὰς πάσας καὶ καττὰν μουσικάν. ψεῦδος δὲ οὐδὲν δέχεται ἁ[12] τῶ ἀριθμῶ φύσις, οὐδὲ ἁρμονία, οὐδὲ[13] γὰρ οἰκεῖον αὐτοῖς ἐντι. τᾶς τῶ ἀπείρω καὶ ἀνοάτω καὶ ἀλόγω φύσιος τὸ ψεῦδος καὶ ὁ φθόνος ἐντί. ψεῦδος δὲ οὐδαμῶς ἐς ἀριθμὸν ἐμπίπτει,[14] πολέμιον γὰρ καὶ ἐχθρὸν τᾷ φύσι τὸ ψεῦδος, ἁ δ' ἀλάθεια οἰκεῖον καὶ σύμφυτον τᾷ τῶ ἀριθμῶ γενεᾷ. καὶ τὰ ἐν τᾷ σφαίρᾳ σώματα πέντε ἐντί· τὰ ἐν τᾷ σφαίρᾳ, πῦρ, ὕδωρ καὶ γᾶ καὶ ἀήρ, καὶ ὁ τᾶς σφαίρας ὁλκὰς πέμπτον.

[6] εἰς ms., corr. Koen: ἐντι Heeren   [7] αὐτοῖς ms., corr. Heeren   [8] εἷς ms., corr. Koen   [9] τούτοις ms., corr. Heeren   [10] σωμάτων ms., corr. Boeckh   [11] δὲ καὶ ms., corr. Meineke   [12] αὖ ms., corr. Iacobs   [13] οὐ ms., corr. Badham   [14] ἐπιπνεῖ ms., corr. Heeren

R49 (< F8a Huffmann) Syr. *In Met.*, pp. 165.33–166.5

ὅλως δὲ οὐδὲ ἀπὸ τῶν ὡσανεὶ ἀντικειμένων οἱ ἄνδρες

anyone, with regard neither to themselves nor to one another, if number and its essence did not exist [cf. **PHILOL. D7**]. But as it is, by producing in the soul accord with perception, this [scil. number] makes all things knowable and adapted to each other according to the nature of the gnomon, composing and splitting the ratios of things, each separately, both those that are unlimited and those that limit [cf. **PHILOL. D2, D3**]. One can see the nature of number and its mighty power not only in the demonic realm and in that of the gods, but also in all human actions and discourses everywhere, in all the arts of craftsmanship and in music. The nature neither of number nor of harmony admits any deception, for it is not akin to them; but deception and envy belong to the nature of the unlimited, unknowing, and irrational, and deception does not fall in any way upon number. For deception is opposed and inimical to nature, while truth is akin and innate to the race of number. And the bodies in the sphere are five in number: the ones in the sphere are fire, water, earth, and air, and the vessel of the sphere is the fifth."

R49 (≠ DK) Syrianus, *Commentary on Aristotle's* Metaphysics

In general, these men [scil. the Pythagoreans] did not begin either from supposed contraries [scil. as Aristotle

ἤρχοντο, ἀλλὰ καὶ τῶν δύο συστοιχιῶν τὸ ἐπέκεινα ᾔδεσαν, ὡς μαρτυρεῖ Φιλόλαος τὸν θεὸν λέγων πέρας καὶ ἀπειρίαν ὑποστῆσαι, διὰ μὲν τοῦ πέρατος τὴν τῷ ἑνὶ συγγενεστέραν ἐνδεικνύμενος πᾶσαν συστοιχίαν, διὰ δὲ τῆς ἀπειρίας τὴν ταύτης ὑφειμένην, καὶ ἔτι πρὸ τῶν δύο ἀρχῶν τὴν ἑνιαίαν αἰτίαν καὶ πάντων ἐξῃρημένην προέταττον, ἣν Ἀρχαίνετος μὲν αἰτίαν πρὸ αἰτίας εἶναί φησι, Φιλόλαος δὲ τῶν πάντων ἀρχὰν εἶναι διισχυρίζεται.

Philolaus as the Source of Plato's Timaeus *(R50)*

R50 (cf. ad 44 A26) Procl. *In Tim.* 3.198a, vol. 2, p. 190.7–10

δέδεικται μὲν οὖν ἐκ τῶν Φιλολάου τὸ πλῆθος τῶν παρὰ τῷ Τιμαίῳ γραφέντων ὅρων, τοῖς δὲ Πλάτωνος τὸ διάγραμμα προβαίνει καὶ ἄνευ τοῦ λόγου τῆς ἀποτομῆς.

An Aristotelian Philolaus (R51)

R51 (< 44 B21) Stob. 1.20.2

Φιλολάου Πυθαγορείου[1] ἐκ τοῦ Περὶ ψυχᾶς

[1] Πυθαγορείου post ψυχῆς mss., transp. Canter

implies at *Metaph.* N1 1089a29–36], but they knew what is beyond the two series, as Philolaus bears witness when he says that god has established the limit and the unlimited, indicating by the limit the whole series that is more akin to the One, and by the unlimited what is inferior to this, and they placed even before the two principles the unitary cause that transcends all things [cf. **R67**], of which Archaenetus says that it is the cause before the cause and Philolaus affirms that it is the principle of all things.

Philolaus as the Source of Plato's Timaeus *(R50)*

R50 (cf. ad 44 A26) Proclus, *Commentary on Plato's* Timaeus

Thus it has been demonstrated that most of the definitions given in the *Timaeus* derive from the writings of Philolaus [cf. **PHILOL. P8**], but in Plato the [scil. musical] scale proceeds even without the ratio of the *apotomê*.[1]

[1] The *apotomê* is the interval resulting from the subtraction of the irreducible remainder (*leimma*) from a tone: 9/8 − 256/243 = 2.187/2.048. Ps.-Timaeus of Locri used it to complete the thirty-four terms of the musical scale that serves as the basis for the construction of the soul of the world in Plato's *Timaeus* by adding two further ones, an addition that Proclus refuses.

An Aristotelian Philolaus (R51)

R51 (< 44 B21) Stobaeus, *Anthology*

From Philolaus the Pythagorean, extract from his *On the Soul.*

Φιλόλαος· ἄφθαρτον τὸν κόσμον εἶναι. λέγει γοῦν οὕτως ἐν τῷ Περὶ ψυχᾶς· "παρὸ καὶ ἄφθαρτος καὶ ἀκαταπόνατος διαμένει τὸν ἄπειρον αἰῶνα· οὔτε γὰρ ἔντοσθεν ἄλλα τις αἰτία δυναμικωτέρα αὐτᾶς εὑρεθήσεται οὔτ' ἔκτοσθεν, φθεῖραι αὐτὸν δυναμένα·[2] ἀλλ' ἦς[3] ὅδε ὁ κόσμος ἐξ αἰῶνος καὶ ἐς[4] αἰῶνα διαμένει,[5] εἷς ὑπὸ ἑνὸς τῶ συγγενέος[6] καὶ κρατίστω καὶ ἀνυπερθέτω κυβερνώμενος. ἔχει δὲ καὶ τὰν ἀρχὰν τᾶς κινάσιός τε καὶ μεταβολᾶς ὁ κόσμος εἷς ἐὼν καὶ συνεχὴς καὶ φύσι διαπνεόμενος καὶ περιαγόμενος[7] ἐξ ἀρχᾶς ἀιδίω·[8] καὶ τὸ μὲν ἀμετάβλατον αὐτῶ, τὸ δὲ μεταβάλλον ἐντί· καὶ τὸ μὲν ἀμετάβολον ἀπὸ τᾶς τὸ ὅλον περιεχοίσας ψυχᾶς μέχρι ⟨τᾶς⟩[9] σελάνας περαιοῦται, τὸ δὲ μεταβάλλον ἀπὸ τᾶς σελάνας μέχρι τᾶς γᾶς [. . .]."

[2] δυναμένου mss., corr. Canter   [3] ἦν mss., corr. Wachsmuth   [4] εἰς mss., corr. Wachsmuth   [5] διαμένων F, διαμένειν P: corr. Heeren   [6] συγγενέω mss., corr. Wachsmuth   [7] περιαγεόμενος mss., corr. Canter   [8] ἀρχιδίου mss., corr. Rose   [9] ⟨τᾶς⟩ Meineke

Examples of Writings Attributed to Archytas (R52–R53)

R52 (cf. pp. 21–32 Thesleff) Simpl. *In Cat.*, p. 2.15–25

Ἀρχύτου γὰρ τοῦ Πυθαγορικοῦ καὶ πρὸ Ἀριστοτέλους τὴν εἰς δέκα τῶν πρώτων γενῶν ποιησαμένου

Philolaus: the world is indestructible. For he speaks as follows in his *On the Soul:* "That is why, indestructible and inexhaustible, it persists for infinite eternity. For no other cause more powerful than this will be able to be found, neither within it nor outside it, that would be able to destroy it; but this world has existed since eternity and will persist for eternity, one and governed by the One that is akin, mightiest, and unsurpassed. But the world, which is one, continuous, traversed by the breath of nature, and eternally turned in a circle from the beginning, also possesses the principle of movement and change. And one part of it is unchanging while the other part changes; the unchanging part extends from the soul that envelops the universe down to the moon, the changing part from the moon down to the earth [. . .]."

Examples of Writings Attributed to Archytas (R52–R53)[1]

[1] **R52** and **R53** are each followed by a citation from Ps.-Archytas derived from Aristotle's *Categories*.

R52 (≠ DK) Simplicius, *Commentary on Aristotle's* Categories

For Archytas the Pythagorean having, even before Aristotle, performed the division into ten of the first genera,

διαίρεσιν ἐν τῷ βιβλίῳ ὃ Περὶ τοῦ παντὸς ἐκεῖνος
ἐπέγραψε [. . .] αὐτὸς ἐν τοῖς προσήκουσι τόποις τὰ
τοῦ Ἀρχύτου παράγων [. . .] καὶ τὴν συμφωνίαν τὴν
πρὸς αὐτὰ τοῦ Ἀριστοτέλους ἐπέδειξε [. . .] διότι φαίνεται
πανταχοῦ τῷ Ἀρχύτᾳ κατακολουθεῖν ὁ Ἀριστοτέλης
βουλόμενος [. . .].

R53 (cf. pp. 15–19 Thesleff) Simpl. *In Cat.*, p. 382.7–9

φαίνεται δὲ καὶ τὰ περὶ ἀντικειμένων Ἀριστοτέλης ἐκ
τοῦ Ἀρχυτείου βιβλίου μεταλαβὼν τοῦ Περὶ ἀντικειμένων
ἐπιγεγραμμένου [. . .].

Other Themes That Feature in the
Pseudepigraphic Writings (R54–R66)
On the Divulgation of the Pythagorean
Doctrine (R54)

R54 (pp. 111, 114 Thesleff) *Pyth. epist.* 2 *(Lysis ad Hipparchum)*, 1 et 7

Λῦσις Ἱππάρχῳ.

[1] μετὰ τὸ Πυθαγόραν ἐξ ἀνθρώπων γενέσθαι
οὐδέποκα διασκεδασθήσεσθαι τὸ ἄθροισμα τῶν
ὁμιλητῶν ἐς τὸν ἐμαυτοῦ θυμὸν ἐβαλόμαν· ἐπεὶ
δὲ παρ' ἐλπίδας [. . .] ἄλλος ἄλλοσε φορεύμενοι
διεσπάρημεν, ὅσιόν κα μεμνᾶσθαι[1] τῶν τήνου
θείων καὶ σεμνῶν παραγγελμάτων, μηδὲ κοινὰ

in the book he wrote *On the Whole*,[1] he [i.e. Iamblichus] cites at the appropriate places what Archytas says [...] to demonstrate the agreement between Aristotle and them [...] since Aristotle manifestly wanted to follow Archytas everywhere [...].

[1] Probably a way of referring to the treatise known under the title (itself variable) *Concerning the Whole System or the Ten Categories*.

R53 (≠ DK) Simplicius, *Commentary on Aristotle's* Categories

It is manifest that Aristotle has likewise borrowed what he says about the opposites from Archytas' book entitled *On the Opposites* [...].

*Other Themes That Feature in the
Pseudepigraphic Writings (R54–R66)
On the Divulgation of the Pythagorean
Doctrine (R54)*

R54 (cf. 46) Lysis, *Letter to Hipparchus*

Lysis to Hipparchus

[1] It never occurred to me that after Pythagoras passed away from among human beings the throng of his disciples would ever be scattered. But since, against all expectation, we have been dispersed, each one in a different direction [...], it would be pious to recall his divine and noble precepts, and

---

[1] ὅσιον κἀμὲ μνᾶσθαι (μεμνᾶσθαι γ) mss., corr. Rohde

ποιεῖσθαι τὰ σοφίας ἀγαθὰ τοῖς μηδ' ὄναρ τὰν ψυχὰν κεκαθαρμένοις. [. . .] [7] λέγοντι δὲ πολλοί τυ καὶ δαμοσίᾳ φιλοσοφέν, ὅπερ ἀπαξίωσε Πυθαγόρας, ὅς γε Δαμοῖ τᾷ ἑαυτοῦ θυγατρὶ τὰ ὑπομνάματα παρακαταθέμενος ἐπέσκαψε μηδενὶ τῶν ἐκτὸς τᾶς οἰκίας παραδιδόμεν. ἃ δὲ δυναμένα πολλῶν χρημάτων ἀποδόσθαι τὼς λόγως οὐκ ἐβουλάθη, πενίαν δὲ καὶ τὰς τῶ πατρὸς ἐπισκάψιας ἐνόμιζε χρυσοῦ τιμωτέρας ἦμεν. φαντὶ δὲ ὅτι καὶ Δαμὼ θνάσκουσα Βιστάλᾳ τᾷ ἑαυτᾶς θυγατρὶ τὰν αὐτὰν ἐπιστολὰν ἐπέστειλεν. ἁμὲς δὲ ἄνδρες ἐόντες καὶ Πυθαγόρα φοιτηταὶ οὐ γνασίως αὐτῷ ποτιφερόμεθα, ἀλλὰ παραβάται τᾶν ὁμολογιᾶν γινόμεθα. εἰ μὲν ὦν μεταβάλοιο, χαρήσομαι, εἰ δὲ μή, τέθνακάς μοι.

On the Universe (R55–R56)
A Pseudepigraphic Summary of Plato's Timaeus:
Timaeus of Locri (R55)

R55

a (cf. p. 207 ad l. 23 Thesleff) Iambl. *In Nic.*, p. 105.10–14 et 17–22

καὶ πρὸ Πλάτωνος δὲ τὰ αὐτὰ διειλήφεσαν ⟨οἱ⟩[1] Πυθαγορικοὶ περὶ αὐτῆς. Τίμαιός τ'[2] οὖν ὁ Λοκρὸς ἐν τῷ

---

[1] ⟨οἱ⟩ Pistelli   [2] δ' Wachsmuth

PYTHAGOREAN RECEPTION

not to communicate the goods of wisdom to those whose souls have not, even in a dream, been purified. [. . .] [7] But many say that you philosophize also in public—exactly what Pythagoras prohibited, he who entrusted his notes (*hupomnêmata*) to his daughter Damo but ordered her not to transmit them to anyone outside his family. And although she could have sold his discourses (*logoi*) for a lot of money, she refused to do so, but thought that poverty and her father's injunctions were more honorable than gold. And they say that when Damo was dying she sent the same letter to her daughter Bistala. But we, who are men and companions of Pythagoras, we are not acting nobly in regard to him, but we are violating the accord. If then you repent, I shall be delighted; if not, in my eyes you have died.[1]

[1] For this letter, see also Iamblichus, *Life of Pythagoras* 75–78.

On the Universe (R55–R56)
A Pseudepigraphic Summary of Plato's Timaeus:
Timaeus of Locri (R55)

R55 (≠ DK)

a Iamblichus, *Commentary on Nicomachus' Introduction to Arithmetic*

And before Plato, the Pythagoreans maintained the same theses with regard to it [i.e. the geometric analogy, cf. Plato, *Timaeus* 31c–32a]. Thus Timaeus of Locri, in his

Περὶ φύσεως κόσμω καὶ ψυχᾶς (ἀφ' οὗπερ ἐφοδιασθέντα Πλάτωνα τὸν διὰ τοῦτο φερώνυμον Τίμαιον συντάξαι λέγουσιν) [. . .] οὕτω πώς φησι: "τριῶν γὰρ ὡντινωνοῦν ὅρων, ὅταν καὶ τὰ διαστάματα κατὰ τὸν αὐτὸν ἐστάθη λόγον ποτ' ἄλλα, τότε δὴ τὸ μέσσον ῥυσμῷ δίκας ὁρήμεθα ποττὸ πρᾶτον, ὅ τι περ τὸ τρίτον ποτ' αὐτὸ κἂν πάλιν καὶ παραλλάξ."

b (p. 205 Thesleff) Tim. Locr. *De nat. mund. et an.* 1.1

Τίμαιος ὁ Λοκρὸς τάδε ἔφα· "Δύο αἰτίας εἶμεν τῶν συμπάντων, νόον μὲν τῶν κατὰ λόγον γιγνομένων, ἀνάγκαν δὲ τῶν βίᾳ καττὰς δυνάμεις τῶν σωμάτων. τουτέων δὲ τὸ μὲν τᾶς τἀγαθῶ φύσιος εἶμεν θεόν τε ὀνυμαίνεσθαι ἀρχάν τε τῶν ἀρίστων· τὰ δ' ἑπόμενά τε καὶ συναίτια ὄντα ἐς ἀνάγκαν ἀνάγεσθαι [. . .]."

A Pseudepigraphic Text of an Aristotelian Tendency: Ocellus of Lucania (R56)

R56

a (48.3) Phil. *Aetern. mund.* 12

ἔνιοι δ' οὐκ Ἀριστοτέλην τῆς δόξης εὑρετὴν λέγουσιν ἀλλὰ τῶν Πυθαγορείων τινάς. ἐγὼ δὲ καὶ Ὀκέλλου συγγράμματι, Λευκανοῦ γένος, ἐπιγραφομένῳ Περὶ τῆς τοῦ παντὸς φύσεως ἐνέτυχον, ἐν ᾧ ἀγένητόν τε

book *On the Nature of the World and the Soul* (which they say that Plato followed and that it is for this reason that he wrote a work of the same title, *Timaeus*) [. . .], says the following: "For when the intervals between any three terms are set in the same ratio to the others, we see that the middle term is to the first one conforming to a rule of harmony as the third one is to this one [i.e. the middle term] and so too alternated."

b Timaeus of Locri, *On the Nature of the World and the Soul*

Timaeus of Locri has said the following: "Of all things there exist two causes: intelligence (*nous*) for the things that happen in conformity with reason; and necessity for those that happen by force, in virtue of the powers of bodies. The former of these causes belongs to the nature of the good and is called god and the principle of the best things, while the ones that come after and are auxiliary causes are related to necessity [. . .]."

A Pseudepigraphic Text of an Aristotelian Tendency: Ocellus of Lucania (R56)

R56

a (48.3) Philo of Alexandria, *On the Eternity of the World*

Some people say that it is not Aristotle who is the inventor of this opinion [scil. that the world is eternal] but instead certain Pythagoreans. As for me, I have read the work of Ocellus of Lucania entitled *On the Nature of the Universe*, in which he not only states that the world is ungenerated

καὶ ἄφθαρτον οὐκ ἀπεφαίνετο μόνον[1] ἀλλὰ καὶ δι᾿ ἀποδείξεων κατεσκεύαζε τὸν κόσμον εἶναι.

[1] μὲν οὖν codd., corr. Turnebus

b (p. 126 Thesleff) Ocell. Univ. nat. 2–3

[. . .] δοκεῖ γάρ μοι τὸ πᾶν ἀνώλεθρον εἶναι καὶ ἀγένητον· ἀεί τε γὰρ ἦν καὶ ἔσται· εἰ γὰρ ἔγχρονον, οὐκ ἂν ἔτι ἦν· οὕτως οὖν ἀνώλεθρόν τε καὶ ἀγένητον τὸ πᾶν.[1] οὔτε γὰρ εἰ γενόμενόν τις αὐτὸ δοξάζοι, εὕροιτο ἂν ‹ἐξ ὅτου γένοιτο, οὔτε εἰ φθαρτόν, εὕροιτο ἂν›[2] εἰς ὃ φθαρείη καὶ διαλυθείη· ἐξ ὅτου τε καὶ γέγονεν, ἐκεῖνο πρῶτον τοῦ παντός ἐστιν, εἰς ὅ τε πάλιν φθαρήσεται, ἐκεῖνο ἔσχατον τοῦ παντὸς ἔσται [. . .].

[1] ἀγένητόν τε τὸ πᾶν καὶ ἀνώλεθρον AM (τε om. M)
[2] ‹ἐξ ὅτου . . . εὕροιτο ἂν› Harder post Rudolph qui scripsit γεννηθείη

c (p. 135 Thesleff) Ocell. Univ. nat. 44

[. . .] καὶ γὰρ αὐτὰς τὰς δυνάμεις καὶ τὰ ὄργανα καὶ τὰς ὀρέξεις τὰς πρὸς τὴν μῖξιν ὑπὸ τοῦ θεοῦ δεδομένας τοῖς ἀνθρώποις οὐχ ἡδονῆς ἕνεκα δεδόσθαι συμβέβηκεν ἀλλὰ τῆς εἰς τὸν ἀεὶ χρόνον διαμονῆς τοῦ γένους [. . .].

PYTHAGOREAN RECEPTION

and indestructible, but also proves this by means of demonstrations.

b (≠ DK) Ocellus of Lucania, *On the Nature of the Whole*

It seems to me that the whole is indestructible and ungenerated, for it has always existed and will always exist; for if it were temporal, it would no longer exist. In this way therefore the whole is ungenerated and indestructible. For if someone maintained that it was generated at a given moment, he would not be able to find ⟨what it was generated from, nor, if [scil. he said that it is] corruptible, would he be able to find⟩ what it was corrupted and dissolved into: what it was born from is the first part of the whole, and inversely what it will be corrupted into will be the last part of the whole [. . .].

c (≠ DK) Ocellus of Lucania, *On the Nature of the Whole*

[. . .] For the capacities, organs, and desires with regard to sexual intercourse that were given to humans by god were not given for the sake of pleasure but for that of the persistence of the race for eternal time [. . .].

EARLY GREEK PHILOSOPHY IV

Political Theory (R57–R62)
The King (R57–R60)

R57 Ecph. *Regn.* in Stob.

a (cf. p. 79 Thesleff) 4.6.22

ἐπὶ δὲ γᾶς ἄνθρωποι[1] ἀπῳκισμένον χρῆμα καὶ πολὺ τᾶς καθαρωτέρας φύσιος ἐλαττούμενον καὶ πολλᾷ τᾷ γᾷ βαρυνόμενον, ὡς ἀπὸ τᾶς ματρὸς αὐτὸ[2] μόγις ἐπᾶρθαι <ἄν>,[3] αἰ μὴ θεόμοιρός τις ἐμπνοίησις ἐλέῳ[4] ζῴῳ συνάψεν αὐτὸ[5] τῷ κρέσσονι μέρει δεικνῦσα τὰν ἱερὰν τῶ γεννάτορος πότοψιν, ὡς ἀδύνατον ἐκείναν θεάσασθαι [. . .].

[1] ἄνθρωπος Delatte [2] αὐτῶ mss., corr. Gesner [3] <ἄν> Meineke [4] ἐλέῳ (ἐλαίῳ A) mss.: ἀιδίῳ Delatte [5] αὐτὸ M: αὐτῶ (vel -ῷ) SA

b (pp. 79–80 Thesleff) 4.7.64

[. . .] ἐν δὲ τᾷ γᾷ καὶ παρ' ἁμῖν[1] ἀριστοφυέστατον μὲν ἄνθρωπος, θειότατον δ' ὁ βασιλεὺς ἐν τᾷ κοινᾷ φύσει πλεονεκτῶν τῶ κρέσσονος, τὸ μὲν σκᾶνος τοῖς λοιποῖς ὅμοιος, οἷα γεγονὼς ἐκ τᾶς αὐτᾶς ὕλας, ὑπὸ τεχνίτα δ' εἰργασμένος λῴστω, ὃς ἐτεχνίτευσεν αὐτὸν ἀρχετύπῳ χρώμενος ἑαυτῷ.

[1] ἁμῶν SM, ἡμῶν A: corr. Gaisford

PYTHAGOREAN RECEPTION

Political Theory (R57–R62)
The King (R57–R60)

R57 (≠ DK) Ecphantus, *On Kingship*, in Stobaeus, *Anthology*

a

On the earth, human beings are something that has been exiled, much worse than its purer nature, and weighed down by a large quantity of earth, so that it could have scarcely risen above its mother if a breath participating in divinity, out of pity for a living being, had not attached it to its better part, showing it the sacred countenance of its begetter, which it was unable to contemplate [. . .].

b

[. . .] On the earth and among us, the human being possesses the best nature; but the king is what is most divine in the nature shared by all, and is ambitious for what is better; he resembles the others in his body, because he comes from the same matter; but he has been produced by the very best artist, who has fashioned him by taking himself as a model.

431

R58 (p. 71 Thesleff) Diotog. *Regn.* in Stob. 4.7.61

βασιλεύς κ' εἴη ὁ δικαιότατος, δικαιότατος δὲ ὁ νομιμώτατος. ἄνευ μὲν γὰρ δικαιοσύνας οὐδεὶς ἂν εἴη βασιλεύς, ἄνευ δὲ νόμω[1] δικαιοσύνα. τὸ μὲν γὰρ δίκαιον ἐν τῷ νόμῳ ἐντί, ὁ δέ γε νόμος αἴτιος τῶ δικαίω, ὁ δὲ βασιλεὺς ἤτοι νόμος ἔμψυχός ἐντι ἢ νόμιμος ἄρχων· διὰ ταῦτ' οὖν δικαιότατος καὶ νομιμώτατος [. . .].

[1] νόμω ‹οὐ› Delatte

R59 (p. 187 Thesleff) Sthen. *Regn.* in Stob. 4.7.63

χρὴ τὸν βασιλέα σοφὸν ἦμεν· οὕτω γὰρ ἐσσεῖται ἀντίμιμος καὶ ζαλωτὰς τῶ πράτω θεῶ. οὗτος γὰρ καὶ φύσει ἐστὶ καὶ πρᾶτος βασιλεύς τε καὶ δυνάστας, ὁ δὲ γενέσει καὶ μιμάσει.

R60 (≠ DK) Porph. *Quaest. Hom.* ad Il. 1.340

οἱ Πυθαγόρειοι κατὰ θεῖον ‹καὶ› κατὰ[1] ἀνθρώπειον γένος ὅλον τρίτον ἐτίθεντο σεβάσμιον τὸν[2] βασιλέα ἢ σοφὸν ἄνδρα, Ὁμήρου πρώτου μεταξὺ θεῶν τε καὶ ἀνθρώπων θέντος τὸν βασιλέα [. . .].

[1] κατὰ . . . ‹καὶ› κατὰ Villoison: καθὰ . . . καὶ McPhail
[2] τὸν secl. Janko

R58 (≠ DK) Diotogenes, *On Kingship,* in Stobaeus, *Anthology*

The most just man would be the king, and the one who complies most with the law would be the most just; for without justice, no one could be king, and without law, justice [scil. could not exist]. For what is just exists in the law and the law is the cause of what is just, and the king is either a law endowed with life or a magistrate who complies with the law. This is then why he is the most just and complies most with the law [. . .].

R59 (≠ DK) Sthenidas of Locri, *On Kingship,* in Stobaeus, *Anthology*

The king must be wise; for it is in this way that he will be an imitator and emulator of the first god. For this latter is by nature both the first king and ruler, while the other [scil. is king because he becomes one] by birth and imitation [. . .].

R60 (≠ DK) Porphyry, *Platonic Questions*

The Pythagoreans, with regard to the divine and human races, posited in general a third one worthy of veneration, the king or wise man, but Homer was the first to place the king between gods and men [. . .].

EARLY GREEK PHILOSOPHY IV

Preambles to the Laws of Zaleucus and Charondas (R61–R62)

R61 (pp. 225–226 Thesleff) Cic. *Leg.* 2.14–15

[Marcus:] [. . .] quod idem etiam Zaleucum et Charondan fecisse video, cum quidem illi [. . .] rei publicae causa leges civitatibus suis scripserint;[1] quos imitatus Plato [. . .].
[Quintus:] Quid quod Zaleucum istum negat ullum fuisse Timaeus [*FrGrH* 566 F130a]?
[Marcus:] At ⟨ait⟩[2] Theophrastus [Frag. 598C FHS&G] [. . .] commemorant vero ipsius cives [. . .] Locri. sed sive fuit sive non fuit, nihil ad rem: loquimur quod traditum est.

[1] scripserunt *mss., corr.* Rob. Étienne   [2] ⟨ait⟩ Müller

R62

a (p. 226 Thesleff) Zaleucus in Stob. 4.2.19

τοὺς κατοικοῦντας τὴν πόλιν καὶ τὴν χώραν πάντας πρῶτον πεπεῖσθαι χρὴ καὶ νομίζειν θεοὺς εἶναι ἀναβλέποντας ἐς οὐρανὸν καὶ τὸν κόσμον καὶ τὴν ἐν αὐτοῖς διακόσμησιν καὶ τάξιν [. . .].

b (p. 60 Thesleff) Charondas in Stob. 4.2.24

τὼς βουλευομένως[1] καὶ πράσσοντάς τι ἀπὸ θεῶν ἄρχεσθαι χρή· τὸ γὰρ ἄριστον, ὥσπερ ἁ παροιμία φατί, τὸν θεὸν ἦμεν αἴτιον πάντων τούτων [. . .].

PYTHAGOREAN RECEPTION

Preambles to the Laws of Zaleucus and Charondas (R61–R62)

R61 (≠ DK) Cicero, *On the Laws*

[Marcus:] [. . .] I see that Zaleucus and Charondas did the same thing [scil. praised the laws in a preamble] when they [. . .] wrote laws for their fellow citizens for the sake of their political community; and Plato imitated these [. . .].
[Quintus:] But what about the fact that Timaeus [i.e. of Taormina] denies that this Zaleucus ever existed?
[Marcus:] But Theophrastus ⟨said [scil. that he did]⟩ [. . .]; and his fellow citizens, the Locrians, mention him [. . .]. But it does not matter whether or not he existed; I am speaking about what is reported.

R62 (≠ DK)

a Beginning of the preamble of Zaleucus, in Stobaeus, *Anthology*

First of all, all the inhabitants of the city and the country, looking at the heavens and the world, and the arrangement and order that are in them, must believe and acknowledge that the gods exist [. . .].

b Beginning of the preamble of Charondas of Catania, in Stobaeus, *Anthology*

Those who deliberate or perform some action must begin with the gods. For the best thing, as the proverb says, is that god is the cause of all these things [. . .].

---

¹ βουλομένως (-μένους L) mss., corr. Meineke

EARLY GREEK PHILOSOPHY IV

The Virtue of Women (R63–R66)

R63 (pp. 195–196 Thesleff) *Pyth. epist.* 5 (p. 166 Städele)

ἀκούω σε τὰ παιδία τρυφερῶς ἄγειν· ἔστι δὲ ἀγαθῆς μητρὸς οὐχ ἡ πρὸς ἡδονὴν ἐπιμέλεια τῶν παίδων, ἀλλ' ἡ πρὸς τὸ σῶφρον ἀγωγή [. . .].

R64 (< 17.1) Iambl. *VP* 132

[. . .] Δεινὼ[1] γὰρ τὴν Βροντίνου γυναῖκα, τῶν Πυθαγορείων ἑνός, οὖσαν σοφήν τε καὶ περιττὴν τὴν ψυχήν, ἧς ἐστὶ καὶ τὸ καλὸν καὶ περίβλεπτον[2] ῥῆμα, τὸ τὴν γυναῖκα δεῖν θύειν αὐθημερὸν ἀνισταμένην ἀπὸ τοῦ ἑαυτῆς ἀνδρός, ὅ τινες εἰς Θεανὼ ἀναφέρουσι [. . .].

[1] δεινωνὼ ms., corr. Scaliger   [2] περιβόητον Cobet

R65 (cf. p. 194.27 Thesleff) Plut. *Praec. conj.* 31 142C

ἡ Θεανὼ παρέφηνε τὴν χεῖρα περιβαλλομένη τὸ ἱμάτιον. εἰπόντος δέ τινος "καλὸς ὁ πῆχυς," "ἀλλ' οὐ δημόσιος" ἔφη.

R66 (p. 142 Thesleff) Perictione *Mul. harm.* in Stob. 4.28.19

τὴν ἁρμονίην γυναῖκα νώσασθαι[1] δεῖ φρονήσιός τε

[1] γυνὰ ἱκανώσασθαι mss., corr. Valckenaer

PYTHAGOREAN RECEPTION

The Virtue of Women (R63–R66)

R63 (≠ DK) Theano, *Letter to Euboule*

I hear that you are spoiling your children. But what belongs to a good mother is not to care for her children's pleasure but to lead them to temperance [. . .].

R64 (< 17.1) Iamblichus, *Life of Pythagoras*

[. . .] Deino, a wise and extraordinary woman, the wife of Brontinus, one of the Pythagoreans, she who uttered that magnificent and admirable saying, "a woman should sacrifice the very day that she gets up from her husband's [scil. embrace]," which some people attribute to Theano [. . .].

R65 (≠ DK) Plutarch, *Conjugal Precepts*

Theano exposed her arm while she was putting on her cloak. When someone said, "Your arm is beautiful!" she said, "But it is not for the public."

R66 (≠ DK) Perictionê,[1] *On the Harmony of Women,* in Stobaeus, *Anthology*

A woman should think that harmony is full of wisdom and

---

[1] Perictionê was the name of Plato's mother.

καὶ σωφροσύνης πλείην· κάρτα γὰρ ψυχὴν πεπνῦ-
σθαι δεῖ ἐς ἀρετήν, ὥστ' ἔσται καὶ δικαίη καὶ ἀν-
δρηίη καὶ φρονέουσα καὶ αὐταρκείη καλλυνομένη[2] καὶ
κενὴν δόξαν μισέουσα[3] [. . .].

[2] καλοννωμένη S, καλον νωμένη M, καλλονωμένη A: corr.
Tr.   [3] μισγέουσα mss., corr. Tr.

Some Neopythagorean Presentations of 'Pythagorean' Doctrines Concerning the Principles (R67–R71)
Eudorus of Alexandria (R67)

R67 (≠ DK) Simpl. *In Phys.*, p. 181.10–30

γράφει δὲ περὶ τούτων ὁ Εὔδωρος τάδε· "κατὰ τὸν
ἀνωτάτω λόγον φατέον τοὺς Πυθαγορικοὺς τὸ ἓν ἀρχὴν τῶν πάντων λέγειν, κατὰ δὲ τὸν δεύτερον λόγον
δύο ἀρχάς τῶν ἀποτελουμένων εἶναι, τό τε ἓν καὶ τὴν
ἐναντίαν τούτῳ φύσιν. ὑποτάσσεσθαι δὲ πάντων τῶν
κατὰ ἐναντίωσιν ἐπινοουμένων τὸ μὲν ἀστεῖον[1] τῷ ἑνί,
τὸ δὲ φαῦλον τῇ πρὸς τοῦτο ἐναντιουμένῃ φύσει. διὸ
μηδὲ εἶναι τὸ σύνολον ταύτας ἀρχὰς κατὰ τοὺς ἄνδρας. εἰ γὰρ ἡ μὲν τῶνδε ἡ δὲ τῶνδέ ἐστιν ἀρχή, οὐκ
εἰσὶ κοιναὶ πάντων ἀρχαὶ ὥσπερ τὸ ἕν." καὶ πάλιν
"διό," φησί, "καὶ κατ' ἄλλον τρόπον ἀρχὴν ἔφασαν
εἶναι τῶν πάντων τὸ ἕν, ὡς ἂν καὶ τῆς ὕλης καὶ τῶν
ὄντων πάντων ἐξ αὐτοῦ γεγενημένων. τοῦτο[2] δὲ εἶναι
καὶ τὸν ὑπεράνω θεόν." καὶ λοιπὸν ἀκριβολογούμενος

temperance. For the soul must really be inspired for virtue, in order to be just, courageous, prudent, embellished by self-sufficiency, and hating empty opinion [...].

Some Neopythagorean Presentations of 'Pythagorean' Doctrines Concerning the Principles (R67–R71)
Eudorus of Alexandria[1] *(R67)*

[1] First century BC.

R67 (≠ DK) Simplicius, *Commentary on Aristotle's Physics*

Eudorus writes the following about them [i.e. the Pythagoreans]: "It should be said that according to the loftiest explanation the Pythagoreans say that the One is the principle of all things, but that according to the second explanation there are two principles of the production of things, the One and the nature that is opposed to it. All things, conceived by opposition, are arranged below: what is refined (*asteion*) under the One, what is base under the nature that is opposed to it. That is why these are not absolutely principles for these people. For if the one is the principle of some things and the other the principle of others, then they are not common principles of all things, as the One is." And he says again, "This is why they stated in a different way also that the One is the principle of all things, since both matter and all things come from it. And it is also the transcendent (*huperanô*) god." And then,

---

[1] ἀστεῖον ἀεὶ E   [2] τοῦτο F: τοῦτον DE

[. . .] "φημὶ τοίνυν τοὺς περὶ τὸν Πυθαγόραν τὸ μὲν ἓν πάντων ἀρχὴν ἀπολιπεῖν, κατ' ἄλλον δὲ τρόπον δύο τὰ ἀνωτάτω στοιχεῖα παρεισάγειν. καλεῖν δὲ τὰ δύο ταῦτα στοιχεῖα πολλαῖς προσηγορίαις· τὸ μὲν γὰρ αὐτῶν ὀνομάζεσθαι τεταγμένον ὡρισμένον γνωστὸν ἄρρεν περιττὸν δεξιὸν φῶς, τὸ δὲ ἐναντίον τούτῳ ἄτακτον ἀόριστον ἄγνωστον θῆλυ ἀριστερὸν ἄρτιον σκότος, ὥστε ὡς μὲν ἀρχὴ τὸ ἕν, ὡς δὲ στοιχεῖα τὸ ἓν καὶ ἡ ἀόριστος δυάς, ἀρχαὶ ἄμφω ἓν ὄντα πάλιν. καὶ δῆλον ὅτι ἄλλο μέν ἐστιν ἓν ἡ ἀρχὴ τῶν πάντων, ἄλλο δὲ ἓν τὸ τῇ δυάδι ἀντικείμενον, ὃ καὶ μονάδα καλοῦσιν."

Moderatus of Gades (R68)

R68 (≠ DK) Simpl. *In Phys.*, pp. 230.34–231.5

ταύτην δὲ περὶ τῆς ὕλης τὴν ὑπόνοιαν ἐοίκασιν ἐσχηκέναι πρῶτοι μὲν τῶν Ἑλλήνων οἱ Πυθαγόρειοι, μετὰ δ' ἐκείνους ὁ Πλάτων, ὡς καὶ Μοδέρατος ἱστορεῖ. οὗτος γὰρ κατὰ τοὺς Πυθαγορείους τὸ μὲν πρῶτον ἓν ὑπὲρ τὸ εἶναι καὶ πᾶσαν οὐσίαν ἀποφαίνεται, τὸ δὲ δεύτερον ἕν, ὅπερ ἐστὶ τὸ ὄντως ὂν καὶ νοητόν, τὰ εἴδη φησὶν εἶναι, τὸ δὲ τρίτον, ὅπερ ἐστὶ τὸ ψυχικόν, μετέχειν τοῦ ἑνὸς καὶ τῶν εἰδῶν, τὴν δὲ ἀπὸ τούτου τελευταίαν φύσιν τὴν τῶν αἰσθητῶν οὖσαν μηδὲ μετ-

explaining precisely [. . .]: "So I state that Pythagoras' disciples admit that the One is the principle of all things, but that in a different way they introduce two highest elements. They call these two elements by many names: the first is called ordered, definite, known, male, odd, right, light; its contrary, disordered, indefinite, unknown, female, left, even, darkness, so that there is the One as first principle, and the One and the indefinite Dyad as elements, the One being in turn both principles. And it is clear that the One which is the principle of all things is different from the One which is opposed to the Dyad, which they also call 'monad.'"

Moderatus of Gades[1] *(R68)*

[1] Second century AD.

R68 (≠ DK) Simplicius, *Commentary on Aristotle's* Physics

As Moderatus too reports, it seems that the first among the Greeks to have had this conception about matter [scil. that matter is distinguished from material realities by the absence of any measurable dimension] were the Pythagoreans, and after them Plato. For he states, in conformity with the Pythagoreans, that the first One is above being and all existing substance (*ousia*), he says that that the second One, which is what really exists (*to ontôs on*) and is intelligible, is the Forms, that the third, which is what belongs to the soul (*to psukhikon*), participates in the One and the Forms, and that the last nature deriving from this, which is that of the perceptibles, does not even participate

ἔχειν, ἀλλὰ κατ' ἔμφασιν ἐκείνων κεκοσμῆσθαι, τῆς ἐν αὐτοῖς ὕλης τοῦ μὴ ὄντος πρώτως ἐν τῷ ποσῷ ὄντος οὔσης σκίασμα καὶ ἔτι μᾶλλον ὑποβεβηκυίας καὶ ἀπὸ τούτου.

Numenius (R69)

R69 (≠ DK) Calcid. *In Tim.* 295, pp. 522–24 Bakhouche (< Numen. Frag. 52 Des Places)

Numenius ex Pythagorae magisterio Stoicorum hoc de initiis dogma refellens Pythagorae dogmate, cui concinere dicit Platonicum, ait Pythagoram deum quidem singularitatis ⟨nomine⟩[1] nominasse, silvam vero duitatis; quam duitatem indeterminatam quidem minime genitam, limitatam vero generatam esse dicere [. . .]. sed non nullos Pythagoreos, vim sententiae non recte assecutos, putasse dici etiam illam indeterminatam et immensam duitatem ab unica singularitate institutam, recedente a natura sua singularitate et in duitatis habitum migrante—non recte ut [. . .] ex deo silva et ex singularitate immensa et indeterminata duitas converteretur.

[1] ⟨nomine⟩ *Wrobel*

in it, but is organized in virtue of the impression produced by them [i.e. the One and the Forms]; the matter in them is the shadow of what does not exist, which in the first place is located in quantity, but it has receded even lower from this last.

Numenius[1] *(R69)*

[1] Second century AD.

R69 (≠ DK) Calcidius, *Commentary on Plato's* Timaeus

Numenius, of the school of Pythagoras, refuting the Stoics' doctrine on the principles by means of Pythagoras' doctrine, with which he says Plato's agrees, says that Pythagoras gave to god the name 'monad' and to matter that of 'dyad'; which dyad he says is not at all generated inasmuch as it is indeterminate, but generated inasmuch as it is limited [. . .]. But some Pythagoreans, who did not understand correctly the meaning of this statement, thought that what was being said was that this indeterminate and unlimited dyad was also produced by the monad alone when the monad recedes from its nature and emigrates into the condition of the dyad—mistakenly, since [. . .] matter would come from god and the unlimited and indeterminate dyad from the monad.

See also **PHER. R18**

Longinus (R70)

R70 (≠ DK) Longin. in Porph. *Vit. Plot.* 20.69–75 (Longin. Frag. 4, p. 147 Patillon-Brisson)

οἱ δὲ καὶ πλήθει προβλημάτων ἃ μετεχειρίσαντο τὴν σπουδὴν τοῦ γράφειν ἀποδειξάμενοι[1] καὶ τρόπῳ θεωρίας ἰδίῳ χρησάμενοι Πλωτῖνός εἰσι καὶ Γεντιλιανὸς Ἀμέλιος· ὃς μὲν τὰς Πυθαγορείους ἀρχὰς καὶ Πλατωνικὰς ὡς ἐδόκει, πρὸς σαφεστέραν τῶν πρὸ αὐτοῦ καταστησάμενος ἐξήγησιν (οὐδὲ γὰρ οὐδὲν ἐγγύς τι τὰ Νουμηνίου καὶ Κρονίου καὶ Μοδεράτου καὶ Θρασύλλου τοῖς Πλωτίνου περὶ τῶν αὐτῶν συγγράμμασιν εἰς ἀκρίβειαν) [. . .].

[1] ἀποδεξάμενοι mss., corr. Toup

*The Variety of Pythagorean Doctrines
According to a (Neopythagorean)
Report in Sextus Empiricus (R71)*

R71 (≠ DK) Sext. Emp. *Adv. Math.* 10

a 262–63

καὶ ὅτι ταῖς ἀληθείαις αὗταί εἰσι τῶν ὅλων ἀρχαί, ποικίλως οἱ Πυθαγορικοὶ διδάσκουσιν. τῶν γὰρ ὄντων, φασί, τὰ μὲν κατὰ διαφορὰν νοεῖται, τὰ δὲ κατ' ἐναντίωσιν, τὰ δὲ πρός τι. κατὰ διαφορὰν μὲν οὖν εἶναι τὰ καθ' ἑαυτὰ καὶ κατ' ἰδίαν περιγραφὴν ὑποκείμενα [. . .].

PYTHAGOREAN RECEPTION

Longinus (R70)

R70 (≠ DK) Longinus, Preface to *Against Plotinus and Amelius Gentilianus,* in Porphyry, *Life of Plotinus*

Those who have demonstrated the seriousness of their writings by the number of problems they discussed and who had their own personal theoretical conception are Plotinus and Amelius Gentilianus—the former, he [i.e. Longinus] thought, gave a clearer interpretation of the Pythagorean and Platonic principles than his predecessors had done (for what Numenius, Cronius, Moderatus, and Thrasyllus say is in precision very far from Plotinus' writings on the same subjects) [. . .].

The Variety of Pythagorean Doctrines According to a (Neopythagorean) Report in Sextus Empiricus (R71)

R71 (≠ DK) Sextus Empiricus, *Against the Natural Philosophers*[1]

[1] The passage from which these two extracts are taken is very lengthy (§248–84).

a

And the Pythagoreans teach in a variety of ways that in truth these are the principles of all things [scil. a version of the theory of principles analogous to the one reported by Eudorus, **R67**]. For among the things that exist, some are conceived in function of their differences, others by way of contrariety, others relatively to something. In function of their difference are [scil. conceived] those that exist by themselves and possess a characteristic that is their own [. . .].

445

b 281–82

τινὲς δ' ἀπὸ ἑνὸς σημείου τὸ σῶμά φασι συνίστασθαι· τουτὶ γὰρ τὸ σημεῖον ῥυὲν γραμμὴν ἀποτελεῖν, τὴν δὲ γραμμὴν ῥυεῖσαν ἐπίπεδον ποιεῖν, τοῦτο δὲ εἰς βάθος κινηθὲν τὸ σῶμα γεννᾶν τριχῇ διαστατόν. διαφέρει δὲ ἡ τοιαύτη τῶν Πυθαγορικῶν στάσις τῆς τῶν προτέρων. ἐκεῖνοι μὲν γὰρ ἐκ δυεῖν ἀρχῶν, τῆς τε μονάδος καὶ τῆς ἀορίστου δυάδος, ἐποίουν τοὺς ἀριθμούς, εἶτ' ἐκ τῶν ἀριθμῶν τὰ σημεῖα καὶ τὰς γραμμὰς τά τε ἐπίπεδα σχήματα καὶ τὰ στερεά· οὗτοι δὲ ἀπὸ ἑνὸς σημείου τὰ πάντα τεκταίνουσιν.

An Example of Doxographic Syncretism (R72)

R72 (> 58B.15) Aët. 1.3.8 (Ps.-Plut.; cf. Stob.) [περὶ ἀρχῶν]

πάλιν δ' ἀπ' ἄλλης ἀρχῆς Πυθαγόρας Μνησάρχου Σάμιος ὁ πρῶτος φιλοσοφίαν τούτῳ τῷ ῥήματι προσαγορεύσας, ἀρχὰς τοὺς ἀριθμοὺς καὶ τὰς συμμετρίας τὰς ἐν τούτοις, ἅς καὶ ἁρμονίας καλεῖ, τὰ δ' ἐξ ἀμφοτέρων σύνθετα στοιχεῖα, καλούμενα δὲ γεωμετρικά· πάλιν δὲ τὴν μονάδα καὶ τὴν ἀόριστον δυάδα ἐν ταῖς ἀρχαῖς. σπεύδει δ' αὐτῷ τῶν ἀρχῶν ἡ μὲν ἐπὶ τὸ ποιητικὸν αἴτιον καὶ εἰδικόν, ὅπερ ἐστὶ νοῦς ὁ[1] θεός, ἡ δ' ἐπὶ τὸ παθητικόν τε καὶ ὑλικόν, ὅπερ ἐστὶν ὁ ὁρατὸς κόσμος. εἶναι δὲ τὴν φύσιν τοῦ ἀριθμοῦ δεκάδα· μέχρι γὰρ τῶν δέκα πάντες Ἕλληνες, πάντες βάρβαροι

b

But some people say that the body comes from a single point. For the flux of this point generates the line; the flux of the line produces a surface; and the displacement of this latter in depth generates the three-dimensional body. But this position of these Pythagoreans differs from that of the earlier ones. For they [i.e. the earlier ones] produced the numbers starting from two principles, the monad and the indefinite dyad, then, starting from the numbers, the points, lines, and the plane and solid figures. But the others construct all things starting from a single point [. . .].

An Example of Doxographic Syncretism (R72)

R72 (> 58B.15) Aëtius

For his part, taking a different starting point [scil. than did the representatives of the Ionian line of descent; cf. **DOX. T20**], Pythagoras of Samos, son of Mnesarchus, the first to have called philosophy by this name, [scil. stated that] what are principles are the numbers and the proportions that exist among them, which he also calls 'harmonies,' while what is composed out of both of these are the elements, called 'geometrical'; again, that the monad and the indefinite dyad are among the principles. Of these principles, according to him, the one tends toward the efficient and formal cause, which is intellect, god, the other toward the passive and material cause, which is the perceptible world. The nature of number is the decad. For all Greeks,

---

1 ὁ MΠ: καὶ m

ἀριθμοῦσιν, ἐφ' ἃ ἐλθόντες πάλιν ἀναποδίζουσιν[2] ἐπὶ τὴν μονάδα· καὶ τῶν δέκα πάλιν, φησίν, ἡ δύναμίς ἐστιν ἐν τοῖς τέτταρσι καὶ τῇ τετράδι· τὸ δ' αἴτιον, εἴ τις ἀπὸ τῆς μονάδος ἀναποδῶν[3] κατὰ πρόσθεσιν τιθείη τοὺς ἀριθμούς, ἄχρι τῶν τεσσάρων προελθὼν ἐκπληρώσει τὸν δέκα ἀριθμόν. ἐὰν δὲ ὑπερβάληται τὸν τῆς τετράδος, καὶ τῶν δέκα ὑπερεκπεσεῖται·[4] οἷον εἴ τις θείη ἓν καὶ δύο προσθείη καὶ τρία καὶ τούτοις τέσσαρα, τὸν τῶν δέκα πληρώσει[5] ἀριθμόν· ὥστε ὁ ἀριθμὸς κατὰ μὲν μονάδα ἐν τοῖς δέκα κατὰ δὲ δύναμιν ἐν τοῖς τέσσαρσι. διὸ καὶ ἐφθέγγοντο οἱ Πυθαγόρειοι, ὡς μεγίστου ὅρκου ὄντος τῆς τετράδος,

οὐ μὰ τὸν ἁμετέρᾳ ψυχᾷ παραδόντα τετρακτύν,
παγὰν ἀενάου φύσεος ῥιζώματ'[6] ἔχουσαν.

καὶ ἡ ἡμετέρα ψυχή, φησίν, ἐκ τετράδος σύγκειται· εἶναι γὰρ νοῦν ἐπιστήμην δόξαν αἴσθησιν, ἐξ ὧν πᾶσα τέχνη καὶ ἐπιστήμη καὶ αὐτοὶ λογικοί ἐσμεν. νοῦς μὲν οὖν ἡ μονάς ἐστιν· ὁ γὰρ νοῦς κατὰ μονάδα θεωρεῖ,[7] οἷον πολλῶν ὄντων ἀνθρώπων οἱ μὲν ἐπὶ μέρους εἰσὶν ἀναίσθητοι ἀπερίληπτοι καὶ ἄπειροι, ἀλλ' αὐτὸ τοῦτο ἄνθρωπον ἕνα μόνον νοοῦμεν, ᾧ οὐδεὶς ἔτυχεν ὅμοιος [. . .]. καὶ ἡ δυὰς δ' ἡ ἀόριστος ἐπιστήμη, εἰκότως· πᾶσα γὰρ ἀπόδειξις καὶ πᾶσα

---

[2] ἀναποδοῦσιν mss., corr. Beck   [3] ἀναποδῶν del. Mau, deest in Arab.: ἀναλαβὼν vel ἀ' μονάδος corr. Usener: ἀναποδίζων Bern.   [4] ὑπερεκπεσεῖται ΜΠ: ἐκπεσεῖται m

PYTHAGOREAN RECEPTION

all barbarians count up to 10 and when they have reached that they revert to the monad. And the power of 10 in turn, he says, resides in the 4 and in the tetrad. The reason for this is that if, reverting (?) from the monad, one constitutes the numbers by addition, one will complete the number 10 by proceeding up to 4. But if one goes beyond the [scil. number] of the tetrad, one will also fall beyond 10. For example, if one posits 1 and adds 2 and 3 and 4 to these, then one will complete the number 10. So that the number is in 10 by the monad [i.e. the unit], but in 4 by its power. And that is why the Pythagoreans proclaimed, thinking that the tetraktys is the greatest oath,

> No, by the man who bequeathed to our soul the tetraktys,
> The source that holds the roots of ever-flowing nature. [cf. **PYTHS. ANON. D16**]

And our soul, he says, is composed out of the tetrad. For it is from intellect, knowledge, opinion, perception, that every art and every science comes and that we ourselves are rational. Therefore the intellect is the monad; for the intellect knows in accordance with the monad; for example, there are many men: but individually they can not be perceived nor grasped and they are unlimited, but we think this very thing, a single man alone, to whom no one else is found to be similar [. . .]. And the indefinite dyad is knowledge, as is plausible: for every demonstration and

---

⁵ πληρώσει Π: πληρώσειεν Mm: ἐκπληρώσει Diels
⁶ ῥίζωμά τ' Wyttenbach   ⁷ θεωρεῖται mss., corr. Usener

449

πίστις ἐπιστήμης, πρὸς δὲ καὶ πᾶς συλλογισμὸς ἔκ
τινων ὁμολογουμένων τὸ ἀμφισβητούμενον συνάγει[8]
καὶ ῥᾳδίως ἀποδείκνυται ἕτερον· ὧν ἡ ἐπιστήμη κατά-
ληψίς ἐστι, διὸ εἴη ἂν δυάς. ἡ δὲ δόξα τριὰς ἐκ κατα-
λήψεώς ἐστιν, εὐλόγως, ὅτι πολλῶν ἐστιν ἡ δόξα· ἡ
δὲ τριὰς πλῆθος, ὡς "τρισμάκαρες Δαναοί." διὰ τοῦτο
οὖν ἐγκρίνει τὴν τριάδα . . .

[8] συνάγει MΠ: ἀνάγει m

Pythagoras in The Assembly of Philosophers (R73)

R73 (≠ DK) *Turba Phil.*

a p. 109.10–15 Ruska

narro, quod magister meus Pitagoras Italus, sapientum magister, vatum caput, tantum donum Dei et sapientiae habuit, quod nemini post Hermetem datum est. discipulos igitur eius iam multiplicatos et per omnes regiones principes constitutos ad hanc pretiosissimam artem voluit congregare, ut eorum locutio sit radix post se venturis.

b Sermo VIII, pp. 72.1–2, 73.4–11 Plessner

inquit Pitagoras: "dico Deum ante omnia fuisse, cum quo nihil fuit, cum fuit. [. . .] et intelligite quod Deus, cum

every conviction belongs to knowledge, and furthermore every deduction brings together, on the basis of certain agreed premises, what is in question and easily demonstrates something else: this is what knowledge apprehends, and this is why it would be the dyad. Opinion is the triad deriving from apprehension, as is reasonable: for opinion belongs to multiplicity; and the triad is multitude, as in the expression 'thrice-blessed Danaans' [cf. Homer, *Od.* 5.306]. This then is why he includes the triad . . .[1]

[1] The explanation of sensation as the tetrad has not been preserved.

Pythagoras in The Assembly of Philosophers *(R73)*

R73 (≠ DK) *The Assembly of Philosophers*

a

I [scil. Arisleus, i.e. Archelaus] report that my teacher, the Italian Pythagoras, teacher of the wise, chief of the prophets, possessed so great a gift of God and of wisdom as was given to no one after Hermes [scil. Trismegistus]. Therefore he wanted to convoke in an assembly his students, who had already proliferated and had been established throughout all the regions as the leaders in this most precious art [scil. of alchemy], so that their discourses would be a foundation for posterity [cf. **ARCHY. R7**].

b

Pythagoras said: "I say that God existed before all things, and together with Him there existed nothing when He

solus fuisset, quatuor res creavit: ignem, aera, aquam et terram, ex quibus iam creatis omnia creavit tam sublimium quam inferiorum rerum, eo quod praedestinavit, quod oportet creaturis ex radice extrahi, a qua multiplicantur et augmentantur, ut inhabitent mundum et sua in eis iudicia perficiant. ideo ante omnia quatuor creavit elementa, ex quibus postea, quae voluit, creavit, diversas sc. creaturas, quarum quasdam ex uno creavit.

existed. [. . .] And understand that God, when He alone existed, created four things: fire, air, water, and earth, out of which, when they had already been created, He created all things, both the upper things and the lower ones, since He had predestined that it was necessary for the creatures to be drawn out of a root, from which they would multiply and be increased, so that they would inhabit the world and fulfill His judgments regarding them. And so before all things He created four elements, out of which afterward He created what He wanted, viz. the different creatures, of which He created certain ones out of one [scil. element]."